Laboring On

BIRTH IN TRANSITION IN THE UNITED STATES

Wendy Simonds

Barbara Katz Rothman

Bari Meltzer Norman

Routledge
Taylor & Francis Group
New York   London

Routledge is an imprint of the
Taylor & Francis Group, an informa business

Routledge
Taylor & Francis Group
270 Madison Avenue
New York, NY 10016

Routledge
Taylor & Francis Group
2 Park Square
Milton Park, Abingdon
Oxon OX14 4RN

© 2007 by Taylor & Francis Group, LLC
Routledge is an imprint of Taylor & Francis Group, an Informa business

Printed in the United States of America on acid-free paper
10 9 8 7 6 5 4 3 2 1

International Standard Book Number-10: 0-415-94663-8 (Softcover) 0-415-94662-X (Hardcover)
International Standard Book Number-13: 978-0-415-94663-6 (Softcover) 978-0-415-94662-9 (Hardcover)

Visit the Taylor & Francis Web site at
http://www.taylorandfrancis.com

and the Routledge Web site at
http://www.routledge-ny.com

Laboring On

Other titles in the *Perspectives on Gender* series, edited by Myra Marx Ferree

Contents

Acknowledgments

All of us offer unending gratitude to the midwives, obstetricians, labor and delivery nurses, and doulas who generously participated in interviews: without their words, this book would not exist. Doors opened for us very easily in this project in several different midwifery communities and organizations. Particular thanks go to Jana Borino at the Florida School of Traditional Midwifery (FSTM), Mickey Gillmor and Susan Stone at The Frontier Nursing School's Community-Based Nurse Midwifery Education Program, Patricia Burkhardt at New York University, Suzanne Schechter at SUNY (State University of New York) Downstate Medical Center, and JoAnne Myers-Cieko at the Seattle Midwifery School for their hospitality and enthusiasm about the work, and for helping us with the logistics of scheduling interviews with students and faculty. Thanks also to Melissa Denmark and Lara Foley, who helped organize the focus groups at FSTM.

We are fortunate to have worked with Myra Marx Ferree as our series editor, and to have had the support of two editors at Routledge, Eileen Kalish and David McBride, and a great production team: Marsha Hecht, Jane McGary, and Sylvia Wood.

Bari Meltzer Norman

The love and support of my parents, Teri Meltzer and Stew Meltzer, provide strength and drive like no one else's. My brother Brad Meltzer is my closest confidant and my rock. He is a talented writer and a true friend, and he has the biggest and warmest heart; he is nothing short of an inspiration and a role model. Cori Flam epitomizes the true essence of family. Jonas Meltzer and Lila Meltzer are just beyond words. Their births were life-changing for me, and the time I've spent with them since, even more so. Parker Norman and Madison Norman warm my heart and make me smile no matter what. Dorothy Rubin is all goodness. Evelyn Meltzer inspires me with her sharpness and her family recipes.

Todd Greenbarg, Michael Moss, and Anneka Norgren are also part of my family, not to mention friends I treasure immensely. Kim Torres made five years of school not only bearable but fun. I also owe thanks to Barbara Katz Rothman and Wendy Simonds for believing in me enough to include me in this project. I am happy to call you both my colleagues and my friends.

Finally, I owe so much to my husband, Will Norman, who cheers the loudest for me at every turn. Whenever I think I'm at the end of my rope, he's there to offer support. He gives meaning to the word "partner," and amazes me every day with his strength and his kindness. I learn from him constantly, and I am grateful to feel so loved by him.

Barbara Katz Rothman

I've been working on this book more or less my whole adult life, which makes writing the acknowledgments feel somewhat like drawing up a "last will and testament." The good part is that you don't have to die to have acknowledgments read; the bad part is that you have no more gifts to give. The book is all there is to show for the help, encouragement, patience, and love of family, friends, and colleagues that went into its making. To keep the acknowledgments from being longer than some of the chapters, I refer you to all the people I thanked in *In Labor*. From my mother to start with, through to the last midwife I spoke to, I thank all the people in my life who have made this work possible.

That said, particular mention must go to Eileen Moran for showing me the central insight of the dissertation research that underlies my work in birth; Mary Cunnane for teaching me how to write books; the midwives Kit Gates, Mary Zwart, and the late Annemiek Cuppen; and — of course, most of all for this book — Wendy Simonds. She drew me back to the work, draws me back from the brink of making a total fool of myself over and over again, and tethers me to reality. And she sets me free again to think, imagine, hope. Thank you, Wendy.

Wendy Simonds

First, to Barbara and Bari — thank *you* for doing this book with me. I am so glad it's finally become what Barbara calls the best kind of book: a *done* one!

A Research Initiation Grant from Georgia State University and the Sociology Department at GSU provided me with wonderful resources for doing this work: money for travel, equipment, and a professional leave for writing. The support of my chair, Don Reitzes, was indispensable, and I am immensely grateful for it. I had excellent research assistants from both the Sociology Department and the Women's Studies Institute over the gestation and writing of the book; they did a range of tasks, including library work, interviewing, coding, and transcription. Nicole Banton, Jennifer Chandler, Michelle Emerson, Hydi Dickstein, Erica Kitchen, Monique Marshall, Courtney Muse, Melissa Travis, and Caroline Wood helped make this book possible. The childcare coverage offered by Joy Dillard, Kendra Sandman, Natalie Spring, Polly Sylvia, and especially Randy Malamud was also crucial to my ability to get the book done; thank you for taking such good care of Jake and Ben.

The GSU sociology staff, Dracy Blackwell, Quanda Miller, and Selma Poage, are wonderful people who spread wondrousness around. Without the indispensable hard work of Dracy Blackwell, I would be mired in an incomprehensible bureaucratic world for which I am ill suited. Dracy, thanks for being my guide in this world, and for being such a fabulous advisor to students. Quanda Miller and Selma Poage also merit gratitude for making my administrative life bearable, and my work life pleasurable!

I am fortunate to have friends (many of whom are work associates too) with whom I've been able to discuss this work, from whom I have gained valuable feedback, and/or with whom I could just bitch about the difficulties involved in research and writing. Many thanks to Dawn Baunach, Elisabeth Burgess, Jennifer Chandler, Denise Donnelly, Chip Gallagher, Behrooz Ghamari, Andy Lowry, Barbara Katz Rothman, Memo Konrad, Judie Malamud, Danny Malamud, Louise Palmer, Ralph LaRossa, Don Reitzes, Gregg Rice, Elisabeth Sheff, Evelina Sterling, Mindy Stombler, Melissa Travis, and Kristin Wilson for your specific assistance in this venture, and for your friendship more broadly.

The writing of this book took place during a difficult time for me, and many people and two cats offered the kind of sustenance that — sappy but true — makes life worth living. I would particularly like to thank Matthew Archibald, Lynn Chancer, Heather Dalmage, Joy Dillard, Marc Eichen, Mark George, Diana Jones, Ivy Kennelly, Bob Konrad, Peter Lindsay, Michael Margaretten, PJ McGann, Joya Misra, Michelle Sas, Bobbie Simonds, Hinkypunk Simonds, Lauren Simonds, Lori Simonds, Glumbumble Simonds, Gordon Simonds, Ben Simonds-Malamud, Jake Simonds-Malamud, and to thank again Andy, Barbara, Denise, both Elisabeths, Gregg, Mindy, and Memo, for your nurturance, your validation of my inner writer (including sometimes reading and commenting on what it/she/I would begrudgingly, belaboredly, and belatedly produce), and your exceptional presence in my life in general: thank you so much for your labors of love!

INTRODUCTION

A Lifetime's Labor: Women and Power in the Birthplace

BARBARA KATZ ROTHMAN

For me there has never been a bright line between my own life and my own work. I was a graduate student, floundering around for a dissertation topic when I decided to have a baby. I found my dissertation topic, and my life's work, in the decision to have a home birth.

Looking Back

My son is now older than I was when he was born; older than my father was when he died. It is, literally for me, a lifetime ago that I first gave birth.

It was a great birth. Even now, looking back as something of a birth aficionado, I would have to say it was not too shabby. Not ideal, I can see now, not quite a perfect birth, but close enough.

There is, I hope you can see, some tongue-in-cheek on that. I've heard so many birth stories now, I've become something of a birth snob. There are unpretentious little births, full-bodied heavy births, births with drama, births with humor, births with pathos — but they all, they *all* linger on the palate, stay with you, last.

There hasn't been a year in all this time that I haven't read, if not written, books and articles on birth, attended midwifery or related conferences, thought long and hard about pregnancy and birth. Sometimes I feel like I've theorized all the juice out of it. Someone tells me a birth story, and however moved or saddened or thrilled or amused I am, I can still slide it into the appropriate box, find the existing analytic category in which to place it. And that is true even of my own first birth, the very first birth I ever saw live and in person.

I came to the decision to have a home birth from feminism, the women's movement of the 1970s, which made us all critical of the ways that major institutions of our society treated women, and in particular of the way that medicine as a profession treated the bodies of women. I also came to the decision after seeing *All My Babies*, a film made in the 1950s to train the "granny midwives," the African American women of the South who were the last vestiges of non-medicalized midwifery. The home birth in that film made a deep impression on me in my undergraduate health education course, and it set me on the path to choosing a home birth.

Mine was, I guess I'd say now, a highly politicized, lightly medicalized birth. It was long on feminism, power, and control; short on spirituality. As am I, so I suppose that's all right.

It was a highly politicized birth because, as much as anything else that was happening that day, I was making a point, proving something. I, who had never so much as seen a baby born, was showing the doctor and the world that birth did not have to be a medical event. It was complicated by the fact that I didn't even understand that it was a "medical event" that I was reacting against. I just knew that the way birth was managed in standard hospitals was not "feminist" enough for me; it did not put the woman enough in charge, and looked awful besides.

It was a lightly medicalized birth because I simply did not have the brains to use a midwife. Or rather, I just didn't know I should. How could I have known? The midwives I had heard of were nurse-midwives working in hospitals. It would be another couple of years before Ina May Gaskin published *Spiritual Midwifery* and I even knew there was a midwifery "movement" going on out there. I went to a Boston Women's Health meeting when my son was still little, and I remember thinking I wasn't that interested in the sessions on midwifery, on the legal status of the midwife, and things like that. It was home birth I was committed to, not one or another breed of practitioners. So I had talked a good feminist obstetrician into attending this birth at home on a right-to-choose basis, and she knew no more about home birth than I did.

Some of her ignorance is just amusing in retrospect, and some kind of scary. She didn't know to tell me to go to the bathroom regularly and empty my bladder. She'd probably always had nurses for stuff like that, so what did she know? She never labor-sat in her life, I bet. But my husband and I had practiced some degree of "bathroom modesty," closing the door when we peed. No good reason; just the way we had done things. I'm sure he'd have had no problem coming in with me while I urinated. But I was in heavy and constant contractions (no doubt made worse by the fact that I was, duh, laboring on a full bladder) and I couldn't get a sentence out, a word even, to raise the issue with him. And I was terrified to be without him for the time it would take to go to the bathroom. I was deep, deep in heavy contact with him, breathing together, hanging on for dear life, and I was going *nowhere* by myself. Not even down the hall to the bathroom. So I went for hours, *hours,* on a full bladder. That was dangerous, and probably had consequences. I'd write more about that now, but I have to go pee first.

Other errors the obstetrician made were just funny. I gave birth on a big comfortable platform rocker, because that's where I was laboring and I wasn't going anywhere. She saw me ensconced there and I think realized it was a better position than the bed she'd had us raise on blocks to spare her bad back. She sent downstairs for two kitchen chairs for me to brace my feet on, and I gave birth in what I now know as the "flying squat" position. At the time, I didn't have the vocabulary for it, and chances are, neither did she. A "supported lithotomy," maybe. She knelt in front of me, sacrificing her bad back as the head crowned. She offered me a mirror — I refused. Hesch, my husband, read my mind. Oh, I don't even know that we had two minds between us that day. He knew what I was thinking, reassured me that it didn't look bloody or gory, and I looked in the mirror. I had my contact lenses in, which for me symbolized the power and control issue more probably than any other single thing. Got your lenses in? You're on top of it. Got your lenses out? You're turning yourself over, for good or for ill, for sex or sleep or very little else, to other powers. So I looked, and I have no memory at all of what I saw. I will never, ever, *ever* forget a thing I felt, but I really don't know what I saw in that mirror.

She, the doctor, thought of a mirror because she thought of the birth as something the mother might want to see. Later I read about midwives who guided the mother's hands to her crotch so that she felt the emerging head with her hands as she felt it with her genitals. I can only imagine what that would have felt like, birthing into my own hand.

She didn't do an episiotomy — not that she didn't offer, mind you, but I still had enough sense to refuse that. It'd be out with another push if she did one, she said, trying to encourage me. What's the rush? I thought. Hell, I'm not ready to be a mother! Five more minutes to collect myself, like cramming before the exam papers are handed out, that's a good thing!

But a few good pushes later, she did catch the baby and hold him upside down over me. I watched him — a gray-blue, kind of scary-looking thing for what seemed a long time to me but not to her — "pink up," turn into a real baby! And as I reached out for him, stretched my arms to hold him, she said "We've got a boy!" and passed him over her shoulder. My mother was there, invited in at the last minute to watch and, lucky mother, standing right where a nurse would have been, right where the doctor automatically passed the baby. So my mother held my son, the child named for her dead husband, my father Danny, and felt her world shift as the almost-a-child that had been my father became the dead grandpa of this baby in her arms. I don't begrudge her the moment. But I was awake, there, reaching for the baby as the doctor passed him back behind her, over her shoulder, expecting, as doctors do, that someone would do the scut work for her: clean him up, handle the details.

That was a mistake, of course. But so was saying "We've got a boy." In those days, we didn't know what we had until we had it; we didn't have sonograms hanging on the fridge. I interviewed a midwife, a really amazing woman, when I was doing my dissertation work on midwifery, who said she never says "It's a boy" or "It's a girl," because "her whole life a woman will remember the sounds of those words, and it should be in the voice of someone she loves." I hear the voice of Marcia Storch, the doctor, and honestly, now, more than 30 years later, with Marcia herself dead, all the history that passed between us gone and buried, it's not so bad that I have that memory. But no, it shouldn't have been her voice, not then.

Interrogating Experience

Rethinking one's own history and life, thinking critically about autobiography, has recently become more respected in sociology (see Mykhalovskiy 1996, Shostack 1996) — not that we haven't all been doing just that all along: sociologists, like everyone else, are inevitably shaped by personal as well as professional experience. I thought it was important when I wrote my dissertation and again when I edited that work into the book *In Labor*, the book that this book has grown out of, that I begin with a personal, autobiographical statement, the experience I had with my own first birth. I used my two births as the brackets, the prologue and epilogue between which I placed my more formal research.

So I sit here now rethinking that first birth, still learning from it. That birth reflected who I was, what mattered to me at that time. That birth was *me, mine.* And that is as it should be, as all births should be: reflections of the woman giving birth. Every birth teaches us about the woman who is birthing — her life, her community, her society. We learn from births at the level of the individual, but we also learn from birth as a society. We shape our births, and our births shape us. That birth decades ago made me who I am today, and that too is probably true of all births: they shape who we become; they show us parts of ourselves; they make us face death and life, the body and the soul; and we're never the same afterwards.

I really believe that. Or at least I believe that birth can be that, all that. In the birth movement, those of us who talk a lot about births, midwives and hangers-on alike, sometimes make fun of a woman who probably doesn't really exist. She's the woman who organizes her birth so it doesn't interfere with her life. Sometimes it's the elective cesarean section scheduled for a convenient work break; sometimes it's the woman who takes business calls or polishes her nails, or both, while in labor with an epidural. She's our version of the Cadillac-driving Welfare Mother, that stereotype created by the right wing to make us think women on state assistance are all wealthy cheaters. These stereotypes are figments of our imagination, straw women we burn in effigy. Such is the woman for whom birth is not a big deal, not a learning experience, not a life-shaping, earth-shaking metamorphosis, but just a day's interruption in a busy schedule.

In truth, I've never met a woman who doesn't recall her births, who can't tell you a birth story in great and crushing detail, no matter how long ago it was. Birth *matters*. Someone ought to write a book with that title, if someone hasn't already. What happens to a woman, how she is treated, how she experiences her birth have consequences for how she experiences her body, her sexuality, her child, her family. The convention is to talk about "maternal-infant bonding" at birth, as if babies and mothers first came together and "bonded," rather than first came apart and separated at birth. But there is often bonding that goes on at a birth — between the woman and those she labors with. The bond I forged with my husband that day continues to carry a lot of weight in my marriage. I trust him: I trust him with my body and my children — and I learned that day that I can. Birth matters in shaping a woman's sense of herself, her own body, and her sexuality, but also her relationships with others. Birth matters in how we as a society, as a community of people, look at women and at motherhood. We in America think of birth on the one hand as a basically medical procedure, and on the other hand as the "arrival" of a baby. We forget, we are unable to see through the medical trappings, that birth is far more than that.

I didn't "bond" with the baby at birth. I was overwhelmed by the whole project, frankly, and the baby was the least of it. What had happened to me, to my body, *that*, as we still said then, "blew my mind." It was a few days later, looking down at the baby lying in a basket on my desk, reaching over to pick him up and feeling the milk let down in a gush, that I thought "Ah, and on the third day the love comes in!"

Nothing that I learned from giving birth to my son, or seven years later to my daughter, was useful to me eight years after that second birth, when I adopted my third child, because birth, as we experience it, is oddly enough not about babies but about the limits and the power of our bodies. What I learned from giving birth did come in surprisingly handy some years later when my stepfather was dying, and I sat by his bedside. I had learned to give comfort with presence, to accept with awe but with a grounded practicality the power of the body in transition. I used much of it when I stupidly broke my ankle and experienced days of shattering pain, and had to surrender to my body or really lose my mind. The lessons we learn in birth are lessons about how to live — and to die — in, with, and through our bodies.

Birth is, I learned and I can say with clarity now, about women. That's what the midwives taught me, and that's what my own experiences have shown me. Birth is not about babies. Babies get born. But women give birth. Giving birth is awesome. Babies are miracles, and cute besides, but birth is an Event. It is Something. It is a life-shaking, developmental moment that makes you who you are, that teaches you who you are. Sometimes people say they want to become midwives because they just love babies. Wrong. Midwives who actually go through with it, the women and a few men who go through all the training, the learning, the growth and change and fear and power of becoming midwives, do it because they love women. They are in awe of the power of the birthing woman.

All of that is missing in the American "managed" birth, the one I had the good sense and the luck of the fool to avoid. I wanted to avoid a place, the hospital. I managed to avoid almost all of medicalization. It was only later, when I was doing my research on midwives, that I came to understand just what that means.

Understanding Birth: Two Models

The key insight that I gained from interviews with medically trained nurse-midwives who were doing home birth in the New York area in the late 1970s (Rothman 1991 [1982]) was that there were very different models underlying practice, and different ways of thinking about birth that resulted in different ways of practicing. I read the obstetrics literature, and I read the literature of the developing American home birth movement — newsletters, conference reports, *Spiritual Midwifery* — what little there was out there on home birth.

Most of the midwives I was interviewing were, in a way, rather like my feminist obstetrician. They had the very best intentions, but they were really out of their depth at home. They didn't know what to think much of the time. They were confused about what they were doing and seeing. I had a study group that I worked with in those years, and we read one another's dissertation work. I kept talking about home birth and hospital birth to my group, but I also kept talking about these hospital-trained midwives and how they were floundering much of the time, unsure of themselves: at home, but not quite *at home* there. I had a hard time articulating the difference between home and hospital birth.

With the help of my study group, and particularly in conversations with my colleague Eileen Moran, I came to see that it wasn't really about "home" and "hospital." A midwife could bring the hospital way of thinking into the home with her, as my obstetrician had done, sometimes treating me as a passive patient and not a capable mother. And a midwife could bring the home way of thinking into the hospital. Many of these midwives would tell me stories of doing home births one day and then hospital births the next, trying to take what they had learned at home and apply it in the hospital. "Midwifery" was a way of thinking to which most of these American hospital-trained nurse-midwives were aspiring. I started calling these two different approaches the "medical model" and the "midwifery model," rather than "hospital" and "home." But the distinction is still grounded in home and hospital as settings of practice, and we mustn't lose sight of that.

The importance of setting lies in where knowledge comes from in the first place. We learn from each other. Models are the way we are taught to think, and that is always in a context. We have learned, for example, that blood circulates, and when we feel a pulse or hear a heart beating, we experience that circulation, a circulation which was not part of the way people understood their bodies just a few hundred years ago. Now the model of the heart-as-pump is so deeply a part of our thinking that it is hard to realize that it was ever possible to think and to experience it otherwise.

Models give you the picture you have in your head, against which you look at the world. You hold up what you know to be true and compare what is before you against that. If the model tells me what a normal labor is like, then what is this labor I am seeing when compared to that? Longer? Shorter? Stronger? Weaker? Or take something very simple: we have learned what a newborn baby should look like. There is a model, an "ideal type" as Weber used the term. A Weberian ideal type doesn't mean an ideal we strive for, but rather a prototype, a representation of a kind of thing. The "ideal type newborn" I refer to is not ideal in the sense of being the "perfect baby" from the baby food ads, but ideal type as in paradigmatic: the essence of new-baby-hood, having the necessary and essential characteristics that mark it as a new baby. Given that model, we can look at any new baby and ask if it varies, and how: In the direction of pathology? Is the head too big? Too small? Are the limbs proportional? How is the muscle tone? Compared to what? Compared to what you know is normal, compared to the model you have in your head of what a baby's muscle tone should be at birth.

So where do models come from? How are they developed? We are accustomed to thinking that we know what we know from what we have observed. But it is just as true that how we practice sets up what we can observe, what is observable in the first place. If every new baby you ever saw was born from a deeply anesthetized mother, what would you know about normal muscle tone in a newborn?

That was the type of problem, if less dramatic, that was confronting the hospital-trained nurse-midwives who were doing home births. Their models did not apply, so how could they know what was normal? Clinical practice in hospitals was structured to avoid the production of just the knowledge they now needed. Want to know how long a placenta could take to separate from the uterine wall and still be healthy? You will never, ever find out if all placentas are removed manually within 15 minutes of the birth of the baby, as all were in the hospital delivery rooms — and as my obstetrician (painfully) did in my bedroom. Want to know if you are looking at a "second stage arrest," a pathological condition, or a normal "rest period" for a woman who has had a difficult labor before she begins the work of pushing forth the baby? If you always and immediately treat any cessation of contractions after full dilatation as second stage arrest and rush to pull the baby out, as they did in the hospitals where these nurse-midwives were trained, you will never, ever observe the rest period or its healthy and spontaneous resolution. The examples fairly flew forth from the midwives in those early years as they confronted the limits of hospital-based knowledge for home-based practice.

Setting — place, location — counts. The differences between medical and midwifery models of birth are not just about "attitudes," and not just a set of guidelines for practice. Different bodies of knowledge are produced in different settings.

Education is about the passing on of knowledge. It would be very difficult to teach obstetrics, that medical model of birth, at home births. It is no less difficult to teach the midwifery model of birth in the hospital. Because American nurse-midwifery has come through the hospital, it has been very hard to become a midwife, to develop a midwife's body of knowledge, in that medically dominated setting. I have brought American nurse-midwives I respect and admire to tears by saying this: a midwifery model does not develop under medical domination. And hospitals are settings where medicine sets the rules.

And so we have developed in the United States two very different models and systems of care: the medical/hospital system on the one hand, and the midwifery/home system on the other. The first is the dominant system, setting the standard of care and the cultural expectations of birth; the second is a still small voice barely heard above the medical roar. The U.S. dependence on the hospital as the place of birth and medicine as its authority encourages Americans to think of birth as apart from daily life. If one thinks of birth in a narrow, medical sense, one focuses on fetal parts, maternal abdomens and pelvises, and there is a certain baby-out-of-vagina sameness in it all. A pelvic arch is a pelvic arch, a fontanel is a fontanel the world over. But it is women who give birth, women whose vaginas, pelvises, and abdomens are being probed and measured and palpated and swabbed. These women are people, with political, social, and occupational as well as family positions in society. To examine systems of birth care from the perspective of the women who give birth within them is to go beyond crude, quantifiable outcome measures such as mortality and morbidity rates, fetal weight, and Apgar scores, and to see birth as an experience in the lives of women.

A Place of Power

Birth at home returns power to the woman.

I learned that lesson as a young woman with a little foresight and a lot of luck, deciding what was important to me in my birth and settling on place as most important of all. I have now learned it anew as a social scientist who, along with many others, has studied birth in America and around the world. What we social scientists have learned permeates this book and now fills many bookshelves. From the earliest studies of American hospital birth, particularly the feminist analysis offered by Nancy Stoller Shaw's *Forced Labor* in 1974, the same year my son was born, through the classic cross-cultural work of Brigitte Jordan's *Birth in Four Cultures* (1983) and the more recent work of Robbie Davis-Floyd (1992), we now have a richly developing sociology and anthropology of birth.

Some of us have looked, as I have, at the sociology of knowledge: How do we know what we know, and who has the power and authority to know? Some of us have looked at interpersonal relations in childbirth. Some have looked at the interprofessional relationships, between midwives and obstetricians, or between the various types of midwives themselves, as Wendy Simonds did for this book, and as Bari Meltzer has done for the newest birth occupation, the doulas, and these other players.

The most significant theme I continue to see is that of power: the very concern with which I started still, for me, drives the issues today. Out of the professional power it has all but monopolized, American obstetrics has developed and used increasingly powerful technologies which in turn increase obstetricians' power over birthing women and over other birth workers. Ultrasound grew out of a conceptualization of the fetus as a separate patient essentially trapped within the woman;

it then reifies that vision, showing us the isolated fetus, the woman erased from the image on our screens and increasingly in our minds. Women struggle to maintain their agency, their power, their control, as Lisa M. Mitchell (2001) has recently shown us, but are presented with the fetus as a virtually external being demanding attention and care — from them and from their doctors.

Prenatal tests of all kinds, I found in my own work on *The Tentative Pregnancy* (1986) — from ultrasound through the more invasive amniocentesis and chorionic villus sampling — (re)create the fetus as both a patient and a potential mistake to be aborted. Women increasingly find their pregnancies, from the earliest moments through to the birth itself, medically mediated, medically constructed, and medically evaluated.

The issues have grown ever more complicated in the years since I began. I look back at what I learned and marvel at my naiveté and my good fortune. I focused on the one thing I thought I might have some control over, the location of birth, and it turned out to be the most significant determinant of how birth is conducted. For today's pregnant women, much of the battle to maintain personal power, autonomy, and control may well be lost long before the birth, as the fetus itself is constructed as a needy patient and the woman as little more than a maternal barrier to its care.

But women are not passive victims of medical care. Rather, women and their doctors and midwives are all part of a larger society in which the way birth is managed reflects the way that birth is thought about; and the way that birth is thought about is reflected in its management.

When I was choosing my own home birth, and when I was doing my research on midwifery, whether I knew it or not at the time, I was part of a movement: a social movement to reclaim birth for women. That movement continues today throughout the world, as midwives and mothers work together to create better births, to take the power that is at the heart of every birth, and put it back in the bodies and souls of women.

We bring you this book out of a conviction that birth matters — not only (only!) in the lives of individual women and their families, but also for us as a community of people, for whole societies of people living, birthing, and dying as human beings.

Introduction

Origin Stories

WENDY SIMONDS

My First Midwife

I have a vivid memory of the sight of my aunt Kit vastly pregnant 30 years ago, on the beach, wearing a bikini. I remember my grandmother muttering to my mother, *"Look at her!"* in a hushed tone that conveyed that Kit had clearly and deliberately done something scandalously excessive. I was eleven; I had never seen a naked pregnant belly that I could remember, certainly never in public. It was impressively large and hard, and her belly button stuck out. Her breasts were huge and the bikini was small. She looked awesomely distorted; I was fascinated.

The next year, when Kit and my uncle Mark visited us with my baby cousin, I remember preliminary discussions about the fact that Kit was probably going to breastfeed in a restaurant where we were going for dinner. Apparently my mother thought she should prepare my younger sister and me — not so much the sight of a naked breast, because we'd seen naked breasts, but for naked breasts in a public place, breasts that would potentially implicate everyone at our table in some way.

"It might upset other people in the restaurant," I remember being told by my mother, "because women don't usually breastfeed in public." (And they didn't breastfeed at all when my mother had us; it was considered lower-class then, she told us.) She emphasized that we shouldn't be embarrassed. I am not sure what else was said, but I remember thinking, "I wonder what will happen when Kit breastfeeds Sarah at the restaurant!"

I waited, waited, waited for Kit to whip out her breast and for a dramatic scene to erupt around us. I was both excited and worried about the prospect. I was pretty sure that, whatever happened, my Grampa would take care of it; he had a commanding arrogance I had seen demonstrated in restaurants when there was a problem (and my grandparents frequently experienced restaurant problems). And then nothing happened. When Kit finally did feed Sarah, you could hardly even tell she was doing it; you certainly wouldn't have noticed it unless you were right next to her, as I was. The restaurant did not split open.

I saw Kit as a rebel, an alien presence in our family. When they first got together, she and my uncle lived together in the Bronx. This was a big deal in my family because Kit and Mark weren't married and because Kit wasn't Jewish. Kit had a matter-of-fact sensibility and a general openness; she didn't talk to us as if we were children. She drank beer and let me taste it. She didn't seem to be afraid of my grandmother (and most people were) or of anything else. Kit and Mark made their own granola, which none of us had even heard of until they brought us some. Kit went with the Peace Corps to Afghanistan, and my uncle followed along to be with her. When they did get married, it was in their living room, and the ceremony was performed by a friend. They read poetry from Kahlil Gibran's *The Prophet*, and Kit wore baby's breath in her hair. That Kit later had her babies at home was just one more fascinating facet of what I saw as her wonderful adventurousness — compared to my family's suburban mundanity ... I thought she was so cool.

Kit is a midwife, the first of many midwives I have known and admired for their coolness. Nevertheless, I don't remember Kit ever talking about what she did in her work, nor did I give midwifery much thought until I was an adult.

The Convoluted Tale of How This Book Came About

When I went to the City University of New York for graduate school in sociology in 1984, Kit said I should look up her friend, Barbara Katz Rothman, who taught there. She said I should read Barbara's book *In Labor: Women and Power in the Birthplace* (1991 [1982]) first. I don't think Kit told me that she had been one of the midwives Barbara interviewed.

The book opened my mind to a subject that was new to me. I had never thought about the social construction or power dynamics of pregnancy and birth, quite simply because I had not thought much about pregnancy and birth — except as events to avoid. (As for family birth stories, I did know my mother had been "asleep" during my birth, and "allowed" to be "awake" for my sister's; she preferred the latter, but neither sounded remotely similar to the home births the midwives Barbara interviewed told about.) Barbara's claim that bringing midwives into the hospital was not much different from putting up floral wallpaper — that the institution was basically not receptive to change — was particularly provocative. I decided I would check out the course Barbara was teaching, "Women and Health Care Institutions." I went into sociology because of my interest in feminism and women's studies, yet I distinctly recall thinking: How could you make a whole course out of that?

When I handed in a paper idea for the course, proposing to look at the portrayal of healers in American fiction, Barbara told me she had a similar book idea germinating: to research the depiction of motherhood loss — miscarriage, stillbirth, and infant death — in popular literature over time. She said she would never have asked me before reading my paper because it seemed sort of nepotistic (because of our connection through Kit), but that she decided it would be logical based on our mutual interest. So would I be interested in being her research assistant? To make part of this long story short, over time — many subway rides, lots of bike rides in Prospect Park, doing research together, drinking coffee together — we became great friends. Barbara was my dissertation advisor. We collaborated on a book based on the research we did: *Centuries of Solace: Expressions of Maternal Grief in Popular Literature* (Simonds and Rothman 1992).

I moved to Atlanta in 1989, and for a decade my research focused on abortion and emergency contraception. I did an interview and ethnography project in one clinic (Abortion at Work, Simonds 1996), and I loved this research mainly because I respected the health care workers I interviewed so much for their devotion to women-centered care. I became increasingly interested in procreative issues and occupational identities, in how professional experiences could be spurred by — or could themselves produce — feminist ideals.

Around this time, a friend of mine named Meg decided to have a home birth. She went to the same HMO as I did, Kaiser/Permanente, and she went to all her prenatal appointments with the Kaiser obstetricians in case she ended up being transported to the hospital during her labor. (At that time Kaiser in Atlanta did not employ midwives.) Meg didn't tell the Kaiser doctors she was trying to have a home birth because she knew that OBs tend to disapprove of home birth. Because home birth midwifery was not licensed or explicitly legal in Georgia (nor is it now), her midwife didn't have back-up arrangements with a physician.

Meg did end up in the hospital after a very long labor. The Kaiser doctor on call figured out what she had tried to do, got angry, and treated her abusively. Meg later told me that she felt like she had post-traumatic shock as a result of that birth experience.

When I got pregnant in 1992, Kaiser had just begun employing nurse-midwives. A home birth would have cost a couple of thousand dollars; at that time in my life, it seemed frivolous to me to pay for something I thought I could nearly have without paying extra. Midwives were midwives, I thought, and midwives would take care of me the way I wanted to be taken care of, wherever I was. Who knows? I might not have the stamina to give birth without medication. The mountain climbing and other athletic accomplishment metaphors that midwives used made me feel discouraged and inadequate; I was not a mountaineer or much of an athlete. Besides, my partner, Randy, had reservations about home birth anyway, especially after what had happened to Meg.

Meg said I should at least talk to her midwife. I'm not sure whether it was my lack of bravery, lack of confidence in my body, my cheapness, or my desire not to have to struggle with Randy over the issue, but I really did believe that nurse-midwifery was a reasonable middle ground: I viewed it as a compromise between what I wanted but felt I couldn't have or might not be able to accomplish (home birth), and what I didn't want (obstetrics). Barbara gently expressed her doubts, but she didn't try to impose her view. At the time, I thought she underestimated the potential of midwives in the hospital.

My pregnancy was delightful, and medically uneventful until near the end.

I watched my "due date" come and go. At 41-1/2 weeks I had a non-stress test. At 42 weeks, I had another, along with a sonogram to check the volume of amniotic fluid in my uterus. (I refused to look at the screen, determined not to see the baby until it was born.) I "passed" the tests, but my midwife, Amy, said to me, "I'm supposed to insist that we schedule an induction for tomorrow." She told me that because I was two weeks past my due date, I would be continually monitored throughout my labor, whether it was induced or not. I cried. I reluctantly agreed to an induction scheduled for when she would be on call two days later. I went home, called Kit, and according to her instructions, began taking castor oil. I took a tablespoon an hour for four hours, and then after another hour, I chugged the remains of the small bottle. Nothing happened. I went to bed.

Two hours later, a little past midnight, I woke up with severe cramps and diarrhea. It took me four hours to realize that I was in labor — convinced, as I'd become, that my body was incapable of doing what it was supposed to do. When I got to the hospital at 5:30 am, my cervix was six centimeters dilated. My dilatation slowed then for several hours, but my contractions remained intense and ranged from two to five minutes apart. I remember looking up at the clock on the hospital room wall all day long, the same sort of institutional clock I had watched through grade school, middle school, high school: Was it time to go yet? At first the clock advanced strangely, zooming ahead in fits and starts, but the more exhausted I got, the slower its hands moved. I had packed Scrabble, a deck of cards, and a portable CD player. I had smuggled in a vat of juice and granola bars. I was going to wear my own clothes. And there I was, doing none of what I'd planned, lost in pain that didn't seem to move forward, based on their measurements of my cervix. The people I didn't know kept saying, "You're doing great!" but I didn't feel great at all.

Suzy, the midwife on call, urged me to try laboring in different positions to make my contractions stay frequent. I lay on one side and then the other; I knelt; I stood; I squatted. By now it was afternoon. I had "made progress," but a rim of my cervix had not receded, despite hours of position changes and a distinctly anti-erotic shower scene where I played with my nipples under hot water. Suzy said I might try pushing if I felt like it. I definitely felt an urge to do something new, something else. Pushing felt excruciatingly painful. The baby's head came forward and receded with each push — for almost two hours. The baby's head was not aligned properly, Suzy thought, but eventually, she said, the contractions would help move it into place. I pushed in a variety of positions, kneeling, crouching, squatting, sitting.

While I was pushing, a doctor from my HMO whom I had never seen before came into the room intermittently and skeptically evaluated my performance. He behaved as if he were in charge of all of us. "You can't keep pushing forever," he announced at about 3:30. He said that if I didn't make progress after another hour, he wanted to "do a section." I felt totally depleted. I knew I couldn't push harder than I had been. Suzy didn't seem too concerned with the doctor's warning, but it seemed clear to me that we could not just disregard him because he obviously thought he was the boss.

My labor slowed down again.

My regular midwife, Amy, was coincidentally at the hospital for a meeting and came in to see me. We told her what had been happening. She advised me to try some pitocin, with an epidural. She said I deserved a rest. I thought: rest? I don't care if I die. (This was not a suicidal death wish, just a desire to have it over with.) None of my birth dreams were coming true; I felt entirely defeated. So I agreed.

When the doctor came back in, I told him what I was going to do. "Maybe this baby can be born from below," he conceded. "But if not, at least you'll be ready for surgery." Whether "from below" or "from above," it made no difference to him. I thought: What an asshole! But

I said nothing. He could be cutting into my body later, after all; it would be practical not to antagonize him.

It took some time for the IV tubes to get going, and for the anesthesiologist to come and get the anesthetic to flow into my spine: a bizarre procedure I never imagined I'd elect to use. The pitocin swiftly cranked up my contractions. I watched with interest as they rose and fell on the fetal monitor display, one on top of the next, feeling only mild pressure as the baby's head pushed against my cervix. Ready? Suzy asked. I had feared an epidural would make me unable to feel how to push, but it didn't. It was clear from my first push that this baby would move forward. Everyone cheered. When the doctor reappeared, Suzy told him, "We don't need you!" First a red face gradually emerged; then the rest of the baby slithered forth in one push. The baby was beautiful, with a full head of hair, and big — almost ten pounds.

I felt victorious that I had avoided a c-section, but I'd averted this outcome via other interventions I hadn't wanted. In retrospect, I came to see this labor as a negotiation process that had been stacked against me.

My second birth was similar in several ways: the baby was "late"; my labor stalled when I got to the hospital; I ended up "choosing" interventions I hadn't wanted to speed it; ultimately I had a vaginal birth; I was euphoric about the baby but regretful about the less than ideal aspects of the birth. To be honest, though, at that time in my life, I wasn't clear about what an ideal birth would be, because despite everything I had read and heard about the wonders and the goddess-like natural ecstasy and total power of home birth, I remained unconvinced that I could pull it off. The first time I was pregnant, midwives saved me from a c-section–threatening doc; the second time, I barely saw the midwife because she was attending several births. Both times, the midwives on call were strangers to me. Both times, I felt that my pregnancies, which went "postdate," were pathologized as "overdue," and this led to medicalization I didn't really want. Both times, I "chose" epidurals I hadn't originally wanted and for which I felt a vague remorse. In the background of my experience, I always heard Barbara's voice in my head, saying, "It's all just wallpaper." Even afterward, I didn't completely believe this, basically because most of the strangers I encountered in the hospital were very nice and respectful to me — but I didn't think she was wrong, either.

What I knew but didn't act upon was that home birth was the best option, the only option where I would truly have had power over the situation of my birth (power that would have been thwarted, nevertheless, by the off chance that something would "go wrong"). While fear of failure was definitely part of what kept me from doing it, I also felt constrained by convention: hospital birth was a much easier alternative to pursue than home birth.

The birth experiences of my friends and family members also seemed full of compromises and capitulations that were rarely named as such. A consistent theme was that the setting had gotten much nicer than in our mothers' day, and that the personnel were also more amicable. The rhetoric was now all about choice, having the birth you want. My social world was rife with yuppie books advocating "birth plans" and alternatives to medical intervention that could be integrated into hospital births. We attended yoga classes that refused Lamaze distractionary techniques and men coaches for a seemingly more direct approach of turning inward and breathing through the pain of contractions slowly, rather than huffing and puffing around it. And yet the power dynamics of the birth place — still the hospital for nearly everyone I knew — seemed not to have changed all that much. And, on closer inspection, even the self-help books promising self-actualizing experiences almost always recommended adhering to medical authority (see, e.g., Eisenberg, Murkoff and Hathaway 1991, Verilli and Meuser 1993).

After my first pregnancy, I began to pay closer attention to the role that time played in women's discussions of their pregnancies, births, and postpartum experiences. I became fascinated by the consistency of what sounded to me like the oppressiveness of medicalized time (for instance, in language about being "late," "early" or "on time," or the medical practice of intervening when medical workers have determined that labor is taking too long), even when the women telling their stories did not articulate it this way. I began to investigate advice offered to pregnant women by a variety of "experts," and offered by experts to each other in medical texts, because I was concerned about the potential of these didactic literatures to shape both expectations and experiences about procreation (Simonds 2002).

Over the past eight years, I have repeatedly taught a course called "Birth and Parenthood." Because *In Labor* was out of print, for many years I used photocopies of my favorite chapters. I was repeatedly surprised at my students' general resistance to the interpretations of the power dynamics Barbara offered there. After reading the book, students knew about midwives if they hadn't before — and many confessed to thinking midwifery was "from the past," an archaic or rural occupation. But most of them didn't come to see midwives as uniquely qualified to attend births, as I felt they should have, so entrenched were they in the medical model's conceptualization of birth as painful and perilous. They argued that hospitals had changed a lot for the better since Barbara had done her research. (The midwives she interviewed in the 1970s didn't even have answering machines, much less beepers and cell phones, so some things certainly had changed!) The students would ask questions like: Why not give birth with women OBs? One student's remark summarized the general view: "When something's wrong with my car, I take it to a car mechanic. When I'm having a baby, why would I NOT go to an obstetrician?" Most students perceived women who had home births and even women who had noninterventionist births as masochistic oddballs, as women to whom they could not relate. They didn't understand why anyone would want to experience the pain of childbirth when it could be avoided. My attempts to shift their focus to thinking about power and control (as Barbara does in *In Labor*) were relatively fruitless. There would be occasional converts, but these tended to be atypical pro-"nature" artsy students, somewhat hippyish themselves. During a class discussion, one such student talked about how she had worked to transform her disgust and annoyance about menstruating into a positive spiritual pleasure in her own body and its moonlike rhythms. I could feel the other students roll their eyes in one collective motion. They knew menstruation was unpleasant, and nothing could convince them otherwise, just as they knew they would trade nebulous power and bodily self-confidence for pain relief. So how could I counter students' acceptance of medicalized pregnancy and birth? Did I want to claim the changes that had occurred didn't amount to much more than pretty wallpaper? It didn't seem to matter if I did, just as it hadn't for me when Barbara had said it to me.

In Labor raised other questions for me (aside from the recurrent wallpaper issue): Why didn't the home birth movement that Barbara described as an apparently growing social force expand — where did it go? The presence of nurse-midwifery must surely mean something — but what? Was it anything more than a check on the episiotomy rate? I decided I wanted to investigate the ways in which things are better now in terms of hospital birth, as well as the ways they had stayed the same or gotten worse. I was interested in finding out about the career paths of midwives. What politicized midwives, and how? Did they see their work as political? Were they feminists?

In 1998, I started trying to convince Barbara to write this book with me. It took some time. She was fairly resistant at first to revisit something she felt that she had been done with decades ago, but she eventually gave in. (I can be very persuasive.) But it was still slow going, because we were busy with other things and got to see each other only a few times a year.

When I imagined doing the research for this book, I didn't know that it would cause me to revisit my own birth experiences, and I didn't imagine that my thinking would change very much. And in a way, it hasn't. Because while I knew a lot of what I now know before I started doing the work for this book, doing it reaffirmed what I already knew — if that makes any sense.

Writing this book forced me to revisit and struggle with my regret over my own birth experiences, and with what seemed like a very central conceptual problem: If someone who knew what I knew — was as informed as I had been — and who truly believed in home birth — let a few state restrictions, a resistant partner, and a couple of thousand dollars stand in the way of the right kind of birth, then how could I possibly persuade other people, most of whom are less dogmatic about the ills of medicine, to think of resisting the System? This is, after all, one of the goals we have for this book, as well as to encourage a broader questioning of the medicalized status quo regarding all aspects of health care.

I'm less optimistic about change at the institutional level than I am about subversion. This is something I love about midwifery: that it can mean a little of both. At midwifery conferences, I heard a plethora of wondrous home birth stories and met midwives who believed that the circumstances and dynamics of one's birth chart the whole rest of one's life. My own birth experiences giving birth (I won't even go into the ways in which my own birth could be sullied by scrutiny) came to seem inferior in comparison. What I heard often made me wonder about the "choices" I had made, about what it would have been like to have given birth in a setting where I was not surrounded by benevolent strangers in a hospital room that was a bizarre mix of midlevel hotel decor and medical machinery.

Ultimately, this book is indebted to, builds upon, and continues the critical tradition of the fine work of many scholars who have written sociohistorical and ethnographic work on the development and practice of health care professions in general, including those writing particularly about birth workers (e.g., Arney 1982, Banks 1999, Borst 1995, Burtch 1994, DeVries 1996, Donegan 1978, Donnison 1977, Ehrenreich and English 1973, Chambliss 1996, Foucault 1973, Fraser 1998, Lorber 1984, Melosh 1982, McGregor 1998, Millman 1977, More 1999, Rosenberg 1987, Roth 1963, Shroff 1997, Starr 1982, Sudnow 1967, Weinberg 2003, Zerubavel 1979), on women's health (e.g., Clarke and Oleson 1999, Fee 1982, Leavitt 1984, 1999, Morgen 2002, Roberts 1997, Ruzek 1978, Ruzek, Oleson and Clark 1997), and on procreative experiences and politics (e.g., Arms 1975, Borst 1995, Casper 1996, Davis-Floyd 1992, Davis-Floyd and Sargent 1997, DeVries et al. 2001, Ferree et al. 2002, Gaskin 1990, Inhorn and Van Balen 2002, Jordan 1993, Kahn 1995, Klassen 2001, LaRossa 1983, Lay 2000, Leavitt 1986, Litt 2000, Martin 1987, Matthews and Wexler 2000, Michie and Cahn 1997, Mitchell 2001, Murphy-Lawless 1998, Oakley 1984, Petchesky 1990, Reed 2005, Rooks 1997, Shaw 1974, Wagner 1994, Wertz and Wertz 1989 [1977]). We are united with these scholars in the view that the deleterious power dynamics involved in health care experiences must be continually examined and exposed if we are ever to achieve any measure of change.

Our Methods and the Organization of This Book

Part One of the book, "Labor in Transition," is based on an updating of Barbara's *In Labor*, and those two introductory chapters, "Laboring

Then" and "Laboring Now," set the stage historically and ideologically for understanding the politics of birth in the United States. With a minimum of sociological jargon, the deeply sociological analysis still stands: birth is what we make it; practices determine knowledge as much as or more than knowledge determines practice; and power relations — between practitioners themselves as well as between practitioners and birthing women — shape the birth experience.

Barbara's original research on this project was done for her dissertation, which was a documentation of the two different clinical models of birth that existed in the United States at the time. One was the standard medical approach. The other was the developing "home birth" or "midwifery" approach. She struggled to find a way to describe these, trying and rejecting Thomas Kuhn's language of "paradigms" (1962), thinking about whether to name these approaches after their places of operation (hospital or home), and finally settling on "medical model" and "midwifery model." Her coinage "midwifery model" became the standard term, the way the midwives themselves now describe their way of thinking about birth.

One part of the research Barbara did was a rich and detailed content analysis of both the obstetric literature and the literature of the home birth movement. But many of the data she gathered, and the source of quotes in her chapters, was participant observation in the home birth movement and the midwifery network for three years, from 1975 through 1978, attending meetings, conferences, informal discussions, and a few births. She focused on the crisis of knowledge — the dawning realization among nurse-midwives and home birth advocates that medical knowledge was simply wrong about birth — and the social activity of reconceptualization as it occurred individually and collectively. In 1978, she did twelve interviews with nurse midwives in the New York City area. That included seven of the eight nurse-midwives who were doing home births in New York City at the time (the eighth was out of the country that year). The other five nurse-midwives interviewed were employed at the only midwife-run out-of-hospital birth center in New York City. She thus had a census of the New York midwives who were most clearly "in transition," moving between the medically based knowledge of nurse-midwifery training and their empirically based knowledge of home births.

In chapter 1, "Laboring Then: The Political History of Maternity Care in the United States," Barbara provides a concise history of American childbirth, tracing the overthrow of midwifery by the newly developed profession of medicine with its aggressive anti-midwifery campaigns, through to the revival of midwifery and home birth in the 1970s. She picks up the story in greater detail thereafter, as midwifery bifurcated into hospital-based nurse-midwifery and the alternative provided by home birth midwives.

In chapter 2, "Laboring Now: Current Cultural Constructions of Pregnancy, Birth, and Mothering," Barbara contrasts the midwifery model of birth with conventional obstetrics. Midwives contextualize birth, seeing the meaning and place of motherhood through the lives of women and their families, as opposed to constructing pregnancy and birth as medical events to be managed. In this chapter, she discusses midwifery and obstetrical approaches to pregnancy, birth, the care and feeding of babies, and the problematic concept of bonding.

Part Two, "Midwives in Transition," is based on interviews conducted between 1999 and 2002 with 115 midwives and midwifery students around the United States. In the late 1990s, when I started my "phase" of the research, I applied for and was awarded a Georgia State University Research Initiation Grant (RIG) that enabled me to travel to midwifery educational institutions and conferences around the United States, and I also began to interview midwives locally in Atlanta. On some occasions, Barbara, Bari, and a few graduate students working with me — Jennifer Chandler, Hydi Dickstein, and Courtney Muse — took part in the interviewing.

Chapter 3, "Becoming a Midwife: Varieties of Inspiration," analyzes midwives' professional origin stories: in it, I explore how and why they came to midwifery. Chapter 4, "Birth Matters: Practicing Midwifery," contrasts midwives' practice ideals and practical realities. I examine what they seek to achieve through their work/art, their rhetorics of "power," "empowerment" and "choice," their views on home vs. hospital births, their discussions of obstacles and aids to achieving ideal practice, their views on intervention and medical technologies in pregnancy and birth, and their assessments of relationships between nurse-midwives and direct-entry midwives, and between midwives and doctors.

These women trained (or were in the process of training) to become midwives primarily in the United States from the 1950s to the 2000s. Their stories are inextricably intertwined with the institutions where they learned (or were learning at the time of their interviews) to practice midwifery, institutions which made and continue to make midwifery possible in the United States.

All in all, we were more successful at gaining entrée to less conventional midwifery programs (institutions that incorporated an anti-institutional flavor into their self-identity): the Seattle Midwifery School (SMS), the Florida School for Traditional Midwifery (FSTM), and the Frontier Nursing Service's (FNS) Community-Based Nurse-midwifery Education Program (CNEP). We spent more time in these places than in the two hospital-based training programs, SUNY (State University of New York) Downstate Medical Center and New York University (NYU), largely because they were especially welcoming to us. Our data thus include more narratives of midwives whose institutional affiliations may promote less mainstream views than they would if we had gained access to more conventional nurse-midwifery programs. We consider this a strength because it allows us to illustrate concertedly critical responses to medicalization. It can also be seen as a limitation, however; we do not fully document the most medicalized aspects of midwifery. Though there is an ethnographic component to our research, we did not attend births as part of this work, nor observe caregiver–client interactions, nor speak to clients about their birth experiences with the practitioners we interviewed.

I visited the Florida School for Traditional Midwifery in Gainesville, Florida in May 1999, and the Seattle Midwifery School in May 2000; and I attended a CNEP training at the FNS in Hyden, Kentucky in June 2000. I conducted focus group and individual interviews with faculty and students at these sites. In December 2000, Barbara and I conducted focus group interviews with faculty (all nurse-midwives) and with direct-entry midwifery and nurse-midwifery students being trained together at Downstate, and an individual interview with a nurse-midwife (with a long activist and home birth midwifery past) who owned a birth center in Brooklyn, New York. Barbara interviewed a group of midwifery students at NYU in March 2002. I interviewed home birth and nurse-midwives in Atlanta between July 1999 and August 2002. (Occasionally, graduate students assisted in these efforts, but only one interview — with the Atlanta nurse-midwife given the pseudonym Lisette Maddox — was conducted by Courtney Muse and Hydi Dickstein together.)

Barbara and I also attended three midwifery conferences: a *Birth Gazette*-sponsored conference at The Farm in Summertown, Tennessee in June 1999, where we conducted several individual and one dual interview; a MANA (Midwives Alliance of North America) conference in Tampa in November 2000; a New York City American College of Nurse Midwives (ACNM) chapter meeting and holiday party in December 2000; and an ACNM conference in Atlanta in 2002. Barbara, Bari Meltzer Norman, and I went to a meeting of a home birth midwives' group in New York City in May 2001 and conducted a focus group interview.

In all, we interviewed 21 direct-entry midwives, 4 direct-entry midwifery activists (some of whom had participated in births in the past but no longer did), 2 direct-entry apprentices, 19 direct-entry students, 22 students in the joint program at Downstate, 22 nurse-midwives (8 of whom also attended home births), and 16 nurse-midwifery students (two of whom had experience as direct-entry midwives).

Part Three of the book, "Disorganized Labor," deals with birth workers other than midwives: the best-known groups, obstetricians and nurses, and perhaps the least-known group, labor doulas. After interviewing about 50 midwives and hearing repeatedly about how CNMs struggled to maintain an anti-medical stance in medical environments (and also spurred by my aforementioned students' continual insistence that women obstetricians were the answer to the overmedicalization of childbirth), I decided to interview a small comparison group of women obstetricians. How much of the institutional mindset would I encounter in their talk, I wondered? I specifically wanted a sample of doctors who were known to be supportive of midwifery, so I asked midwives and midwifery-oriented nurses to recommend doctors they thought were "good." How different would women OBs deemed to be "good" by midwives be from midwives? How different would they be from conventional obstetricians, whose authoritarian and invasive practices, described by the midwives we interviewed, are well documented in the literature (e.g., Arms 1975, Arney 1982, Borst

1995, Davis-Floyd 1992, Davis-Floyd and St. John 1998, Goer 1995, 1999, Langton 1994, Litt 2000, Rothman 1982, Shaw 1974)?

Chapter 5, "Women in White: Obstetricians and Labor and Delivery Nurses," is based on interviews with ten "good" doctors and five nurses (also deemed "good" by midwives). By no means do I wish to suggest that this group represents women obstetricians or labor and delivery nurses more generally, or that it is a group comparable to that of the midwives we interviewed for this book. But their views do offer many points of comparison, and their reflections on their experiences elucidate a path to birth work entirely different from those of the midwives and midwifery students.

In the past decade or so, labor doulas have emerged in the popular press as a potential solution for excessive intervention rates. Doulas, who generally can receive training in a few days, claim to provide woman-centered, nonjudgmental labor "support." Chapter 6, "The New Arrival: Labor Doulas and the Fragmentation of Midwifery and Caregiving," is based on qualitative, in-depth interviews with 30 doulas. Bari conducted individual interviews with doulas during two separate phases of data collection. The first phase of her data collection consisted of interviews with 20 doulas from New York City and its surrounding suburbs between January and May 2001. The second phase of data collection included follow-up telephone interviews with the initial group of respondents and in-person interviews with a second group of ten labor doulas between January and July 2003. The second group of doulas all practiced in the Miami metropolitan area. Bari's interviews focused on the movement of individuals (doulas) within an institution (the medical institution) and the resulting effects on those individuals' moral identities, the people they serve, and their developing occupation. (Further discussion of demographic characteristics of the doulas can be found in chapter 6.)

Though I attempted to collect demographic data on all the midwives, midwifery students, nurses, and doctors who participated, sometimes — especially during focus groups — people would take the demographic data sheets with them and fail to return them. Since we do not claim to establish any sort of representative sample of midwives, OBs, or nurses, I will not dwell too long on the particulars. Seventeen of the 125 participants defined themselves as members of racial/ethnic minorities or as mixed race, and the rest called themselves white or Caucasian (and several didn't answer the question). The biggest racial/ethnic diversity was among the doctors, of whom three out of ten were African American, and the least racial/ethnic diversity was among the nurses, of whom all five were white. Participants ranged in age from the mid-twenties to late sixties; most were in their thirties and forties at the time of their interviews. Student-midwives, unsurprisingly, tended to be younger than midwives or doctors and nurses. About two-thirds of the participants had children. Among those who reported incomes from midwifery, nurse-midwives made the most money, with $85,000 a year the highest salary and $22,000 the lowest reported by those working full time. Direct-entry midwives doing home births reported making between $10,000 and $35,000 annually; a few direct-entry participants were not working as midwives at the time of their interviews because they could not find work, or had not yet begun to work after graduating. Many direct-entry midwives supplemented their income from midwifery with other work, but none of the other participants did. The doctors who gave us information about their incomes made over $100,000 annually, and the nurses made about a third of that (less than nurse-midwives).

The names of all participants used in this book are pseudonyms.

The Trials and Tribulations of Research

For the most part we had very little difficulty recruiting midwifery participants because Barbara's contacts with midwives around the country opened doors. Faculty members at all the schools knew her work, and many knew her from her decades-long involvement with midwifery politics. Once I began interviewing midwives in Atlanta, I gained local contacts and my sample snowballed nicely. Through one of these women (given the pseudonym Mel Sallinger here), I gained access to CNEP students and faculty.

But contacts were not always enough. The difficulties involved in research can be telling. In our case, they illustrate some of the very differences among midwives and differences between midwifery and obstetrics that we sought to investigate. The more medicalized the setting, the more difficult it was for us to gain entrée. This was partly because of us.

For instance, it seemed logical and convenient for me to try to do interviews at Emory, a local, well-known, well-established nurse-midwifery school. I had interviewed several local nurse-midwives who trained there, and I wanted to include a counterpoint to the programs training direct-entry midwives and to CNEP, which is known for its unconventional self-directed, distance-education approach to nurse-midwifery training. Following are two excerpts from the notes I kept on my attempts to gain access to Emory nurse-midwifery students and faculty.

3/27/00: About a month ago, I wrote to the director of the program. Then, when I didn't hear back, I called her, and she was very pleasant on the phone. She said they were having a meeting the next week and that she would raise my request with the faculty. I sent her my application for the RIG at her request. I called her after the meeting, and she told me that the matter was now in the hands of [the program director]. I started trying to reach [this person]. When I finally did reach her, she had a list of questions. The main issues were: What would happen with the research? How was it to be used? Faculty members had "concerns" about the proposal — "many" felt that we were making assumptions — like that nurse-midwifery was more medicalized than direct-entry midwifery! And what was I going to do to achieve rigor?

5/8/00: About a month ago [the director] called me to say YES, the faculty would participate in a focus group interview. We tentatively agreed that I would do a focus group this week. In the interim, I sent her a brief project description for her students along with a note asking her to collect their responses; they could fill out the bottom if they were interested in participating, and then I would contact them. I heard nothing back, so I e-mailed her to see what was up. Well, they hadn't met again as a faculty, so they hadn't scheduled a time they could do the group. She had given her students the handout I sent her "so they could get in touch with me" — as if that's how research gets done in this sort of situation — or ever! I e-mailed her back saying that if a focus group wasn't convenient now I could wait, or I could interview people individually. She e-mailed me that she forwarded my e-mail to the faculty. So what now?

After one more attempt at reaching the director, I gave up. I decided I didn't want to continue to pursue a research opportunity where I sensed disinclination and suspicion on the part of the faculty. They weren't wrong about us. We *did* believe nurse-midwifery was more medicalized than home birth midwifery. (How could it not be?) Still, I felt I was open to hearing that hospitals were no longer medicalized, if that would be the viewpoint participants would bring to the table. My goal wasn't to sabotage anyone. Yet I couldn't allay concerns that my critical view would conflict with theirs. I was asking to take their words and use them for my own purposes: this is what research is all about. And the director was worried about my stance, because I already had one and wasn't hiding it. As for "rigor," this was not a double-blind study, nor did we intend it to be. Though we were on the phone, I felt I could *hear* the smirk on the director's face when I expounded on the virtues of qualitative research, trying to explain that rigor was not a particularly meaningful concept for me, and that I thought it was a smokescreen for the inevitable subjectivity of sociological research.

Interviewing doctors was the most challenging aspect of the research project for me. The first two doctors I interviewed were people I had met casually who showed interest in the research (called by the pseudonyms Mindy Fried and Lois Silverman in chapter 5), who told me they had enjoyed working with midwives, and who were endorsed by midwives I'd interviewed. They were eager to participate. During the summer of 2000, I interviewed these two women and two other obstetricians, and I unsuccessfully attempted to set up interviews with six others.

Arranging these interviews with doctors was much more difficult than setting up interviews with midwives (with the exception of the Emory midwives, described above). First of all, one cannot call doctors directly. Whether or not they would return my calls depended on how their communications systems with staff were organized. Often I would speak only to staff members several times before getting to a doctor, and in some cases, the staff member would arrange

the interview entirely or I would give up after three attempts, without
ever speaking to the doctor. The doctors who did return my calls often
would grill me about the content of the proposed interview. Of course,
participants have every right to ask questions. Many of the midwives,
too, had asked a lot of questions before agreeing to an interview. But
something felt different here. I perceived two disparities: first, like
the Emory midwifery administrators, the doctors were suspicious and
reluctant; they sometimes sounded like they basically didn't want to
do it. I felt that I was coercing or pushing them to participate, and I
didn't like that feeling. Second, they clearly thought they were doing
me a big favor, and that participating would be quite an inconvenience.
In fact, they *were* contemplating doing me a big favor, but as in the
Emory case, being treated as if I were imposing made me feel that I
would rather not pursue the interview opportunity.

At this point, I simply lost my energy for this part of the project
and abandoned it in frustration at myself and at obstetricians in general. I wrote:

> I feel strange doing these interviews, uncomfortable when the doctors
> do what we want them to do, which is give voice to the medical model
> (which most do, at least at some of the time), and demonstrate that they
> are not like midwives (which most are not, most of the time). I feel
> uncomfortable when they express an uncritical acceptance of medical
> procedures or interventions, or when they demonstrate medical arro-
> gance. These are nice women. I like them. I am suddenly struck by a vast
> distance between us. I have the vague feeling that I am setting a trap in
> asking these women to talk honestly about obstetrics. (Fieldnotes)

After about a year, my dissatisfaction at not having accomplished
my goal of interviewing OBs resurfaced. I conferred with Barbara and
Bari, and as a result, Bari volunteered to make all the arrangements
for Barbara and me to do a focus group interview with obstetrical
residents at a hospital in New York. I planned a trip to New York in
May 2001. When Barbara and I arrived at the hospital seminar room
where our group was scheduled to meet, bearing refreshments, the
residents were nowhere to be found. We waited in the empty room
where they had "just been," according to the very nice secretary with
whom Bari had arranged the meeting. She said maybe they would

be back, because she was certain they knew about the interview. We waited and waited. It was like waiting in a doctor's office, only we both felt fairly certain we would never see the doctors.

And we never did see the doctors. The secretary returned after more than half an hour, abashed, apologetic. The residents had stood us up! Their instructor had told them they could go, and so they went. "They just went?" I sputtered. "But they knew we were coming?" "Herd mentality," Barbara muttered under her breath. They probably wouldn't be back, the secretary said, but we could wait a couple of hours and see, if we liked. We exchanged annoyed looks and soon decided that rather than look back on this experience and laugh, we would just go ahead and laugh, and eat some of the pastries we had brought.

After this point, I felt that there was no way we were going to get even a small group of interviews with obstetricians or obstetricians-to-be. When I discussed these difficulties with my department chairperson, he suggested that perhaps doctors might respond to a financial incentive. "Would they do it for $50 an interview?" he wondered. He encouraged me to apply for departmental research money to fund such a venture, but I bridled at the thought of paying obstetricians to talk to us when midwives, who make much less money on the whole, had participated for free.

In 2002, I had two willing and able graduate students working for me, Hydi Dickstein and Courtney Muse. I told them about my experiences and cautioned them about the persistence they would need to get interviews scheduled, and they agreed to try. They then embarked on conducting the second group of five interviews with OBs over the next nine months. To get to an even number with double digits (ten), I conducted one more interview in 2002, with an OB working in a large HMO, given the name Lydia Salvo in chapter 5.

All the doctors who participated in this research (except for Mindy Fried, who was on a leave from her job, and who had me over to her home on a weekend) fit the interviews into their work schedules. Since each of them was very busy in her practice, being "fit in" to a schedule often meant being crammed in. Interviews were often interrupted – by phone calls, office staff, or doctors' colleagues — and they usually had to be compressed into less than an hour and occasionally were cut short. The interviews with midwives and midwifery students, in contrast, were much more relaxed. (Ironically — or maybe not — these time variables echo the two professions' approach to time during labor and birth.) The doctors who did participate were less likely to sound mistrustful and inconvenienced, but their demeanor was still different from that of midwives, who were usually eager to expound on their professional experiences at length, and who clearly saw themselves as advocates for midwifery.

Dilemmas and Hopes in Writing

The writing of my parts of this book occurred in fits and starts. Writing felt futile to me at times. What could it accomplish? Change is slow, I would argue with myself, trying to get myself to just sit down and write this book that we had a contract for and whose deadline loomed and then passed. Books *have* changed my thinking — yet not always quite firmly enough that I put what I believed into action. I would go back and forth with myself. I would let the pile of interviews sit, and leave half-baked chapters half-baked.

Then I would come back and reread the interviews and be reminded of what amazing philosophers midwives could be, and recapture my awe at activists truly and idealistically focused on one thing. I would also regain my fascination with those who expressed a more muddled view: women who still stood for midwifery ideals in a loose way, tilting at windmills, but also chipping away at things that seemed written in stone.

For instance, take episiotomies. Midwives' opposition to episiotomies appears to have had an effect on the episiotomy rate, which has declined gradually as nurse-midwives have entered the realm of hospital birth. Now, episiotomies are not the biggest deal in the surgical world by any means. But they are instructive for precisely that reason. Think of millions of women a year, for decades, needlessly having their perineums slashed — because that's what an episiotomy is: Doesn't that seem like a crime to fight? When you think about it that way, you might wonder why millions of women have seemingly willingly walked into hospitals, lain down on beds, spread their legs, and allowed doctors to slash their perineums. But when you learn that the cutters truly believe that the cutting is good for women, that complicates it a bit. Sometimes — ever so occasionally — they're right. The cutters are surgeons; cutting into the body is the central element of their job. So in a world where slashing into the body is a norm, where bodies are conceived as a conglomerate of parts that can be improved when slashed into, midwives can appear to be quite unusual: for the most important part of their job, their sole goal is to enable the actions of others. The politics of birth, and of medicalization in general, can seem insurmountable, a battle that has been waged in different ways for centuries between those with power and those without, over the definition of knowledge, of organizing principles. Yet change is constant, even if not progressive. Social movements and institutions grow, evolve, adapt, make compromises. As a movement settles into the larger culture, cracks appear along its own original fault lines. Our book tells the story of midwifery and childbirth reform in the United States and places them within the larger women's health and feminist movements, as well as within the 1960s counterculture, in New Age spirituality, and even in the rise of conservative Christianity. We will tell the stories of all of these movements and show how they influence childbirth practice and experience.

In the childbirth movement, as in the rest of the women's health movement, much has been made of the "empowerment" of women: giving (or returning) to women power that medicine had usurped. The home birth movement was very clear about this: only women had the power to give birth. Doctors did not deliver babies, mothers did. Birth was not something done *to* women, but something women *do*. What happens to a radical reconceptualization like this one as it settles into the larger culture? "Birth is only 10% in the pelvis, 90% in the head," a midwife told Barbara, explaining that change had to take place in the culture to make birth better. Many midwives and home birth activists agree that the problem lies in the way women are taught to think about birth. But this conceptualization, too, can become one more responsibility, one more potential failure: if a birth does not go as a woman plans and desires, the blame lies with the woman for not being "strong enough."

Often during the research for and writing of this book, when I would talk to people about the ideological differences between midwifery and obstetrics, they would get defensive, as if my goal were to impugn or denigrate their birth experiences. It isn't. And, as I've discussed, over the course of this project I have experienced this sort of defensiveness myself. Ultimately, I have found it most productive when this defensiveness can be transformed into anger. One of the things that happened during my prolonged writing (and not-writing) process was that my anger would sometimes shift into exhaustion, and that is not a particularly productive emotional base from which to write. But luckily, I would always get pissed off again.

And that's my goal. I want you to be pissed off too. This book is the closest I'm ever going to get to home birth. I'm glad I got the energy I needed to push.

PART ONE

LABORING IN TRANSITION

1

Laboring Then

The Political History of Maternity Care in the United States

BARBARA KATZ ROTHMAN

Introduction

When it comes to motherhood, we live in a world that makes no sense. We have seen the return of the midwife, and the rise of the cesarean section. For 50 years there were almost no midwives to be found in most of the United States. Then, during the same period when nurse-midwives began practicing in U.S. hospitals, while hospitals introduced "birthing rooms" to replace operating room-like delivery rooms and the "natural childbirth" movement flourished, we also saw the cesarean section rate rise from slightly over 5% in 1970 to an astonishing and unprecedented rate of 29.1% in 2004; it increased by 41% between 1996 and 2004 (Curtin and Kozak 1998, DeClercq et al. 2006, Hamilton et al. 2004, Martin et al. 2005).

Since the development of modern obstetrics, there has never been more talk of birth as a "healthy natural event," yet each individual birthing woman is now acquainted with her personal "risk factors," which doctors tell her make *her* birth less than healthy and far less than "natural." Of women who birth in hospitals, 85% are strapped to fetal monitors (Martin et al. 2003), despite evidence that such monitoring produces unnecessary interventions (see Goer 1999: 244–47 for a summary of the medical literature on this issue).

Hospitals, where virtually all of our births take place, hire lactation consultants, show breastfeeding videotapes, and offer breastfeeding classes. They also provide formula companies with mailing lists, so that samples once given out in maternity wards are now simply sent by mail.

Childbearing at forty is considered chic, childbearing at fifty and up is the new frontier of procreative technology, but childbearing at eighteen is considered pathetic — chances lost. And we have one of the highest teenage pregnancy rates in the developed world.

Ultrasound examinations are used as moments for women and families to "bond" with their babies. Sonographers like to talk about the baby waving, sucking its thumb, even "looking at" the mother looking at the screen. And those same ultrasounds are used to screen fetuses for selective abortions.

In the name of "family values," family needs are going unmet: every attempt to provide family services, from maternity leave to day care, is being cut by conservative politicos, all while they're calling for a return to family values.

How did we come to this paradoxical position we now occupy, where all of these contradictions are part of our everyday life? Understanding these contradictions and the other strange twists and turns of contemporary U.S. maternity care is the goal of this book. As sociologists, we believe that understanding these situations requires placing them in the larger context in which they occur. To unravel the contradictions surrounding U.S. maternity care, we will consider the meaning of pregnancy, of birth, and even of parenthood itself. When we look at the use and misuse of technologies in maternity care, we will consider the *meanings* we attach to the human body, as machine, as organism, and as the embodiment of personhood.

Pregnancy and birth have different meanings for different people. What, after all, is a pregnancy? Pregnancy is sometimes a contraceptive failure, a side effect of a not very reliable method of birth control. Pregnancy is also the effect of a successful treatment for infertility. Pregnancy is a condition of a woman's body, to be distinguished from ovulation, menstruation, and menopause. Pregnancy is the presence of a man's baby in a woman, as when a man wants a woman to bear him a son to carry on his name. W. I. Thomas famously said, "Situations defined as real are real in their consequences." How do we define pregnancy and birth, how do we give meaning to them? Who has the power to define?

The meaning of pregnancy is, like everything else, in the eye of the beholder, and in the United States, the foremost "beholder" of pregnancy is the obstetrician. The obstetrical perspective on pregnancy and birth is held to be not just one way of looking at it, but to be the truth, the facts, science: other societies may have had beliefs about pregnancy, but we believe our medicine has the *facts*. But obstetrical knowledge, like all other knowledge, comes from *somewhere*; it has a social, historical, and political context. Medicine does not exist as "pure," free of culture or free of ideology. The context in which knowledge develops and is used shapes that knowledge. Doctors see pregnancy, childbirth, and women's entire procreative lives from their own perspective. This book examines that perspective and compares it with the perspective that was developed by home birth advocates and midwives. These two perspectives are very different; in some ways, they are diametrically opposed. Pieces of both perspectives have come into U.S. popular culture. It is in the conflict between these two perspectives that the contradictions surrounding birth in this country arise. And it is in the negotiation of those two perspectives that contemporary midwives and doulas struggle.

Two Models of Care

The questions we are asking in this book are about birth and pregnancy and babies, about motherhood and midwives and doulas. But they are also some basic questions in sociology: How do people know what they know? How do social groups — movements like the home birth movement or established professions like obstetrics — arise, gain power, and maintain themselves?

The popular view of what is happening in maternity care in the United States is that obstetrics provides safety, and good technical care, but at the cost of warmth. We have, however, listened carefully to what home birth advocates, midwives, and doulas are saying, and to what obstetricians are saying. In contrast to the ideas that home birth is for socio-emotional reasons and hospitals for safety, obstetricians for science and midwives for spirit, we hear midwives offering scientific, evidence-based criticisms of obstetrics. It is not just being more "humane" or more concerned with emotional needs that differentiates the home birth movement from contemporary obstetrics in the United States: these people are seeing things in different ways. Both groups are taking the same objects — things like fetus, milk, placenta, term, or labor — and forming different ideas about them. They respond differently, they treat things differently, because they see them all differently.

We are taking a "sociology of knowledge" approach here, heavily influenced by the work of Thomas Kuhn on how science moves by "paradigm shifts." But we are not going to talk about "paradigms" because we are talking about "clinical" work, not science. Both obstetrics and midwifery are applied practices, clinical rather than scientific work. Clinical work may cloak itself in the mantle of science, but it is a fundamentally different kind of work. So we will talk not about "paradigms" but about "models" of care, the underlying, sometimes unstated sets of assumptions practitioners make about the objects of their work.

And what shall we call these models? One is easily called the "medical model," since obstetrics draws so heavily on underlying medical approaches. We could think of the other model as the "home birth model" since we are very concerned with the importance of place. But back when I first began this work in the 1970s, I saw that there were midwives who had worked very hard at bringing into the hospital the essence of what home is about in birth: autonomy and woman-centered control, not flowered sheets. Medicine too has had a long history of bringing hospital management into the home. A mid-1950s obstetric textbook by Alan Guttmacher shows a photo of a woman tied up in sheets, rigged up like a nightmare with her legs spread and tied, her hands restrained, in her very own bedroom. So, with much deliberation, I chose the term "midwifery model" to contrast with the "medical model," to express two different bodies of knowledge and practice that have developed in U.S. maternity care.

Ideologies of Technology and of Patriarchy

The primary characteristic of the modern medical model of health and illness in general is that it is based on the ideology of technology, that ideology appropriate to technological society, with its values of efficiency and rationality, practical organization, systematizing, and controlling. The application of a technological model to the human body can be traced back to René Descartes's concept of mind/body dualism. For Descartes, the body was a machine, the structure and operation of which fell within the province of human knowledge, as distinguished from the mind, which God alone could know. Even though the Hippocratic principles state that the mind and body should be considered together, most physicians, whatever their philosophical views on the nature of the mind, behave in practice as if they were still Cartesian dualists (Dubos 1968: 76). The Cartesian model of the body as a machine operates to make the physician a technician, or mechanic. The body breaks down and needs repair; it can be repaired in the hospital as a car is in the shop; once "fixed," a person can be returned to the community. The earliest models in medicine were largely mechanical; later models worked more with chemistry, and newer medical writing describes computer-like programming, but the basic point remains the same. Problems in the body are technical problems requiring technical solutions, whether it is a mechanical repair, chemical rebalancing, or "debugging" the system.

A second major ideological basis of the medical model comes from medicine's history as a men's profession, growing out of a patriarchal history. Its values are those of men as the dominant social power; medicine sees pregnancy and birth through men's eyes; even now, as more and more women are trained in obstetrics, that history continues to cast its shadow. Medicine treats all patients, male and female, as "machines," in conformance with the ideology of technological society. The treatment of women patients is further affected by the ideology of patriarchal society. I mean something more subtle here than just "men rule." In a patriarchy, it is men *as fathers* who rule, and families take their names and their identities through fathers. Our society is not, of course, a simple patriarchy, but the history of patriarchy colors our understandings of birth and family. We can see this become increasingly important with the development of new reproductive technologies, which focus entirely on getting "seeds" to grow, the essential patriarchal concern. Relationships, even the relationship between a pregnant woman and the baby in her belly, take second place to the genetic ties, the "seed."

But just in terms of pregnancy and birth care, one important consequence of its patriarchal history is that medicine has fared no better than other disciplines in arriving at a working model of women that does not take men as the comparative norm. Medicine has treated and in many instances overtly defined normal female reproductive processes as diseases. Certainly U.S. medicine is disease-oriented and has been since its early formal organization. That is very true; and that particular critique of medicine, and medical management of women's reproductive functions especially, has been made over and over again. Yes, doctors are illness-oriented, and yes, they did and sometimes still do treat pregnancy, birth, menstruation, and menopause as diseases. But knowing that is not enough. We must go beyond that and ask *why*. Medicine does not, after all, treat all of our biological functions as diseases: the digestive system, for example, is usually considered well unless shown otherwise. Neither a full nor an empty colon has been seen as a disease-like state, and normal bowel movements are not medically monitored. Why, then, are female reproductive processes singled out to make women "unwell," in a "delicate condition," constantly moving from one disease-like state to another?

The source of the pathology orientation of medicine toward women's health and reproduction is a body-as-a-machine model (the ideology of technology) in which the male body is taken as the norm (the ideology of patriarchy). From that viewpoint, reproductive processes are stresses on the system, and thus disease-like.

In earlier times, through the mid-twentieth century, the language of illness was quite frankly used when discussing women's reproductive systems, with pregnancy seen as a disease, menopause as a deficiency disorder, and childbirth as a surgical procedure. Contemporary physicians do not usually speak this way any more, regularly asserting that female reproductive functions are normal and healthy. However, they make these statements within the context of teaching the medical "management," "care," "supervision," and "treatment" of these "conditions." From the "diagnosis" of pregnancy, through the "management" of its "symptoms," on to "recovery" from childbirth, the disease imagery remains and continues to influence obstetric thinking and practice.

The contemporary midwifery model of birth grew in response to this medical approach. Coming together out of the "back to nature" movements of the 1960s, "hippie" communal life, the feminist movement, the patient's rights movement, religious fundamentalism, and radical individualism — from a variety of strangely interrelated and sometimes apparently unrelated sources — a new midwifery began to appear in the United States. Where the obstetric approach was "technological," the midwives were "holistic"; where the obstetricians were patriarchal, the midwives were "women-centered." In home births and birth centers, in midwifery practices in and out of hospitals all over the United States, midwives worked to redefine birth and to offer a different place to stand, a new — and maybe a very old — perspective on pregnancy, birth, mothers, and babies.

Meddlesome Midwifery: The Entry of the Men

When Americans look back at the history of birth and maternity care, midwifery seems like a branch of medicine, and the midwife an untrained forerunner of the obstetrician. We are going to tell a different story.

The recorded history of midwifery goes back as far as any recorded history. The wife of Pericles and the mother of Socrates were midwives, and in the book of Exodus, Moses' midwives, Shifrah and Puah, were rewarded by God. Every culture in the history of the world has had its midwives; wherever there have been women, there have been midwives.

Two important things happened in the history of midwifery: midwives lost autonomy, control of their work, to doctors; and doctors and midwives allocated patients according to notions of appropriate "territory." The two problems are interrelated. Doctors carved out as their territory pathological or abnormal births. They then went on to define all births as either inherently or at least potentially pathological and abnormal, so that there was no room for the midwife. Even today, midwifery care in the United States is seen as suitable only for "low-risk" births, while more and more births are being defined as "high-risk."

The focus in this chapter will be the background of the American midwifery story. Midwives came over with the Pilgrims, and indeed the native peoples had their midwives before that. What is different about the United States, compared to other countries, is that it was virtually unique in the world in largely abolishing midwifery before reinventing it in a new form, as a branch of nursing. Other industrialized countries, such as France, Germany, Japan, and the Netherlands, maintained some form of midwifery. In some the midwives had more power and in some less, but all have a continuous history of practicing midwives. There are continuing midwifery traditions all over the world, but their independence and their relationship to medical practice directly reflects the history of imperialism and colonization. The history of midwifery reflects world history: America won World War II, and Japanese midwives lost status and power as Americans restructured Japanese hospitals; East and West Germany went separate ways in birth practices; countries colonized by the Dutch show a different midwifery than those colonized by the British. But it is in the United States that we see an attempt simply to abolish midwifery completely.

The beginning of the end of American midwifery goes back before the establishment of the United States and has its roots in British and European history. The earliest sign of encroachment on midwifery came from the development of the barber-surgeons' guilds. In England, for example, under the guild system that developed in the thirteenth century, the right to use surgical instruments belonged officially only to the surgeon. Thus, when giving birth was absolutely impossible, the midwife called in the barber-surgeon to perform an embryotomy (crushing the fetal skull, dismembering it in utero, and removing it piecemeal), or to remove the baby by cesarean section after the death of the mother. It was not within the technology of the barber-surgeon to deliver a live baby from a live mother. Not until the development of forceps in the seventeenth century were men involved in live births and so became a genuine challenge to midwives. Interest in abnormal cases increased throughout the seventeenth century and especially the eighteenth; this may have been due to rapid urbanization and the resultant increase in pelvic deformities caused by rickets. (For a history of American midwifery, see Donegan 1978 and Donnison 1977; for a history of European midwifery, see Bullough 1966.)

In the early seventeenth century, the barber-surgeon Peter Chamberlen developed the obstetrical forceps, an instrument that enabled its user to deliver a child mechanically without necessarily destroying it first. The Chamberlen family kept the forceps secret for three generations, for their own financial gain, and only let it be known that they possessed some way of preventing the piecemeal extraction of an impacted fetus. The right to use instruments resided exclusively with men, and when the Chamberlens finally sold their design (or the design leaked out), it was for the use of the barber-surgeons and not generally available to midwives.

It has frequently been assumed that the forceps were an enormous breakthrough in improving maternity care, but on careful reflection that seems unlikely. The physicians and surgeons did not have the opportunity to observe and learn the rudiments of normal birth and were therefore at a decided disadvantage in handling difficult births. And whereas in pre-forceps days a barber-surgeon was called in only if all hope of a live birth was gone, midwives were increasingly encouraged and instructed to call in the barber-surgeon prophylactically, whenever birth became difficult.

The midwives of the time expressed their concerns. Sarah Stone, an eighteenth-century midwife and author of *The Complete Practice of Midwifery*, alleged that more mothers and children had died at the hands of raw recruits just out of their apprenticeship to barber-surgeons than through the worst ignorance and stupidity of the midwife (Donnison 1977: 31). The noted midwife Elizabeth Nihell, author of *A Treatise on the Art of the Midwife*, in 1760 questioned the value of instrumentation as a result of her training in France at the Hôtel-Dieu, where midwives practiced without male supervision or intervention (Donnison 1977: 33). Instruments were, in her opinion, rarely if ever necessary. The forceps of that time were of a primitive design, not originally curved to fit the birth canal; they were what is now called "high" or "mid" forceps rather than the "outlet forceps" that became more commonly used in modern times, and so went high up into the birth canal; and instruments were not sterilized. A journalist of the time, Philip Thicknesse, agreed with Elizabeth Nihell that the growing popularity of the man-midwife, the barber-surgeon, and his instruments resulted not from his superior skills but from the power of men to convince women of the dangers of childbirth and the incompetence of the midwives. The men were aided by the growing prestige of employing male birth attendants as a symbol of higher social status, possibly because of their higher fees. Not only did the men use their instruments unnecessarily, resulting in maternal and infant mortality and morbidity, puerperal fever, and extraordinary birth injuries, but, Nihell complained, they were so adept at concealing errors with "a cloud of hard words and scientific jargon" that the injured patient herself was convinced that she could not thank the man enough for the mischief he had done (Donnison 1977: 34). "Meddlesome midwifery," as it was called at the time, was the forerunner of what later became known as "interventionist obstetrics."

Spurred on by the development of basic anatomical knowledge and increased understanding of the processes of reproduction, surgeons of the 1700s began to develop formal training programs in midwifery. Women midwives were systematically excluded from such programs. Women were not trained because men believed women to be inherently incompetent. The situation was far from simple, however, and some men surgeons did try to provide training for midwives, sharing with them the advances made in medical knowledge. Such attempts failed in the face of opposition from within medicine, supported by the prevailing beliefs about women's ability to perform in a professional capacity. The result was a widening disparity between midwives and surgeons. As men developed newer and more sophisticated technologies, they kept them from the women.

We cannot assume that midwives would have been incompetent to use these technologies. Rather, their basic experience with normal birth probably made them eminently more capable than the inexperienced men. For example, some historians believe that the first cesarean section recorded in the British Isles in which both mother and child survived was performed by an illiterate Irish midwife, Mary Dunally (Donnison 1977: 49). The training, experience, and competence of the midwives of the seventeenth and eighteenth centuries varied enormously and went largely unregulated. The same was true of the training, experience, and competence of the physicians and barber-surgeons.

As physicians gained nearly complete ascendancy, the midwife was redefined from being a competitor of the physician-surgeon to being, in her new role, his assistant. Midwives lost autonomy over their work throughout most of Europe and in England, to a greater or lesser degree losing control over their own licensing and training requirements and the restrictions under which they functioned. Once physicians came to be *socially defined* as having expertise in the management of difficult or abnormal birth, midwifery effectively lost control over even normal birth. And it is a "social definition," not a simple fact of acquiring greater expertise. The iatrogenic (caused by medical practice) ill effects of the new obstetrics probably outweighed its benefits, particularly for normal and healthy pregnancies. The rise of obstetrics in Great Britain, in Europe, and in cities throughout the United States was not associated with improved outcome for mothers and babies.

But once the surgeon or physician is held to be necessary "in case something goes wrong," then the midwife becomes dependent on the physician and his goodwill for her "backup" services. When physicians want to compete with midwives for clients, all they have to do is withhold backup services — that is, refuse to come to the aid of a midwife who calls for medical assistance. This is a pattern that began in the earliest days of the barber-surgeon and continues right through to today.

Even when physicians are not in competition with midwives but really need midwives to handle the cases that the physicians wish to avoid — such as tending to the rural poor or tediously normal births — physicians still control midwives by setting the standards for training and regulating which instruments and procedures they may use, and for which procedures they must call on their backup doctors. While these decisions are ostensibly made to bring about best possible health care for mother and child by preventing "unqualified" persons from providing particular services, that is certainly not the way it has always worked out. Again, this is a problem that repeats itself over and over in different eras. In a work written in 1736 as a question-and-answer session between a surgeon and a midwife, tellingly titled

The Midwife Rightly Instructed, the surgeon refuses to tell the midwife how to deal with a hemorrhage. The surgeon warns the midwife not to aspire beyond the capacities of a woman, saying, "I never designed, Lucina, to make you a Doctoress, but to tell you how to practice as a Midwife" (Thomas Dawkes, cited in Donnison 1977: 24). There is almost no way for a doctor to be called in quickly enough to save a hemorrhaging woman, even assuming he knew how to do it. Clearly the health of women and children was sacrificed to the furtherance of medical control over midwifery.

The U.S. Situation

The balance of power that has been achieved between medicine and midwifery varies across the world. It is only in the United States, however, that midwifery actually failed to survive. When in 1966 a joint study of the International Confederation of Midwives and the International Federation of Gynecology and Obstetrics compiled a report on maternity care, it was necessary to treat the United States as a "special case" in the tables "because of its tendency not to recognize midwifery as an independent profession" (Brack 1976: 21).

In the nineteenth and early twentieth centuries, midwives and physicians in the United States were in direct competition for patients, and not only for their fees. Newer, more clinically oriented medical training demanded "teaching material," so that even immigrant and poor women were desired as patients (Ehrenreich and English 1973). Doctors used everything in their power to stop the midwives from practicing. They advertised, using racist pictures of "drunken, dirty" Irish midwives and hooked-nose, witch-like Jewish midwives. They played on immigrant women's desire to "become American," linking the midwives with "old country" ways of doing things. The displacement of the midwife can be better understood in terms of this competition than as an ideological struggle or as "scientific advancement." Physicians, unlike the unorganized, disenfranchised midwives, had access to the power of the state through their professional associations. They were thus able to draw women in with their advertising, but also to control licensing legislation, in state after state restricting the midwives' sphere of activity and imposing legal sanctions against them (Brack 1976: 20).

What did the medical takeover of birth mean for women and babies? Medicine would have us believe that it meant, above all, a safer birth. The profession of medicine claims that the decline in maternal and infant mortality experienced in the twentieth century was a result not so much of women's hard-won control over their own fertility, or even of better nutrition and sanitation, but rather of medical management per se. Medical expansion into the area of childbirth began, however, *before* the development of any of what are now considered to be the contributions of modern obstetrics: before asepsis, surgical technique, antibiotics, or anesthesia. At the time when physicians were taking over control of childbirth in the United States, the non-interventionist, supportive techniques of the midwife were safer for both the birthing woman and her baby.

In Washington, D.C., as the percentage of births reported to be attended by midwives shrank from 50% in 1903 to 15% in 1912, infant mortality in the first day, first week, and first month of life all increased. New York's dwindling corps of midwives did significantly better than did New York doctors in preventing both stillborns and puerperal sepsis (postpartum infection). In Newark, New Jersey, a midwifery program in 1914–1916 achieved maternal mortality rates as low as 1.7 per thousand, while in Boston, in many ways a comparable city but one where midwives were banned, the rate was 6.5 per thousand. Infant mortality rates in Newark were 8.5 per thousand, contrasted with 36.4 in Boston (Kobrin 1966: 353). The situation was similar in England, where an analysis of the records of the Queen's Institute for Midwives for the years 1905–1925 found that the death rate rose in step with the proportion of cases to which midwives called doctors (Donnison 1977: 120).

In sum, during the course of the late 1800s through the early twentieth century, medicine gained virtually complete control of childbirth in the United States, beginning with the middle class and moving on to the poor and immigrant populations. And it did this without any indication that it was capable of doing it well. Midwifery almost ceased to exist in this country, and for the first time in history, an entire society of women was attended in childbirth by men.

What did this medically attended birth look like, feel like, to the women who experienced it?

The standards for obstetrical intervention that gained acceptance in the 1920s and 1930s remained in place through the 1970s, and shadows of those practices remain with us today. These practices can be traced back to a 1920 article in the *American Journal of Obstetrics and Gynecology*, "The Prophylactic Forceps Operation," by Joseph B. DeLee of Chicago. DeLee's procedure for a routine, normal birth required sedating the woman through labor and giving ether during the descent of the fetus. The baby was to be removed from the unconscious mother by forceps. An incision through the skin and muscle of the perineum, called an episiotomy, was to be done before the forceps were applied. Removal of the placenta was also to be obstetrically managed rather than spontaneous. Ergot or a derivative was to be injected to cause the uterus to clamp down and prevent postpartum hemorrhage.

Why were DeLee's procedures, rather than allowing the mother to push the baby out spontaneously, so widely accepted by the 1930s? On one level, we can answer this in terms of the needs of the still-developing profession of obstetrics: the need for teaching material; the need to justify both the costs and the prestige of obstetrics by providing a special service that midwives and general practitioners had not provided; and the need to routinize patients in a centralized facility. Consider, however, the medical rationale, the reasons doctors themselves gave. They thought that what they were doing was a reasonable response to the demands of labor. Just how did they understand labor, and what was this medical model of birth?

The use of forceps was to spare the baby's head, DeLee having famously compared labor to a baby's head being crushed in a door. The episiotomy was done to prevent tearing of the perineum, something that is almost inevitable with the use of forceps. Even without forceps use, however, U.S. physicians were finding tearing to be a problem, most likely owing to the use of the American-style delivery table, which required the supine position, with legs in stirrups (Haire 1972). The clean cut of the episiotomy was held to be easier to repair than the jagged tear. DeLee further claimed that the stretching and tearing of the perineum resulted in such gynecological conditions as prolapsed uteri, tears in the vaginal wall, and sagging perineums. It wasn't until 1976 that an empirical study was done to determine the long-term effectiveness of episiotomies, and the results indicated that episiotomies caused rather than prevented these conditions. (Brendsel, Peterson, and Mehl 1979). Episiotomies are still the most widely performed surgical procedure on women, and every few years another study comes forth showing that they do not work (most recently, Hartmann et al. 2005). Most intriguingly, perhaps, DeLee claimed that the episiotomy would restore "virginal conditions," making the mother "better than new." All through the 1970s obstetricians were heard to assure husbands, who were just then starting to attend births routinely, that they were sewing the woman up "good and tight."

For the baby, according to DeLee and his many followers, labor was a dangerous, crushing threat, responsible for such conditions as epilepsy, cerebral palsy, "imbecility" and "idiocy," as well as being a direct cause of death. For the mother, birth was compared to falling on a pitchfork, driving the handle through her perineum. Using these analogies, DeLee was able to conclude that labor itself was abnormal:

> In both cases, the cause of the damage, the fall on the pitchfork and the crushing of the door, is pathogenic, that is, disease-producing, and anything pathogenic is pathological or abnormal. (DeLee 1920: 40)

The implication of the DeLee approach to birth for the mother is that she experienced the birth as an entirely medical event, not unlike any other surgical procedure. At the beginning of labor she was brought to the hospital and turned over to the hospital staff. The sedation of the 1930s, 1940s, and 1950s was "twilight sleep," a combination of morphine for pain relief in early labor, and then scopolamine, believed to be an amnesiac. A woman under twilight sleep can feel and respond to pain; the claim is only that she will not remember what happened. Women in twilight sleep therefore had to be restrained lest their uncontrolled thrashing cause severe injuries, as the drugs left them in pain and disoriented. Obstetrical nursing texts offered warning pictures of women with battered faces who had been improperly restrained and threw themselves out of bed.

The birth itself was not part of the mother's conscious experience because she was made totally unconscious for the delivery. Such women required careful watching as they recovered from anesthesia. They were in no way competent to hold or even see their babies; it might be quite some time before they were told the birth was over (Guttmacher 1962). The babies themselves were born drugged and required careful medical attention. That drugged, comatose newborn was the source of the popular imagery of the doctor slapping the bottom of the dangling newborn, attempting to bring it around enough to breathe. It could be several hours, or even days, before the mother and baby were "introduced."

That essentially the same management existed through to the 1970s in U.S. obstetrical services was documented by Nancy Stoller Shaw in her observations of maternity care in Boston hospitals (1974). Shaw reported that obstetrics residents went by the book, and the book (the "Procedures and Policies" of the hospital) said:

> The use of premedication for labor and anesthesia for delivery are an integral part of the philosophy of this hospital. ... It is the conviction of this institution that the use of adequate medication for labor and anesthesia for delivery serve the welfare of the mother and baby best, not only when difficulties develop suddenly, or unexpectedly, but also in uncomplicated situations. (Shaw 1974: 75)

With regard to the interventionist management of labor and delivery, Shaw wrote:

> The Maternity Division staff strongly believes in an activist controlling approach to labor designed to make it as short as possible. Synthetic labor stimulants (oxytoxics) are injected into the woman, especially the primipara (first time birthers), to stimulate labor. ... In addition, during (the) expulsive stage of labor (delivery) the obstetrician is expected to *routinely* use "episiotomy and low forceps delivery to minimize damage to maternal soft parts, to diminish the need for subsequent gynecologic surgery, and to *shorten the duration of pressure on the fetal head*." (73; emphasis in original)

Shaw's observations led her to conclude: "These patients become totally alienated from their birth experience. They are treated like lumps of flesh from which a baby is pulled" (1974: 74). But women are most assuredly not lumps of flesh: women are also political actors, people who take control over their own lives and circumstances. While women were sometimes co-conspirators with doctors in the development of twilight sleep, so-called "painless" labor, and medicalization, other women were fighting this turn of events. When the DeLee approach developed in the 1920s and 1930s became dominant throughout the United States by the 1950s, a counter-voice was raised, calling for a return to more "natural" childbirth.

Making Pain the Issue

"Natural childbirth" is a slippery concept: one would be hard put to claim that anything people do is "natural." In the world of birth, "natural" is used for anything from a vaginal (as contrasted to a cesarean) birth, whether or not the woman was conscious, to a completely "non-medicated" birth. "Prepared childbirth" is a more useful concept for viewing U.S. hospital births; it has come to mean the use of breathing and/or relaxation techniques, and particularly taking some "childbirth preparation course," perhaps six evenings, perhaps one or two days over a weekend, to learn about birth — or perhaps, to be more accurate, to learn about the medical management of birth: Most of the preparation courses, many offered by the hospitals themselves, are designed to prepare the woman for the hospital experience she is expected to have.

And what is that experience? Largely, it is understood in terms of pain: pain experienced and pain avoided. There are a number of reasons why pain became a central issue in hospitalized births. For one thing, birth in hospitals is almost certainly experienced as more painful than birth outside hospitals. Before the pressures of the prepared childbirth movement brought husbands or other companions into the labor room, laboring women were routinely left alone. Their only companionship might be another laboring woman on the other side of a curtain. A nurse would stop in now and again, but for hour upon hour the woman lay alone, with no one to comfort her, hold her hand, rub her back, or just talk to her, and nothing to do to take her mind off her pain. Consider what a toothache feels like in the middle of the night, when you're all alone and just lying there, feeling it ache and watching the clock tick away the hours.

Second, the physical management of birth made it more painful. Confinement to bed prolongs labor, and the comparatively inefficient contractions in the horizontal position may make it more painful. When a woman is upright, each contraction presses the baby down against her cervix, opening up the birth passage. When she is lying down, the weight of the baby presses on her spine, accomplishing nothing except to increase her discomfort.

Third, the mother's experience needed to be conceptualized as pain in order to justify medical control. Conceptualizing the mother's experience as *work* would have moved control to the mother. This was clearest in the medical management of the second stage of labor, delivery, in which the woman was so positioned as to make the experience as painful as possible and at the same time to minimize the value of her bearing-down efforts. When the mother was in the lithotomy position, as she almost invariably was from the 1930s on through the 1970s, flat on her back with her legs in stirrups, the baby had to be moved (pushed or pulled) upward because of the curve of the birth canal. Doctors felt that this position gave them the most control, with total access to the woman's exposed genitals. But doctors' control came at the expense of mother's control. The lithotomy position rendered her totally unable to help herself, feeling like "a turtle on its back" or a "beached whale."

This is not to say that labor, even under optimal conditions, is not painful. It is. But there is a difference between experiencing pain and defining the entire situation only in terms of pain. Pain may be one of the sensations people experience in sexual activity, for example, but most do not take it as the key element in sex. Any particular stimulation or pressure produces many complex sensations, and pain may be part of what one feels. What would be taken by itself as a painful sensation when felt at orgasm may be incorporated into the orgasm and never felt as pain at all. And birth does have much in common with orgasm: the hormone oxytocin is released; there are uterine contractions, nipple erection, and, under the best circumstances for birth, an orgasmic feeling (Gaskin 2003). But the lithotomy position, like the "missionary" position, put women flat on their backs and made attaining an orgasm a lot less likely.

Pain itself — felt pain, real pain — can be handled in different ways. It can be met with chemical pharmacological techniques (at its extreme, rendering people unconscious so that they do not feel pain — or anything else); with physical contact and comfort, as we rock a baby with a bellyache; with reassurance of the pain's normalcy and its passing ("There, there, you're okay it's almost over now!"); or any combination of these. The techniques medicine used to handle pain in labor were, and still are, often not the most appropriate. Most remarkably, obstetricians recommended the strongest pain relief after the point of strongest pain had passed: women report late labor ("transition") as the most painful part, and the "delivery," actually pushing the baby out, as not usually nearly as painful and often quite pleasant or exciting. But health workers offered women mild sedatives in early and later labor, and spinals and anesthetics for "delivery."

Dick-Read: Childbirth without Fear

There were instances of American women's rejecting one or another aspect of modern obstetrics long before any "movement" began. Margaret Mead, for example, writes in her autobiography, *Blackberry Winter* (1978), of her attempts to re-create for herself in a U.S. hospital the kind of natural, unmedicated birth she had seen so often in the South Seas. The first major thrust of the childbirth movement, however, was the publication of *Natural Childbirth* by Grantley Dick-Read in 1933 (the U.S. edition was released in 1944). Dick-Read was an English obstetrician, and so his work must be understood in the light of a different cultural experience surrounding birth. English midwifery survived the growth of obstetrics, and English obstetricians, quite possibly balanced by the existence of midwifery and relatively uninterfered-with births, never became as interventionist as U.S. obstetricians.

Dick-Read developed his concept of "natural childbirth" as a result of a home birth experience. He attended a woman in labor in a leaky one-room hovel lit by a candle in a beer bottle. As the baby's head was crowning (beginning to emerge) he offered the mother a chloroform mask, which she rejected. She went on to have a calm, peaceful, quiet birth. When Dick-Read asked her later why she had refused medication, she gave an answer that became a classic statement of the natural childbirth philosophy: "It didn't hurt. It wasn't meant to, was it, doctor?" (Dick-Read 1944: 2).

In the years that followed, Dick-Read decided that no, it was not "meant to hurt," and developed a theory of natural childbirth:

> Civilization and culture have brought influences to bear upon the minds of women which have introduced justifiable fears and anxieties concerning labor. The more cultured the races of the earth have become, so much the more dogmatic have they been in pronouncing childbirth to be a painful and dangerous ordeal. This fear and anticipation have given rise to natural protective tensions in the body and such tensions are not of the mind only, for the mechanisms of protective actions by the body include muscle tension. Unfortunately, the natural tension produced by fear influences those muscles which close the womb and prevent the child from being driven out during childbirth. Therefore, fear inhibits: that is to say, gives rise to resistance at the outlet of the womb, when in the normal state those muscles should be relaxed and free from tension. Such resistance and tension give rise to real pain because the uterus is supplied with organs which record pain set up by excessive tension. Therefore fear, pain and tension are the three evils which are not normal to the natural design, but which have been introduced in the course of civilization by the ignorance of those who have been concerned with attendance at childbirth. If pain, fear and tension go hand in hand, then it must be necessary to relieve tension and to overcome fear in order to eliminate pain. (Dick-Read 1944: 5–6)

In a nutshell: "If fear can be eliminated, pain will cease" (Dick-Read 1944: 19).

Dick-Read's is a fairly sophisticated statement of psychosomatic relationships, and notably one that does not "blame the victim." Unlike many other statements by physicians that held the "weakness" or "delicacy" of "civilized" women to blame for pain in childbirth, Dick-Read placed responsibility with birth attendants for the "evils" of fear, pain, and tension. The pain, he acknowledged, was real, but it was not necessary.

For Dick-Read, motherhood was women's "ultimate purpose in life" (8), her crowning achievement. He saw the laboring woman as drawing closer to God as she worked to bring forth her baby — and Dick-Read definitely viewed labor as work, "hard work." This is hardly what most of us in the United States think of as modern feminism, but it was a kind of woman-centered approach, a spiritual focus on motherhood and a respect for the work laboring women do. It is a far cry from the dominant medical approach, which saw the laboring woman as essentially no different from someone in the hospital for gall bladder surgery.

Dick-Read's philosophy had considerable appeal in the United States as well as in Great Britain, and it is its Americanization that concerns us here. *Childbirth without Fear: The Principles and Practices of Natural Childbirth* was published in the United States in 1944, one generation after DeLee introduced the full-blown American birth. In 1947 the Maternity Center Association invited Dick-Read to the United States for a lecture tour. While Dick-Read's book and method appealed to many American women, the Americanization of Dick-Read was, in practice, something of a disaster.

Dick-Read called attention to the socio-emotional context in which birth takes place: he did not speak only of its psychological meaning for the individual woman. Having a "good attitude" was not enough. Dick-Read taught women relaxation techniques now familiar to many of us: how to find and then release muscle tension throughout the body by unwrinkling the brow, letting loose the hunched shoulders, and unclenching the fists. He taught those techniques before labor but then reaffirmed that teaching throughout labor. He stated: "No greater curse can fall upon a young woman whose first labor has commenced than the crime of enforced loneliness." In a now familiar comparison, he related his own fear during a wartime battle in which he "learned the meaning of loneliness" (Dick-Read 1944: 155). He said that women needed *continual* comfort and emotional support during labor.

The majority of women in the United States who attempted to follow Dick-Read's advice did so under hostile conditions. They were confined to labor beds, they shared labor rooms with women who were under scopolamine, and their screams, combined with the repeated offering of pain-relief medication by the hospital staff, reinforced the very fear of birth that Dick-Read set out to remove. The results were generally perceived as failures of the method or failures of the individual woman.

What was needed was a childbirth method designed to meet the needs of hospitalized women in the United States. Women needed preparation not just for the physical event of the birth itself, as Dick-Read provided, but for the birth as it occurred in hospitals. The Lamaze or psychoprophylactic method met those demands.

Lamaze: Childbirth without Pain

Lamaze, known as the "psychoprophylactic method," grew out of Pavlovian conditioning techniques. Uterine contractions were held to be stimuli to which alternative responses could be learned. Most women had learned pain and fear responses; it was believed that with training these responses could be unlearned, or deconditioned, and replaced with such responses as breathing techniques and abdominal "effleurage," or stroking. It is Lamaze technique that introduced the rhythmic "puffing and panting" that characterizes, or maybe caricatures, the portrayal of birth in popular media. It was held that concentration on these techniques — techniques based on the methods used by midwives — would inhibit cerebral cortex response to other potentially painful stimuli. In contrast to Dick-Read's evocation of God and the spiritual, this approach was couched in the language of science. The method was developed in the Soviet Union and in 1951 was established there as the official method of childbirth.

In that same year, 1951, two French obstetricians, Ferdinand Lamaze and Pierre Vellay, traveled to Russia and observed obstetrical practices. After making some relatively minor changes, Lamaze introduced the method in Paris. In 1956 he published a book on the method, *Painless Childbirth*, and Pope Pius XII sanctioned its use. Worldwide acceptance followed swiftly. (For a fuller discussion of the history of Lamaze, see Tanzer and Block 1972.) The method was brought to the United States not by an obstetrician but by a mother, Marjorie Karmel, an American who gave birth with Lamaze in Paris in 1955. In 1959 she published *Thank You, Dr. Lamaze: A Mother's Experience in Painless Childbirth*. In 1960, Karmel, along with a physiotherapist, Elizabeth Bing, and a physician, Benjamin Segal, founded ASPO, the American Society for Psychoprophylaxis in Obstetrics (Bing and Karmel 1961, Vellay 1966).

ASPO, unlike the Dick-Read approach, was specifically geared to the American hospital and the American way of birth. The only challenge ASPO offered to the status quo concerned the use of anesthesia. ASPO substituted psychological for pharmacological control of pain. While the difference between consciousness and unconsciousness may be all the difference in the world for the mother, from the point of view of the institution, that single factor is relatively minor. The original ASPO training course, written by Bing and Karmel and published in 1961, stated:

> In all cases the woman should be encouraged to respect her own doctor's word as final ... It is most important to stress that her job and his are completely separate. He is responsible for her physical well-being and that of her baby. She is responsible for controlling herself and her behavior. (1961: 33)

This certainly poses no threat to the control of birth by obstetricians. As Vellay himself, one of the French developers of the method, wrote in 1966:

> We have always maintained the *Painless Childbirth belongs above all to the obstetrician*. They can estimate and understand better than anyone else the very special behavior of the pregnant woman. (50).

Even on the question of pain medication, the doctor's rather than the woman's perceptions were to be valued and trusted: "If your doctor himself suggests medication, you should accept it willingly — even if you don't feel the need for it — as he undoubtedly has very good reasons for his decision" (Bing and Karmel 1961: 33). Note that this was written long before obstetricians were familiar with the technique and so could not possibly be accurate in their judgment of the need for pain relief — if in fact one person can *ever* judge another's pain.

The physical trappings and procedures surrounding the American birth were written into the original course, including perineal shaves, enemas, delivery tables (although women were taught to request politely that only leg and not hand restraints be used), episiotomies, and so on. Even more basically, ASPO accepted the medical model's separation of childbirth from the rest of the maternity experience, stating in this first manual that rooming-in (mother and baby not being separated) and breastfeeding are "entirely separate questions" from the Lamaze method.

Were Bing and Karmel really this naive? Elizabeth Bing has been an active participant in the childbirth movement for more than half a century, an intelligent, thoughtful woman. Undoubtedly, they were making the same kinds of political compromises midwives and doulas are making today.

ASPO managed successfully to meet both the demands of women for a "natural" childbirth and the demands of obstetricians for "good medical management." The issue became resolved over *consciousness*. The title of the first book published by an American obstetrician supporting the Lamaze method makes the point: *Awake and Aware: Participation in Childbirth through Psychoprophylaxis* (Chabon 1966). Control came to mean simply control over one's behavior (notably pain response). At first glance, the Lamaze method may appear to center on the woman's autonomy, but that confuses consciousness and pain control with power. Women, especially the middle-class educated women of the 1960s and 1970s who used the method and made it so popular, may have felt that it met some of their desire for control over their bodies. But this was a deceptive thing, a *false consciousness*. The method succeeded where Dick-Read had failed because it was the only practical method designed to deal with the hospital situation.

Lamaze courses were designed as six weekly sessions, evening courses for six or seven "pregnant couples," husbands and wives. Husbands' participation was considered advantageous but not initially considered necessary for the use of the method. "Enforced loneliness" was not considered an insurmountable handicap, though for many women the real battle they fought was to bring a husband or someone else into the labor room with them, and not the right to breathe in rhythm. Over a period of almost 20 years, it became entirely acceptable first for husbands, and later for other companions of the woman's choice, to enter first the labor room and later the delivery room. In

Lamaze training in the United States, the husband acted as his wife's "labor coach," a position held by the *monitrice* in the French version of the Lamaze technique, and arguably now held by the doula. The coach provided the continual emotional support that Dick-Read talked about but was seen by ASPO as really being there to provide very specific coaching in the method, reminding the woman to pant, to take cleansing breaths between contractions, to relax her muscles. Since there was no *monitrice*, no member of the hospital staff assigned to help the laboring woman, the husband took on both roles in the American version, and so he had to be trained along with the wife. This fit closely into the approach to marriage and "togetherness" popular in the 1950s and early 1960s.

In essence, the method keeps the woman quiet by giving her tasks to do. Being a "good" — uncomplaining, obedient, cooperative — patient is the woman's primary job, "controlling herself and her behavior," while the doctor does his task (Lorber 1975: 220). As is not uncommon for relatives of institutionalized people, the husbands are co-opted into doing the staff's work, moving the patient through the medical routines as smoothly as possible. In the classic Lamaze birth, Mother, coached by Father, behaves herself while Doctor delivers the baby.

Lessons from Childbirth Education

"Childbirth without Fear" and "Childbirth without Pain" were not the only "childbirth methods" introduced in the United States. But they were the *first* attempts, and then the first *successful* attempts, to "manage" birth by birthing women. What do we learn from the failure of Dick-Read and the success of Lamaze? The contrasts between Dick-Read and Lamaze can be understood only in the social contexts within which each method developed. Dick-Read saw birth as a woman-controlled event, something that a woman works to bring about. The women Dick-Read saw were only minimally medicated and were physically unrestrained. Because at least on occasion he dealt with women at home, in their usual social setting, Dick-Read was able to see the influence of a supportive environment. Furthermore, he saw birth in the social context of motherhood. Immediately after birth the women were *mothering* — holding, talking to, comforting, nursing, playing with their newborns. The baby, in Dick-Read's view, was the woman's prize for her work.

Those who dealt exclusively with hospitalized births, and particularly American managed births, saw birth as a physician-controlled event, something that physicians work to bring about. The women the U.S. childbirth movement saw were both heavily medicated and physically restrained, as well as cut off from all social support. Birth was thus seen as a mechanical-surgical event. After birth, the babies were taken away and the mothers sent to recovery rooms. Birth was to be witnessed, rather than "done," by mothers: the Lamaze method introduced the use of the mirror in the delivery room. The orgasmic and spiritual nature of birth of which Dick-Read spoke was replaced by a businesslike matter-of-factness. Emotional support was traded in for technique coaching; spirituality for athletics. The crisis nature of birth was retained from the medical model, and childbirth, as practiced by the Lamaze prepared-childbirth instructors, continued to be defined in terms of medicine rather than motherhood.

The most profound lesson to be taken from this history of childbirth education is that within the institution of the hospital, medical dominance, and thus the medical model of birth, is so powerful and entrenched that it successfully resists modification. Attempts at reform either fail outright or become so co-opted that they end up supporting the system.

2

LABORING NOW

Current Cultural Constructions of Pregnancy, Birth, and Mothering

BARBARA KATZ ROTHMAN

And what about now, in the early years of a new millennium? American society has experienced a major feminist movement, women moving into medicine in general and obstetrics in particular, a childbirth movement, a revival of midwifery, a new science of fetal and newborn development, and a renewed appreciation of breastfeeding. What is it like to labor and give birth in America today?

This chapter examines contemporary American experiences of pregnancy, childbirth, and newborn care. As I reviewed the work I had done on this decades earlier, I was constantly aware of what had changed (sometimes a lot) and what had not (also a lot). That sense of things changing and yet remaining the same permeates these chapters. So much of what the feminist and midwifery revolutions taught has been incorporated into American culture, into our *beliefs* about birth, but so little of it has actually changed medical *practice*. The juxtaposition of, on one hand, an ideology of birth as a natural thing and of women as powerful competent beings, and on the other, of birth as a medical procedure performed on patients forms the theme of these next chapters.

Pregnancy

Whenever I am talking about home birth or midwifery care, some woman speaks up wistfully: "I'd have loved to have done that, but my pregnancy was high-risk." Everybody, it sometimes seems, is "high-risk." Like the fabulous children of Lake Wobegon, all of whom are "above average," the pregnancies of U.S. women all seem to be of above-average risk.

Not everybody who gets pregnant can be a tall, well-nourished, Rh positive 24-year-old who has never miscarried or had a stillborn, has never been sick except for rubella and toxoplasmosis many years before, and has given birth vaginally three years earlier to a healthy baby weighing between seven and nine and a half pounds. Yet virtually any deviation from this ideal makes a woman "high-risk." Even though she and her doctor may accept in principle the idea that pregnancy is a normal and healthy condition, the many tests, the careful watching, and the constant screening will help her think of her own particular pregnancy as being precarious, even dangerous. If she is 35 years or older, she will be encouraged to have amniocentesis to test for genetic disorders and will be watched for obstetrical complications. If she is too young, has had no children or too many, even if she is simply poor, she may find herself classified as "high-risk," an exception to the supposed norm of pregnancy as healthy.

In fact, even if a woman does have all the healthy characteristics medicine can ask for, she still won't be called healthy, or even normal. She will be classified as "low-risk." In that sense, all of us are at some risk for developing virtually any disease and even dying of it in the next year. But what if you went for an annual check-up, and instead of being told you were healthy, you were told that you were at low risk of dying of leukemia, lung cancer, or heart disease this year? Virtually any house can be struck by lightning: Do you care to think of where you live as being "low-risk" for lightning? This is just what contemporary medicine has done to pregnancy. It has distinguished between "low-risk" and "high-risk" pregnancies, with the emphasis always on risk, and then gone on to define an ever-increasing proportion of pregnancies as "high-risk." Some of the risk factors are engendered by the changes of pregnancy itself, such as the phenomena of "preclinical diabetes," or "mild pre-eclampsia." Other risk factors are natural characteristics of women, such as parity (number of previous pregnancies) and age.

Ever since the introduction of the "risk" approach to pregnancy, obstetrics has broadened the "high-risk" category. For example, a grand multipara is considered a high-risk patient. Until the 1970s, obstetrics defined a woman as a grand multipara when she had had five or more previous births. Once women started having fewer children, they redefined "grand multipara" to mean having had three previous births. Presumably the objective and inherent risk of a fourth or a fifth pregnancy had not increased just because it became a less frequent occurrence, yet it was a newly defined "high-risk" situation. Similarly, the age for amniocentesis for genetic disorders moved from 40 to 35, and in some locations 33 or even younger. As the categories expand, more and more pregnancies are subsumed under the heading of "high-risk," until by now more pregnancies are high-risk than are low-risk.

The Medical Model of Pregnancy

Obstetrics used to define pregnancy itself simply as pathological, a condition of illness, quite frankly a disease. That was how doctors gained control over the management of pregnancy. They justified requiring medical care during pregnancy by calling it a disease state. Doctors are, after all, society's experts on disease. Having called childbirth a pathological condition and moved that under medical control, their next step was to call the entire pregnancy pathological and to develop medically oriented prenatal care. By the 1970s, only remnants of this language remained. A physician introducing a discussion of an aspect of normal pregnancy said in 1974, for example: "For those who regard normal pregnancy as a disease, the terms 'physiological' and 'normal pregnancy' will probably appear as contradictory or even mutually exclusive" (McKay 1974). By 1980, the official position, as stated in the classic obstetrics textbook *Williams Obstetrics*, was that "A priori, pregnancy should be considered a normal physiological state." But the next sentence goes on, "Unfortunately, the complexity of the functional and anatomic changes that accompany gestation tends to stigmatize normal pregnancy as a disease process" (Pritchard and McDonald 1980: 303). By the 2001 edition of *Williams*, concerted effort had been made to move beyond the disease approach:

Chapter 8 is called "Maternal Adaptations to Pregnancy" and begins by stating that "the anatomical, physiological, and biochemical adaptations to pregnancy are profound" (Cunningham et al. 2001: 168), and "because of these physiological adaptations, in some cases there are marked aberrations that would be perceived as abnormal in the nonpregnant state. Physiological adaptations of normal pregnancy can be misinterpreted as disease, but they also may unmask or worsen preexisting disease" (168). Through the 1970s, in discussions of one or another phenomenon of pregnancy, the word "normal" was frequently used to refer to the nonpregnant state, as in the hormonal level in pregnancy being "higher than normal," or the uterus in pregnancy being contrasted to its "normal state." The current editors of *Williams* carefully contrast the changes of pregnancy to the "original" status of the body, showing the continued medicalized if not fully pathologized view they hold of pregnancy.

The seductive vocabulary of illness continues to color all discussions of pregnancy in the medical literature. The determination of pregnancy itself, for example, is still routinely called the "diagnosis" of pregnancy, and the changes of normal pregnancy its "symptoms."

The Fetal Parasite

Until the 1960s, medicine in the United States viewed the pregnant woman as a body with an insulated, parasitic capsule growing inside it. The capsule within was seen as virtually omniscient and omnipotent, knowing exactly what it needed from its mother-host, reaching out and taking it from her — taking vitamins, minerals, protein, and energy, at her expense if necessary — while protected from all that was harmful.

The pregnancy in this model was almost entirely a mechanical event in the mother, who differed from the nonpregnant woman only by the presence of this thing growing inside her. Differences other than mechanical changes, such as the enlarging of the uterus, were accordingly seen by physicians as symptoms to be treated so that the woman could be kept as "normal" as possible throughout the "stress" of pregnancy. Working with this model, obstetricians did not consider pregnancy as necessarily unhealthy, but pregnancy was frequently associated with changes other than the mechanical growth of the uterus and its contents: these changes the doctors *did* see as unhealthy. For example, the hemoglobin count, which is lower in pregnant women than in nonpregnant women, makes pregnant women appear (by nonpregnant standards) to be anemic. The result was that doctors treated this anemia with iron supplementation. Water retention, or edema, is greater in pregnant than in nonpregnant women. Obstetricians treated this "condition" by placing limits on salt intake and prescribing diuretics. Pregnant women tend to gain weight in addition to that accounted for by the fetus, placenta, and amniotic fluid. Obstetricians then treated women for this weight gain by putting them on strict diets and sometimes prescribing "diet pills." Knowing that these changes were very likely to occur in pregnant women, American doctors set out to treat all pregnant women with iron supplements, limits on salt and calorie intake, and diuretics, all in the name of "preventive medicine."

What were the sources of this model? How did pregnancy come to be considered as a stress situation — as not normal? How did the fetus come to be thought of as a parasite and the mother as a host? One answer is that medicine as a profession gained control over pregnancy by calling it a disease. The other answer lies in the essentially patriarchal ideology of medicine in its definitions of pregnancy and parenthood. Medically, pregnancy was viewed as being a man's baby growing inside a woman. When the fetus was seen as a product of the male's body, it followed that its presence in the female body must be an intrusion. Hughes entitles the chapter on the fetus in his 1972 *Obstetric-Gynecologic Terminology* "The Fetus (Passenger)." And even today, the current edition of *Williams* says: "The fetus is a demanding and efficient parasite!" (2001: 22; exclamation point theirs). Looking at the way that embryonic and placental tissues produce hormones and affect the course of pregnancy, *Williams* concludes:

> These are but a few examples to indicate unambiguously that the embryo-fetus, estraembryonic fetal tissues, or both, direct the orchestration of the physiological adaptations of pregnancy. The maternal organism passively responds — even at times to her own detriment. (2001: 22)

The dominant organizing belief for medicine about pregnancy was that daddy plants a seed in mommy. Thus, for doctors, pregnancy was and still is an adversarial relationship, in which the needs and interests of the mother-host are pitted against those of the fetus-parasite.

The Vulnerable Fetus

In 1961–1962 an unprecedented outbreak of phocomelia, a congenital malformation characterized by severe defects of the long bones, resulting in what were commonly called "flippers" or missing limbs, was observed in West Germany primarily, and throughout Europe and the United States to a lesser extent. At least 5,000 infants were involved. It was later documented that the defects were related to the use of a tranquilizing drug, thalidomide, during the thirtieth to fiftieth day of pregnancy. In many cases, thalidomide was taken on prescription from obstetricians for the control of nausea during pregnancy.

That thousands of infants were dramatically damaged by a substance ingested by their mothers directly contradicted the earlier medical model, which believed the fetus to be insulated and protected within the womb. The placenta, as a result of this experience, was no longer seen as a shield or barrier for the infant; instead, it came to be seen as what the renowned doctor Virginia Apgar called a "bloody sieve" (Apgar and Beck 1973).

At first, this seemed really to threaten the medical management of pregnancy, which involved using a lot of drugs of one sort or another to "treat" the many changes of pregnancy. The 1971 edition of *Williams Obstetrics* stated:

> The most important practical lesson to be drawn from the experience with thalidomide is that no drug should be administered to the pregnant woman *unless it is urgently indicated*. This injunction applies particularly to drugs administered during the first half of pregnancy for nausea and vomiting. (1971: 1069)

Just a few years later, though, editors of the sixteenth edition, in 1980, substituted "in the absence of a real therapeutic indication" for "unless urgently indicated," somewhat softening the statement. But in both of those editions of *Williams*, 600 pages earlier, in a discussion of nausea of pregnancy, several drug recommendations are made, including one that *Williams* reported may be teratogenic (causing malformation), although "evidence is not convincing" (1980: 344). *Williams* had painted the thalidomide disaster as graphically as possible: a photograph of an entirely limbless baby, a formless column of flesh with a baby's head, appeared in both of those editions. On the one hand, these doctors understood the profound risks of tampering with pregnancy; on the other hand, they found — and still find — it very difficult to believe that drugs doctors prescribe could cause such problems. Not 20 years after thalidomide's effects were discovered, the evidence that another drug prescribed for nausea was teratogenic had to be "convincing" enough before the editors of this basic obstetrics textbook would stop recommending it.

Rapidly on the heels of the thalidomide discovery came a new awareness of the danger to the fetus from radiation. While some acknowledgment of the hazards of radiation resulted from the Hiroshima and Nagasaki bombings and their effects on fetal development, in the early 1960s chest X-rays were still considered an important part of good early prenatal care, and X-rays were used routinely to determine fetal position (and number, where multiple pregnancy was suspected), to measure the pelvis, and even to determine pregnancy itself. By the later 1960s, however, doctors recognized that exposure to radiation in utero greatly increases the incidence of malignant disease in the exposed children.

A further blow to the model of the protected fetus came from the DES research, in which diethylstilbestrol, a synthetic hormone given to some women in the 1940s and 1950s to prevent miscarriage, was found in the 1970s to have caused cancer in their daughters decades later. This revelation that a baby who appeared fine might nonetheless have been profoundly damaged by a prenatal exposure further rocked the idea of the fetus as being insulated. But medicine never really feared tampering with the prenatal environment, which would have led it to avoid absolutely all but life-saving medications, radiation, and other procedures. There was, rather, some increased selectivity. For example, while radiation was used less and less frequently, sonography became widespread, along with the claim that sound waves, unlike X-rays, are not harmful. The technique became routine long before there was, or could have been, any long-term follow-up.

The use of drugs for pregnancy-related complaints did not quickly — nor yet — disappear. For example, compare two major obstetric texts published in 1975. One included, on its list of drugs so widely used as to be considered safe, meclizine (Winship 1975). The other listed several that have been shown to cause birth defects in animals and should thus be avoided; included in this list is meclizine (Quilligan 1975). The 2001 *Williams* includes meclizine in a fairly long list of antiemetics (antinausea or antivomiting drugs) currently used during pregnancy (1028).

The story of Bendectin™ is even more informative. For many years it was considered a perfectly safe treatment for the nausea of pregnancy. A parents' lawsuit in the 1980s raised the safety issue. They claimed that the thalidomide-like damage done to their child was caused by Bendectin. Other lawsuits followed, and the drug was withdrawn. The current *Williams* tells this tale as an example of "nonscientific and biased reporting" that removed a "useful" drug from the market. In one of the very rare examples of attempted humor to be found in *Williams*, the editors cite a researcher who concluded that "although a drug may not be a teratogen, it may be a litogen!" (a made-up term meaning "causing litigation") (2001: 1008). Twenty pages later, they write that Bendectin can "essentially be constituted by ingesting vitamin B6 along with an over-the-counter sleep aid, doxylamine, neither of which is considered to have teratogenic potential," citing a 2000 reference. Oddly, their overall conclusion on drugs for nausea cites two very old studies, one from 1971 and one from 1977, to conclude: "There is no evidence that any antiemetics are associated with an increased risk of congenital anomalies" (1029).

It is tempting to track drug after drug, year after year, as they swing in and out of favor. But what is the larger lesson here, the forest lost among all these trees? To some extent, it is that drugs prescribed by doctors are innocent until proven guilty — that the drugs *they* offer are safe, or safe enough, unless proven otherwise. About one antihypertensive drug, *Williams* concludes: "There are no large epidemiological studies in early pregnancy, but its many years of use attest to its safety" (1024). That standard does not apply to what *Williams* groups as "Natural (herbal) remedies." For those, in spite of generations of use, they conclude that "Because it is not possible to assess the safety of various herbal remedies during pregnancy, pregnant women should be counseled to avoid these substances" (1029).

It seems that there has been more widespread public than medical acceptance of the idea of the permeability of the placenta and the care that women are therefore obliged to take with what they eat and drink. Many people seem to be aware of the hazards of smoking or drinking alcohol or possibly of using caffeine, and many hesitate to use any over-the-counter medications without (or even with) the recommendation of a physician. Some women find that they are more cautious than their physicians are about using medications. The current *Williams* reports that women overestimate the risk of exposure to teratogens and underestimate the background risk of birth defects in the general population. Their conclusion on counseling for teratogen exposure is:

> With few notable exceptions, most commonly prescribed drugs and medications can be used with relative safety during pregnancy. For the few believed to be teratogenic, counseling should emphasize *relative risk*. All women have about a 3 percent chance of having a child with a birth defect, and although exposure to a confirmed teratogen may increase this risk, it is usually increased by only 1 or 2 percent or at most doubled or tripled. (2001: 1011)

Risk is such a slippery concept. When a 35-year-old woman has a three in one thousand, or 0.3%, risk of having a baby with Down Syndrome, medical workers tell her that she is high-risk. When a drug doubles "or at most" triples the background 3% risk of fetal anomalies up to 6% or 9%, six or nine in *one hundred*, the counseling emphasis shifts from "high" to "relative" risk. This is quite a change from the "most important practical lesson to be drawn from the experience with thalidomide!"

Not having evidence that a drug does cause birth defects is not the same thing at all as having evidence that it does *not*. More than 90% of the drugs that have been approved by the FDA since 1980 have an "undetermined" risk of causing birth defects It wasn't until 2002 that the FDA issued guidelines for medical manufacturers to create registries to track the effects of drugs on pregnant women and fetuses. Pregnant women are excluded from drug trials, but doctors do prescribe these drugs to them once the trials are completed and the drugs are on the market. Between the very few known and proven teratogenic drugs and the very few known and proven safe drugs are a vast number of drugs whose safety in pregnancy is simply not known. Until those data are in, should pregnant women use such drugs? Should doctors prescribe such drugs? How do they decide?

Doctors tend to err on the side of assuming that what they are doing is safe, or safe enough. Women, it seems, tend to err on the side of "not taking chances," to assume higher risks of teratogenicity than might actually exist, and even when fully informed of all of the risks, to try very hard not to take risks with the fetus. It is not unheard of, for example, for women to refuse treatment of life-threatening cancers until they have completed a pregnancy. The drugs we have been talking about, which medicine prescribes so freely, are for things like nausea and heartburn, ordinary discomforts of pregnancy. The midwifery model tends to avoid any unnecessary "unnatural" interference in the normal changes of pregnancy. The stance the midwives take, in marked contrast to that of the physicians, is one of humility: we do not know enough to try to "improve" on nature.

Laboratory Definitions of Normal

Physical discomforts like nausea are not the only "symptoms" of pregnancy that receive medical attention. Pregnancy is a total body condition in its physical effects; virtually no part of the body is unaffected. Of all these changes, a number have been seen by medicine as pathological deviations from the norms for the nonpregnant, including some deviations that show up only on laboratory tests.

Along with the development of techniques for measuring body functions, such as urinalysis and blood tests, came a set of standards for measurement defining not only what is, but also what should be. Laboratory screening became routine in pregnancy by the mid-twentieth century, and to some extent what we know as prenatal care became the measuring of that which is measurable and the treatment of deviations from the norm.

There was, even by the early 1970s, some self-consciousness in medicine about the way that standards are used in clinical practice. The authors of a volume called *Diagnostic Indices in Pregnancy* lamented that many clinicians, as was clear from any review of the medical literature, had come to rely so heavily on laboratory tests that deviation from an accepted range of measurements was in itself sufficient to justify treatment (Hytten and Lind 1973). That is, if a person looks and feels well but has laboratory values outside the normal range, she must be treated anyway. It is a debatable approach under any circumstances. Should someone with no symptoms and no problems be treated if her blood sugar, for example, is above or below normal? Increasingly, the medical consensus is yes, that it is just a matter of time before symptoms appear. An alternative would be to observe for a longer time before treating, partly because we do not know what is normal for any particular person.

In pregnancy, the situation is even more confusing. The physiological situation changes continuously. What is normal for nonpregnant women may not be normal at all for those who are pregnant. Normal measurements, one could argue, can be defined only as they occur in normal pregnancy. What is more, medical attempts to deal with normal physiological changes and adjustments in the pregnant woman may in fact harm her and her baby.

Changes in the blood are typical of those that showed up in the laboratory testing of pregnant women and were often treated as deviations from the norm. Blood is like an enormously varied soup, of which plasma is the stock. Most blood tests are measures of concentrations of a particular ingredient in a given amount of blood. Just as we can speak of one soup as having more vegetables and fewer noodles per cup than another, so too can we speak of blood as having varying concentrations of red blood cells, white blood cells, platelets, and so on. If you add half again as much stock to the mixture, obviously the concentration of the other ingredients is going to lessen. This is the basis for what obstetrics called "physiological anemia of pregnancy." Hemoglobin is measured in grams per 100 ml of blood, like ounces of carrots per cup of soup. (The hematocrit is another measure of the same thing.) In nonpregnant women a hemoglobin level between 12 and 16 is normal, with 13.5 to 14 a good, healthy average. A non-pregnant woman with a hemoglobin level of 11 or 12 could be just borderline anemic. But what happens in pregnancy?

Starting at approximately six to eight weeks after conception, the amount of plasma in circulation begins to rise, until by the twenty-eighth to thirty-fourth week there is approximately half again as much plasma as in the nonpregnant woman. The pregnant woman needs the increased blood volume not only because of the blood flow to her uterus and breasts, but also to enable her skin and kidneys to eliminate the extra wastes of pregnancy in increased urine and per-spiration. The increased blood flow to her skin eliminates the heat generated by the pregnancy. The increased flow to her kidneys helps them function more effectively to remove the wastes of the fetus as well as of the mother. Both require plasma rather than whole blood for these functions.

In pregnancy the actual amount of hemoglobin increases by about 33 percent. But plasma increases by about 50 percent. The conse-quences show up in hemoglobin or hematocrit measures. Here we have the basic dilemma: If a woman goes to a doctor and has a blood test showing a hemoglobin of 11.5 and is not pregnant, she would be treated with iron supplements. But what if she is pregnant? Is she or is she not anemic?

For many years, obstetricians regarded this lowered hemoglobin as a measure of anemia and called it "physiological anemia," requiring treatment. But the 2001 *Williams* acknowledges that "physiological anemia" is a "major misnomer" (168). And what are the consequences of this reevaluation for clinical practice? After full consideration of the phenomenon of "hypervolemia," or increased blood volume, and a discussion of the iron stores and iron requirements of pregnancy, the conclusion, printed in bold type, is that "The amount of iron absorbed from diet, together with that mobilized from stores, is usually insuf-ficient to meet the demands imposed by pregnancy" (178), thus neces-sitating supplemental iron. The upshot? It is not anemia, but it does require treatment.

The diagnosis of anemia based on a blood sample, and its treatment with iron or folic acid supplements, appears to be relatively harmless, if not necessarily helpful. Other diagnostic procedures and treatments may not be so benign, however. Testing for diabetes is a good example here. On the one hand, diabetes is an endocrine disorder that makes the maintenance of a healthy pregnancy more difficult. On the other hand, pregnancy makes the management of diabetes more difficult. Pregnancy may also trigger diabetic reactions in some previously non-diabetic women. This is where the question of standards for normal becomes even more complicated. Does a blood sugar level that would be classified as diabetic in a nonpregnant woman indicate diabetes in a pregnant woman? Are the same standards of measurement for diagnosis appropriate in pregnant and nonpregnant women? Medicine's answer has been "yes" to both questions. Many women who show no signs or symptoms of diabetes prior to pregnancy are diagnosed as having "preclinical" or "chemical" or "gestational" diabetes, a diabetes that shows up only on laboratory testing during pregnancy. The diagnosis is based entirely on laboratory tests.

Diabetes is, according to *Williams*, the most common medical complication of pregnancy: 2.6% of all live births were "complicated" by diabetes. But 90% of those cases were "gestational" diabetes, diabetes diagnosed for the first time in pregnancy, and the diagnoses themselves represent the complication (2001: 1361). Despite more than 30 years of research, it is still not clear who should be screened (1362), nor is there agreement as to which tests to use or what values to use for diagnosis (1363). *Williams* reports that with gestational diabetes that doesn't respond to dietary management, more than 90% of practitioners start insulin therapy — usually requiring hospitalizing the woman. They also report, though, that the studies do not show that prophylactic insulin in these gestational diabetics improves outcome (1366).

What a diagnosis of gestational diabetes does unquestionably do is move the woman into the "high-risk" category. This makes it a difficult issue for midwives. Midwives claim their expertise in helping normal women through normal pregnancies. If a woman is not healthy, a physician should be managing or consulting on the case. A diabetic woman, by definition, is not a normal, healthy woman. But how to define normal when medicine has the monopoly on defining and treating illness remains problematic. In the 1970s, when widespread diabetes testing was being introduced, midwives expressed their skepticism over the frequency with which preclinical or gestational diabetes was being diagnosed in pregnant women, and what precisely that diagnosis should mean for the management of pregnancy.

The question of anemia has also been somewhat problematic for midwives. Good nutrition has been one of the strong points of prenatal care in the midwifery model, and midwives see eating properly as the most important thing women can do for themselves in pregnancy. Many midwives adopted the hematocrit as a measure of nutritional status and prided themselves on setting and achieving higher levels than did physicians. Some still do. Others feel that this would be following the same policy as medicine: not establishing health and normality standards on pregnant women for pregnant women. Some midwives recommend iron supplements; some stress the importance of getting all nutrients from a "natural" diet. Midwives in the early home birth movement reported using hematocrit "almost as a threat" to make women eat well, setting levels women had to achieve. Some felt it became a ritual, measuring hemoglobin as a way of acknowledging the importance of nutrition and self-care. It is a way of showing how the woman can take care of herself and her baby by eating well. As one midwife I interviewed in the late 1970s, who was active in the early home birth movement, said of hematocrit testing: "It becomes symbolic for everything that food means in our culture: Are you treating yourself right?" Within the midwifery model, the laboratory value itself has been less an issue than is its use as a symbol for nutritional status, and nutrition has had different meanings in the midwifery model than in the medical model.

Weight Gain

U.S. medicine, as its critics have often pointed out, has not been concerned with nutrition. This was very evident in the case of pregnancy, even though obstetricians supervised the diets of pregnant women. Nutrition became one of the chief battlegrounds between standard medicine and the many "alternative," holistic approaches that grew up in the 1960s and 1970s — certainly including midwifery.

Up through the 1970s, the main dietary concern of obstetricians was with limiting weight gain, which grew out of concern over what was then called "toxemia," a disease of pregnancy now mostly known as pre-eclampsia and eclampsia. Eclampsia refers to convulsions, the most severe form this disease takes. "Toxemia" is a disease unique to pregnancy and, interestingly, almost unique to human pregnancy.

One of the early symptoms of toxemia is generalized edema (swelling), which shows up as a sudden weight gain. Obstetricians screening for the sudden weight gain of toxemia began to be critical of any weight gain whatsoever in their patients.

Not all of the increased fluid in pregnancy is in the blood. The increased fluid in the body cells, edema, is frequently noticed in swelling of the ankles and legs, which when limited to these areas is called "dependent edema." Blood pools in the legs because of the pressure of the uterus, and water retention combines with this to make the legs swell during the day. At night, as the woman lies on her side, allowing better circulation, the water is returned to the kidneys, frequently necessitating several trips to the bathroom. By morning the dependent edema is gone, or almost gone, and the buildup starts again. Each leg may accumulate one liter or more of water during the day. Some obstetricians regarded any sign of edema as abnormal, as indeed it would be in the nonpregnant, and treated it with salt restrictions and diuretics. Yet the midwives found it hard to reconcile the idea of edema as "pathological" with the fact that it occurs in 40% of normal, healthy pregnancies resulting in the birth of normal, healthy babies.

Edema, however, can also be a symptom of toxemia. A generalized edema — noticeable swelling of the face and hands as well as the legs — was frequently the first sign doctors saw of toxemia. The second major part of the syndrome was a rise in blood pressure, and the third, the presence of protein in the urine (proteinuria). Most obstetrical prenatal care was organized around screening for those signs: edema, elevated blood pressure, and protein in the urine. At a standard obstetrical prenatal visit, the woman was weighed (sudden weight gain is indicative of water retention), her blood pressure was taken, and her urine tested.

This regime developed even though there really was no clear-cut agreement on just what was and what was not the beginning of toxemia or mild pre-eclampsia. Just how much edema, how much of a rise in blood pressure, or how much protein in the urine were all subject to debate. Each author, researcher, or physician stated clearly what the standards were, yet no two stated exactly the same thing. Some authors believed that any one of those three conditions was sufficient for diagnosing a woman as pre-eclamptic, while others stated that the woman must have high blood pressure and either edema or proteinuria or both in order to be diagnosed as pre-eclamptic. Given this difficulty in defining the terms, research studies were of course confusing. Some studies, for example, looked at women with edema and no other symptoms. For these reasons, as well as the variations in populations being studied, the incidences of pre-eclampsia reported in the medical literature were as low as 2% and as high as 29%.

Edema is a "soft" measure, not easily quantified, and as the mid-wives long claimed and *Williams* now acknowledges, edema "occurs in too many normal pregnant women to be discriminant" (2001: 568). Not surprisingly, it has finally fallen out of favor, and hypertension, defined as blood pressure of 140/98 mmHG or higher, has become the key item in diagnosing the early stages of the phenomenon that used to be known as toxemia. The chapter in which eclampsia is discussed in the current *Williams* is "Hypertensive Disorders in Pregnancy," and "gestational hypertension" (elevated blood pressure alone) is distinguished from pre-eclampsia, which is marked by proteinuria in addition to high blood pressure.

Women who develop toxemia recover if the uterus is emptied in time, but it is an important cause of maternal and infant deaths. The earlier in pregnancy and the more severe the toxemia, the greater the likelihood of fetal death. The decrease in blood flow to the uterus associated with toxemia results in fetal malnutrition, yet the fetus may be too premature to be delivered with a good chance of survival. In a sense, toxemia or eclampsia is the prototypical obstetrical disease: the fetus and the mother are endangering each other, and they can be rescued from each other by the doctor.

Because of the various ways obstetrics defined pre-eclampsia, the outcomes of the disease were found to be very different. The same researcher who claimed that generalized edema alone is a sign of mild pre-eclampsia not surprisingly stated that mild pre-eclampsia is not associated with increased fetal or maternal loss. Those physicians who thought that edema was itself pre-eclampsia tried to prevent edema and used the same techniques that would be used with nonpregnant people: limiting salt intake and using diuretics. Salt restriction and the use of diuretics came to be widespread in obstetrics as preventive measures, yet there were absolutely no data to show that this regimen prevented anyone from developing eclampsia. Salt restriction was not helpful for expanding blood volume, and the use of diuretics was out-and-out dangerous.

Especially because of toxemia, but also in order to maintain "normal" standards throughout pregnancy, obstetricians stressed weight control. An average full-term infant weighs about seven and a half pounds (though midwives claim and research shows that a well-nourished mother will produce a larger baby), a placenta weighs about a pound or a pound and a half, the amniotic fluid and the fully developed uterus each weigh about two pounds, and the breasts together gain about one and a half pounds during pregnancy. Add a few more pounds for the increased blood volume, and a weight gain of 15 pounds can be "accounted for" in the entire pregnancy. Accept that a few extra pounds of fat are stored for energy for lactation, and the figure goes up to 20 pounds. Physicians who worked with the model of pregnancy in which women "contain" pregnancy as a host contains a parasite expected to see a weight gain among their patients of only 15 to 20 pounds. Larger weight gains were seen as symptoms of pathology, especially because of their similarity to the weight gain of toxemia. Here we have the basis for the scenario prevalent from the 1940s through 1970s of the eight-months-pregnant woman nibbling lettuce and cottage cheese because she had to step on the scales at the doctor's office the next day.

Birth weight, however, is the single most important factor in the health and survival of newborns. And birth weight is directly related to maternal nutrition. Better-nourished mothers have better-nourished infants. This became almost a mantra, a deep commitment of the home birth movement: Nutrition intrinsically connected taking care of the mother with taking care of the baby. To make a healthy baby, you make a healthy mother, and nutrition is one of the ways to actively make people healthy. A focus on nutrition is not just the "avoidance" of disease; it is the positive acquisition of health, and one of the most basic ways people "take care" of each other.

Almost from the inception of medically based prenatal care on into the 1970s, medicine believed that pregnant women should aim for a weight gain at term of their ideal weight plus 15 to 20 pounds. That is, a woman 10 pounds overweight would be allowed a weight gain of 5 to 10 pounds in the course of her pregnancy, and a woman 30 pounds overweight would be asked to *lose* 10 to 15 pounds. The omnipotent, omniscient fetus was expected to draw its needs from the maternal store. Maternal nutrition, medicine remarkably believed, had no bearing on the birth weight or the condition of the baby.

The 1962 edition of Alan Guttmacher's widely read *Pregnancy and Birth* was fairly typical of the advice obstetricians were giving to pregnant women. Guttmacher offered three reasons why weight gain should not be "excessive" during pregnancy: "First, it may impair health. A definite correlation exists between excessive weight gain during pregnancy, especially when rapid, and the development of high blood pressure complications" (1962: 91). "High blood pressure complications" refers to toxemia or eclampsia. The correlation does exist, but it works the other way: it is the toxemia that causes the sudden weight gain of fluid retention. "In the second place, excessive weight gain makes the pregnant woman more clumsy and prone to stumble or fall" (Guttmacher 1962: 91).

The issue here was weight gain limited to 20 pounds, as opposed to unrestricted weight gain, which is usually not much higher than 30 to 35 pounds. Having pudgy thighs does not make one accident-prone. "Finally," Guttmacher concluded, "the pregnant woman ought to control weight within normal bounds for vanity's sake alone" (1962: 91).

In the late 1960s and early 1970s, enough studies had begun to appear indicating that birth weight and maternal weight gain were positively correlated, and that in newborns, bigger really is better to begin to seriously penetrate obstetric thinking. The working group of the National Academy of Sciences stated in 1970:

> Current obstetrical practice in the U.S. tends to restrict weight gain during pregnancy. In view of the evidence available, one may raise the question of whether this practice is in effect contributing to the larger

number of low birth weight infants and to the high perinatal mortality rates. (National Research Council 1970)

This was another major attack on the medical model of the fetus as located within yet somehow separate from the mother. If the fetus is a parasite, it is, at any rate, not an especially effective parasite, not the all-knowing and all-powerful being medicine had thought it was.

The weight gain now suggested in the medical management of pregnancy for a woman of "normal" weight before pregnancy is around 25 to 35 pounds. But what is most heartening to see in *Williams* in 2001 is almost exactly what midwives were saying in the 1970s — it depends on the woman, and no objective measure can be set: "Perhaps the most remarkable finding about weight gain in pregnancy is that a wide range is compatible with good clinical outcomes and that departures from 'normality' are very nonspecific for any adverse outcome in a given individual" (2001: 232).

The Midwifery Model

The home birth movement and the revival of midwifery were developing as the research on the relationship between maternal weight gain and better infant health was becoming available, and that may explain part of the midwifery model, in which nutrition is the single most important aspect of pregnancy care. But that is a superficial explanation at best. Midwifery rejected much that was part of then-current medical knowledge. And midwives weren't talking about pounds at all, apart from requiring some reassurance that a woman was gaining steadily throughout her pregnancy. Weight gain expectations were not discussed in the midwifery literature, but good nutrition was and remains a recurrent theme. The midwifery approach to nutrition — that good maternal nutrition is essential to the health of the baby as well as that of the mother — accords with the underlying ideology of the midwifery model as woman-centered. In this model, the baby is part of its mother. Caring for the mother is therefore the best way of reaching the fetus. Unlike the medical model, the midwifery model consistently sees the needs of the mother and the fetus as being in harmony, the two as one organic unit.

Thus, there is not in the midwifery model a sense that the needs or desires of the mother must be sacrificed for the good of the fetus, or that the mother would indeed have needs that are other than good for the fetus. For example, midwives repeatedly state that if the mother gives up "junk food" and eats better food for the baby's sake (less refined, more "natural" foods), the mother will feel better and healthier. There has always been much talk in midwifery and alternative-birth circles about a woman's "getting in touch with her body." That makes sense only if pregnancy is viewed as a normal condition of the female body. The introspection, the psychological turning inward and self-absorption that may accompany pregnancy, is seen as an opportunity for the woman to learn more about her body and its needs and rhythms. A woman's pregnant body is still very much her own in this model, and it is not a host to a parasite. Where the medical model sees pregnancy as a stress and a drain on the mother, the midwifery model sees it as a period of physical and emotional growth and development for both mother and fetus.

What, then of the "discomforts" or "complaints" of pregnancy? The position that pregnancy is a healthy and entirely normal condition for mammals is of course politically necessary if midwives are to claim that they, as nonmedical people, are competent to attend to the needs of pregnant women. How, then, do they respond to these common physical complaints of pregnancy? Being nauseated certainly does not *feel* healthy. How can midwives maintain that this is a normal and healthy part of pregnancy? The primary resolution involves, on one hand, minimizing these complaints, and, on the other, responding to them as nutritional problems. Discomfort is not denied, but it is minimized because it is not seen as "symptomatic" of disease. In interviews with the midwives in the home birth movement of the 1970s, they never raised the question of how they dealt with the physical discomforts of pregnancy until they were specifically asked, and even then it went unanswered until they were pressed. Typically, they would say something like "It passes," or, with more elaboration:

> I would help you to understand your basic physiological mechanisms involved so you could take a very active role in dealing with some of

these minor discomforts, especially through nutritional and dietary management.

One midwife, trained as a nurse-midwife very much in the medical model and who had then started to do home births and reevaluate her approach, said:

> Women do get heartburn, but it's a very small issue. I just don't find it a big deal. I remember, though, in (the) training I had that's all we did — we spent days studying heartburn. Maybe five minutes of a visit is spent on that kind of thing.

Visualizing the Fetus: Bringing Forth the New Patient

When I began looking at pregnancy care back in the 1970s, the fetus was being thought of as a patient, but it was still quite an abstraction. No longer. When I give a talk about prenatal care, sometimes I ask the audience to picture a fetus and then "draw it" in the air with their hands. You get arms waving in the air, forming a big circle for a head with a curled-up body beneath. Then I ask them to put the pregnant woman's belly button right on that fetus. Just point where it would be. And the room is still. People have no idea where that woman's belly button would be. Of course if they were to draw the pregnant woman around the fetus, she'd be standing on her head. The fetus has been turned around to a more baby-like position. Oddly, as real as the fetus is, it's the pregnant woman who has become the abstraction. Ultrasound is a near-perfect example of an ideology made real, a set of beliefs reified with a technology. Obstetricians think of fetuses as separate patients more or less trapped within the maternal environment, and ultrasound was developed as a technology to get through that maternal barrier and show the separate fetus lying within. The baby becomes an entirely separated image, floating free on the screen, tethered only by the umbilical cord. The woman is erased, an empty surround in which the fetus floats.

But we are not surrounds: we are living people experiencing these pregnancies, with all the contradictions the technology brings.

Women are asked to take a moment of profound psychological separation and differentiation, when they first see inside themselves to the being that is growing within, and make of that a moment of attachment, a "bonding" experience. The baby on the screen is made "real," more real than the baby within, the experienced pregnancy. Making baby, a fetus, real with ultrasound includes but is not limited to "sexing" it, assigning fetal sex to the blur on the screen. "It" becomes "she," she becomes named, an abstraction becomes a baby.

I'd had my own pregnancies before this technology. So while I knew, sort of, what it must mean for women, it's nothing I really understood until I read Lisa M. Mitchell's study of the use of ultrasound in pregnancy in Quebec (2001). Quebec is the Canadian province most like the United States in its highly medicalized maternity care and in its highly politicized abortion context, and Mitchell's study made me see what U.S. women are experiencing.

Back when I was pregnant, we did not actually have fetuses — we had pregnancies, which resulted in the birth of babies. I remember a half-joking, half-fantasy, dreamlike image I had of myself, the night before my first baby was born, searching around frantically for the eyebrows, the fingernails, all those details, much like the last few footnotes on an overdue paper. The baby I imagined within was amorphous, unstructured, unfinished.

Not so today's fetus. It has every little detail in place. From that grey blur on the ultrasound image, a fully formed fetus is read into being. The sonographer works to construct fetal personhood, "talking about the image and encouraging the parents to see and to bond with a sentient and acting 'baby'" (Mitchell 2001: 118). The irony is that this construction occurs in the very same moment the sonographer is looking for the signs and symptoms that would indicate the fetus is not developing normally. In that case, the woman would be encouraged to consider abortion, and the "baby" would be quickly de/reconstructed as a "fetus" or even a "genetic mistake," an "abnormality."

But for most women, most of the time, the fetus passes its inspection and "fetal personhood," or more accurately "babyhood," is narrated into being — with or without the participation of the mother. Some women resist: "I think we'll forget the picture. It looks like a deep sea animal," Marie Claude says during her 32-week scan. And the technician responds: "Can you see that? The foot. Little toes." And as Marie Claude and her husband peer into the screen, the technician continues "tickling" the toe on the screen, "It's so cute" (Mitchell 2001: 125). Who could resist?

With the routine scan, done shortly before most women would feel fetal movement, the observed fetal movement on the screen is maybe not anthropomorphized; maybe "baby-ized" would be the term. Mitchell observed technicians using terms like "dancing," "playing," "swimming," "partying," or "waving" to describe fetal movement. A rolling fetus is "trying to get comfortable," one with an extended limb and arching back is "stretching." Not moving doesn't spare the woman and her partner the process: Without movement, the fetus is described as "sleeping, resting." A fetal hand near the mouth turns into "The baby is sucking his thumb," even though sonographers told Mitchell that actual thumb sucking is rarely seen. Parents, the sonographers told her, like to think that is what the baby is doing (2001: 127).

Who knows what it is parents like to think? Sonographers, along with the rest of medicine, apparently know quite well what they *should* think. In Quebec, as elsewhere, a racialized script exists: Some women (black, first nation) "never show anything," are impassive and unemotional. Other women are too emotional, giggling loudly, shedding tears, showing "excessive" joy. Both groups are punished by silence: sonographers give them only brief descriptions (135), saving their rich descriptions that call a baby forth into being for the good mothers, the ones who respond "appropriately."

Women tend to take silence during the exam as a sign of a problem. And, for all the commercialization of the process, the pictures for sale, the souvenirs to take home and to share, ultimately searching for a problem is the reason the technology is being used. Women have reason to worry. Perhaps they ought to worry more: informed consent has been notably lacking, and many women don't even realize what the implications of having this ultrasound could be until the sonographer is suddenly silent, seeing something unexpected on the screen.

Somewhere between tickling toes on the screen and clinical coldness, there must be a way of handling the use of this technology better. But no one seems to have found it — not Mitchell, not the other social scientists who have studied the new ultrasound diagnostic technologies in pregnancy (see, e.g., Summers Scholl), not the Dutch midwives I have interviewed who tried really, really hard (Rothman 2000), and not the U.S. and Canadian midwives who are working on it. In one generation we have truly changed pregnancy from a time of "expecting" a baby to a time of containing a fetus. And who can resist?

Prenatal Care in Sum: Two Approaches

The differences between the models of pregnancy developed by obstetrics and by the home birth movement and midwifery are based on both their underlying ideologies and their political necessities. Medicine had to emphasize the disease-like nature of pregnancy, its "riskiness," in order to justify medical management. Midwifery, in contrast, had to emphasize the normal nature of pregnancy in order to justify nonmedical control in a society in which medicine has a monopoly on illness management.

The first major difference between the two models is that while medical management organized itself around a search for pathology, the midwifery model approached pregnancy as essentially normal and healthy, a period of psychological as well as physical growth and development. Ideologically, medicine developed as a patriarchal institution that embodied the religious and cultural views of western European society. It consequently focused on the presence of the fetus during pregnancy, and it saw that fetus as the child of the man. Pregnancy, then, is a stress and disease-like state caused by the presence of the fetal parasite. In the midwifery model, the focus is the perspective of the woman, and pregnancy is understood as a normal condition for women. Women are not compared to a hypothetically stable, noncycling male system but are expected always to be in one or another phase of reproductive life. There is no single "normal" from which to judge deviations: ovulation, menstruation, pregnancy, lactation, menopause — these are not deviations from some abstract norm, but are themselves normal states.

Medicine thus attempted to maintain the normalcy of the mother throughout the stress of the pregnancy, viewing deviations from normal (nonpregnant) status as symptoms of disease states. This, of course, justified medical control. Midwifery, in contrast, viewed the changes as demonstrating the health of the mother. Rather than seeking to change the mother back in the direction of nonpregnant normality, midwifery's goal was to provide the best possible environment in which the changes of pregnancy could occur.

In the medical model, prenatal care is the *management* of pregnancy, like the medical management of any (other) disease. How did obstetrical prenatal care come to take its current form? Much of it, as stated earlier, revolved around screening for what was called toxemia. The standard that evolved from the introduction of prenatal care, mostly by nurses and social workers, to obstetrical management called for increasingly frequent visits. By the 1970s, the pregnant woman was expected to see the obstetrician each month during the first two trimesters, twice a month for the seventh and eight months, and weekly for the last month. No research ever showed such a schedule to be of particular value. In fact, as heretical as it may sound, it is hard to find any evidence that prenatal care improves birth outcomes (Fiscella 1995: 468).

Even now, the "prenatal care" that obstetricians offer women is basically a screening program. The visits typically take 10 to 15 minutes or less, in which the woman is weighed, her blood pressure taken, and her urine tested. Blood is drawn for yet more screening and testing. She lies on an examining table and the fetal heart rate is noted, as is the position of the baby. If she has symptoms to present, these are noted, and remedies may be prescribed. As is often the case in physician visits, a prescription handed over is a way of resolving questions and terminating the interview. Time, one feels, is of the essence as the doctor moves from one examining room to the next.

The prenatal care that the midwives of the home birth movement developed grew in response to this approach. Screening for pathology is part of the care they offered, but not where the emphasis was placed. Nutrition, self-care, and education were stressed, and the psychological meaning of the pregnancy was particularly important. As one midwife doing home births in the 1970s put it:

I'm usually interested in why they wanted the pregnancy in the first place; why they want to do it at home and what that means to them, this is a decision for responsibility that they've taken; their relation as a couple; how they relate to the baby — these are the principal issues to deal with, usually at the first meeting.

The second major difference between the medical and the midwifery model is in the conceptualization of responsibility. In the medical model, responsibility is something shouldered by the doctor. This is, of course, not unique to obstetrics but has long been part of the traditional clinical mindset. In the medical model, practitioners see themselves as responsible for the outcome of treatment, and since pregnancy is a disease-like state, its care comes under the treatment model. The physician "manages" the pregnancy, attempting constant, usually minor adjustments in order to bring the physiological picture of the woman back to "normal." In the midwifery model, the woman herself holds the responsibility for her pregnancy and makes her own decisions. The midwife sees herself as a teacher and a guide for the pregnant woman and her family.

Thus, while a physician might spend 10 to 15 minutes at each prenatal visit (or even less, if ancillary staff do part of the work), a routine midwifery prenatal visit takes 30 minutes, an hour, or even more. Essentially the same physical screening procedures are performed (frequently by the mother herself), but the midwives also discuss and evaluate the socio-emotional context of the pregnancy. The sense of rush and efficiency in medical care may be heightened under "managed care" and the general speed-up in medicine, but it is also deeply rooted in the logic of the medical model. The job of the physician is to diagnose and to treat, and in the relatively straightforward work of pregnancy management, these routines are handled quickly.

The goals of the midwives doing home and birth center births are more time-consuming and far more complex. Getting to know women and their families, educating and sharing information, all take time and involve the midwives in the lives of clients to a greater extent than does drawing blood. As one midwife in a 1970s birth center summed up the work of prenatal care:

We strive to create a milieu that is safe and supportive in which individuals can discover for themselves what it means to give birth. To open
themselves on physical, emotional and spiritual levels to another person
— to give birth.

Childbirth

The Social Construction of Birth

The first thing to remember is that obstetrics is a surgical specialty. In
surgery, the ideology of technology is dominant. Perhaps more clearly
than anywhere else in medicine, the body is a machine, the doctor a
mechanic. In the typical surgical situation, the unconscious patient is
waiting, like a car on a hydraulic lift, when the surgeon arrives, and
is still in that condition as the surgeon leaves. The surgeon and the
rest of the medical staff may care about the person whose body lies
before them, but for the duration of the surgery, the mind/body dualism theorized by Descartes is a reality. Marcia Millman, in a classic
study of observations of surgical wards, reported that when patients
have been given local rather than general anesthesia for an operation
and are thus awake, their serious remarks about the operation or their
attempts to take part in the doctors' conversations as the surgery is
underway often bring the staff to laughter (Millman 1977). To them,
the talking patient is incongruous, almost as if a car had sighed while
one of its flat tires was being replaced.

When women were sedated through labor and made unconscious
for delivery, the only possible description of birth was as an "operation"
performed by a surgeon on a patient. And this was the basic model for
birth for more than 50 years. In the early days, scopolamine, known
as "twilight sleep," was the standard anesthesia for labor, with general
anesthesia used for birth. In the 1970s the approach to anesthesia
shifted towards spinal anesthesia, or the more contemporary epidural,
both of which leave the woman conscious but numbed from the waist
down.

Nancy Stoller Shaw (1974) described the physician-directed, in-
hospital deliveries she observed in the 1970s in Boston as all following
the same pattern. The patient was placed on a delivery table similar in

appearance to an operating table. The majority of patients had spinal anesthesia or an epidural. The woman was placed in the lithotomy position and draped; her hands were sometimes strapped to prevent her from "contaminating the sterile field." She could not move her body below the chest, and her "active participation" in the birth was effectively over. Shaw wrote:

> This does not mean that the woman becomes unimportant, only that her body, or more specifically, the birth canal and its contents, and the almost born baby are the only things the doctor is really interested in. This part of her and, in particular, the whole exposed pubic area, visible to those at the foot of the table, is the stage on which the drama is played out. Before it, the doctor sits on a small metal stool to do his work. Unless he stands up, he cannot clearly see the mother's face, nor she his. She is separated as a person, as effectively as she can be, from the part of her that is giving birth. (Shaw 1974: 84)

Much has gone on in the past few decades to "humanize" birth; hospitals not only let significant others be present at birth but actually welcomed the mother back. People do talk to women giving birth now: even cesarean sections can be "family-centered." Mirrors abound. So much has changed since the days of the scopolamine-drugged, leather-strapped, isolated woman of the 1950s. And yet birth itself, the actual process of laboring and delivering a baby, is believed to have remained the same, untouched by anything other than evolutionary forces. How people "manage" birth changes, but does birth?

The Birth Process

The medical literature defines childbirth as a three-stage physiological process. In the first stage the cervix, the opening of the uterus into the vagina, dilates from being nearly closed to its fullest dimension of approximately 10 centimeters (almost 4 inches). This is referred to as "labor," and the contractions of the uterus that pull on the cervix are known as "labor pains." In the second stage, the baby is pushed through the opened cervix and through the vagina, or birth canal, and out of the mother's body. This is the "delivery." The third stage is the expulsion of the placenta or "afterbirth."

In any situation the possibility exists for alternative definitions of the event, different versions of what is *really* happening. Which version is accepted and acted on is a reflection of the power of the participants. Those with more power can have their definition of the situation accepted as reality. Often this involves some bargaining or negotiating between the people involved. Take, for example, a child with a sore throat who doesn't want to go to school. The parent may say the throat is not *that* sore, and the child counters with, "But my head hurts too." Might the child be experiencing some soreness and pain? Certainly. But is it bad enough that the child should stay home from school? That depends. Medical authorities may function just like the parent in this situation. Some of the classic work in medical sociology has addressed just this: how doctors and patients negotiate reality. Patients recovering from tuberculosis claim that they really are well enough to have a weekend pass (Roth 1963), and patients and doctors in mental hospitals negotiate over the patients' mental health (Goffman 1961). These are not, as we might assume, just "medical" judgments, but interpersonal negotiations.

Similarly, pregnant women frequently come to the hospital claiming that they are in labor, but by medically established judgment they are not. The state of being in labor, like any illness or any deviance, is an ascribed status; that is, it is a position to which a person is assigned by those in authority. But one can also negotiate to try to achieve that status or have one's claim to it recognized.

When people have negotiated a definition of the situation, that becomes reality for them, and they have to work within that reality. Let us take as an example a woman at term having painful contractions at 10-minute intervals, who has not yet begun to dilate. Whether she is or is not in labor will depend on whether she then begins to dilate, or the contractions stop and begin again days or weeks later. Whether a woman is in labor or "false labor" at Time One depends on what will have happened by Time Two. If she presents herself to the hospital claiming that she is in labor, and by weeping and pleading, or just because she seems educated and middle-class, she gets admitted, the medical acknowledgment that she is in labor will have been established. If she does not begin to dilate for 24 hours, and then 12 hours after that — 36 hours after her admission — she delivers, that woman will have had a 36-hour labor. On the other hand, if she is denied or delays admission and presents herself to the hospital 24 hours later for a 12-hour in-hospital labor, she will have had a 12-hour labor preceded by a day of discomfort. From the point of view of the institution that is "responsible" for her labor, and thus her pain, only from the time of her admission, the latter is preferable, the longer labor being easily perceived as institutional mismanagement. Yet from the point of view of the woman, the *physical* sensations in both cases are precisely the same; it is the *social* definition — calling it "labor" or not — that makes the difference between a terribly long labor or a pretty average labor with some strange contractions beforehand. Because medicine wanted to define labor as a situation requiring hospitalization but at the same time wanted to avoid prolonged labor, "real" labor got defined not in terms of the sensations the woman experiences but in terms of "progress," or cervical dilation. A dilation of 3 centimeters was generally required to be admitted.

The pregnant woman thus wants to be accurate (in medical terms) about defining the onset of labor. Otherwise, if she gains early admission she will have helped to define the situation as an overly long labor. In addition to the stress inherent in thinking oneself to be in labor for 36 hours, the medical treatment she will receive presents its own problems. Laboring women have been routinely confined to bed in hospitals, a situation that can be disturbing psychologically and physically. Not only is the labor perceived as being longer, but the horizontal position physically prolongs labor, as may the routine administration of sedatives during a long hospital stay. In addition to the variations in treatment during the first hours of labor, the treatment she will receive is different in the last hours, when the woman is hospitalized in either case. Women who have been in a hospital labor room for 30 hours receive different treatment than do women who have been there for only six hours, even if both are equally dilated and have had identical physical progress. Which woman, after all, is more likely to have a cesarean section for overly long labor — the one who got there just six hours ago, or the one who has been there through three shifts of nurses? What the woman experienced before she got to the hospital — how strongly, how frequently, and for how long her contractions have been coming — does not enter into the professional decision making nearly as much as what the medical attendants have seen for themselves.

It is also important for the pregnant woman to be accurate in identifying labor because, if she presents herself to the hospital and is denied admission, she begins her relationship with the hospital and her birth attendants from a bad bargaining position. Her version of reality is denied, leaving her with no alternative but to lose faith in her own or the institution's ability to perceive accurately what is happening to her. Either situation will have negative consequences for the eventual labor and delivery. That is why childbirth education classes frequently spend considerable time distinguishing labor from so-called false labor.

In U.S. hospitals, until recently, the first and second stages of labor were seen as sufficiently separate to require different rooms and, frequently, different staff. Women attended to by nursing and house staff throughout their labor might not have seen their own obstetricians until they got to the delivery room. When women were moved from one room to another to mark the transition from one stage of labor to another, the professional staff had to make a distinction between laboring and delivering, and then apply that distinction to the individual woman. A cut-off point had to be established at which a woman was no longer viewed as laboring, but as delivering. If the point was missed and the woman delivered, say, in the hall on the way to the delivery room, then she was seen as having "precipped," having had a precipitous delivery. If the point was called too soon — if the staff decided that the woman was ready to deliver and the physical reality was that she had another hour to go — then concern would be aroused about the length of second stage because she had spent that extra hour in a delivery rather than a labor room. As hospitals permit the mother to labor and birth in the same room, hospital staff pay less attention to establishing the moment of entry into second stage.

Even today the editors of *Williams*, in bold print, state: "One of the most critical diagnoses in obstetrics is the accurate diagnosis of labor" (Cunningham et al. 2001: 310). Why? They offer two reasons: "If labor is falsely diagnosed, inappropriate interventions to augment labor may be made" (310). But home birth midwives do not intervene just because a clock tells them a labor is long. They look at the condition of the mother and the fetal heart tones, and if all is well, all is well. The second reason *Williams* offers is that if labor is not diagnosed, "the fetus-infant may be damaged by unexpected complications occurring in sites remote from medical personnel and adequate medical facilities" (310). The birth may, that is, occur at home.

What if there were no hospital, no labor room, no delivery room? That, of course, has been the case for most of human history, and it is what the midwives doing home births faced. There were no *institutional* demands to define labor, or to distinguish the very end of first stage from the start of second stage. If a woman is having painful contractions and feels she needs her midwife, then her needs are real, whether or not her labor is "false." If you're not moving her from one place to another, does it really matter what "stage" she is in? Can just being in any given stage for "too long" itself make a birth unsafe? For midwives in the early home birth movement, these were important questions. Those who were trained as nurse-midwives and those who were self-taught had very little in the way of "midwifery" knowledge to draw upon. There was only "obstetrical" knowledge. And many "facts" of obstetrical knowledge turned out to be "artifacts" of obstetrical management.

The Active Management of Labor

There is something enormously appealing about the phrase "active management" applied to labor. The notion that labor can be managed, is manageable — what a reassuring thought! When women face labor, they often think about managing it: How will I manage, they ask, how will I cope? That question is really about managing oneself. The labor arrives, happens, unfolds, descends — and one manages or copes as best one can. "Best" here often means being a good patient, not complaining, being cooperative, not making a fuss.

When physicians think about it, they like to think of themselves as managing the labor itself: steering its course, speeding it up or slowing it down, "handling" or "managing" it much as one "manages" a car on a highway. When you add in the word "active," you're really onto something. Then physicians can think of themselves as managing the labor not reactively, responding to or coping with what happens, following the bends of the highway and keeping the wheels on the road, but in a way people now like to call "proactively," actually taking charge. Now we are not talking about fine tuning or steering between shoulder and side rails, but about piloting in open seas, controlling the labor by taking its power into one's own hands.

Either notion of managing labor — managing one's reactions to it as a laboring woman or taking charge of it as a physician — assumes the labor itself as the object of attention. Labor, in this medical way of thinking, is something that happens to women, rather than something women *do*. This is a way of thinking about labor that encourages what is called "prepared" childbirth, preparing the woman to cope with the labor as it is managed. Labor and its active medical management are something that happens to a woman, with which she can learn to cope.

From the physician's perspective, when all is said and done, there is not much that can be done to "manage" labor. Doctors cannot make, produce, or guarantee healthy babies or healthy mothers. The two areas they have had some success with are the management of the pain of labor and the management of its length. One can absolutely guarantee a woman a painless labor, if one is willing to use the medications to ensure it, whatever their costs. That was the direction medical management first took: from chloroform onward, it promised painless labor.

By the early 1970s, the costs of pain control — both psychological and physiological — became increasingly apparent. At that point, two things happened. The most common form of pain relief switched from sedation and general anesthesia to more localized pain relief. Epidural anesthesia has become the most widely used medical form of pain relief. According to the Maternity Center Association's report *Listening to Mothers*, 59% of women having vaginal births reported using epidural analgesia for pain relief during labor (DeClerq et al. 2002: 1). For an epidural, a fine plastic tube is inserted in the lower back just outside the spinal cord, and numbing drugs are dripped in. An anesthesiologist is necessary to insert the epidural, and the availability of on-site anesthesiologists is the single most significant factor in a hospital's epidural rates. Epidurals are more commonly inserted during daylight hours, and Ina May Gaskin reports that often women accept epidurals they don't really feel they need at the time because the anesthesiologist tells them he'll be leaving shortly and it's their last chance (Gaskin 2003: 236). Epidurals have the enormous advantage of allowing the woman to be fully present mentally: she can observe the proceedings. When they work — and 15% of women do not get full pain relief from the epidural — they numb her. Some women feel pressure and an urge to push with an epidural; some do not and then become "bystanders" to their own labor. For many women, that is the ideal situation: they can have essentially the same experience being offered their husbands — a chance to watch their baby being born. Of course it is *not* the same experience when it is your own body you are watching give birth, but epidurals absolutely do resolve the problem of "managing" the pain and the intensity of labor and birth.

The other change in medical management that occurred was a shift in energy from managing the *pain* of labor to managing its *length*. In 1968 a Dublin hospital introduced "the active management of labor" as an obstetrical approach focused on providing control over the length of labor. As long as one is prepared to stop the labor with a cesarean section, one can guarantee a labor no longer than any arbitrary time limit one chooses: 12 hours seems to have become the standard figure. In the United States today, according to the *Listening to Mothers* survey, almost half of mothers had a caregiver try to induce labor, and these inductions successfully started one-third of all labors. Just over half of all the women reported that they were given drugs to strengthen (speed up) contractions, and more than half had their membranes artificially ruptured, also to speed labor (DeClerq 2002: 1).

It's All in the Timing

The standard obstetrical model of labor is best represented by "Friedman's curve," a "graphicostatistical analysis" of labor introduced by Emanuel A. Friedman in seven separate articles between 1954 and 1959 in the major American obstetrical journal (see summary in Friedman 1959). "Graphicostatistical analysis" is a pompous name for a relatively simple idea. Friedman observed labors and computed the average length of time they took. He broke labor into separate "phases" and found the average length of each phase. He did this separately for primiparas (women having first births) and for multiparas (women with previous births). He computed the averages and the statistical limits — a measure of the amount of variation. Take the example of height. If we computed heights for women, we would measure many women, get an average, and also be able to say how likely it was for someone to be much taller or much shorter than average. A woman of over six feet tall is a statistical abnormality.

What Friedman did was to make a connection between *statistical* normality and *physiological* normality. He used the language of statistics, with its specific technical meanings, and jumped to conclusions about physiology: "It is clear that cases where the phase-durations fall outside of these (statistical) limits are probably abnormal in some way. We can see now how, with very little effort, we have been able to define average labor and to describe with proper degrees of certainty the limits of normal" (Friedman 1959: 97). Once the false and misleading connection is made between statistical abnormality and physiological abnormality, the door is opened for medical treatment. *Statistically abnormal labors are medically treated.* The medical treatments include rupturing membranes, administering hormones, and cesarean sections. Using this logic, we would say that a woman of six feet one inch was not only unusually tall, but also that we should treat her for her "height condition."

How did this work in practice? Obstetrics has held very closely to these "limits of normal" for labor. The first phase of labor Friedman identified was the *latent* phase. This, he said, began with the onset of regular uterine contractions and lasted to the beginning of the *active* phase, when cervical dilation is most rapid. But how can one know when contractions are "regular"? There is no way to examine a particular contraction and identify it as "regular." It can only be determined retroactively, after contractions have been *regularly* occurring for a while. This brings us to the confusion over "false labor." The only difference between "false labor" and "true labor" is in what happens next: true labor pains produce a demonstrable degree of effacement (thinning of the cervix) and some dilation of the cervix, whereas the effect of false labor pains on the cervix is minimal. The difference is then one of degree: how *much* effacement and dilation, and how *quickly*.

The concept of "false labor" served as a buffer for the medical model of "true labor." Labors that display an unusually long "latent phase" or labors that simply stop can be diagnosed as "false labors." Doctors could continue to believe that labor does not stop and start, even after they had seen it happen, because they could retroactively diagnose the labor as "false." Friedman himself pointed out that the latent phase may occasionally be longer than the time limits, yet the active phase may be completely normal. He explained these "unusual cases" by saying that part of the latent phase must really have been "false labor." That way, his tables of what is statistically normal still work out. These are techniques that are used to prevent anomalies from being seen, to "normalize" events so that they conform to the medical model.

Midwives attending home births, in contrast, see labors start and stop; they see women stop in labor, be reassured in some way, and have their labor start again. Ina May Gaskin has pointed out that doctors themselves used to know these things. They even knew that labor could reverse itself, that "progress" is not an inevitable direction. A partially opened cervix could tighten back up. She cites a dozen medical textbooks published between 1846 and 1901 in which doctors knew and taught that their presence, their entry into a woman's birthing room, could disturb the labor (Gaskin 2003: 140–141). By the mid-twentieth century, that knowledge was lost. Birth had moved into the hospitals, and doctors never saw the consequences of their own presence because they had nothing to compare it with. If a woman's labor appeared to stop, then the doctors decided it had never really started; it was a "false" labor. If labor appeared to reverse itself and the cervix closed back up, then they decided the admitting nurse had measured wrong. A fact that didn't fit into the theory was simply not a fact, just a mistaken measure.

Home birth midwives, in contrast, saw these things happen. They saw a birth slow down when the mother was made uncomfortable, saw the effect that social and emotional factors had on labor, and began to reevaluate the medical definitions of labor itself. Eventually, in the midwifery model, strict time limits were abandoned: each labor is held to be unique. Statistical norms may be interesting, but they are not of value for the management of any given labor.

Consider, too, the situational politics of home birth. When a midwife has a woman at home or in a birth center, there is a very strong incentive to keep her out of the hospital. Arbitrary time limits can be "negotiated," and the midwife looks for *progress*, some continual change in the direction of birthing. It was hard for nurse-midwives who started to do home births to "let go" of their medical training. One midwife I interviewed in the 1970s expressed her ambivalence: "They don't have to look like a Friedman graph walking around, but I think they should make some kind of reasonable progress." Another expressed the concern in terms of the laboring woman's subjective experience, a more woman-centered understanding: "There is no absolute limit — it would depend on what part of the labor was the longest and how she was handling that — was she tired? Could she handle that?"

A third midwife described her technique for dealing with long labors:

> Even though she was slow, she kept moving. I have learned to discriminate now, and if it's long I let them do it at home on their own and I try to listen carefully, and when I get there it's toward the end of labor. This girl was going all Saturday and all Sunday, so that's forty-eight hours of labor. It wasn't forceful labor, but she was uncomfortable for two days. So if I'd gone and stayed there the first time, I'd have been there a whole long time; then when you get there you have to do something.

"Doing something" is the cornerstone of medical management. Every labor that takes "too long" and cannot be stimulated by hormones or by breaking the membrane will go on to the next level of medical intervention, the cesarean section. Breaking the membranes is an induction technique that is particularly interesting in this regard. The sac in which the baby and the amniotic fluid are enclosed is easily ruptured once the cervix is partially opened. Sometimes that happens by itself early on in labor, and "the waters breaking" may even be the first sign of labor. But once broken, the membrane is no longer a barrier between the baby and the outside world. The *Listening to Mothers* survey reports that 55% of women experienced artificially ruptured membranes. (*Williams* states, "If the membranes are intact, there is a great temptation even during normal labor to perform an amniotomy [rupture them]" [Cunningham et al. 2001: 315].) It is not a temptation that home birth midwives feel. Once the membrane is ruptured, the chance of infection increases — more so in hospitals with frequent vaginal examinations, but in any case more than if the membrane remained intact. Once the membrane is ruptured, it is important that the labor proceed more quickly to avoid infection. Thus the intervention, the "doing something" to speed the labor itself, demands that the labor indeed be sped up.

Length of labor is not a basic, unchanging biological fact but is subject to social and medical control. Even before the introduction of the Dublin-style "active management of labor," which guarantees a labor of no more than 12 hours, there has been a kind of "speed-up" of hospital labors. Looking at *Williams* in its different editions, the reported length of labor dropped from an average first stage of labor in first births of 12.5 hours in 1948, down to 10.5; and from 7.3 hours for second and subsequent births in 1948 down to only 5 hours by the 1980 edition.

The speed-up was even more dramatic for the second stage, which dropped from an average of 80 minutes for first births in 1948 to only 50 minutes for first births, and from 30 minutes in 1948 down to 20 minutes for subsequent births. Third stage is barely measurable in time, with some obstetricians practicing "routine manual removal of any placenta that has not separated spontaneously by the time they have completed delivery of the infant and care of the cord in women with conduction analgesia" (Cunningham et al. 2001: 323). In 1980, *Williams* said that if the placenta has not separated within three to five minutes of the birth of the baby, "manual removal of the placenta should probably be carried out" (Pritchard and McDonald 1980: 425), and in 2001, "Manual removal of the placenta is rightfully practiced much sooner and more often than in the past". In a home birth, the birth of the baby is itself such an important event, so demanding of human response and attention, that unless there is particular cause — like excessive bleeding — midwives are content to wait a while for the woman to expel the placenta spontaneously. At home, babies are usually put to the breast or brought up to the breast by the mother, and the suckling stimulates contractions that expel the placenta.

A midwife in the 1970s told me a story of one of her first home births. The birth went well, and the mother and baby were doing fine, but after almost an hour, the placenta had yet to appear. The midwife went into the kitchen and, barely restraining her panic, called a colleague who was far more experienced with home births. "Is there any chamomile tea in the house?" the calm voice on the phone asked. Rummaging through kitchen cabinets, still clutching the phone, the midwife found a box. "Well, then, make a strong cup and sit down and drink it." The placenta, the experienced midwife assured her, will come when it's ready. It takes a few minutes, but what's the rush?

The rush is largely institutional: births in hospitals need to be meshed together to form an overarching institutional tempo. Predictability is important; timing matters, as staff moves from birth to birth, as women are moved from place to place. There have been many studies of the variations in interventions by time of day, time of week, even by football schedules: interventions increase when doctors are rushed, whatever the reason.

One good, careful recent study of more than 37,000 live births in Philadelphia hospitals shows that women who give birth during the day are much more likely to have obstetric interventions than those who give birth during the "off peak" hours of 2 am to 8 am. Looking only at low-risk women admitted in active, non-induced labor, and excluding labors involving fetal distress or "prolonged, obstructed or abnormal labors," the researchers found that women who gave birth during peak hospital hours were 43% more likely to have forceps or vacuum extraction and 86% more likely to have drug-induced labors. They were also 10% more likely to have an episiotomy (Webb and Culhane 2002). The institutional tempo slows down at night, and staff allow birth to take a bit longer.

"Active management," managing labor by the clock with interventions as necessary to speed it up, is part of the medical ethos. Although they may often have to watch the clock the obstetricians have set for them, it is not part of the midwifery approach.

Giving Birth or Being Delivered?

Physicians control birth in hospitals because it is done in their territory, under their expertise. That control over their work space is what makes them "professional." As the senior professionals around, they obviously control all the other workers, including midwives and doulas, along with nurses, orderlies, and aides. But they also control the patients. The medical management of birth means the management of birthing women: to control or to manage a situation is to control and manage individuals.

The alternative to physician and institutional control of childbirth is childbirth outside medical institutions, outside the medical model. In this alternative, birth is an activity that women *do*. The woman may need some help, but the help is, for the most part, in the form of teaching her how to do for herself.

The word "deliver" exemplifies the medical model: it is a service delivered. The word "birthing" clarifies the midwifery model: birthing, like swimming, singing, and dancing, is something people do, not have done for them.

Home birth midwives struggled to redefine birth, but also to define their *own* role — what they do at a birth. Nancy Mills was a direct-entry midwife in the 1970s, not a nurse but a midwife who began by helping a friend during labor. By the time she had attended more than 600 births, she had come to see her role at birth as this:

> I see myself going in and being a helper, being an attendant. Sometimes I play with the kids, or I do some cooking. Sometimes I sit with the woman. Sometimes I help the husband assist the woman. Some families need more help than others, but it is easy to go in and see where you are needed and how you can fill that role. (Mills 1976: 131)

The birth is not made to fit the routine, but the attendant to fit the birth. The birth is something the mother does by herself, but

> It is important for that woman to be able to look at you, to know you are there, to hold your hand, to be reassured. I know it helps when I say to a woman, "I know how you feel. I know it's harder than you thought it was going to be, but you can do it.'" (Mills 1976: 134)

What do midwives actually do when they get to a birth at home? They come in, say hello, introduce themselves to anyone they don't know, just as any guest in a home would do. And in that entry, in that way of entering the home, they make the statement that they are not there to "do" the birth. One midwife, when asked what she does when she first gets to a birth, said:

Nothing, first. Which is very important, because they expect me to do something, like I'm supposed to do something. But they're doing it already and that's what we're going to be doing, so I find it very important to just come in and sit down.

This approach is a radical departure from the medical model, in which the entry of the doctor signifies the start of the performance, or the admission of the woman to the hospital signifies the official start of the labor. Judy Luce, a Vermont midwife who has been practicing for over 25 years, likes to show people a birth film made in Australia. In this film, the woman is seated on a big lounge chair, and casually brushes away the midwife's hand. The camera watches as slowly, without any touching, the vagina bulges and the baby emerges. It reminds her, she says, that whatever midwives are doing or not doing with their hands and their skills, it is women who give birth.

This is not to say that midwives don't have and use their skills. They do vaginal exams during labor, but not usually on a clocked schedule. They will, on a more regular basis, listen for fetal heart tones. The role is to keep a check on the physical changes, and not to interfere with personal interactions. Often that means that the midwife has to "support the support person," providing reassurance not only to the woman but also to her support people that labor is progressing normally, and occasionally offering advice on how to give support. People often are not fully prepared for just how painful labor can be or how needful the laboring woman may become. The midwife provides reassurance that her condition, however distressing, is normal, and suggests positive ways of coping.

At home there are no changes in room (labor to delivery room) for the second stage of labor, but there is usually a marked change in the ambience. The end of active labor (transition), as the woman reaches full dilation, is usually quite painful for the mother and difficult for the support person. The pushing stage is usually exciting, climactic. The mother may be semi-sitting at the edge of or on a bed, braced by her support person, or she may be squatting, lying on her side, on a chair, or on her hands and knees, depending on her comfort and the suggestions of the midwife. The mother is in no way physically restrained. Sometimes the midwife encourages the woman to reach down, to push the baby out into her own hands. After the baby emerges, into either the mother's hands or the midwife's, the mother draws the baby up to her. One of the home birth midwives I interviewed in the 1970s said:

> There are at least thirty seconds of both mother and baby looking at each other and going, 'who are you?' Then everybody usually starts climbing all over the baby and we usually back off at that point, just back off a bit and keep an eye on the placenta, what's going on.

The ability to "back off" is raised almost to an art by some midwives. One said that she never lets herself call out "It's a boy" or "It's a girl" because "all of her life a woman will remember the sound of those words, and she should hear them in a voice she loves."

After a few minutes the midwife will either cut the cord herself or may help the father, or less commonly the mother or someone else, to do so. The baby will be wrapped in warm blankets and given back to the mother to put to the breast. Suckling usually stimulates uterine contractions, and the mother will hand the baby to someone else while she expels the placenta. After checking the placenta and showing it to the mother if she is interested in seeing it, as most women are, the midwife will check the mother for tearing and for excessive bleeding. In the unlikely event of a tear or an episiotomy, the midwife will do the repair with a local anesthetic. If all is well, the mother might get up and bathe or shower while other people dress the baby and weigh it.

Midwives stay for some hours after birth, depending on the needs of the family and the condition of the mother and baby. Many families celebrate the birth with the traditional glass of champagne, some with birthday cake. People are frequently ready for a meal, and a party atmosphere may prevail. At other births the family may just want to sleep. The midwife eventually bids goodbye; as one said:

My aim is that when I leave that family feels they birthed it. I was there and I helped, but they did it…so that in their whole recollection of the experience I will be very minimal. That's my goal and that's my aim.

That role and that goal are very different from the role of the doctor in a hospital birth, which Shaw, in her observations, summed up as being "the director and the star" (1974: 87).

The Importance of Place

It is not just a matter of moving from place to place as we examine birth under different circumstances. Under different systems of care, we are not just doing the same thing in a different place. Different meanings make birth a different event. Teeth, tongue, jaw, and intestines are all pretty much the same thing the world over, but the meaning of a meal could not be more different as we move from a famine in a country under siege to a food court in a suburban U.S. mall, from a Passover Seder to a fast-food lunch, from high tea to a steak house. So it is with childbirth: the social and cultural variation overwhelms the physiological sameness.

Institutionalization — any institutionalization — disempowers, drains power from the birthing woman and gives it to the institution itself, as it homogenizes the experience. Annemiek Cuppen, an extraordinarily fine midwife in the Netherlands, shared the following illustrative story. She had attended a birth in which the woman planned to give birth in the hospital. While the Netherlands has a 30% home birth rate, midwives do attend births in both places. Annemiek Cuppen came first to the woman's home for the early labor. As she came in the door, she was greeted by the woman, who told her husband to go and get the midwife a cup of coffee, sent her children and mother-in-law scurrying on errands, and generally bossed people around and remained the center of her home. And then came the move to the hospital — a move chosen, remember, by the woman herself. As they entered the hospital room, the woman sat herself quietly on the edge of the bed. With a new demeanor now, looking up at Annemiek, the woman asked, "Uh, excuse me, do you think it would be OK if maybe we opened the window please?"

It is not only at this individual level that an institution drains power from women. Once institutionalization is inevitable for birth, once all births move (as they have essentially done in the United States) out of the home and to a specialized site, that site, the institution itself, comes to seem necessary. And once it seems necessary, it seems causal, as if the birth itself depends on the institution. That is how it is now in much of the world where home birth is not so much unavailable as unthinkable. Most Americans cannot imagine home birth.

That is one reason that maternity homes or birth centers are often suggested as a compromise for places like the United States that have lost their home birth traditions. Even if there is absolutely nothing that makes a particular birth center any safer than a home birth, people who are now several generations removed from home birth can accept the possibility of a maternity home or birth center. Just going there will somehow make birth safe and possible in a way that simply staying in one's bedroom will not, because to trust the home as a place for birth is fundamentally to trust the woman to give birth — and that is the fundamental trust that most of this country now has lost. The power that is the birthing woman's has been drained from her and given to the institution in which she is placed.

Giving birth at home returns that power to the woman.

Of Babies, Breasts, and Bonds

The most obvious, dramatic truth of a birth is that one being becomes two. But nothing is ever quite that simple. The distinct kicks of the fetus in late pregnancy; the hiccups the baby has that the mother can feel but are not, after all, *her* hiccups, the struggle to find a comfortable sleeping position accommodating the weight of the fetus — all are growing indications to the mother that the baby within is already a distinct being. And at the moment of birth? There is, actually, no single moment of birth. Over the course of several moments the baby emerges — usually a head comes forward first, eyes may or may not make contact, a sound may or may not be heard even before the rest of the body is born. The pulsating cord slows, stops. A fully awake, undrugged, unrestrained mother reaches for her baby, and the baby reaches, in its own way, for the mother, even crawling, creeping, pulling itself up to her breast. Living material passes from the mother's skin to the baby. The living cells of colostrum and later of milk move into the baby's body, transferring the mother's immunities. Certainly one being becomes two. But maybe it takes a bit of time; maybe it is a process, not an event.

That's not the way that doctors have seen it.

The development of separate medical specialties of obstetrics and pediatrics and the subspecialty of neonatology, the care of newborns, may be both a reflection and a cause of the medical view of mother and child as being entirely separate "problems in medical management." Medicine separated, both physically and conceptually, the mother from her infant, denying the biological as much as the emotional relationship and interaction that home birth midwives see as continuing in the postbirth period. That the development of separate specialties reflects the conceptual separation is obvious. One reason for this may be the nature of medical education. With their "rotations" through the various specialties, physicians — and nurses — learn about mothers and babies in different places and at different times, and about other family members, notably fathers, not at all. The moment the cord was cut may very well have been the last time any physician saw mother and baby together in the hospital.

Home birth midwives, on the other hand, maintain responsibility for both mother and baby as an interdependent unit in the hours and days after birth. The responsibilities that the midwives expect mothers and their support people to take for the birth extend to their responsibilities for the baby. After it is ascertained that the baby appears well and normal, further primary responsibility for the baby at a home birth is passed to the parents. Midwives carefully point out the problems and signs to look for (notably infant jaundice, which might not be obvious to an untrained eye), but being alert for the signs of a problem and seeking assistance are parents' responsibilities. The assumed competence of the parents to observe their own babies contrasts strongly with the current medically defined "necessity" of keeping infants under medical observation immediately after birth, the reason many doctors and hospitals give for objecting to same-day discharges, so-called drive-through deliveries (see Kelleher 2003

for fuller discussion). The midwives see it differently. As one I interviewed in the 1970s said:

> When the mother is really the first human being to have contact with
> the baby and that contact is continuing within several hours, she is the
> expert for her baby, and feels it, and develops a tremendous amount of
> confidence, even skills: fathers too, and others. They all feel very close to
> the baby, very responsible for the baby. There is no third party interfer-
> ing with this. The role of the midwife in that instance is really just to
> point out little things, to enhance this feeling of responsibility.

In the medical approach, the needs of the infant and mother, not
necessarily perceived as harmonious during pregnancy, are certainly
not perceived as interactive after birth. For example, since pregnancy
and birth are thought of as illnesses or crisis situations, the mother is
expected to "need her rest," to recuperate or recover. Consequently,
in most U.S. hospitals, mothers were sent to "recovery rooms" from
the delivery rooms. Infants, however, are perceived as "demanding"
attention and feeding. The infant's "demands" are then counter to the
mother's "need for rest." Since rest in a hospital is defined as something that takes place quietly and in solitude and infant care is seen as
an activity, the two are contradictory. That is why mother and child
were routinely separated immediately after birth, just when the desire
and need for intimacy are greatest.

Within the midwifery model, however, both maternal and infant
needs are defined quite differently. The mother's need for rest is
defined as the need to be free from everything but herself and her
baby. The infant's needs are perceived as body contact, colostrum,
and then milk. Far from being contradictory, these needs all come
together as the mother lies in bed, dozing and nursing her baby:
"Then when we leave, the family can all get into bed together and
get some rest."

Maternal Bonding and Cultural Binds

Motherhood is a biological relationship in a social context and
a social relationship in a biological context. It is hard to say how
much of mothering behavior, especially in the first few hours and

days after birth, is the result of biology, and how much the result of social learning and social pressures. Those who emphasize the importance of biology in motherhood often refer to animal studies. Many animal mothers, if separated from their newborns immediately after birth, will reject them when they are returned. It is only immediately after the birth that the mothers will accept, or bond to, their young. Similarly, newborns of some species, such as chicks, will bond to their mothers only in the first few hours after hatching, the so-called critical period. If separated during these first critical hours, the chick will not display the normal behavior of following behind its mother and staying close to her. On the basis of these and other animal studies, some people have suggested that there is a similar critical period for maternal-infant bonding in humans and have attempted to demonstrate this experimentally.

Very widely reported and influential studies on maternal-infant bonding were done in the 1970s. The original study, reported in the prestigious *New England Journal of Medicine*, involved 28 mother-infant pairs. Variation in the amount of contact in the first three days of life was shown to affect interaction a month later (Klaus et al. 1972). Fourteen mothers received what was then standard hospital treatment in the United States. The babies were removed to a separate nursery after the mothers had just a brief glimpse of them in the delivery room and were not returned to the mother for six to twelve hours, and then were allowed only 20-minute to half-hour visits every four hours. The other 14 mothers were allowed to have their babies for one hour within the first three hours after birth and then followed the same every-four-hours pattern, except for an extra five-hour visit each afternoon for the three days of hospitalization. The only difference between the two groups was the 16 hours of "extra" contact permitted the "experimental" group. In retrospect, what is probably most striking is how little contact both groups of mothers had with their babies. None of these mothers had even the level of contact that standard maternity care offers these days, and nothing like the contact home-birthing mothers have. And, in a study that purports to look at "instinctual behavior," it is fascinating to note that all babies in both groups were bottle-fed. The researchers used only bottle-feeding mothers so that the additional contact would have no effect on the amount of milk available and thus not confound the findings. It is amazing to think about drawing conclusions about maternal instincts when babies were removed, washed, dressed, and returned "within three hours" for only an hour, and not ever put to the breast.

The mother-infant interactions were observed under three separate circumstances by independent researchers a month later. The "extended contact" mothers were more reluctant to leave their infants with someone else, usually stood and watched during the pediatric examination, showed greater soothing behavior, and engaged in significantly more eye-to-eye contact and fondling. Differences between the two groups continued to be seen at two years of age (Ringler et al. 1975). The findings were widely reported.

In itself, it was an interesting study, but it came at an even more interesting moment. It was a moment in which "sociobiology," an attempt to combine the insights of evolutionary biology with those of sociology and anthropology, was being developed. It was a moment when feminism, and the beginnings of anti-feminist backlash, were much in the public eye. And it was a moment when the home birth movement and midwifery and the women's health movement were all trying to change U.S. hospital practices.

The sociobiologists were eager to find "maternal instincts." The feminists were eager to deny them. The midwives were eager to increase women's access to their babies in hospitals. The study was cited by one and all.

Those who argued for "instinctive" or "natural" maternal behavior contended that the "extended-contact" mothers were freer to follow their instincts, while the other mothers had their mother-child relationship disturbed or interrupted, their instinctual patterns blocked by the enforced separation. It was not an unreasonable explanation. An alternative, equally plausible explanation is that mother-child interactions are learned, not instinctual, but that mothers do need the presence of the baby, and the baby that of the mother, to learn how to interact. If the mother is denied her baby except for a few minutes at times based on neither the baby's needs nor her own, learning does not take place, or, even more important, incorrect learning occurs. The baby learns that comforting is unrelated to the need for comfort, and the mother learns that she is superfluous to the child's needs.

In either case, the implications for mothering are the same. If there are "maternal instincts," they may be fragile and disturbed by mother-child separation. If the behaviors are learned, they need to be learned in the beginning, before other patterns are learned — by mother or baby — and interfere.

But why was the whole discussion focused on mothers? This study was not looking at the biological part of early mothering: all the babies were bottle-fed. Would a father who'd spent time in the first hours with a baby behave differently from one who hadn't? A grandmother? There really is no reason not to think that this research on newborns applies to *anyone* who will be caring for the child — mother, father, siblings, adoptive parents — but as long as all the research was done on mothers, the term "maternal-infant bonding" rather than "adult-infant bonding" was used.

And what of a baby's attachment to and need for its mother? The research on that was also based on deeply gendered assumptions. Some classic studies were done in the late 1950s on love, milk, and infant monkeys. Researchers noted that rhesus monkey infants raised in laboratory cages became deeply attached to the cloth pads in the cages, showing real distress when these were removed for cleaning. "The behavior of the infant monkeys was reminiscent of the human infant's attachment to its blankets, pillows, rag dolls or cuddly teddy bears" (Harlow 1973). What these observations suggested to Harry F. Harlow were some experiments. Infant monkeys were raised alone in cages with two wire dolls, one covered with soft terrycloth and one left bare. Half the monkeys received milk from a breast-level rubber nipple in the wire doll, and half from a similarly placed nipple in the cloth doll. All the infants gained weight and grew normally. All of them spent time cuddling the cloth doll.

Harlow, in the 1950s before the term took on its newer connotation, called both of the dolls "surrogate mothers." Of course, calling a wire contraption a "mother" does not make it a mother. An equally plausible alternative would be to call the milk-producing doll "mother" and the non-milk-producing doll "father." That way we could say that each monkey had two surrogate parents, a father and a mother, rather than two surrogate mothers.

Harlow found that "those that secured their nourishment from the wire mother showed no tendency to spend more time on her than feeding required, contradicting the idea that affection is a response learned in association with the reduction of hunger or thirst." The cloth dolls were a source of reassurance when the infants were frightened, while the wire ones gave no comfort, no matter which one supplied the milk. We could then say that monkey infants preferred a cloth to a wire parent, regardless of the "sex" of the parent. Or, to put it another way, half of the monkeys preferred their mothers, and half their fathers.

The question Harlow was asking was: "What is it about mothers that infants love?" It is a loaded question. What his experiments demonstrated is that "contact comfort" is more important than breasts or nursing in the development of infant attachment. Harlow did not question the basic assumption of the 1950s that is *only* their mothers whom infants will love.

If love in infant humans is like love in infant monkeys, then being a biological mother, including breastfeeding, does not have to mean being the sole caretaker, the central person in a baby's life. This contradicted virtually all of the literature on breastfeeding and mothers, which linked breastfeeding to full-time, all-encompassing mothering in which the mother is fully engrossed in the child and the child in the mother; the father encompasses them both with his love and protection.

It is interesting to reflect that mid-century — at just that time when breastfeeding was at the lowest rate it has ever registered in any group in history, when so few women were nursing their babies that it was necessary for those who were doing so to form a "club" to encourage and help each other — at that same time our society was at the height of the "feminine mystique" (Friedan 1963). Women stayed home and made mothering a full-time job, taking care of children, waxing kitchen floors, and sterilizing formula.

Some women may find it helpful to remember that breastfeeding is a natural behavior shared by all mammals. It can be comforting to lie in bed and nurse a baby and feel like a mama cat with her kittens. And sometimes it can be nice to have sex like a cat — mindless, thoughtless, wordless, and careless. But people are not cats. We don't let our babies wander off when they're weaned and forget about them, and we don't choose a mate because we are in heat. We have values, beliefs, language, thoughts. We have a culture. Breastfeeding, like birth, sex, death, and the other biological facts of life, takes its meaning from the culture that defines it. In our culture we have made both too much and too little of breastfeeding. We have ignored its physiological importance for both mother and baby, thinking that technology could do the same thing better, faster, and more efficiently. At the same time, we have taken for granted and subsequently overemphasized its importance in adult–newborn bonding and the symbolic implications of breasts for child care. The irony is that we have allowed ourselves to be limited to the idea of family centered on mothers as the "natural" caretakers of infants and young children, while allowing anything natural in the relationship to be overrun by hospital regulations, pediatricians' orders, and the baby-food and formula industry.

Breastfeeding

A picture is indeed worth a thousand words, but what powerful words do is evoke pictures. Picture this: *milk*. People in our world now picture "milk" and see a glass container filled with white liquid. You see a "glass of milk." Maybe you see a bottle? Perhaps a pail? You cannot, do not, see "milk," but milk-in-a-container.

What was it like to picture "milk" before the development of glass, before the domestication of cows and goats for their milk? What does "milk" conjure as a picture for people who did not ever put the milk of other species into containers and drink it?

It's beyond our imagining.

That picture we now have of milk — a flowing, pouring, splashing liquid moving from container to container, from container to mouth, leaving behind its well-advertised "milk moustache" — that picture forever changes the way we think about an infant at the breast. "At the breast" is a rather archaic expression itself. "Breastfeeding" is what we say now. The image of baby at the breast is itself a powerful picture, conjuring up Mary and the infant Jesus, and a host of Madonnas and their suckling babies. We don't speak of the "breastfeeding" Jesus, or of Mary breastfeeding the infant Christ.

Two separate vocabularies come into play: *suckling*, or *at the breast*, for the Madonna and child; *breastfeeding* for the woman down the street, the mother in the postpartum unit, the baby in the mall.

When we use the language of "breastfeeding," we are conjuring up the image of the milk: we see the woman feeding milk from her breast to her baby. The milk is the essential element. When we use the word "suckling" or the phrase "at the breast," we are not talking about the milk but about the activity that mother and baby are engaged in, the interaction, the *relationship*. "Nursing" — derived from the word "nourish" — is another word we used to use for that activity: mothers nurse their babies, babies nurse. Those words have all become rather old-fashioned, and "breastfeeding" is more common in everyday use, "lactation" in more medical use. Go online and do a search for "breastfeeding" and you will find pages and pages and pages of listings, most about problems and the things you can buy to solve them. Search for "nursing" and you will get mostly the job, the lady with a lamp, the RN. Search for "suckling" and you get a poet, Sir John Suckling, and a bit about suckling animals.

So what? Words change, evolve, shift. Does it mean anything? I think it does. I think that the language we are using is both shaped by the pictures we have in our heads and also shapes those pictures. The words we use to name this activity shaped and are shaped by our understanding, and our understanding has moved from "process" to "product," from the relationship between mother and baby to the milk itself as a product.

Lactation is interesting in this way because it is the sole reproductive process that has a widely based, routinized commercial competition. The substitution of artificial for natural infant feeding is a recent phenomenon, available on a widespread basis only since the development of the rubber nipple and the creation of a dairy industry capable of meeting the needs of an urban population. In the history of evolution, that is very recent indeed. To date, women's other reproductive services, notably the incubation of embryos and fetuses, are not yet widely available commercially. IVF clinics, which offer the early incubation of embryos, and "surrogacy" arrangements are just beginning to enter the sphere of the market. But so far, infant food is a unique commodity, essential for human procreation and available through two distinct production systems: as a human biological product, and as an industrial product.

As a biological product, milk can be viewed — and midwives, home birth advocates and La Leche League have all tended to view it — as part of mothering. As an industrial product, in contrast, milk is a commodity, a product rather than a relationship, subject therefore to "comparison shopping," to advertising and to technological refinement. Of crucial importance, and very well studied, has been the role of producers of artificial formulas and the sales methods they used to compete with breast milk (see, e.g., Palmer 1993, Hausman 2003). The profession of medicine has a history of acting in support of commercial interests and has done so with infant formula just as with the drug industry: by patient education, formal and informal, and by selective prescribing. Medicine, most importantly, has adopted underlying assumptions about maternal and infant health that are entirely in accord with those of the formula industry. The medical model has followed commercial and industrial needs. Milk, in this model, is a product, something that can be synthesized and, with technological know-how, quite possibly improved on.

For more than 50 years, standard American medical practice strongly encouraged artificial feeding. Jacqueline Wolf (2000) traces the social and medical construction of "lactation pathology" back to the 1880s. The new "germ theory turned mothers into vigilant guardians against unseen dangers: disease lurked everywhere, and only scientific practice could protect the family. A massive education program of 'scientific housekeeping' taught women to be afraid and on guard against this invisible danger" (Tomes 1998). Unsafe, dirty cow's milk was a real danger, but breast milk could be dangerous too. The Chicago Assistant Commissioner of Health, F. W. Reilly, urged women to breastfeed but also warned that if a mother is overheated or even if she has simply not breastfed for two or more hours, she should express and discard some milk, "implying that the milk nearest the surface of mothers' bodies could easily sour — like cow's milk left on a porch during the summer" (Wolf 2000: 98). As more attention was paid to the cleanliness and storage of artificial milk, it came to be seen as safe, maybe even safer than breast milk. Similarly, as more attention was paid to the production of artificial formula, its unvarying, standardized content contrasted favorably with the supposed variability of breast milk, which could be "inadequate" or "too rich." Pediatricians, eager to create a professional niche for themselves, were more than happy to take over the task of creating scientific infant feeding, and middle-class mothers, in their new role as consumers, were made to believe that would be best.

By the 1920s, educated and middle-class women were abandoning breastfeeding, leaving it to their poorer, less educated sisters. Fast-forward 70 years, and the situation reversed: breastfeeding was again recommended by doctors, as it had been before the 1880s, and middle-class women became more likely than their poorer counterparts to attempt breastfeeding.

"Attempt" is the operative word here: ever since the "social and medical construction of lactation pathology" in the 1880s, breastfeeding has remained an elusive goal, a practice fraught with failure. Volumes and piles of academic and scholarly articles have been written to explain that. Rather than explore the reasons for breastfeeding failure, here let us focus on what "breastfeeding" — as success or as failure — has come to mean. It has come to mean the production, transmission, and ingestion of breast *milk*. The focus on the milk, the *product*, changed our understanding of the *process*. Suckling or nursing became breast*feeding*, getting the milk made and transported into the baby. Obvious? Not if you didn't have that image of milk — milk splashing into its glass, stored in cartons and bottles, milk in pails and vats.

Minutes and Ounces

So how does this picture of milk enter into our experiences of breastfeeding? What are the practical consequences of having created "milk" as the kind of object it now is?

One of the things medicine did as a result of thinking about "milk" was to concern itself with ounces. Having the idea of "milk," but not having the milk visible, doctors wanted to find a way of measuring how much of the milk made it to the baby in a breastfeeding session. With bottle-feeding, they could measure the amount of milk in the bottle at start and finish and have a number to assign. The invisible milk of the breast was a problem to overcome: How can you get a comparable measure? Enter the scale: weigh the baby at the "start" and at the "finish" of each breastfeeding session. And that is, quite literally, what doctors used to recommend. Gesell, Ing, and Ames (1943), for example, told mothers to weigh babies before and after every single feeding, to record the weight difference and thus know just how much the baby got. That recommendation was not for babies who were not gaining or to reassure anxious parents, but for normal, healthy babies throughout the duration of nursing.

Their classic book on infant care was written in the 1940s when breastfeeding was declining rapidly, especially among middle-class women — the very people most likely to read child-rearing literature and to seek medical advice. When the authors of that book tried to explain why breastfeeding was being abandoned, they not very surprisingly blamed mothers who said, "Why bother?"

And were the mothers wrong? Why bother, indeed? Why bother breastfeeding if breastfeeding is such a bother? And the way that doctors told women to breastfeed from the time they began giving their advice all the way through the 1970s made it quite a bother. Babies were put on an arbitrary time schedule, which is hard enough with a bottle-fed baby but almost impossible with a breastfed baby. If you can't *feed* the baby for another two hours, how can you pick it up, comfort it, while milk is soaking through your shirt and the baby is nuzzling in? Close the door, walk into another room, and hope your milk dries up?

When the baby was finally put to the breast, another clock began ticking: the baby's time at breast was limited to the arbitrary number of minutes that doctors thought it ought to take the baby to empty the breast. And they did use words like "empty the breast," showing that they were thinking of it as a container for the milk, and the only point of the suckling is getting the milk out of the container and into the baby.

Breastfeeding, in their minds, was really a substitute for bottle-feeding, and not the other way around. The doctors did not try to find ways of making bottle-feeding more like breastfeeding, but breast more like bottle. And it didn't work: Gesell's study found that even those babies who were being nursed were weaned within a few months.

Physicians thought in terms of scheduling feedings not just because of the widespread importance of the clock in industrial societies, but specifically because their contacts with newborns were in hospital nurseries, where feedings are scheduled according to bureaucratic demands: eight-hour shifts do not lend themselves to three-hour feedings. Was the four-hour recommendation just a coincidence?

On a schedule of limited four-hour feedings with — hard as it is to believe — no night feedings from the day of birth, breastfeeding was very difficult to establish, and so the physician had very little positive experience with it. As one doctor pointed out in the mid-1970s: "The prevailing attitude is that the mother is assuming an impossible and insurmountable task" (Applebaum 1975: 104). As indeed it pretty much was. Dr. Alan P. Guttmacher's popular book of the 1960s on pregnancy and birth described early breastfeeding to mothers this way:

> Babies are offered nothing by mouth the first twelve hours. During the remaining twelve hours of the first day they nurse each breast for two or three minutes every four hours. On the second and third days the child suckles for three to five minutes on each breast, and ten minutes on each breast thereafter. The four-hour schedule is continued, the baby being put to both breasts but alternating the starting breast. As long as the baby gets little milk, it may be offered two ounces of five percent glucose water after each nursing, especially in hot weather. (Guttmacher 1962: 251)

This language sounds like a prescription for administering medicine. In the mid-1970s, *Williams* was still advising a four-hour schedule for newborns, with only "five minutes at each breast for the first four days, or until the mother has a supply of milk. After the fourth day, the baby nurses up to ten minutes on each breast" (Hellman and Pritchard 1976: 393).

That just won't work: a few minutes every four hours? With glucose water? This is a prescription for weaning, not for nursing. It is suckling that stimulates milk production; if that were not the case, women would produce large amounts of milk from their first pregnancies throughout the rest of their lives. If babies don't suckle, the breasts stop making milk. But Guttmacher prescribes:

If after several days the child does not get enough breast milk to satisfy its needs, discovered by weighing before and after several nursings, the mother's breast milk is supplemented by offering the baby three ounces of formula. If after forty-eight hours of mixed feedings the mother's milk does not increase sufficiently to meet two-thirds of the baby's needs, it is wise to discontinue breastfeeding and put the baby on full bottle feedings. (1962: 251)

The idiosyncratic rhythms of mothers and babies, the pleasures and intimacy of suckling, cannot survive the mechanical regulation, the weighing and measuring and timing. Breastfeeding fails. Mothers fail. It was an impossible task anyway. And there you have it: it is not that physicians ever adopted the principle that women should not nurse their babies. Rather, they took up the more insidious practice of telling women how to nurse their babies, and making it all but impossible.

La Leche League: Lessons in Demedicalization

On a July day in 1956, two mothers at a Christian family movement picnic in Franklin Park, Illinois, sat under a tree and nursed their babies. Throughout the afternoon, mothers at the picnic walked over to them and said, "I had so wanted to nurse my baby, but…"

"That's when it really hit us that the problems we had in trying to nurse our babies were common to a lot of mothers," Marion [Thompson] recalled. "It wasn't just Mary's particular rare problem or my particular rare problem." (Lowman 1977: 11)

That kind of mental leap between one's personal problem and a common, socially structured situation has variously been called the sociological imagination (Mills 1959) and (by feminists) consciousness raising. These two women, along with five others, took that idea and joined together in what eventually became La Leche League International, with hundreds of groups in the United States and other countries.

La Leche League started by offering the support and encouragement for breastfeeding that women were not getting elsewhere. The League set out to provide support groups, a telephone "hot line" for individual counseling, and role models. Any interested woman, whether she was pregnant, nursing, or neither, could come to La Leche League meetings and watch other women nurse and hear their discussions. She could see for herself healthy five-month-old infants who had never gotten any nourishment other than breast milk.

In the 1950s, Americans were at least a full generation removed from midwifery and home birth. Grandmothers of the 1950s had more often than not given birth in a hospital, attended by a physician. They had likely had their own babies on scheduled feeding and weaned them early to a bottle. The League provided in a more formal structure what the family was unable to provide informally: some counterbalance to medical advice.

La Leche League began to come up with specific, concrete suggestions for infant care and parenting that directly countered prevailing medical advice, including taking the baby into the parents' bed for night feeding, "baby-led" weaning, and the late introduction of solid foods. Doctors thought that babies needed solid food early, and that breast milk could not really sustain a baby beyond the first six weeks or so. League mothers trusted the baby to indicate when it needed more than milk and trusted the mother to recognize that need. Rather than coaxing and patiently pushing in spoonfuls of "baby food," League mothers said it was fine to wait till babies reached out for food. It took almost two generations before medical advice changed to catch up with La Leche League, to recognize that breast milk alone is best for babies in the first six months, and the bananas and cereals were pointless.

The League mothers began to deal with these questions of baby care in political terms, asking not only what is best for babies but also asking *who knows best*: "We were bucking the whole medical establishment when we recommended late solids. These were the problems we dealt with at board meetings" (Lowman 1977: 27).

It was no small thing for a group of fairly traditional women in the 1950s to take on the "whole medical establishment." Dr. Spock had been considered fairly radical in the 1940s when he offered a *Commonsense Guide to Baby and Child Care*. Spock's recommendations broke from the rigid weighing and scheduling and suggested that the baby himself (in the early days of Spock, the babies were always gendered male) might offer a guide to feeding needs:

If he is on the bottle, draining every one, and regularly waking early, consult the doctor about increasing the formula. (Spock 1946: 28)

If he's regularly not getting enough, he'll probably cry for more. Take his word for it, and get in touch with the doctor. (29)

True, the judgments were to be left, in the end, to the doctor: "The baby's doctor is the one to make the decisions and prescribe [sic] the formula" (38), but the baby's judgment also counted for something. The only person whose judgment was clearly not to be trusted was the mother's.

And this was the prevailing tone of the times for the middle-class mothers to whom the League was responding. Even when medicine itself began to create the idea of easing up on schedules, it was not the mother's judgment they relied on but the baby's. Think about what it means when we use the term they offered, "demand feeding" — that the newborn makes demands, which the mother then meets. This is like the model of the fetus in pregnancy as a consuming parasite. How different it is if we instead think of "need feeding," babies being suckled when they need it. La Leche League provided continual reassurance that the mother knows her own baby and is able to interpret its needs.

These were radical insights, true consciousness raising. The League history describes a process much like that the *Our Bodies, Ourselves* collective went through a decade or so later, questioning not just the facts of medical knowledge but the very authority of medicine to offer those "facts." For example, with regard to when to wean from the breast:

We started giving a lot of thought to weaning and discovered that although the medical textbooks said it should take place no later than nine months; they didn't offer a solid reason why. It gradually dawned on us that we were asking the wrong people. Doctors were men, and why should they know more about it than mothers? Since it wasn't a medical question, their medical education was of no help. That was why no good answer could be found in the medical books. We decided that it would be much more likely to be a woman, a mother, who would know. (Lowman 1977: 12)

But if the League was a forerunner, a mother to the women's health movement, it was also the daughter of the midwives of earlier time. Elizabeth Nihell, the eighteenth-century midwife, felt it was ludicrous for men to try to take control over birth. Whatever would come next?

> I should not despair of seeing a great he-fellow florishing [sic] a pap-spoon as well as a forceps, or of the public being enlightened by learned tracts and disputations, stuffed full of Greek and Latin technical terms, to prove that water-gruel and scotch-porridge was a much more healthy aliment for new-born infants than the milk of the female breast, and that it was safer for a man to dandle a baby than for an insignificant woman. (Nihell cited in Donnison 1977: 36)

Beyond Milk

We never entirely escape our moment in history, our time, our culture. As radical as some of the things they said were, as much as they rejected medical authority, La Leche League was, most pointedly and assuredly, not a feminist organization in any of the modern meanings. It did not challenge gendered divisions of labor, but did assert women's primacy within the gendered sphere of mothering.

And even the advice League members offered, the language they used, was inevitably informed by the language of medicine that surrounded them, which established the grounds of discussion. Compare the League's 1997 recommendations for breastfeeding at birth to what the doctors had been prescribing:

> Keep in mind that, in the beginning, nursing frequently — every two hours or so from the beginning of one feeding to the beginning of the next — is easier on the nipples and at the same time stimulates the production of milk. The length of a breastfeeding session should be determined by the baby's interest and response. (La Leche League 1997: 56)

Though offering advice to counter medical dogma, La Leche League nonetheless speaks in the terms medicine proposes: "frequent nursing" is anything more than the four-hour intervals. If La Leche League calls every two hours frequent, how is a new mother to assess the baby who seems to want to breastfeed more often, as newborns often do? The baby's "interest and response" may be her guide, but she may well perceive the baby as greedily demanding to "feed" more than it rightfully should, if every two hours is "frequent." Both the medical and the alternative discourse offered by La Leche League constructs breastfeeding as a time demand — in terms of both frequency and duration — to which the mother submits as directed: by the doctors, by the League, by the baby, or by some combination of these varied authorities. And both construct suckling as breast*feed*ing, focusing on the feeding, the milk being produced.

What if we dropped the language of time, of hours, even of *feeding*, and thought instead of the baby "at the breast." Babies need to suckle. They nuzzle in, they grasp the nipple and suck, doze off at the breast, reach for it again, get interested in something else and turn away, come back, suck, sleep. Are these "feedings"? "Sessions"? And is the only point of all this suckling just to build up a milk supply? Some babies get a lot of milk — from a full breast, from a bottle nipple with a big hole — and still want to suck. They suck thumbs, their father's shoulder, blankets, pacifiers, whatever comes to the mouth. Some mothers enjoy long hours of quiet time with a newborn baby at and near the breast, and some do not.

We've come to understand something about "baby-centered" mothering. But focusing on the baby as they do, most advisors — from medical professionals to La Leche League — present breastfeeding in ways that make women feel inadequate as mothers and as women, make men feel marginalized, and exacerbate the gendered division of labor that heterosexual couples tend to enact after the birth of a first child (Walzer 1998: 78–79). Can we even imagine what a woman-centered mothering would look like?

Mothering has so often and in so many ways been a source of oppression to women; that hardly needs restating here. But isn't it possible to imagine motherhood very differently? Given the time, the space, the money, and taking away the fear of loss of self, of loss of autonomy, of loss of identity, couldn't *mothering*, the intense experience of early mothering, be a source of pleasure and joy? For some of us it certainly is and has been. Our motherhood has not been something that makes us less, but something that makes us more. Rather than experiencing the threat to our autonomy that motherhood can be (and most often is; see Blum 1999 for a rich discussion of this) some women, sometimes, are privileged enough to be confident enough in their autonomy, their selfhood, to just enjoy those first few months of early mothering.

But enjoying it requires a level of trust: in ourselves, our bodies, our lives, and our world. Women have learned, have been carefully taught, not to trust themselves — not to trust their bodies, not to trust their spirits either, and certainly not to trust their world. We have learned that we have to be taught how to take care of our babies, taught to pay attention to them, taught even to want to take care of them. That has been one of the concerns of both professional staff and new mothers about early discharge: that mothers are simply not ready to take care of their babies, that they don't yet know how and won't learn if someone does not teach them (see Kelleher 2002 for fuller discussion).

We are not offering an argument about the "natural" or the instinctive here, not arguing for "bonding" theories. But there is something to be said for a new commonsense approach, one that trusts mothers, trusts women. This is, after all, not all that complicated. You could, without a scale, without a clock, and even without a book, figure out how to take care of a newborn baby. And it is even easier if you don't have to think in terms of "feeding" it, but simply letting the baby suckle when you — your full breasts, your aching heaviness — and the baby, its reaching, grasping, nuzzling self, want to suckle.

Of course, that won't work if you can't trust your world to let you do that for a while without enormous personal sacrifice: if you have to get back to work within a couple of weeks or maybe a couple of months or watch your carefully built career go down the drain; if no one is going to pay you for that time; if the only person to tend to the three-year-old is you; if nobody's going to make dinner if you don't; and if you think if you're not careful you'll turn into, well, a 1950s full-time Mommy!

And so the milk comes back in again: the milk as the problem and the milk as the solution. Breastfeeding — not suckling, not an intimate, maybe delicious, maybe sensual relationship, but *breastfeeding*, feeding the baby breast milk — becomes the way out.

There is no doubt that breast milk is the best possible thing to feed a new baby; and there is no doubt that producing breast milk has health benefits for women. But breast milk, expressed with a pump, stored in a freezer, and fed to the baby by someone hired to do that task, is not the same as nursing or being nursed, suckling or being suckled.

Linda Blum, in *At The Breast* (1999), describes the wry amusement with which some women, particularly the African American women she interviewed, look at the white middle-class women who have totally "bought" the breastfeeding idea. There they are at work, waxing idyllic at the naturalness of breastfeeding, and running off to pump while their babies are at home. The medical profession, Blum points out, solved the wage-earning/breastfeeding dilemma by glibly advising mothers to use breast pumps:

> What had once seemed a deeply embodied and interdependent act has fast become something that can occur without the mother being physically present….The mother is disembodied, as if she *is* the milk; by providing this milk, she still qualifies as an exclusive mother, as *if* mother and baby are still monogamous and physically tied; the mother in her body, her pleasures and needs, satisfactions and pains, has largely been erased. (Blum 1999: 53–55)

One striking aspect of all this is the commercial aspect, evidence of the newest way in which women's bodies are commodified. It used to be formula, a substitute for breast milk, that was being marketed, and of course it still is. But now, even those who are breastfeeding are seen as a market. Breast milk can substitute for the woman's being present, thanks to consumer goods like breast pumps, special storage bottles and bags and containers and thermoses. Even when she is physically present and nursing, a range of consumer goods has been introduced: special pillows, chairs, creams, clothes. The clothes themselves produce that magic erasure: the woman can breastfeed without appearing to breastfeed, with clothing artfully hiding the act. A bottle of breast milk is an acceptable sight; a nursing breast exposed is not.

Just as the invisible fetus became the center of maternity care, the mother rendered invisible in ultrasounds and in practice, so now the invisible milk is made visible and the mother erased.

Ideology in Practice

The alternative managements of infant feeding, presented as the "breast or bottle" choice, are about a lot more than milk. These two approaches represent genuine differences in ideology. Even phrasing the issue as a simple choice like that of using cloth or paper diapers requires that one sees the mother-infant relationship in a particular way. If one sees the mother and baby as an interdependent unit, still part of each other, then the "breast or bottle" question is almost silly, like asking whether the baby should be maintained in the womb or in an incubator for the last six weeks of pregnancy.

In the medical model, the mother is host to the fetus but her interests and those of the fetus are not seen as necessarily harmonious. At birth they are freed from each other and separated quite literally and totally. In standard American medical management from the early twentieth century through the late 1970s and the introduction of "rooming in," the baby was sent to a nursery, where specially trained personnel kept it under observation and cared for its needs. Babies need to be kept warm, so baby warmers were used, little incubator-like boxes. Babies need nourishment, so glucose water and artificial formulas were provided. If the babies became sick, antibiotics were available. Mothers after birth were given hormones to contract the uterus and sent to recovery rooms where their sleep was not disturbed by their babies.

In the home birth, the fetus is part of the mother and babyhood is a transitional stage physiologically as well as emotionally for both mother and baby. At birth the baby goes directly to its mother's arms. She becomes familiar with what her baby looks and feels and smells like, and along with those who share her life, she is expected to recognize any problems. The mother's body provides warmth for the baby, and her colostrum and milk provide immunity and nourishment. The suckling provides for the release of hormones that contract the mother's uterus and prevent hemorrhages. While for the physicians the two were separate problems in medical management, for home birth advocates and midwives, mother and baby are an interdependent pair.

Conclusion: Winning the Battles and Losing the War

There is something profoundly heartening about picking up the current copy of *Williams Obstetrics* and seeing so much of what embattled midwives were claiming in the 1970s moved into standard obstetric knowledge in 2001. But, like seeing the one woman among the six current author/editors of the volume, it is equally clear that whatever progress has been made, however far we have come, we still have a long way to go.

Back in the 1950s and 1960s, when childbirth activists were still fighting to get fathers into labor rooms and then into delivery rooms, when women were still restrained in delivery tables with leather straps on hands and legs, when semi-unconscious babies were pulled with forceps from the bodies of unconscious mothers, it was probably unimaginable that within 50 years 70% of first-time mothers would have taken childbirth education classes (DeClerq 2002: 3), and that not only fathers but other family members, friends, and even young children, and video cameras besides, would all be found at births in hospitals. But it would have been just as hard, or even harder, to imagine that within that space of time the rate of cesarean sections would have gone from just over 5% to just over 29% in American hospitals.

This is a glass-half-full kind of problem for some: we have things to celebrate and things to mourn. But for us glass-half-empty kind of people, it's worse than that. Fetuses — as patients, as objects of political and social concern — were invented and changed the way we think about pregnancy and birth. Mothers and even babies slipped into the background as obstetrics focused on visualizing, testing, treating, and removing fetuses.

When feminists like Barbara first studied birth, they were hopeful, thinking maybe we could bring midwives back, put mothers in the center of their own births, and surround them with families and friends and love and hope. But now we have to wonder. Listen to the nurse-midwives and women obstetricians whom Wendy interviewed for this book and the doulas Bari interviewed, and you too will wonder. And worry.

PART TWO
MIDWIVES IN TRANSITION

3

Becoming a Midwife

Varieties of Inspiration

WENDY SIMONDS

The midwives and midwifery students we interviewed told how a variety of conditions and events coalesced to shape them into midwives. They spoke about their profession as both a serendipitous journey and a predestined destination. They described achieving passion, self-realization, spiritual heights, and moral satisfaction through their "paths" to midwifery, no matter how circuitous the route. They seldom agonized over whether midwifery was right for them once they decided on it or it decided on them: they tended to achieve such a deep affinity for midwifery that questioning became unnecessary.

Consider these diverse remarks from several participants:

> I had an epiphany one day. … It's something I am very compelled to do. It's not a rational decision and it's not a decision. (Greta Mallory, midwifery student, Seattle, Washington)
>
> Would it sound strange if I said it was a call? You've probably heard it before. (Ginnie Lanford, home birth midwife, Atlanta, Georgia)
>
> I felt myself more drafted, you know, than called. (Liz Jeffords, midwifery activist, Gainesville, Florida)
>
> I think a lot of us became midwives by accident. (Elaine Jacobs, nurse–midwife, Brooklyn, New York)

Even those who stumbled into midwifery seemingly accidentally stressed its power to guide their course in life. Many participants talked about the events that brought them to midwifery as if they were accidents that didn't *feel* accidental at the time, and which, in retrospect, they came to see as fated.

Their sense of who they are as midwives intertwines with their views about gender, gender politics in medicine, and sometimes feminism. They would sometimes wax essentialist, speaking about women's "natural" abilities to birth babies and idealizing womanly traits such as maternal behavior, nurturing, caregiving, or intuitiveness about health care. Yet they also would portray their work socio-historically, telling how they were motivated to pursue midwifery out of anger at the ways in which masculinist, patriarchal, paternalistic, and capitalist institutions have constrained women's bodies, opportunities, and life experiences.

In this chapter, I explore midwives' "origin stories." Their stories contain several ironic dialectics: external forces direct and ultimately effect identity transformation; accidental events synthesize into inevitability; an essentialist view of womanhood as static combines with a vision of changing oppressive institutions to make a better world.

I begin with a discussion of two historical starting points for midwifery in the United States: the Frontier Nursing Service (FNS) and The Farm. Our interviews allowed us to tap into a variety of communities of midwives that can be considered the progeny and diaspora of these institutions. We interviewed two longtime Farm midwives, one CNM (certified nurse–midwife) student, and three CNMs attending a conference at The Farm (one of whom practiced in a hospital, one of whom did home and hospital births, and one of whom owned a birth center). We interviewed ten students and five faculty members at FNS's direct descendant, the Community-Based Nurse Midwifery Education Program (CNEP). We also visited indirect descendants of both these places. We interviewed ten students and six faculty members at the Seattle Midwifery School (SMS), nine students and ten faculty and board members at the Florida School of Traditional Midwifery (FSTM), 22 students and four faculty members at SUNY (State University of New York) Downstate Medical Center (Downstate), and five nurse-midwifery students at New York University (NYU). Additionally, we interviewed six home birth midwives and two home birth apprentices in Atlanta, Georgia (trained through apprenticeships), six nurse–midwives in Atlanta (who trained at a variety of programs, and only one of whom attended some births outside of hospitals), and seven nurse-midwives with home birth practices in and around New York City, also with a variety of educational backgrounds.

Home birth activists founded the Seattle Midwifery School (SMS) in 1978. By 2006, SMS had graduated more than 200 midwives, 3000 doulas, and 50 doula trainers (Seattle Midwifery School website 2006). The SMS takes up part of an old school building in a working-class neighborhood of Seattle not far from downtown.

The Florida School of Traditional Midwifery (FSTM) was incorporated in 1993 after Florida laws became suddenly favorable to direct-entry midwifery, and was modeled on its older "sister," the SMS. Like the SMS, the "institution" is homey and unassuming. It is located in a ranch-style five-room house next to a massage school, at the side of a four-lane highway several miles from downtown Gainesville. Both SMS and FSTM offer three-year midwifery programs that train midwives primarily for out-of-hospital births.

The FNS's nurse-midwifery education program has trained more midwives in the United States than any other program (more than 1000 by 2005). Students travel to FNS for several sessions over the course of their training and stay on the campus, a small group of buildings in the hills above the tiny town of Hyden, Kentucky, many of which housed the original Frontier Nursing Service in the 1920s and 1930s.

Downstate and NYU are both housed within medical facilities in New York — large complexes in Brooklyn and Manhattan, respectively, in which hospitals, medical offices, classrooms, and labs often share the same or connected buildings. Downstate began training nurse-midwives in 1932 and since then, like FNS, claims to have trained more than 1000 midwives.

Our Atlanta interviews were not institutionally based, though many of the interviews were conducted in medical buildings and hospitals. The groups of health workers we interviewed in Atlanta began with personal contacts and evolved into "snowball" samples.

The narratives of all these midwives show how common threads weave through the past century to create distinctive professional identities for midwives. I discuss origin story themes that illustrate the diversity of participants' interpretations of their paths to midwifery.

Last, I relate the paths to the two predominant types of midwifery, home birth (or direct-entry) and nurse-midwifery.

The Frontier of Nurse-Midwifery

"I had an immense drive as a girl that I was not allowed to put in any constructive channel, so I took it out in adventure whenever I could," Mary Breckinridge, the founder of the Frontier Nursing Service (FNS) wrote in her autobiography (1981 [1952]: 36). Breckinridge came from a well-known, elite, politically and socially well-connected Southern family. Her family traveled a great deal during her youth, both in the United States and abroad, but she had a special fondness for Kentucky, where she would visit family every summer.

Breckinridge's first husband, Henry Ruffner Morrison, died of appendicitis less than a year after their wedding in 1904. She went to nursing school and married again (to Richard Ryan Thompson) in 1912. They had two children who died, Polly at birth in 1916, and Breckie two years later, at four years old. Breckinridge writes that the deaths of her children eventually revealed to her a new purpose for her life: "There is a work beside which all other strikes me as puerile — the work which seeks to raise the status of childhood everywhere, so that finally from pole to pole of this planet all of the little ones come into that health and happiness which is their due" (1952: 74). Breckinridge divorced Thompson and began working to develop what would become the Frontier Nursing Service.

First, she continued her own training by volunteering with the American Committee for Devastated France as director of Child Hygiene and District Nursing after World War I. This is where Breckinridge first encountered nurse-midwives, and she was immediately impressed by their skills and methods. When she returned from France, Breckinridge took courses in public health nursing at Teachers College of Columbia University.

In her social history of the FNS, Nancy Dammann writes:

> Breckinridge selected mountainous Leslie County for her experiment because of its extreme isolation and poverty. She felt that if her program could succeed in Leslie County it could succeed anywhere. At

that time there were no roads within sixty miles of Hyden, the county seat; horseback and mule travel were the only modes of transportation. There were no hospitals, no licensed physicians; just granny midwives and herb doctors. The one room schools were inadequate and most of the population were semiliterate. There was no industry in the area and very little money. (Dammann 1982: 1)

Breckinridge spent the summer of 1923 in Kentucky, assessing the health needs of the population. She felt that a description of the inadequacies of current practices would serve as evidence to attract potential funders; one of the ways in which she detailed these problems was to write a report about local midwives. She issued faint praise for some of the 53 midwives she interviewed, writing, for instance, that "Contrary to popular impression, many of the midwives were intelligent women whose homes were tidy and gay with flowers" (1952: 116). For the most part, though, Breckinridge depicted these midwives as backward, inadequate caregivers because of their lack of formal education. "Here it suffices to say that the care given women in childbirth and their babies ... was as medieval as the nursing care of the sick in the public hospitals of France" (1952: 116). Breckinridge was not alone in her denigration of rural midwifery practices.

> Pursuing professional self-interest and a desire to decrease maternal and infant mortality [early 20th century nurse-midwives] ... joined obstetricians in a campaign to eliminate the traditional midwife. In pursuit of these goals, they ignored the reality that traditional immigrant and African American midwives had better maternal outcomes than the general practitioners delivering babies at that time. (Dawley 2003: 92)[1]

Breckinridge worried that her descriptions of rural midwives might turn off potential funders. She "feared that thoughtful men and women ... would wonder whether the eighteenth century conditions she described were attributable to ... a low native intelligence" (Dammann 1982: 7). So she hired Ella Woodyard, a friend from Teachers College, to come to Kentucky and give IQ tests to children. Woodyard concluded that the Kentucky children were slightly more intelligent than the national norm (Dammann 1982: 8).

Breckinridge sought funding from the American Child Health Association to establish an infant and maternal health demonstration project in Kentucky. Her proposal was not funded because of the opposition of Dr. Annie Veech, the head of the Kentucky Bureau of Maternal and Child Health, who thought the program would be too expensive and recommended investing in training local women to be midwives instead (Dye 1984: 333). Nancy Schrom Dye writes:

> Professional rivalry and the customary opprobrium physicians displayed toward midwives also colored Veech's objections. "If high type young women want to be of real value in isolated areas," she asked, "why do they not prepare themselves by taking a medical degree? They could then practice obstetrics instead of midwifery and meet the other medical needs of the people they wish to help" [Veech wrote]. (Dye 1984: 333)

Breckinridge resolved to pursue her plan despite both this opposition and her inability to secure governmental funding. She went to London to become a midwife herself. While abroad, she traveled to the Scottish Highlands to observe a public health service that would serve as a model for her own project: the Highland and Island Medical and Nursing Service was "a decentralized health care organization staffed by nurse-midwives that provided skilled care to an impoverished population" (Dye 1984: 330).

In 1925 Breckinridge began to raise money for the Kentucky Committee for Mothers and Babies (renamed the Frontier Nursing Service three years later). Ever the empiricist, she set out to conduct a census of the area. She hired a Scottish demographic surveyor, a local teacher, and two British-trained American nurse-midwives, and together they interviewed 1645 families scattered over 376 square miles of topographically rugged terrain with unpaved roads. Her final report "listed malnutrition, anemia, hookworm, tuberculosis, typhoid, and serious accidents as the region's most common health problems" (Dammann 1982: 14). This was the first of many demographic investigations conducted under the auspices of the FNS with the goal of improving public health.

Breckinridge sought to avoid conflict and competition with medicine. Dye writes:

She did not envision an organization that directly challenged the medical system. The Frontier Nursing Service, Breckinridge repeatedly stressed, was designed for impoverished "remotely rural areas" without physicians. Indeed, Breckinridge may well have realized that given many physicians' hostility toward nurse-midwifery and their fears of nurse-midwives as potential competitors, an impoverished rural area offered the only location in which she could carry out her project independently. ... To the limited extent that nurse-midwifery has been adopted in the United States, it has been largely along such lines. (1984: 388)

Breckenridge's strategic choices worked. Rural Appalachia appealed both to philanthropists and to young women looking for adventure. By 1930 the FNS employed more than 30 staff nurses and had built six outpost nursing centers in Kentucky's Leslie and Clay counties, which together served over 700 square miles. Raising money from private sources would not always be so easy. Over time, the FNS gained international acclaim and medical approval, despite many periods of financial instability (Dye 1984: 337). The FNS had registered more than 64,000 patients since 1925 (Center for Nurse Advocacy 2003). FNS began training its own midwives in 1939, when many staff members left Kentucky to go back to Britain at the start of World War II.

I happened to visit Hyden to interview students and faculty during celebrations of the 75th anniversary of the FNS. There I met Bonnie Stanton, a retired nurse-midwife who trained at the FNS in the 1950s and has been a CNEP staff member intermittently since then. Stanton happily reminisced about her past. She began by telling me about her nursing student days in the 1950s. She had no interest in birth nor knowledge of midwifery. Everything she had seen of obstetrics repelled her. She describes how women in labor were routinely given scopolamine, an amnesiac:

It was just terrible to see women screaming and climbing the walls. ... You had to even tie them down! 'Course, they never remembered any of this. But *I* remembered it! And it was terrible. And besides that, we almost never saw a birth without forceps — and high forceps. And lots of tears, and awful conditions — ruptures — everything under the sun that ... should never happen I saw as a student. No wonder I didn't like obstetrics! I knew I never wanted a baby of my own, I can tell you that!

During her senior year, while browsing in the library in search of inspiration for a paper topic on "Current Trends in Nursing," she discovered the FNS:

> There on the periodical rack was this picture on the front of a magazine ... of a nurse on a horse fording a river. And it was the *Frontier Nursing Service Bulletin*. Well, I picked that up, and once I got into that, I forgot about everything else except that: "This is exactly what I want to do!" But it had nothing to do with midwifery at that time! [She laughs.] So I wrote to the Frontier Nursing Service, and surprisingly, got an answer from Mrs. Breckinridge herself. And she had included ... a bunch of materials. And I wrote this paper on the Frontier Nursing Service. I got an A. And my nursing director was a friend of Mrs. Breckinridge. They were contemporaries. And the next thing I knew, I was getting ready to graduate, and on my way to Kentucky.

What originally compelled Stanton was the opportunity to ride horses in the wilderness. The FNS offered independence and a rustic adventure typically inaccessible to young middle-class women in the mid-twentieth century. Marriage was the expected life course. The FNS enabled women to subvert or delay conventionality and join a bold band of frontierswomen.

Stanton loved the FNS. She spoke of Mary Breckinridge and other members of the Service with reverence undiminished by the passage of half a century. Going to Kentucky was clearly a wonderful life-changing experience for her.

One night, one of the midwives asked Stanton if she wanted to ride with her to a birth. Always keen to go along for a ride, she agreed.

> So we saddled up the horses and off we went. And the next thing I knew, I was in this cabin, way over the mountains — up a creek. And of course there was no electricity, no running water. It was very primitive. They had a kerosene lamp and the fire going in the fireplace — coal fire. ... And I could smell chicken frying. [laughing] And there were two enormous beds in this one room cabin. And in the one bed, there were four little children sound asleep. ... And in the other bed, that had been all prepared ahead of time with the feed-sack cloths over the newspapers as padding, and of course, the nurses, during the prenatal

period had ... shown the women how to prepare for their birth at home. And bedsheets were clean — you know, everything was just fine. And the nurse put her saddlebags over a chair, and laid out newspaper padding, and then got her pack out ... then started getting her instruments ready. Put on her cap and her mask and her gown — I mean, this was *full* regalia. Got everything ready for the newborn. And she just told me to "just stand over there and ... don't say a word," you know, "be quiet." And that was fine with me. And so I just watched.

And the most *extraordinary* thing: the mother herself never uttered a peep. She — it was the most *quiet* birth. And I wasn't used to it. I mean, I had never seen a birth like this — a natural birth. ... I *hated* obstetrics when I was a student nurse. I had no use for it at all. I thought it was *barbaric*.

But when I came and saw *that* — it was like a total transformation! Women really *can* give birth! And sure enough, it was the most joyous occasion! That baby came out screaming, was beautiful. The midwife took care of everything — cleaned up, put that baby to breast right away, and propped the woman up. And then the children. ... Well, they woke up a little bit when we first came in, but went back to sleep, and slept through the whole thing until the baby started to cry. Then we had a great big fried chicken, biscuits, gravy breakfast in celebration of the baby's birth. And I was *transformed*, and said, "I want to be a midwife too!"

Stanton describes beauty and simplicity in an event she had thought of previously as horrible and dehumanizing for women. Though the midwife was in control, she did not control the birth. Stanton's awe of the silent but fully conscious birthing woman and her admiration for the meticulous midwife who "took care of everything" were immediately motivating. The woman accomplished it by herself.

For Stanton, midwifery combined the ideal of service with spiritual intensity. She found satisfaction nurturing women and taking part in what she now saw as the wonders of birth. Becoming a midwife provided her with the opportunity to engage in a physical and emotional quest for knowledge and meaningful experiences. Various aspects of Mary Breckinridge's and Bonnie Stanton's stories recur throughout the narratives of midwives we interviewed: serendipity, mentorship, the compelling and transformative forcefulness of a dramatic life event (in Breckinridge's case, the death of her child, and in Stanton's case, the birth she witnessed in the cabin), a sense of mission, and a desire to help others through service.

Birth on The Farm

Fast-forward nearly half a century, out of the wilderness of Kentucky to the wildness of San Francisco in the late 1960s. Stephen Gaskin taught English at San Francisco State and held regular evening events there that eventually came to be called Monday Night Class, and that were open to the public. These sessions fit the times; they "focused on putting the group's shared psychedelic experiences into the perspective of the world's religions. There was a strong emphasis on compassion, developing personal character, self-reliance, and the awareness of the interconnectedness of all life" (Fike 1998: vii). Stephen Gaskin achieved guru-like status among regular Monday Night Class attendees. "And by 1969, weekly attendance at Monday Night Class had reached several thousand people" (Fike 1998: vii). An American Academy of Religion conference held in San Francisco spurred an invitation for Stephen Gaskin to go on tour around the country to speak at mainstream religious congregations, with the hope that his presentations might "help heal the rift growing between generations" (Fike 1998: vii). About 250 of the Monday Night Class followers wanted to go too. So these hippies bought a small fleet of old school buses, and thus, in October 1970, the Caravan was born.

The Caravan provoked an occasional media stir as it rolled across the country; members were portrayed as quintessential immature iconoclasts, unfettered by conventional norms and thus a source of amusement, a potential threat, or both — as when a Nashville TV newscaster proclaimed "The hippies are coming! The hippies are coming!" (cited in Baker 1987: 918). Imagine traveling across the country this way, following the lecture tour of a man whose words you find inspirational. Imagine the nerve to believe you can restructure social life, relationships, community — make your own — inclusive of anyone who believes similarly. To me, it seems like an amazing organizational feat to start up a traveling mini-society like theirs. I am struck by both the haphazard casual sensibility and reckless idealism conveyed in the recollections I've read and heard, as well as by the strength of members' commitment to the holism and holiness of the group experience.

Stephen Gaskin's notoriety and charisma spurred the initial journey. But in my view, the most compelling and notable charismatic phenomenon to emerge from the Caravan was midwifery. Ina May Gaskin was central to the development of midwifery in the group and was responsible for writing *Spiritual Midwifery*, which has remained in print since 1977 and is now in its fourth edition. In her book, Gaskin describes how the Caravaners' involvement in birth arose out of their countercultural politics:

> Several of us had given birth in hospitals previous to the Caravan and had been unsatisfied with the way we and our babies were treated. We wanted our men to be with us during the whole process of childbirth … and we didn't want to be anesthetized against our will, and we didn't want to be separated from our babies after their births. We were already looking for a better way. (Gaskin 1990: 17)

The first births on the Caravan were completely improvisational events that served as inspiration to the community. One of the Farm midwives we interviewed, Marnie Griffin, described what these first Caravan births were like for her:

> I didn't even know about midwifery until I was, you know, twenty-seven, twenty-eight-years old, and living in San Francisco, and … some of my friends were pregnant. And there was a lady in the house who was delivering babies. And that was my first kind of knowledge of it. And then when we were on the Caravan, I remember when I got pregnant, I thought, well, I'm not going to go to a hospital! There's no way! You know, either my husband will deliver the baby or one of my friends. And then Ina May and I knew each other, and we started helping each other out. And … the first birth she called me to, I didn't go because … I was just about ready to have a baby. … But she called me again. And so the second time I went. … And once I saw that first baby and it came out so lovely and all pink and everything, I thought: well, I can do this! You know, I can help women. And then of course, [with] the next baby we

had had some problems [but it was ultimately all right]. And we had to
— we realized that we, you know, this wasn't to be taken lightly.

Sometimes doctors they met along the way would help them out,
giving them supplies and medical books and teaching them techniques.
By the time the Caravan returned to San Francisco four months later,
eleven babies had been born. Ina May's own baby, the tenth born on
the Caravan, died after a premature birth:

> He lived for twelve hours ... and then he died in my arms, probably of
> hyaline membrane disease, the most common cause of death in pre-
> mature babies in those days. I was filled with grief. At the same time,
> I knew he had taught me something I was never going to forget. I was
> also relieved that if we had to lose a baby that it was mine and not some-
> body else's. (Gaskin 1990: 77)

In *Spiritual Midwifery*, birth and loss are portrayed as part of the
same whole.

Gaskin portrays her calling as a way to tap into "female" power: "I
spent so much time as a kid feeling cheated by being female, because
I saw that this was not the powerful sex. I saw that it was a man's
world." After reading Grantley Dick-Read's book *Childbirth without
Fear* (first published in the United States in 1944), when she was six-
teen, Gaskin says, "I saw that it took some sort of gathering of courage
to go ahead and have a baby and I thought, 'OK, maybe there's some
sort of power in that.' And that little hunch certainly turned out to be
true" (cited in Wickham 2002: 38).

The Caravaners bonded so strongly over the course of their trip
that they decided not to disband. "The Caravaners had become
a community — a church. The decision was made to pool their
money, head back out across America, and buy some land. ... South
of Nashville, a thousand acres were purchased in the backwoods of
Lewis County, and The Farm was born" (Fike 1998: vii). Members
signed vows of poverty and saw their lives together as a common
emotional venture that was far more meaningful and honest than
conventional social relations. Fike reminisces that life on The Farm
in the early days was "sort of a never-ending encounter group,"
devoid of boundaries (1998: viii), yet his collection of narratives

also shows that the conventional gender and sexual arrangements in U.S. society recurred on the commune (most members engaged in monogamous marriage, and there was a pretty conventional division of labor between men and women).[2] Stephen Gaskin was the spiritual leader, but the group and its practices were aggressively democratic:

> Your inner business was everybody's business. Each person had the responsibility to suggest changes for others while gracefully (in theory) accepting input about themselves, in order to elevate their consciousness. ... The "teachings," as they came to be called, were a mix of common-sense virtues filtered through Christian, Buddhist, Hindu, Sufi, Jewish, and Native American traditions. Through a process of trial and error, the community continuously refined its agreements to be compassionate, nonviolent, and vegan ... to avoid tobacco, alcohol, and hard drugs; to shun consumerism; to be a good planetary citizen, a "voluntary peasant." (Fike 1998: viii–ix)

It is difficult for me to imagine all of this rich intensity, invention, and initiative now, without firsthand experience of the cultural context that created the loose spirit of adventure and righteous rebellion that fueled this group's actions. Theirs was a time when leftist social action was strong and visible and large-scale progressive change seemed possible — much more possible than it does now. Amid civil rights activism and antiwar protest, anti-authoritarianism flourished. People apparently really did believe they could stop racism, end the war, forge a revolution. The Caravaners sought meaningful lives in a way that was radical, yet emblematic of aspects of "Americanism" that have been celebrated over centuries: adventurous wilderness wanderlust and independence of thought. Their desires echo Thoreau's transcendental retreat from American politics and war-mongering into the woods of Massachusetts to live simply, and they resonate with the commune movement of the early twentieth century. Their motivations also resonate with those of Mary Breckinridge and Bonnie Stanton. Like these women, the Caravaners sought a better, morally profound, and satisfying way of living. The Caravaners' quest also had a distinctive late-1960s, early-1970s activist/hippie flavor. In Stephen Gaskin's words:

I can't put my attention into a city scene anymore. Because the worst thing happening on the planet is the cities. Like the cities are the major cause of warfare, poverty, totalitarian police state, whatnot. ... [We're] going to take off to Tennessee and get a farm. Because what you put your attention into you get more of, and I need more trees, more grass, more wheat, more soybeans, more healthy babies, more goodlooking sane people, people that can work. ... That's why I want to go out and really get into it with the dirt. (Gaskin 1972: n.p.)

Now Stephen's words sound dated; readers today could mistake them for a parody of hippiness injected with a little Puritan ethic. Ironically, this is how many Americans think about home birth midwifery — as a hippie throwback, as a glorification of unnecessary pain. Nowadays, most people who have heard of The Farm know about it because of midwifery, not Stephen's more general countercultural philosophy. "Isn't that that home birth commune in Tennessee?" many people have asked when I've mentioned it — as if home birth were radical enough to give rise to its own theme commune.

Ina May Gaskin attributes her path to midwifery to Stephen's influence:

When I decided to learn about midwifery and was attending those first births, I applied the principles I had learned from him. He taught me respect for life force and truth and holiness, how to manage spiritual energy, how to be compassionate even when it's hard to be that way, how not to be afraid, and how to help people relax. (Gaskin 1990: 16)

Women on The Farm who were drawn to birth or interested in health found a niche at the Clinic, especially during the early years of high fertility among Farmers. Evelyn Carter described how her childhood interest in medicine and the body combined with her later "hippie" inclinations and prepared her for a life on The Farm:

It seemed like all my life I was attracted to anything kind of medical, and anatomy, and things like that. ... One day I picked up [my older sister's] ... first-aid book. And the last chapter was "Making an Emergency Childbirth Kit," for women who lived in rural areas and who might ... deliver before they could get to the hospital. ... And it totally fascinated me. So I put one together. And I was in seventh grade, and my home ec. teacher gave us an assignment to write about ... different time periods of child rearing, and one of the periods of time was birth to a year. And kind of all I heard was the word *birth*. And so I brought in the emergency childbirth kit ... and demonstrated it, and talked about what was in it. And I knew I wasn't going to be a doctor, because I didn't like school enough to go to that many years of schooling, and at the time I thought, I'm just gonna carry this kit around with me all the time, because some day, I'll be prepared if there's a woman having a baby, and nobody knows [what to do], you know, *I'll* be prepared [she laughs].

And then, I guess when the hippie movement kind of started, I started hearing about people having their babies at home. And I got married when I was 17, and got pregnant when I was maybe 18 or 19. And I knew I wanted to have my baby at home, but I didn't feel like my husband and I — I mean, we were pretty young — that we knew what we were doing. And then I heard about The Farm and that they had midwives. And so I was like, "Oh, great!" ... Right about then ... I saw a poster. It said Stephen and The Farm Band [were] coming to the town I lived in. So I went, and I sat on the front row. And when Stephen got to question and answers ... I raised my hand and I said, "Can I come and have my baby there?" And he said, "yes". ... We wrote [to him], and before we got the answer, I had a miscarriage. But by then, we had, you know, decided that we'd come visit. And we visited several times. And we moved to The Farm. And a year later, I had my first baby on The Farm. So, it just was kind of a gradual thing, you know. And I knew that I wanted to be a midwife by the time I had my baby here.

Carter first worked in the lab at the Farm clinic, and gradually gained technical skills like drawing blood and starting IVs. When she felt her children were old enough for her to leave them for longer periods, she started doing midwifery. Though she doesn't explicitly use the term "calling" to describe her evolution into a midwife, she portrays her life as moving in that direction from the time she was a child.

Farm members see practicing midwifery and giving birth as spiritual acts that are deeply meaningful and that connect women to each other. As Carolyn, one of the Farm women whose birth stories appear in *Spiritual Midwifery*, said: "I flashed on all the mothers around the world who must be having babies at the same time, and felt telepathic with them. Then I felt it all go back in time to include *all* mothers. It just felt like giving birth is such a pure, eternal thing, always happening somewhere, always Holy" (cited in Gaskin 1990: 187).

The FNS and The Farm exemplify the roots of the two basic paths to midwifery that exist today in the United States. The original nurse-midwives, similar to their sister practitioners in social work, saw their mission as ministering to the poor, assisting them with basic life skills and supplying them with information and medical care that would improve their lot. Though nowadays midwives do not serve exclusively disadvantaged women, a general sense of midwifery as altruistic practice does persist. Mary Breckinridge's canny avoidance of conflict with medicine and concomitant dedication to the promotion of midwifery as a profession in collaboration with medicine resonates in the current tactics and policy statements of the American College of Nurse-Midwives (ACNM). As when nurse-midwifery first arrived in Kentucky, relationships between groups of midwives remain complex: sometimes uneasy or antagonistic, sometimes distant, and sometimes collaborative and trusting — a range of dynamics still exists now.

In contrast to nurse-midwives' quest to modernize the "wilderness" of Appalachian "lay" midwifery, the Farm women deliberately re-created wilderness-style home birth for their community and transformed themselves into midwives by practicing it. Their Arcadian goal was to avoid the worst of medicalization and to get back to nature, whereas Frontierswomen carried out their work as a pragmatic medical public health mission. In contrast, the Farm women stressed the spirituality of both midwifery and birth. Yet women trained in both settings learned empirically to respect the simplicity of birth and generally to employ a hands-off approach. The motivations and dreams of the midwives and midwifery students we interviewed are historically and ideologically rooted in those of the Frontierswomen and Farm midwives who set the stage for midwifery in the twenty-first century.

Calling All Midwives

Many participants in our research spoke about coming to midwifery as responding to a "call" or as the result of an "epiphany," a compelling indication that midwifery should be their mission in life. Most of the women who talked about midwifery as a calling described what I label an "empirical calling," an event that precipitated the certain knowledge that they were meant to be midwives, such as birth experiences (their own or someone else's). Others described what they saw as more otherworldly epiphanies, which I label "mystical callings." Callings can be both empirical and mystical at once.

Viewing one's work as a calling seems characteristic of a simpler, more religious, less corporate time than now, as in Weber's discussion of the historically Protestant notion of "calling" as divinely ordained and righteous work in the real world: "the fulfillment of duty in worldly affairs as the highest form which the moral activity of the individual could assume" (Weber 1992: 80). A search of sociological literature and occupational journals turned up several articles on experiencing a "calling" at work, but most of these treated having a calling as synonymous with achieving a sense of personal fulfillment in one's work, as a sort of volitional act of reinvigoration. For example, in "Nursing Care as a Calling" Ritva Raatikainen defines a calling as "a deep internal desire to choose a task or profession which a person experiences as valuable and considers her own" (1997: 1111). And in "Hearing the Call to Nursing," Elizabeth Jeffries outlines techniques nurses can use to "uncover or clarify" their callings (1998: 34). In these articles, authors portray callings as manipulable aspects of selfhood.

Midwives and midwifery students' talk of "callings" is more in line with Weber's conception, though usually secularized. They often describe their awareness of professional opportunities as awakenings that set them on the righteous path to midwifery. Loosely interpreted, most midwives' stories can be seen as including a "calling" narrative, in the sense that they all believe midwifery is righteous practice, and right for them. In this section, though, I include only those who describe their paths to midwifery as sparked by an unvolitional revelatory incident.

Empirical callings often occurred during incidents that involved awe-inspiring exposure to birth. Lisette Maddox described seeing her first birth in a hospital: "I was in nursing school in 1995 and was doing my OB rotation, and saw my first baby being born . ... [I] was in absolute *awe* at the creation of life and God's power in seeing this baby come to life, and just cried, and said, 'I want to do this! I want to do this!'" Julie Blum's enchantment occurred in a stable: "I had been living in Israel actually, and experienced some *livestock* births ... that were inspiring to me. ... I spent a whole night watching a horse give birth, and I wept through the whole thing. It was just incredible." Both of them would eventually become nurse-midwives.

Empirical callings could emerge out of negative exposure as well; women could be suddenly inspired to become midwives by first-hand or indirect encounters with medicine that angered or distressed them. Shana Hess, a graduate of and faculty member at SMS, recalled the exact date of her epiphany:

> Eight years ago, March 22, I happened to be reading an article in *Mothering* magazine about interventions in labor. And they were talking about electronic fetal monitoring and scalp electrodes and they had — that's what they had done with me in that [my second] labor. But they didn't tell me. There was no informed consent. They just said, "We need to put this thing on your baby, because its heart rate is messed up" or something. ... So I was reading this article and I became really *angry*, you know, that they did this to me and they didn't ask me, and so I just continued reading on in the magazine and I happened on an article about midwifery, and they were talking about the Seattle Midwifery School, and that was in 1992, and I had no idea that women were still using midwives, that it was even legal, that, you know, anyone would ever consider having their baby out of the hospital. Both my labors were natural childbirths. I didn't want an epidural, and I knew that. I don't know where I got that from, but I just *knew* it. So I called the Seattle Midwifery School, and came up and got more information, and that's kind of how I decided to do this [she laughs]. You know, I think it was more of a calling for me realizing that there was a better way.

Shana Hess was motivated by a sudden awareness of the lack of disclosure of medical personnel during her own birth experience, and her anger motivated her to work to promote this "better way." Like Hess, Ariana Lessing, an SMS student, related how anger charged her experience of a calling when she was thumbing through a Leboyer book on natural childbirth:

I opened it to the picture of the doctor holding that screaming baby up by the ankles, and the baby's just *screaming*, and he [the doctor] just has the happiest look on his face. ... It was just like, I felt this physiological change inside me and I was like, "Oh, this is *disgusting*! How could they hit — you know, [how could] this man be treating this new life this way?" And it pretty much, I was like, yeah, I'm going to — I'm going to be a midwife! I need to make a difference and this is where it's going to be.

Like Hess, Lessing felt so invigorated with anger that she acted on her strong reaction by becoming a midwife.

Several women described realizations, pivotal moments, when midwifery became evident to them as a perfect or obvious fit, even though they might know little about it. This was Paula Daniels's situation. She described a vague, general "sort of attraction to health care even as a child," but said that she lacked direction, and didn't know what to do with her life. It was a pivotal conversation with her parents that sparked her sense of a calling:

I got into a pretty heated discussion about childbirth in our culture with my parents. My father's a Western doctor and he always has ... opinions on things when it comes to health care. And we just got in pretty deep conversations about childbirth: how it is here, how it could be different. And my mom said, "seems like you have a lot of strong feelings about this. Have you ever thought of being a midwife?" And I was like, "Ahhh [she gasps]!" And all of a sudden I just felt like there was nothing else that I should do at all — that that was *it*! And it made so much sense. It brought together everything that I ever believed in. ... My political feelings, and my social service background, and my ideas of alternative health care, and — it just like brought together every piece of my life all at once. I was like, "Oh, my gosh! Of course!". ... Then I just started researching different paths to midwifery, and how to become educated.

The sudden realization that one should be a midwife could set events in motion to dramatically change the life of someone who had been floundering previously. Daniels's epiphany felt perfectly attuned to her beliefs and passions; all of a sudden she had a direction in life. Like Hess, she pursued her goal at SMS. Another SMS student, Nova

Rousso, described drifting around in the mid-1990s and deciding to try massage school, which is where she had her magical moment:

> It sounds really silly when I say it, but the first time I laid my hands on a pregnant woman, I had a vision and I had a completely religious experience. I was, at that time, I was in a very intensive spiritual program. ... And the next day, I went to a psychic and a tarot reader and asked her ... : "I had this really powerful experience, and what do you think?" And she flipped out, and was like, "Oh my God, that's it! You found it!". ... Everything just started falling into place right at that point. ... I don't feel like it is something I have chosen to do as much as something that has been chosen for me to do, that I was *supposed* to do.

Rousso's vision emerged out of empiricism and then was confirmed for her mystically, through consultation with a "psychic." These experiences redirected her life. She had found what she didn't even know she was looking for — or, as she interprets her "vision" and its aftermath, midwifery had found her.

Callings often combined empirical and mystical elements. That is, no calling was purely mystical, hitting someone completely out of the ideological or empirical blue. Those who described religious or mystical events as the catalysts that set them on the path toward midwifery also talked about life events or political involvements that were pointing them in that direction already, even if they didn't know it yet. For example, Tori Gustafson, another SMS student, saw her route to midwifery as beginning with a realization that occurred when she sought prenatal care:

> Well, I guess I'll share my epiphany moment. ... I did go immediately to college for a year after graduating high school, and I did do pre-med for that year, and then dropped out. (I think I would have dropped out regardless, whether I was doing pre-med or not.) And very soon after, I became pregnant. And I knew nothing about childbirth, and I knew almost nothing about babies ... I called an obstetrician to make an appointment. And I walked into the office, and decided as I was sitting there that I couldn't birth the baby in any place that was like this! [The group laughs.] So she walked in — after me waiting for half an hour — and she said a few perfunctory words, and I said "Can I have my

baby at home with you?" And she gasped out loud! ... I just said "I can't have my baby in anywhere that looks like this. Can I have my baby at home? That seems logical." I knew *nothing* of the home birth movement at that point. I knew *nothing* about birthing at home. She said "No, no, no, no! You need to leave." So I left! And as I walked out of her office, I walked underneath this cedar tree and I found this beautiful, beautiful owl feather. And I thought that I am obviously supposed to do something with it. So I found a midwife after that point.

Gustafson doesn't specify what it was about the doctor's office that so turned her off, yet it seems clear that the institutional impersonality just struck her abruptly, and the "logic" of home birth did too, despite her ignorance about it. This empirical calling incident includes a mystical touch. Gustafson kept the owl's feather; in retrospect she saw it as a talisman portending her future in midwifery.

The firm decision that midwifery was the right path could emerge suddenly within unsettled, confusing lives or it could entice women to move gradually in its direction. Serena Davis, who had given birth at home and was already interested in midwifery, came to consider it as a profession for herself after a bizarre exchange with a stranger:

What happened was I was buying a car from this lady who I didn't know very well but she was part of the community — our community — and I had seen her several times. ... One evening when I was doing the last payment ... in purchasing the car ... the two of us, we were sitting in the car together, the woman and myself, and before I was leaving out the car, she told me that she had a vision that she wanted to share with me. Now, I'm not one that usually goes out looking for readings or anything like that. This just happened to happen just the way I'm telling you. So I said, "Okay." So she told me — in about two hours time — that she saw me becoming a midwife. ... I haven't seen her since then. It was just pretty much that she was delivering a message to me and then off she went.

The message, in Serena's view, was divine. And whatever divine presence brought the message continued to guide her. Not long after this strange conversation, the opportunity presented itself, in a serendipitous way, for Serena to attend her own midwife's birth as a "support person":

And because she [my midwife] had already hired somebody to be her midwife and there were other women that were there, it was basically me trying to find what it is I can do to be of some need or some help, you know, and nobody was offering her any comfort with their hands. ... You know, that's what I did ... [I was] massaging her, her shoulders, her hands, whatever seemed like it was tensing up — and talking with her. And after the birthing was over ... I stayed a little longer [than everyone else] and so she reached out to me and she says, "Let me see your hands." And so I showed her the palms of my hands and she said, "You know, you have the hands of a midwife. I would like to train you."

Part of what women express when they describe a sense of a mystical calling is the notion that midwifery is bigger than they are. The sense of being chosen exists along with the notion that one becomes a vehicle for midwifery and, in so doing, an agent of social change. In this focus group at the FSTM, the links between divine purpose and political mission blur:

Jessie Harris (midwifery activist): Part of my inspiration was my mother, but a very big other part was really *divine.* And it reminds me of ... the grand midwives, feeling like they were called by God. ... So there was a lot of like, divinity, you know, kind of a calling, because I ended up being in exactly the right place but without ever being told where to go.

Wendy Simonds: Do others of you feel that way — like you had a calling?

Celeste Waters (RN and direct-entry midwife): I don't think I had a calling. ... I was in the right place at the right time, it seemed like ...

Liz Jeffords (activist, direct-entry midwife, physician's assistant): I felt myself more *drafted,* you know, than called. ...

Waters: That's how it seemed. It just seemed like I *fell* into the right place.

Liz Jeffords described an activist pull rather than a spiritual one, which she cast as arising out of a sense of duty. Yet it seems to me that to say one is "drafted" has the same sense of inevitability about it as to say that one is divinely called (as Jessie Harris did). Both ways of describing the move into midwifery connote a lack of will or overt decision making on the part of the women, and a sense of service to an ideal. Similarly, Celeste Waters's sense that she "fell into the right place" also strikes me as a way of representing a change that feels externally imposed and unvolitional, yet morally and personally fitting. Harris's spiritual calling, Jeffords's being drafted, and Waters's "fall" into midwifery all seem inevitable and random at the same time. The categories I'm employing for considering midwives' and midwifery students' origin stories are not mutually exclusive. Women who become midwives "accidentally" may not talk of a calling, but they do tell of predilections, or a sense of a right fit with midwifery. Encounters with birth change women's lives in unexpected ways, as luck or fate would have it.

Accidents and Self-Actualization

Several of the women we interviewed traced the beginnings of their journeys to midwifery back to childhood and described a knowledge that was part of who they had been for as long (or nearly as long) as they could remember. For example, Athena Cuthbert, a nurse-midwife who owns a birth center in Trinidad, was exposed to birth early by her grandmother:

> Well, I became a midwife because of my grandmother. My grandmother was one of those lay midwives — as they call it in America, but we don't in Trinidad. They're known as midi- or granny midwives. And she did that ... all her life. ... And as a little child, I've been going around with her for all the deliveries. You know, you go to visit your granny, she takes you everywhere. And my family ... were into law and medicine. And my father really thought that is what I would have done. But coming to school in England, I ended up doing the midwifery. And that was it. You just gravitate to something that you love. And irrespective of what your other family do, you do what you want to do.

Cuthbert saw herself as following her heart to carry on a family legacy. Though her father would have preferred that his daughter enter a higher-status profession, she chose what suited her.

Like Cuthbert, Laurie Green described how exposure to birth during her adolescence led her eventually to become a midwife. Green, the daughter of a serviceman stationed in Naples, Italy, described how, at twelve years old, she had been told only negative things about birth: "My mother had four children at that point, and what I had heard was, you know, martyrdom, you know, you go through the valley of the shadow of death, and all that stuff. But she had them in the twilight sleep, strap-'em-down, knock-'em-out, drag-'em-out time." One day, Green was home from school, and opportunity knocked:

> The portiere's wife was in labor, and the midwife sent the oldest kid around to knock on doors to see if there were any women home to come help because her assistant wasn't there with her. And I was the first door that they knocked on. ... And so I went. And it was totally different from what I had in *my* mind. ... Here was a woman laying in the bed, and another woman helping her. And she showed me where to put my hands to support her back. ... And a baby came out. I mean, the sheets weren't even clean, but a baby came out! And it was just — in my mind, up until then, I thought you had to have all these people *make* the baby come out. ... I thought it had to be made to happen. And she [the midwife] must have seen a glint in my eyes of something, because she would call again if she was in the neighborhood to see if I was home. So I got to help with a couple more. And I learned a bunch from her, but more than anything, was her infectious calm, you know, just that this wasn't a crisis. ... *Babies come out.* So then, we [my family] went back to the States, and at that point, I guess I was thirteen, and decided — I *knew* — that was what I wanted to do. I just — it gets you off or it doesn't. It scares you or it just feeds you.

Even though she was an adolescent when she had this transformative experience, Green recalls the sense that doing birth work was just right for her. It appears that she also sensed that it would sustain her emotionally from the very start ("it just feeds you"). Green started as a home birth midwife and eventually became a nurse-midwife through CNEP so that she could remain the primary caregiver of women who were transported to the hospital and attend clients who wanted to birth in the hospital.

Donna Parker, a home birth midwife, described a childhood interest, though hers apparently first manifested itself as an interest in babies rather than in birth:

> Well, I guess the decision to be a midwife was always there. ... When I was small I always wanted to be involved with babies — and skipped church services to go play in the nursery, work in the nursery. And when I was twelve, we moved to Hong Kong. ... When I was thirteen, I started going to the hospitals, and volunteering or just playing in pediatrics. Whatever they needed me to do. At school ... I would skip study halls and even some classes and go down to the clinic and work with the nurse. And she realized that there was quite a few of us that, you know, had that bent ... so she got correspondence courses from the States for us to become nursing assistants. And after school every day she did a class for us, and we became nursing assistants. ... You know, if there's something you really want to do, you're going to do it. ... And she also found the hospital there that would let us do clinicals. So, right at fifteen I was in surgery working, you know, as a nursing assistant. And my goal was to get into labor and delivery. And they had a rule — I think they made it when teenagers started coming in — you had to be sixteen to be in labor and delivery. So my sixteenth birthday, I went into labor and delivery and showed 'em my ID and said, "I'm sixteen now." And so I saw three births on my sixteenth birthday, and I've been going to births ever since.

Donna Parker's remarkable dedication to nursing as a teenager led her clearly but circuitously to midwifery. First, the hospital-based nursing school program in which she enrolled upon returning to the United States proved objectionable:

> I was still hospital-ingrained, you know, and nursing was what I thought I was going to be doing. So — until geriatrics! And I just — it really made me ill. I mean, I would come home, I would take my uniforms off. I would ... boil 'em, you know, boil 'em and gag. I couldn't get the smell out of my nose. And it's so funny because ... at *births* ... there's plenty of smells associated with that, but for some reason it just really, really bothered me [in geriatrics]. So I withdrew from nursing school

and started — went to school to become a medical assistant, and then, when I graduated, started working for a pediatrician.

This pediatrician taught her all about newborn care. Next, Parker got married and "just ended up being a housewife for a little while, and got pregnant." Her first child was born in the hospital; the labor was induced and she had an epidural. After the birth of her child, she got involved with a local La Leche League (LLL) group:

> And they were having home births. ... There was one midwife here and basically, she worked with the doctor. If the doctor didn't okay you for the home birth, she couldn't do the birth. And if they didn't like you, if there was personality conflict — anything — then you were out. And so I had a friend who ... wanted a home birth [her first birth was in the hospital with twins]. And the doctor wouldn't agree to it and she was going to do it anyway. She asked me if I would be there. "Sure! You know, why not?" God protects fools and babies! So that was my first home birth, in 1977, maybe '78.

Before joining LLL, Parker said that she considered unmedicated labor and home birth "so far out there." But her friendships with the women she met in LLL opened her to these new ideas. And once she attended her first birth at home, there was no going back. "After a while, and some more babies being born, I decided, you know, this is getting ridiculous, because I really should learn, you know, figure out what I'm doing if I'm going to be doing this." She sought an apprenticeship arrangement with the local midwife, who strung Parker along for a while without taking her on. Fortuitously, another midwife moved to town, and Parker worked with her for about a year before starting her own home birth practice in the early 1980s; through it she has trained many other local midwives over the years.

An early interest in midwifery or birth was less common among those we interviewed than "awakening" to midwifery in early adulthood. This may have been a matter of access. Living outside the United States gave girls like Donna Parker, Laurie Green, and Athena Cuthbert an opportunity to see births that they would not have had living in the United States during the 1950s and 1960s. Though each tells about circumstantial factors that led her toward midwifery, each also describes a fit, a sort of inevitability in her choice that resonates with the sensibility of midwives who explicitly named their experiences "callings." What is different in these narratives, though, is that the women detailed how they recognized and then followed their desires, rather than talking about an external or inexplicable source of motivation.

Participants who described an attraction to birth that began when they were young were not children who capriciously decided "this is what I want to be when I grow up," but girls with a deep desire to be present at births. Exposure to midwifery and birth during girlhood would shape the course of the rest of their lives.

Many of the most recent cohort of midwives and midwifery students we interviewed, especially those who had been college students in the 1990s, told us about academic experiences that initiated their interest in midwifery. Greta Mallory recounted how seeing a film of childbirth in a freshman biology class fascinated her: "Everybody [else] was really grossed out, and I thought it was just the most amazing thing in the world." Most of the women who got turned on to midwifery during college encountered it in women's studies or sociology courses, where they were exposed to the politics or history of childbirth, as Allie Connell recounted:

> I first discovered midwifery when I was a college student, studying women's studies. I was interested in sexuality issues and reproductive health issues, and had a soc class that I needed to write a paper for. And went down to the library stacks and was just kind of running my fingers along the books, and some of these books leapt out at me! And I'd never heard of midwifery, and was completely blown away as I started to do research. … And it was kind of towards the end of, I don't know, maybe my junior year, that I started to think, you know, maybe I'm interested in this more than just intellectually.

In the United States, young women rarely encounter pregnancy and birth as academic subjects before college (other than in biology or sex education courses, where they are typically proscribed). To learn about the medicalization of birth — or of anything else, for that matter — at a time in their lives when they are perhaps recognizing gendered power arrangements for the first time can also be a heady experience.

A few women told of how their attraction to midwifery emerged from disillusionment with educational experiences, notably pre-med studies. For instance, Nell Lowry said:

> I was studying pre-med … and was really having a hard time in the program. My grades were fine, but the program was *extremely* competitive, and I couldn't find anybody to study with me. I mean, people wouldn't study with one another, and there was all this competition, and right before an exam, people would be verbally abusing each other, like, "I'm going to kick your ass!" … I was having a really difficult time, and for lack of the better word, the whole program was really "macho."… But I stuck with it. I was eating lunch one day with a friend of mine who was in nursing school, and she said, "I think after I'm done with nursing school, I am going to go study to become a midwife." And I remember getting chills. And I didn't know what one was. I'd never heard of a midwife … but I remember thinking "Oh my God, I have to go find out what that is. That's what I have to be! That's who I am! I have to go do that!" And because I was so embarrassed that I didn't know what it was, I ate my lunch as fast as I could, and I ran to the library and got on the Internet and put in "midwife" and found all these schools. I remember seeing pictures, and words like *cooperation* and *share,* and I was like "Oh my God, I have to go!" And I dropped out of school that semester, and started looking to see if I wanted to do nurse-midwifery or licensed midwifery, and trying to figure out the differences between the two.

Lowry's experience exemplifies the ways in which the empirical and mystical can come together into a feeling — she didn't call it a calling — like a premonition, which then serves as an impetus to begin the path toward midwifery. So many of those we interviewed who didn't employ the fated calling trope told stories of quite similar revelatory experiences.

Many women told about how their own birth experiences initiated their desire to pursue midwifery, stories similar to those of women who felt "called" to midwifery as a result of their own births, but without the sense of fatedness or external intentionality:

Clarissa Kephart (NYU nurse-midwifery student): With my third child, I had a midwife as my practitioner, and it was such a good experience that I decided I wanted to become a midwife.

Kendra Wolf (Downstate student): My second home birth was inadvertently unassisted, and my husband caught the kid. After this
 kid was born was the first time I became interested in midwifery. I just felt that if my body was so delightful that it could
 pop out a nine-pound three-ounce kid into my husband's
 arms in a bathtub in Brooklyn, that I felt a little evangelistic
 that maybe other women should know this is possible.

Wendy Simonds: Did others of you come to it through personal birth
 experiences also?

Lisa Suttles (Downstate student): … I had a terrible birth trauma when
 my first son was born, and I realized that there was no reason for it. … Women should be treated a lot better. One
 of the reasons why I became a midwife [was to] never let
 anybody go through that, and to take care of people like I
 wanted to be taken care of.

So women can decide to advocate for or against experiences like their
own. Paradoxically, delight over a good birth experience and bitterness
over a terrible one could set women on the same path. The route was
typically indirect; moving from critical birth experience to a midwifery
career could take years. Kaye Pringle, an NYU nurse-midwifery student, told about how her "wonderful" and "completely natural" birth
experiences inspired her to become a labor and delivery nurse, and then
her experiences as a nurse spurred her to pursue midwifery:

> I went to school to become a nurse and started working in a labor and
> delivery setting about ten years ago. … I loved being with patients and
> I loved taking care of them while they were in labor, but I became more
> and more disenchanted because of all the interventions. And then I
> became exposed to midwives about eight or nine years ago and really
> liked the way they did things, that it was … less hands-on, actually.
> Less interventions, more natural, more caring. And decided that, you
> know, was what I wanted to do, so that I could actually be a part of that
> myself and have a voice in how women should be cared for.

Like Lisa Suttles, Pringle wanted to become an advocate for pregnant
and birthing women, to provide them with nurturant and non-invasive

care, and had come to this decision as a result of coming to perceive the "disenchanting" aspects of medical care.

Personal or professional experiences other than birth could as easily lead women to midwifery. Jenna Barkson, a fellow student of Pringle's, told how she decided to move from cardiac nursing to midwifery:

> I guess I would say it was … the concept of midwifery that I was attracted to. Nursing as a career — I didn't like how far away it felt from the patient and the bedside. Technology would get involved … and I wanted something that was more about the patient. And I was very intrigued by women's health and there was a whole model of midwifery that was something I really believed in, something I really wanted to learn about. … It wasn't like: This is … *exactly* what I'm going to do. It was just kind of a path that I had been drawn to.

Though her narrative lacks the dramatic intensity of epiphanies or revelations, midwifery fit the bill for Barkson for the same reasons it did for so many other participants: it countered what she had come to see as too much impersonal technology with a woman-centered model grounded in human connection. Similarly, Celia Robinson told her story as a confluence of her own apparent predilection for caregiving and handling emergencies that came about as a result of idiosyncratic events:

> My first draw was to service in health care. I saw a book — when I was seventeen and going to school in France — by Frederick Leboyer. I loved it. … That was stage one. Stage two, I was living in Morocco. A girl got blown up in her cave, and they knocked on our door to take her to the hospital. And I didn't have a car. And I knew in that moment that I wanted to be able to save her and I would not be satisfied unless I did something to make sure that the next time something like that happened I could be the one who could do it. And then very synchronistic, really, my sister was living in Denmark. She was a lesbian. … I was visiting her and she kind of roused my political awareness about women. … And I just decided I was going to do midwifery, because I wanted to do something that had no built-in obsolescence, that could relate to really — that all over the world would never separate me from the human race, such as computers — there would be no educational rift or whatever. … I've been doing this since I'm 22 — and [it is] not at all the product of

having given birth. I was extremely virginal and young and maiden-like at 22! It was *service*. And then the first birth I attended, the midwife was late and the friend who was supposed to be helping was screaming, and I'm like: "*You!* Get out!" And I said to the mother — (I'd never seen a birth before) — "God, you're doing *great*! It's perfect! Here comes the baby!" I called the midwife up, boiled the instruments. I'm like, "I *felt* it." [laughing] Same thing with people on the side of the road. ... My sister's girlfriend got hit by a car. Who took control? Me. "Call 911. Get a blanket. Don't move her." I just knew inherently what to do.

Robinson's serendipitous self-awareness of her capable response to emergency situations and her sister's political influence caused her to gravitate toward midwifery. Like Barkson, Robinson felt midwifery offered her a way to connect with others through experiences unmediated by machinery. Midwives want to touch people's lives and to be touched by them in the process.

Activism and Feminism

At a conference at The Farm, in a session entitled "Moving Midwifery Forward," Pam Maurath proclaimed, "We're saving the world one birth at a time." While this may seem hyperbolic — would that midwives *could* gradually "save the world" by handily catching babies — this sense of heroic mission comes through both in midwives' narratives about being called and in their more explicit talk of the political agenda of midwifery. Midwifery is, ideally, activist work. Whether this means that midwives see themselves as promoting large-scale social change or taking incremental steps in a better direction, all the midwives and midwifery students we interviewed saw midwifery as having reformatory or revolutionary potential. The philosophy of midwifery, even in its least radical incarnations, contests some aspects of the dominant, antifeminist, hegemonic discourse of obstetrics. Many of these participants also *explicitly* invoked feminism (even before we asked). Even the minority among our participants who were reluctant to self-identify as "feminist" voiced what I consider to be feminist ideals. Quite simply, midwives are woman-centered. In a cultural environment that generally devalues women's bodies, desires, and experiences, midwives honor them. Ideally, midwives recognize diversity and depth in women's lives and try to protect them from a reductive, homogenizing, and oppressive institutional climate.

"Feminist experiences" could lead women to midwifery, as with the women who learned about the politics of birth in women's studies or sociology courses. Among older cohorts of midwives (those trained before the mid-1980s), feminist experiences were empirical rather than academic and tended to involve some sort of political involvement and/or group affiliation. For instance, Elaine Jacobs, who runs a birth center in New York, credited her involvement with La Leche League as helping her to formulate the politicized consciousness that eventually would move her toward midwifery:

> As a young mother, college-educated, I found a certain way of thinking and approaching family and motherhood, of really asking questions, of having my consciousness raised, and the challenging of the medical establishment came in those [La Leche League] groups. I never would have had the nerve to do it unless I had that kind of network of people that [agreed]: Yes, this is all right. Yes, these things did happen to us with our first births. Yes, we were treated this way.... And all of a sudden we were saying: *No!* ... Just about that time, the early seventies, the feminist movement was happening, [and] we already had our own little feminist movement.

In the 1970s, the "big" feminist movement's focus, when it came to health care issues, was on achieving access to contraceptives and abortion — freedom *from* motherhood. Jacobs said: "There was no joining of the two groups. We were the outcasts. They didn't see us as feminists because we were talking about motherhood." LLL, an organization founded by stay-at-home mothers, seemed reactionary to feminists who saw motherhood as a dead-end job in which women sacrificed their identities through the act of caring for others and, in so doing, cemented their financial dependence on men; see, for example, the bestselling work of the liberal feminists Betty Friedan (1963) and Germaine Greer (1970), as well as the work of the radical feminist Shulamith Firestone (1970), whose ideal vision was procreative machinery to free women from the barbaric prison of biological procreation. The women's health movement and a "strand" of feminism now called "cultural feminism" were exceptions (see, e.g.,

Boston Women's Health Collective 1971 and Rich 1995). Most feminist activists avoided discussing motherhood as anything other than a barrier to true self-development. Jacobs said that she felt a sense of "empowerment that happened in just being a mother — and I don't mean *just* being a mother — to me it was ... very important. ... It was through my being a mother that I came to be a midwife, that I found my career." In retrospect, she lamented the divide between self-labeled feminist organizations of the 1970s and LLL as unfortunate because the women in both groups bonded through their experiences *as* women, and both proclaimed resistance to patriarchy, albeit to different aspects of it. Jacobs's LLL group forged a bond similar to that among Farm women or FNS staff. They engaged together in purposeful action to promote what they saw as meaningful social change in women's health care experiences.

Mel Sallinger told how her procreative experiences informed her sense of herself as a feminist, which would eventually inform her sense of herself as a midwife:

> [My experiences] taught me a lot about how little power you have, my own limitations about what I was willing to do, what I, you know, what I was willing to put up with because of the medical situation. ... I think having had two cesareans has given me a lot of empathy for the women that I take care of who have ended up with cesareans. ... I also had an abortion when I was nineteen, and knew that that was not the time for me to be having a baby. And it was also not a time when you could get a legal abortion. ... And I had the *Cadillac* of illegal abortions because my father arranged it for me and it was with a gynecologist who knew what he was doing, but ... the guy was kind of psychologically sadistic. ... The worst, I think, was that when I woke up from whatever he gave me — and I think it must have been sodium pentothal because I was like out [snaps her fingers] and then [snaps again] back in again. He was ... just finishing up, and he said to me, "Are you ready for me to start?"... And he was *done*, you know. ... Many women experienced much worse — much, much worse. You know, I mean, women *died*.

Having been through situations where she felt vulnerable and powerless politicized her. Sallinger felt that, in the long run, these experiences made her a more empathetic and nurturant midwife, more aware than she would have been otherwise of the variety of reactions women have to getting pregnant in the first place, and deeply committed to preserving women's dignity and agency in medicalized environments. When asked to discuss what feminism meant to her, Sallinger started with general observations and then moved into telling about the students whom she taught through CNEP and their drive to become midwives:

> Women ... bring unique attributes to the world as *women* that need to be valued. ... There's something about midwifery that attracts women who want, you know, who are interested in *that* kind of relationship with women. ... Midwifery students come with a whole load of *spirit* is all I can quite say about it. They *come* with this vision of midwifery. Most — almost all — of them have this idea about being *with women* and supporting women, empowering women, or allowing them to be empowered by themselves. ... And they all don't have exactly the same vision of what that means, but there is some common ground. ... I still see a lot of nurses with this vision, you know, a feminist vision. I mean, some of them come at it from a very different place than I do, and we have a lot of very Christian women coming into midwifery which is a very different avenue than I took! [She laughs.] ... They wouldn't define themselves as feminists but there is a feminist line in there somewhere for almost all of them.

When asked to describe what being a feminist meant to them, many of the midwives would respond in this same manner: they would start with a general statement and then segue into a discussion of midwifery as feminist praxis. They used midwifery as a lens to describe feminist ideals:

> *Renie Daley:* Being a feminist? Empowerment and egalitarian communication styles and leadership styles. The value of women's experiences. So all the way I practice.

> *Laurie Green:* What that [being a feminist] means to me? I guess keeping an eye out for women, kind of protecting them and supporting them in any way I can. Not in a way of women *instead* of men. Not in the way of demanding equal. Because it's different. But in the sense that women inherently do not believe in themselves. And very often, just someone

else just looking them in the eyes, and saying, "*You* did that. You had that baby. You can do *anything*." I've seen women change. I've seen them change their lives. And that's — that feeds me. It feeds me a lot. [She is teary here.] It's just — it's amazing. It's a beautiful thing to watch. It's beautiful to watch a woman who … in our society would not be considered beautiful *become* beautiful in labor. And look at her and say, "you're *so* beautiful!" And have her just *become* more beautiful in front of your eyes because basically you saw it and acknowledged it, and it helped her. … It's just amazing what can happen to people. It really is.

Feminist midwifery, as Green sees it, can help women feel transformed and capable and beautiful. For these women, as for all the midwives and midwifery students who participated in our research, the idealized goal of midwifery is to create a context in which a meaningful experience can unfold. Many also expressed a belief in women's specialness — an essential specialness based on our procreative capacity— that midwifery, at its best, would enable them to explore. As Carrie Ward said, "I believe that women are wonderful. That's why I work with women. … They're great. … I think when I was a teenager, I … was more into equality and being the same. [But now] I don't want to really be the same as men! [laughing] I value *women's* strengths."

Like Laurie Green, many midwives told about how a good pregnancy and birth experience could empower women for life, and how past bodily traumas like sexual abuse could even be addressed in a healing way through a good birth experience. In rare instances, participants essentialized birth into an Ur-experience for the baby, from whence all else would flow. As Sonia Miller, an FSTM student, said, "I have a core belief that how you come into this world sets the stage for the rest of your life. … It's about how you move through the world, personally, as a person. How you take on or don't take on pain or pleasure. … It's a very spiritual level." Mostly, the women we interviewed celebrated the potential of birth less dogmatically than Miller did, considering it an event that should be meaningful, that could forge a collective spirit among women, and that could set the stage for confident mothering. As Hannah Silverman said, "When I had my second baby at home, I felt this tremendous spiritual connection with *all* of the women on the planet. ... Listen, I usually don't talk like this, but you know, it's true. ... So I felt very strongly that I wanted to help women do that."

Lara Foley and Christopher A. Faircloth write that midwives "use a discourse of medicine in constructing a legitimizing narrative of midwifery" in three ways:

> First, it is used as a contrast device to set midwifery practice apart from the medical establishment. Second, the discourse is employed in the description of the midwife's daily work, building bridges with the medical community while having the "best of both worlds." Third ... midwives use a discourse of collaboration to establish themselves as professional equals of physicians. (Foley and Faircloth 2003: 166)

In contrast, we found that most of the midwives and midwifery students we interviewed stressed differences between feminist or woman-centered midwifery and masculinist medicine, rather than claiming commonalities or attesting to collaborative goals. They typically portrayed midwifery as superior to obstetrics. Indeed, the participants who became midwives during the home birth movement of the 1970s and their "descendants" into the twenty-first century pursued midwifery *because* they saw it as embodying a refutation of the medical model, a broadly different approach to "moving through the world." This motivation to work against the medical model was often the most crucial aspect of their genesis as midwives.

Most of the nurse-midwifery students we interviewed had past or current experience as labor and delivery nurses. Frustration with the power dynamics they observed between OBs and their patients, as well as with those they themselves experienced as nurses with doctors, motivated these women to become midwives. Labor and delivery nurses who came to see women as wrongly pathologized by conventional medicine developed critiques of obstetrics that ranged from cautious to scathing, as these excerpts from focus groups with nurse-midwifery students at CNEP and NYU (respectively) demonstrate:

Carly Norwood: The hospital I'm at — this is an example — you know, their protocol is continuous monitoring. So every time that I want to ambulate a patient, you know, I have to give specific order to let her off the monitor, you know, and those kind of things. And at that hospital, I ... was trying to teach child-birth education as an empowerment tool, and ... would bring up intermittent monitoring, and suggested they talk to their doctors. You know, I actually was called on the carpet for it and had to quit teaching that portion of the class. ... I was told by my nurse-manager that we are to teach the childbirth classes as to what's going to happen when they come to *our* facility to have their baby. And I just totally disagreed with that. ...

Terri Barilla: I would have to say that, along that same line, the conflict that I — if anything — that I have run into, is my personal inner conflict with anesthesia protocols. I — I really feel that women aren't given a choice there. ... They're asked to come in for an anesthesia interview and told how wonderful they're going to feel with anesthesia. But yet, limited information is presented to them on all of the effects of ... the anesthesia they may be given. So, my own conflict, I think, is more a personal conflict that I try to — try to be very objective about, but find myself in a personal conflict over that issue. ...

Norwood: I think she's got a good point about the inner conflict, you know, that you experience as a labor and delivery nurse when you see things, you know, policies in effect and practices in effect. You know, it's not that they're *wrong*, it's not that, you know, they will *harm* anyone. It's just that the women are never told the other side. And never given a *full* picture of what's going on. ...

Barilla: That's what concerns me: the consistency of women being ... told the *full* scope of what's going on is maybe not always there. And that presents me with an inner conflict of feeling like I know this woman has been told *this.* I don't want to present something in a negative way because of my own conflict of what is — what I feel is — the right thing to say in the position of a *nurse.*

Jenna Barkson: [OBs are] just like, up front and in your face. They're very personable to you and tell you they're giving you the best care, but, you know, they are just quick to cut and they're not really — they don't value a woman's body in any way.

Bari Meltzer Norman: So how do you deal with that?

Barkson: It's really hard. It's *really* really hard because, you know, my way is trying to be with her as much as you can, be as much of a voice. But you find in this area that you have such a limited voice because of malpractice and because of the way that these physicians have practiced for so long. It's just their way. ...

Norman: Is there anything in your program here that kind of helps you prepare for these kinds of situations? . ...

Cindy Butler: I don't think so because the role that I have as a nurse is, you know, pretty much defined, so I may have a voice, but ... they look at you and say, "*I'm* the physician and this is *my* patient."

In the first excerpt, CNEP students Norwood and Barilla soften their objections to the conventional practices of doctors and hospitals by referring to their perceptions as "inner conflicts" and by speculating that these routine methods are most likely benign. They know that constant monitoring and lack of ambulation together produce more interventions than intermittent monitoring and encouraging ambulation. They know that anesthesia carries risks, and that any of these interventions (or combinations of them) can lead to a cascade effect of interventions that puts women at greater risk of surgery and morbidity. They know that interventions inhibit birthing women's control over their birth experiences. They tread carefully and avoid condemning obstetrics as harmful or misogynist. Yet when I listen to them talk, that's the critique I hear, in a masked and convoluted way (as Barilla's passive-voice, equivocal statement beautifully demonstrates: "the consistency of women being ... told the *full* scope of what's going on is maybe not always there"!).

In contrast, the NYU students depict doctors as territorial and duplicitous creatures of (bad) habit. Jenna Barkson says they don't "value a woman's body in any way"; she means, I think, that they don't value women as people, period. Conceptualizing people as easily cut open entails depersonalizing them. Surgeons don't see cutting as unwanted or unwarranted bodily intrusion, Barkson recognizes, because they have normalized this objectified view of women's bodies. Midwifery is different.

As these excerpts show, when nurses object to medicalizing practices, there is little they can do about it. They answer to physicians. They can, in fact, get in trouble if they are caught educating women in ways that do not cohere with institutional practices (as Norwood did). They hope that in the future, as midwives, they will have more power. Indeed, this hope fuels their determination to become midwives; as Barkson said:

> I think that when you're in that role, you're going to be the one that's going to be delivering this baby. You're going to be the provider of care. You're going to be the one that's going to decide, like, what this woman needs, what kind of interventions, so you're deciding, which is great, ideally, what you want. It's not like you're standing there and you're being the main support and you have no say in what's going to happen to her body and to her self.

Barilla was less optimistic:

> It's a system that's been in place. … [As a midwife,] I may find myself in a different form of that conflict. I may have a bigger voice as a nurse-midwife than I certainly ever had as a labor and delivery nurse. However, I'm not sure my voice is quite big enough to make a significant change. The change will be made in the way that I present things to my *own* clients in a nurse-midwifery manner. … As a nurse-midwife, it will put me in a different position because that client is *my* responsibility.

Even as these nurse-midwifery students voice their commitment to opposing the system, they portray their future midwife-selves as protecting women by making decisions about treatment options, rather than as assisting women who are making decisions about their own births. Clients will now be their "responsibility" rather than that of doctors. As nurse-midwives, they plan to do their best to fight within the system, and this is simply the best they can imagine in that context: a shift in authority from doctors to midwives safeguarding women as they see fit. In their remarks, as in those of other nurse-midwifery students and nurse-midwives, midwifery comes across as a heroic underdog representing women's best interests.

The women we interviewed often spoke about midwifery as a redemptive or restorative practice that could revive lost collective ideals or heal past individual damages. This was particularly true of home birth midwives. They know direct-entry midwifery has a rich history, and a longer history than obstetrics or nurse-midwifery. Shana Hess, for instance, considered it her mission to work toward revitalizing invaluable African and African American cultural practices:

> In the African-American community and in African communities, too, there's this rich history of midwifery, and it's kind of been lost. You know, we don't really hear about it. You know, midwives are not really considered health care — *legitimate* health care — professionals in some areas, and that's kind of what attracted me to it. ... When I decided to go to midwifery school, my *goal* — ultimate goal — was to, you know, bring midwifery, the knowledge of midwifery, back to the African-American community and other African communities in the Seattle area. We have a large contingent of East African — Somalian, Eritrean — women in this community and they're used to home birth. They're used to midwifery care. But when they come here, they're not even told it's an option. ... And so I really feel like that community of women — what they need is their own midwife, and that's really what I'd like to do is, you know, give them the knowledge and the information so that they can send somebody to the [Seattle Midwifery] School, you know, to be a midwife for their community. I don't, you know, pretend to be able to, you know, know the intricacies and the, you know, the culture and how that works, and so I don't feel like I'm the *best* person for that. But I feel like we do share something in common, that I can sort of be a catalyst for getting that going. So ultimately, that is my goal.

Other midwives we interviewed also described their desire to make midwifery more accessible to particular communities of women as clients and as midwives-to-be; sometimes these were communities in which they participated, and sometimes not. In addition to the notion that midwifery meant a reclamation of cultural practices, there was a general sense among midwives that poor women and women of color were least likely to have their desires and needs met by conventional medicine as clients, and that they therefore had the most to gain from midwifery. Along with Hess, several midwives mentioned that midwifery would be more appealing to poor women and women of color if they could encounter midwives of color. For instance, Renie Daley discussed her frustrations with the exclusivity and whiteness of the profession of nurse-midwifery, which she attributed to the style of its educational programs:

> The way we educate nurse-midwives is very elitist ... and so we end up with a whole bunch of white nurse-midwives. And we really need midwives of color — more, many many many more, midwives of color. And I don't see it happening. ... [The] CNEP program where they keep women in their communities is hopeful. But the Emory kind of model, you know, got to come to campus and you have to go there and you have to be a student, and the only way you get socialized is by doing that academic life [isn't working].

She told me she had been working with a local black women's health advocacy group to try to advance opportunities for black women in her area. Another white nurse-midwife, Carrie Ward, gave a specific example of witnessing racism in nurse-midwifery school (at Yale): "When we compared our tests ... I had the same answer as this other woman who was a woman of color, and she got less points for it than I did! And it wasn't just that one question. You know, it was consistent." The students got together and brought the issue up to the faculty, alleging racism. "And the faculty were *furious*. They were just furious. And they decided they weren't going to speak to us." This episode soured her experience in midwifery school, and in her view, was "painful" for everyone in the program, including the faculty, at that time. A commitment to diversity and antiracism in midwifery education (for both direct-entry midwives and nurse-midwives), as participants described it, was developing slowly.

Despite this limitation, midwives and midwifery students saw their profession as ideal in many other ways because of its woman-centered philosophy. Midwives and midwifery students served as advocates for midwifery however they could. One reason why they were willing, indeed eager, to participate in this research was that they want people to know about midwifery. They want people to understand that midwifery is more than just a friendlier option than obstetrics. It's a different paradigm, a different worldview.

Along these lines, Alona Golden told me about being invited by a friend of a friend to attend a local reading group comprised of wealthy suburban Jewish women who had just read Chris Bohjalian's best-selling novel *Midwives* (1998). In the novel, a home birth midwife attending a birth in rural Vermont during an impassable blizzard uses a kitchen knife to perform a cesarean section on a woman she thinks is dead, but who really isn't — until the midwife unwittingly kills her. The women in the reading group were much more interested in hearing about Golden's work than in discussing the book (which is really a page-turner). Golden told me she felt that the women in the reading group saw her as an exotic curiosity. They had never considered home birth as viable before, but her presence apparently made it much more conceivable to them than it had been before they met her, regardless of the brutal depiction of the woman's death in the book. Golden and I discussed how ironic it was that she had this opportunity to promote home birth midwifery as a result of a book that offers such a negative portrayal. Her experience reminded me of consciousness-raising groups in the 1970s. Maybe group experiences that create intimacy and openness really can help forge incremental social change.

Midwifery, as many midwives conceive of it, can be revolutionary feminist practice. As Ina May Gaskin put it: "You know I've always been convinced that as a society we're doing it all wrong and that we need to utterly change it" (cited in Schlinger 1992: 19). In spreading the word about their worldview, that's what midwives hope for.

Different Routes, Different Groups

At the group level, midwifery has distinctive flavors that are much less evident than in interviews with individuals. The general sensibility of most midwives is quite similar, whether they practice in the hospital or at home, or somewhere in-between. I wanted to know how midwives decided what sort of midwives to become — nurse or direct-entry — and why, and how they felt about the "tracks" or "routes" in midwifery at the educational and organizational levels.

As of this writing (July 2006), there are ten direct-entry programs in the United States that are accredited by the Midwifery Education Accreditation Council (MEAC), and 42 U.S. nurse-midwifery education programs currently listed on the website of the American College of Nurse Midwifery (three of which are listed as "preaccredited"). Two of the 39 accredited programs also offer ACNM-endorsed non-nurse midwifery training: Baystate Medical Center in Springfield, Massachusetts, and Downstate, in Brooklyn, New York. (Regarding midwifery education, see Myers-Ciecko 1999 and Tritten and Rosenberg 2002.)

Laws explicitly prohibit direct-entry midwifery in ten states, but licensure or some other form of state registration or certification is available to midwives in only 23 states. Two of the latter allow licensure only to certified midwives (CMs) trained by ACNM-endorsed CM programs, of which there are currently two, Baystate and Downstate. Midwives can receive Medicaid reimbursement for home birth in only ten of these states.

Most of the nurse-midwives and nurse-midwifery students we interviewed never considered direct-entry midwifery as a route. Simply, they wanted the credibility and legal sanction that comes with a nurse-midwifery (CNM) credential. Occasionally, though, CNMs or CNM students would talk about having considered the direct-entry route. For instance, we interviewed a group of nurse-midwives with home birth practices in New York, and two discussed weighing the implications of taking each of these paths:

Hannah Silverman: I have six kids altogether and most of them were born at home. And I had actually, very strongly considered pursuing the lay midwifery route, and after … starting to participate in that kind of training, there were just a lot of things that I was uncomfortable with, like the dichotomy in educational levels, as well as the legal climate. … Especially socially, I felt like I wanted to be able to tell everyone what I do, because I really love doing it. So that's when I decided … to go back to school and become a nurse, you know, and go through all that, and then becoming a nurse-midwife in order to be able to come back and do home births... .

Celia Robinson: I felt as if my entire career could be taken away [as a direct-entry midwife] — because I witnessed a trial in the health department [having to do with a case of] a midwife and maternal mortality — and I said, "Wow, I could devote sleepless nights, yada yada, years of dedication, and then have this *removed*!" So I decided to get a CNM.

These women came to see direct-entry midwifery as lacking social and legal legitimacy. Practice possibilities, in their view, would be limited and more risky without the nurse-midwifery degree. Robinson saw the CNM credential as offering her more legal protection against prosecution than she would have without it.

Many of the nurse-midwives and nurse-midwifery students who participated in our research disliked some aspects of nursing education; others took issue with what they saw as the cut-throat and competitive culture of nursing education programs. Several told me it was well known that "nurses eat their young." A few described nursing and nurse-midwifery school as philosophically objectionable because it was medicalized (see also Davis-Floyd 2002). These perceptions could prompt women to leave nursing or nurse-midwifery school to take a different path, pursuing a less fractious, less elite, or less medicalized program such as CNEP.

A few of the CNMs we interviewed at CNEP and The Farm began as direct-entry midwives and then decided to pursue more mainstream training. Sheila Marks[3] was training as a direct-entry midwife in Texas when she applied to the nurse-midwifery program at Columbia University on a whim. She felt very uncertain about her decision to attend Columbia, and her experience there confirmed her ambivalence. What she saw as central to midwifery was neglected in the Columbia program. "It's not about midwifery. It's about mini-OBs. It's: 'okay, let's be really good at reading this fetal monitor and watching for the warning signs.' They teach fear, you know." Marks was grounded in a different philosophy and did not want to compromise her ideals in midwifery school or as a nurse-midwife, so she left the program for CNEP. Similarly, Traci Roeg said:

I came to CNEP because I had been at Columbia. That's where I did my nursing degree. And I was really pretty disgusted by the way that program was going. I felt like there was no support. ... I felt like it was a medical model of midwifery school. ... It was really, really, really high-tech. ... For me, it felt very important, as I was learning, to really keep the focus on *normal*, and try to be in a birth center setting or home birth setting. And really, really get what normal is.

Most CNEP students and faculty cherished the hope that positive birth experiences, safeguarded by midwives like them, *could* happen in hospitals, if medicalization could be avoided, subverted, or overcome — even as they participated in an institution characterized by intransigent control and ignorance of what *they* saw as most important.

Nursing offered what several women considered to be a more reputable and more flexible base than direct-entry midwifery for a broader practice spectrum. Sheila Marks explained:

I want to provide well-woman care throughout the lifespan as well. I mean I want to be able to do more health-work than just midwifery with women. And I also want to do a lot of political stuff and international work and I felt like the nursing would give me sort of a just — really a piece of paper that people respect *more* or something, and recognize more, just because that's the way our culture is. ... I wanted to do more than just home births also. ... I wanted to have the niche, you know, of bringing midwifery to wherever the women want it. You know, I wanted it to be easy for me to practice anywhere. That I could expand the world of midwifery to more of the population because, while it's great that there's one percent of the population having home births, it's like there's *so* much work to be done. ...

Wendy: So you felt it would give you more credibility than a direct-entry midwifery program?

Marks: Not — I mean I don't like to say it like *that* because somehow it sounds — I mean, I guess that's true, though. I mean that is kind of what it is. But at the same time, I mean, in *my* mind they're [direct-entry midwives are] *more* credible. ... But in society's mind, that's not the case, and ... I definitely want to be an agent of change for that as well.

Many CNMs said, as Marks did, that they could reach more women as nurse-midwives than they could as direct-entry midwives. Marks, unlike most other CNMs who raised the issue of the higher level of credibility of nurse-midwifery, felt that direct-entry midwifery was more ideologically attractive and a "purer" form of midwifery.

Several of the nurse-midwives and nurse-midwifery students we interviewed went to nursing school only because they wanted to become midwives, as opposed to becoming nurses first, and then becoming attracted to midwifery. For them especially, nursing school was a difficult hurdle because of the atmosphere and the scope of the training. For example, Julie Blum hated nursing school but stuck with it because she wanted to be a midwife:

> The first year medical surgical nursing training was *awful* for me. I'd never been in hospitals. I don't like sick people. ... I don't like mucus. I don't like slime. ... I'm ick-aphobic. I'm a compulsive hand washer. What can I say? . ... "How can you like, be doing births?" That's healthy ick, and it doesn't bother me. ... [I was] totally turned off when I was at the VA hospital my first year of nursing school. I was dying. It was awful. I would get home and spend twenty minutes in the shower trying to get clean. It was just, the whole unit smelled. And all of these old men at the VA hospital ... all their illnesses were really self-inflicted, you know, emphysema, they had liver problems from alcohol abuse. It was very depressing. I had people ... who were smoking out of their tracheotomy holes. I mean, it was *really* — it was *all* very icky.

Donna Parker told of a similar visceral disgust to aspects of nursing training that exposed her to pathology (cited earlier in this chapter); unlike Blum, Parker dropped out of a hospital-based nursing program, and ended up pursuing direct-entry midwifery via apprenticeship. After informally apprenticing with a doctor who attended home births in North Carolina, Diane Eastman moved to Atlanta to pursue nurse-midwifery:

> My love was home birth. I thought, at that point, that I was going to pursue my master's as a CNM. ... The official position of the ACNM on home birth is actually quite positive. And based on that, we moved to this area. I was accepted at Emory [nursing school]. And very quickly found the reality of the situation, which, at that point, was that you

literally did not *mention* home birth. ... Even when I was at Emory, I immersed myself in the home birth community here and began right away to attend some births with some other midwives, and began actually to move into a realm where I was practicing on my own, and left Emory rather quickly in the whole course of things. I mean, it became apparent that home birth practice was really not an option [for nurse-midwives here].

The informal apprenticeship route to direct-entry midwifery is much less common now than in the past. Professionalization efforts and formal education programs go hand in hand. A collaboration among the North American Registry of Midwives (NARM), the Midwives Alliance of North America (MANA), and the Midwifery Education Accreditation Council (MEAC) to produce "core competencies" for certification for direct-entry midwives in the mid-1990s produced national standards, which all of the direct-entry midwives and midwifery students we interviewed endorsed.

Initially, though, many direct-entry midwives resisted the introduction of standards and certification. In her history of MANA, Hilary Schlinger cites several examples:

Anne Frye: To certify ourselves, even with the best of intentions, we would run the risk of merely creating a new class of birth professionals, and quickly lose sight of the very thing which most requires transformation. We would be in danger of becoming part of the system which no longer serves us. (Schlinger 1992: 98)

Carol Leonard: Why do these women think that they have to have permission from daddy in order to do what they know, in their blood and in their heart and in their soul? That's part of where I do this other dance on certification, because I was born a midwife. I knew the first birth that I even attended that I had done it a thousand times and I knew exactly what to do. And why would I have to ask some guy to give me permission to do what I already have in my blood and in my heart? (Schlinger 1992: 103)

The groups involved in formulating the certification standards were attentive to the reservations and desires of their constituency. As Davis-Floyd writes:

CPM [Certified Professional Midwifery] certification is competency based; *where* you gained your knowledge, skills and experience is not the issue — *that you have them* is what counts. In keeping with MANA's values, NARM has been as inclusive as possible, honoring multiple routes of entry into midwifery, including self-study, apprenticeship, private midwifery schools, and university-affiliated programs. (2002: 78)

Some students in Washington state said they didn't approve of all the regulations governing home birth practices there, and home birth midwives in Georgia said they had set up informal networks that satisfied them. Nonetheless, all the direct-entry midwives we interviewed supported state licensing of home birth midwives as ultimately preferable to operating outside the law, and many worked as activists to advance this cause. State regulations, whatever they are, take on a life of their own once they are codified, and this life is apparently inextricably intertwined with the possibility of being sued — which is not so different from what direct-entry midwives fear without state regulation. One SMS student, Ariana Lessing, commented:

There hasn't been a week that I've been in school that someone hasn't said: "Oh, but you better be careful to do this to protect yourself from being sued." Or "One day when you get sued, you want to make sure you do this so you don't look bad in court." ... And on one aspect, I'm really grateful for that [advice], and I'm like, "You know, thanks for letting me know these things now before I'm in that situation, and then I am screwed because I didn't do the things I should have done." But at the same time, it's like: *ooh*! And it makes me kind of want to drop out and say, "Forget it! I don't want to live my life in fear and paranoia."

Midwifery school faculty members attempt to prepare students for the practical realities of the difficulties of working in a profession that, though legal in certain states, remains tenuous in terms of its status. Even within the seemingly non-exclusive, non-elite direct-entry world, SMS clearly had a distinctive status; one SMS student compared the school to the elite college she had attended (Vassar), and several said they had applied specifically because of the "academic reputation" of SMS.

I imagine that college-educated women going into direct-entry midwifery in the future will be increasingly likely to seek out educational programs than to make less formal apprenticeship arrangements, and the educational route could eventually entirely replace the apprenticeship route. It is also likely, I think, that states will increasingly endorse institutionally trained midwives as a result of organized efforts on the part of midwives, and continue to block the way of those with less conventional training.

We did interview midwives who had apprentices working with them, some of whom were also enrolled in distance-education programs for direct-entry midwives, and all of whom were planning to pursue NARM certification. All formal direct-entry midwifery programs require "clinical" or "preceptorship" placement in out-of-hospital settings, except for the ACNM-approved programs like Downstate. Many home birth midwives speak out for the benefits of apprenticeship and self-study as a wonderful training method (see, e.g., Bastien 2002 and Wells 2002).

Women who trained via apprenticeship before the 1990s, like Donna Parker and Diane Eastman, described their experiences as much less systematic and more haphazard than did those involved in apprenticeships more recently. For instance, Alona Golden said:

> I was really one of the first apprentices to come through here — in Georgia — and one of the only ones that did start and finish. There is such a high attrition rate among apprentices. People come in and think it's groovy and glamorous, and you realize it's really a lot, and it's demanding emotionally. ... Because my apprenticeship was in the early days of the midwifery renaissance, there weren't the standards and expectations [we have now]. There were a lot of times where I would ask someone what does something mean, and they would be like, "Oh, look it up! Who knows?" because they just didn't *have* the level of academic knowledge that even those same midwives have now. ... Basically the requirement was that you observed at ten births, you assisted at ten births, and you primaried ten births, and then you were on your own. ... Sometimes I think that we were winging it a little too much.

These "older" midwives we interviewed had all met the NARM core competencies and were certified — even those who lived in Georgia, where their certification was not recognized.

Many of the direct-entry midwives and direct-entry midwifery students we interviewed, especially the younger ones we met in formal educational programs, rejected nurse-midwifery specifically in favor of direct-entry midwifery. They either got into midwifery wanting to do home births from the outset, or, after careful consideration, rejected nurse-midwifery as too medicalized. Greta Mallory said:

> I spent about nine years trying to decide if I wanted to be a CNM or … a licensed midwife, or an unlicensed midwife, or a naturopathic midwife, or a naturopathic obstetrician, and all that stuff. I decided — I was pretty convinced that I wanted to do home birth, and in Oregon at the time, CNMs who did home births weren't allowed to have hospital privileges. And I thought if I wasn't going to be able to have hospital privileges, why even bother going through this whole thing about being a CNM?

When they talked about the differences between nurse-midwifery and direct-entry midwifery, many direct-entry students and midwives depicted nurse-midwifery as co-opted, increasingly drifting away from the ideals of *true* midwifery. Consider these examples:

> *Erica Atwell (Faculty member at SMS):* I have one friend . … She was a nurse, and she went on several births with me before she went on to midwifery school. She was like my second pair of hands. Then she went to [nurse-]midwifery school. And then she got out, and she got a job in a hospital here. And I was going through case questions that my senior students were doing here. … I said "How would you handle this situation? You are an hour and a half out from the hospital, you've got a woman who is hemorrhaging, and a baby that doesn't look so good. What do you do?" And she goes "*Oh my God!* I don't know!" That was her *first response.* And I thought that sort of was a metaphor; that sort of is the difference between direct-entry and nurse-midwifery. I think nurse midwives are more comfortable in hospital settings. They are more used to having other people around to help them when there's a problem. LMs [licensed midwives] kind of hit the ground running. We

are kind of like those one-man-band things. We have all these different skills at our disposal, so that if we need a neonatal resus [resuscitation], or we can start an IV, or whatever we need to do, we are equipped to do that. And we have that in our minds, that any of those [things] ... could happen — and we are equipped to deal with it, are ready to handle it.

Diane Eastman (home birth midwife in Atlanta): I can only generalize, and I'll state from the onset ... that I *am* generalizing. There are wonderful CNMs out there. And in general, I really respect the work that CNMs do, because for those women that are birthing in hospitals, you know, very often CNMs are making the best of situations and certainly, *certainly*, providing better care and better outcomes for women than ... if the nurse-midwifery care were not available. But having said all of that: in general, I feel that nurse-midwifery care is very much an arm of obstetric care, and that very often, nurse-midwives practice more as mini-obstetricians or as obstetric technicians than they do truly as midwives. ... From what *I* observed from my time at Emory and in nursing school, and the nurse-midwives that I now also have relationships with: many nurse-midwives because they, you know, from day one, they are born and raised within the medical model of obstetric care. That *is* their model. They have integrated that, and they don't really have, within themselves, a true sense of normal birth, or any sense of the midwifery model of care. ... Even if somehow a nurse-midwife *has* managed to attain more of a true sense of normalcy in childbirth, very often her hands are tied and she's constrained by a variety of limitations. ... Nurse-midwives virtually always have to have malpractice insurance and they have to follow those guidelines. And then there are always the protocols imposed by the institution. ... Add all that together ... what it boils down to doesn't relate very strongly to what *I* know and practice as midwifery care.

Nina Lawrence (recent graduate of FSTM): My decision to do direct-entry was very political. And I, you know, wrote this thesis on it for my women's studies degree. Just coming from a feminist perspective — you know, the nursing thing is all about following the doctor's orders. And that's not what midwifery is about. So why am I having to jump this hoop to do that? And the other aspect of it that I was looking at was, well, am I going to kind of work for change within the system or work for change outside the system? And just for me, I felt like, oh, I'll do the outside thing. Like, both are valid. And it seems like nurse-midwives are definitely more within, and they're *still* fighting. They're still working for change.

Whereas nurse-midwives see nobility in going where the women are, direct-entry midwives express pride in not selling out their ideals to practice in institutions where such ideals are difficult or even impossible to realize. Women in both groups often expressed admiration for each other and talked about how all paths were valid or working for change in the same general direction. This is clearest in the comments of Nina Lawrence above. But many direct-entry midwives, like Erica Eastman and Diane Atwell, were quite critical of nurse-midwifery. They see nurse-midwifery in hospitals as accommodationist at best and assimilationist at worst. They see nurse-midwives as narrowly confined by a fear-based pathological approach to pregnancy and birth, rather than able to practice in a holistic and creative manner. Their take on the situation, in short, is that nurse-midwifery in the hospital is better than nothing, but it's not *really* midwifery.

Alas, midwifery isn't always all sweet sisterly love and cosmic cataclysmic connections. Social divisions and mutual suspicions among midwives — between nurse-midwives and direct-entry midwives as groups — were there from the first; they've changed shape over time, but their substance remains. While it is not our goal to air dirty laundry, the tensions among the groups illuminate the difficulties involved in organizational identity formation and achieving feminist goals.

Over the years, groups of midwives have also bonded and banded together at the local and national levels, and have sought to foster connections. Nurse-midwives sympathetic to home birth can join MANA. The ACNM, in contrast, has treated direct-entry midwives in a variety of ways over the course of its existence since 1955: as rather embarrassing lower-class relatives; as completely unrelated non-professional practitioners who give midwifery a bad public image (similar to Breckinridge's stance); and occasionally as comrades-in-arms. Non-nurse midwives can join the ACNM only if they have graduated from an ACNM-endorsed program:

In 1994, ACNM members voted overwhelmingly ... to create a direct-entry certification process; in 1995, they chose CM (certified midwife) as the name of this new type of practitioner; and in May 1997, they passed a resolution making this new CM a full-fledged voting member of the College. Only two DOA-accredited educational routes of entry to the CM credential are available: university-based programs and university-affiliated distance learning programs. These routes will not include apprenticeship programs or non-university affiliated programs. CM entry-level requirements are based on entry-level CNM requirements; the exams taken by CMs and CNMs are the same. ... Many ACNM members feel they have now "opened up" their profession, allowing easy ingress to all those who want to be midwives but just don't want to be nurses. ... In contrast, many MANA members do not see ACNM's move into direct-entry as an opening up but rather as a closing down, an exclusionary move to redefine direct-entry on ACNM's terms and shut out MANA-style direct entry midwifery. (Davis-Floyd 2002: 81)

At the same time that it was planning to initiate the program for direct-entry midwifery at Downstate, the ACNM also supported legislative changes in New York state that made practicing home birth midwifery legitimate only for direct-entry midwives who would graduate from this program or others similarly established and certified by ACNM. As a result, many practicing direct-entry midwives felt that the ACNM now wanted to take over and co-opt direct-entry midwifery.

According to Mel Sallinger, most members of ACNM support home birth and respect direct-entry midwives, but the leadership tends to be more conservative and controlling. One exception was Dorothea Lang, a past president of ACNM. Even as president, Lang felt she could not alter the institutional mindset of ACNM:

In the latter part of the seventies there was an obvious need for someone to represent or to be an umbrella for all the midwives that were not called nurse-midwives ... and whom ACNM would absolutely not consider part of their fold. ... I always said that ACNM should have a broader scope. ... A lot of us said that we must open our hearts and minds to a different type of entre [sic] into professional midwifery. There was always the movement within the college [ACNM] to say that we're not extended nurses, which I fought tooth and nail to preserve.

... We are not a sub-group of nursing. With that in mind I became a president, and two or three members of my board fought tooth and nail that I was not allowed to use the word "midwife" when I represented the ACNM; I always had to use "nurse-midwife" or I would be impeached. ... In California by that time they had something like 2000 women who called themselves midwives who were doing births in the area of San Francisco. In the earlier days, the ACNM was trying to distinguish itself as being different from the granny midwives in the South. (Lang cited in Schlinger 1992: 12–13)

So divergences between the midwives had at first a racist and classist basis: "granny midwives" — known now by the more respectful term "grand midwives" — were old, black, poor, or working-class women, and the new nurse-midwives were white middle-class women. Now most of the "grands" are retired or dead, and most direct-entry midwives are white and middle-class. The former class difference now tends to play out as a status difference based on educational credentials or professional style. This comes out in quirky, mostly subtle ways, very different from the overtly disparaging treatment nurse-midwives often accorded direct-entry midwives (whom they tellingly referred to as "lay" midwives) in the early twentieth century. On the ACNM website, in a "Fact Sheet" entitled "State Laws Governing Direct Entry Midwifery," in a footnote it says: "Direct entry midwives enter the profession of midwifery without a nursing credential." This was the only place I found a definition of a different type of midwife from a nurse-midwife or a CM — a certified midwife who has graduated from an ACNM-endorsed program for non-nurses.

At the Downstate program, the direct-entry program is merged with the nurse-midwifery program, for the most part. When we asked women in the first such class to graduate from this first ACNM-endorsed program to discuss the differences between direct-entry and nurse-midwifery, a strange conversation ensued:[4]

Student One: We don't have separate programs here. We have a single program. We're getting a midwifery education. We all come out of this beginning level midwives. ... We are getting midwifery training as distinct from nursing training. We, the 23 of us, will come out of here beginning midwives. So there is no split.

Student Two: As a non-direct-entry — I think that, I think that all of us feel there's no difference between all of us as a group. The only difference might be in hand skills. Some of us have, some of us might be more comfortable starting IVs than others. ... Some nurses might not feel as comfortable as some other nurses in the group. Or some people might feel more comfortable with, like, certain medical technology, or you know, there are like totally minute details that don't affect the quality of your care that you provide or your ability to be a good midwife. I think we probably all feel that way — direct-entry, non-direct entry.

Student Three: I think that really the only difference is where we place our anxieties. Direct-entries must, I think, have anxiety about the skills we lack. They're sort of vague and evasive, and they're out there. And the nurses have the same anxieties but they call them other things because their background is different. ...

Student Four: I think it's sad because I think in reality there's a lot of divisiveness and division between different types of midwives in this country. And I think it's very unfortunate because I think that if you scratched away the surface enough and dug down, we all hold the same essential beliefs in common, which are: love for women, respect for women, a desire, you know, to protect them and you know, to facilitate positive transitions throughout their lives. ... I think we all have something to bring to the table, and I'm talking about lay midwives with no formal education on paper whatsoever, all the way up to, you know, nurse-midwives with many decades of experience and Ph.D.s. I think it's a little ludicrous, ridiculous, how much we get hung up on titles, the route to the education. ...

Student Three: I'm very surprised at the hierarchical structure that's supporting this divisiveness. I think it's male hierarchical structure. I did not expect to find it and I find that very disturbing. ...

Student Five: I think what makes me uncomfortable is anyone within a profession that is practicing outside the guidelines of what that profession is. ... I just have a hard time with anyone that's practicing illegally, regardless of what the profession is. I don't feel that's someone I can trust.

In this discussion, students clearly present a unified front while also acknowledging that "divisiveness" exists outside, in the professional world of midwifery. At the same time that they express solidarity and lament hierarchical differences, a couple of them differentiate between themselves and the wrong kind of direct-entry midwife, the kind who practices illegally. They do not interrogate the law, which strikes me as peculiar for women about to practice in a state that had recently outlawed any practitioners not credentialed by their own school, and in a country where most states do not license midwives. They also differentiate themselves from certain direct-entry midwives by using the term "lay midwife," and by referring to a hierarchy where lay midwives are at the bottom, and "all the way up" at the top are nurse-midwives with Ph.D.s. Though they are at times critical of medicalization (as when Student Three blames the conflict among groups of midwives on the "male hierarchical structure"), their talk also shows the strength of the medical model and the anxiety they have as they prepare to do birth work based on an opposing philosophy. Student Five's talk about the untrustworthiness of midwives practicing illegally shows the tendency among those in oppressed or low-status groups to reify the dominant group's stereotypes to separate themselves from problem members who reflect badly on the whole group. In their conversation, I can see both promise for increasing solidarity and continuing divisiveness among midwives.

Time will tell. As Carol Leonard opines in *Circle of Midwives*, the narrative-based history of MANA by Hillary Schlinger:

I think all this divisiveness is really not only dumb but dangerous. We have so much to learn from each other. We're not going to go away, and they're not going to. It's the same thing where the lay midwives think the nurse–midwives are too medical, and the nurse midwives think the lay midwives are too Birkenstock, flaky, whatever. Somewhere in the middle there's got to be a realization that we are all working to improve outcome and that we all have an idea of a midwifery model. It doesn't really matter what your route of entry. (1992: 142–143)

It will be interesting to see what happens within direct-entry midwifery now that there are essentially two tracks, the ACNM-sanctioned programs and the others. As Robbie Davis-Floyd writes:

Although they are willing to drop a nursing degree as a requirement, they will keep all other aspects of their educational standards by creating ACNM's version of direct-entry midwifery in the image of nurse-midwifery. To succeed within medicine, as they are doing, they must mirror the standardized education of all medical professions. Their leadership believed that success within the technocracy requires a college degree. (2002: 68)

Before doing this research, I had imagined occupational identity to be the product of a combination of chance and social-structural opportunities and limitations: the result of serendipitous (or unlucky) events, the influences of others, the privilege (or lack thereof) to make decisions about individual socially constructed desires and needs, financial, emotional, or intellectual. Midwives and midwifery students tell stories that do include this sort of haphazard meandering, serendipitous accidents, structural opportunities and limitations. But at the same time, they often present their professional trajectories as fated opportunities to express their most passionate selves. They describe midwifery as a craft they learn out of devotion, and an art they often believe they are destined to practice. Whether it was a decision clearly made or gradually arrived at or imposed from outside, sparking an internal transformation, everyone we interviewed portrayed midwifery as gratifying worthwhile work.

Becoming a midwife means acting on the desire to care for or nurture others; pursuing an interest in how the body works; loving birth for its ecstatic, glorious, and awesome potential; maintaining an antipathy toward conventional medicine; learning to deal with crisis situations calmly; and articulating a political-personal desire to serve women and help them feel strong and in control.

Once they choose or accept this path, are midwives able to keep their ideals alive? In the next chapter, I turn to the practical realities involved in the worklives of midwives.

4

BIRTH MATTERS

Practicing Midwifery

WENDY SIMONDS

Introduction: My Ganglion Cyst

Let me start this chapter by considering the issue of medicalization through a subject less potent than birth. A few years ago, a surgeon removed a small ganglion cyst (a hard benign lump that can form from the repetitive motions of daily life) on my wrist. Here's how I remember it.

I arrive early in the morning to be prepped. I fill out forms; I don a hospital gown open in back, and I am allowed to wear no clothes underneath — not even underwear. (I think about Goffman's work to calm myself!) I am wheeled around in a bed, rendered helpless to walk where we're going not because of anything to do with the cyst on my wrist, but because this is the method of transportation prescribed in hospitals: once a patient, one is nonambulatory, a reclining passenger. One can go only where one is taken. A stranger parks me in a holding area.

After a while, a young man whom I've never met comes over to me and introduces himself as a resident working with "my" surgeon. He shakes my hand. He will be assisting with the operation, he tells me. He strikes me as very smiley; I can't tell if his smiles are fake or earnest. He goes away.

After a while I am wheeled into a bright room, where some nurses greet me briefly and then begin to separate my arm from the rest of me with white sheets. I can't see my arm; it lies on the other side of this curtain on a metal table, taped into place.

After a while, they give me an oxygen mask to put over my face. I have prearranged not to have any sedatives because I'm breastfeeding. They tourniquet my arm above the elbow and then inject a local anesthetic. I think they would be tourniqueting my arm if I were sedated, too, but I'm not sure. I think it keeps my blood from gushing out when they cut into me, but they don't tell me why and I don't ask, because the encounter is structured by their being busy, curt, and only really handing me bits of information when I ask for them or when they notice me — which they mostly seem not to do as they scurry around. I ask if the tourniquet will hurt, and the nurse says that I will feel "some pressure." This pressure turns out to be very painful indeed.

After a while, I hear the two doctors on the other side of the curtain. They don't greet me. They are having a friendly conversation as if I am not in the same room.

When the cutting starts, I can feel it. "That hurts!" I say. "I can feel that!" They ignore me. It hurts some more; now it hurts a *lot* more. *"That hurts a lot!"* I say in a high-pitched panicky voice that resounds inappropriately in the bright white, cold room. The doctor says to the nurse: "What did she say?" as if I'm speaking a foreign language or my words are slurred. "She said she feels it," the nurse says, adding: "She's not sedated." "Why isn't she sedated?" he asks, in an annoyed tone. "She's breastfeeding. She didn't want sedation," the nurse answers. (I had discussed this issue with him the week before in my pre-surgery visit and he had agreed that sedatives were best kept out of breast milk, but he had apparently forgotten.) "Oh, right," he says. He sounds annoyed that they have to stop the surgery to give me more local anesthesia.

When they start up again, they talk about the young resident's vacation. Interspersed with this, the older one, "my doctor," quizzes and sometimes directs the younger one. Apparently the younger one is cutting into my wrist and doing the work of removing the cyst. I hope he knows how to do this right. It sounds like maybe he hasn't done it before. Things are happening to my hand that I — now, thankfully — cannot feel. Then the doctors go out without saying goodbye.

After a while, the nurse says, "I'm wrapping your hand now." I figured as much. Still, it's nice to have verbal confirmation that she's wrapping it rather than sawing it off.

Eventually, the nurse removes the curtain. I am surprised to see my arm in a cast up to my elbow. Someone wheels me to a recovery area, where I sit inside a room comprised of curtained partitions and read a book. I have to sit here for 45 minutes and have my blood pressure and temperature checked several times. I can hear other people talking, a child crying. I have to go to the bathroom; the nurse tells me to stay in the bed for ten minutes more. She tells me a reason for this rule, but I can't remember it now. Now all I remember is trying to suppress the intense urge to piss, and feeling infantilized but not fighting back. A nurse gives me information sheets on infection and papers to sign, and offers me a prescription narcotic. I tell her I am breastfeeding and she seems startled, as if this is not something she usually hears. "Will Tylenol help? Is it going to hurt a lot?" I ask. She says that I "may feel some discomfort" — ! I am always surprised when they use this word because it's as if they're performing a self-parody. "Discomfort" is such an evasive way of portraying pain. Ibuprofen would probably help more, she says. My arm "will be sore for a few days," she says.

And it is. Not mild soreness either: throbbing pain. Before scheduling the surgery, I had asked the doctor about what I might expect in terms of pain and disability. He had said, "It's outpatient surgery. You can be back at work the same day if you want to be." I guess I misinterpreted. I *could* be at work feeling this pain, but my arm was unusable for several days because it hurt so badly. I had asked, "Can I use my arm afterward?" and he had said "Yes." I had mistakenly assumed this meant no cast, and that pain would not prohibit or greatly inhibit the use of my arm. But it really, really hurt. It was difficult to breastfeed my baby on the right side; I couldn't support his head, much less lift him with that arm for several days without experiencing sharp, intense jolts of "discomfort." I had to devise an elaborate pillow scheme to compensate. It was hard to sleep. I couldn't fasten my clothes or cut my food or drive for several days, and the strong "discomfort" did not abate for well over a week (at which point it transformed into quite unpleasant itching).

My minor surgery exposed me to the institutional dynamics of medicine in an immediate and personal way. Through my own body and pain, I experienced how medical workers and hospitals treat bodies and pain. Objectification and routinization made me feel fragile and anxious; I felt totally alone. As we — and many others — have pointed out before, medicine is uncaring in certain ways to everyone (see, e.g., Chambliss 1996, Frank 2004, Simonds and Rothman 1992, Sudnow 1967, Weinberg 2003). What happened to me was minor as medical degradation goes, but emblematic.

Over the course of this medical experience, I was always treated politely when spoken to, yet I was also generally ignored. If I *had* been sedated, I might not remember at all the doctor and nurse talking about me as if I weren't there in-between them, or the docs sounding as if they were having a cup-of-coffee chat as they cut into my wrist. First, reduced to my body, I felt inconsequential as a person: for them, I was a disembodied arm with a cyst on its wrist that needed excising. Doctors conceptually fragment the bodies they treat, focusing in on the part or parts deemed pathological or improvable or removable; everything else is secondary, even inconsequential.

Next, my non-routine demand (no drugs, breastfeeding) led to unanticipated pain; my consciousness became a problem for medical workers to negotiate. My idiosyncrasy, my sentience, and my pain disrupted the standard treatment regimen. It was a hassle for them: I was the hassle. Yet none of the people objectifying and routinizing me did anything overtly evil or willfully malicious. Routinization and objectification are inherent to institutionalization. No one acknowledged my fear of being processed by the institution, of being taken to unfamiliar places where strange things were done to my body. This sense of alienation born of powerlessness and its accompanying vulnerability seem to be central elements of institutionalized care; yet, as far as I know, the people doing the work of these institutions avoid acknowledging this aspect of medicalization in their interactions with patients. Perhaps they don't see, or stop seeing them. After all, I wasn't the only one suffering under the burdens of routinization and institutionalization, but I'll never know whether the other participants in this event ever thought or now think about these aspects of their work.

Even though I had asked questions, I didn't really know what to expect before the surgery: the doctor had been dismissive when I asked about pain, and he and the nurses used a particularized language to deflect my concerns about pain throughout the experience. Because of this, I felt that I was overreacting when the anesthetic didn't work and I announced my pain. It is also significant that I had only superficial relationships with everyone with whom I came in contact that day. The doctor and I had never engaged in a conversation as two people, but always as expert authority and ignorant patient. The nurses functioned like mediator/translators, friendly middlewomen between the power and me.

Afterward, I mused about the centrality of lumps to medicine. Surgery, the highest-status specialization among medical practitioners, boils down to the removal of lumps (medically known as cysts, growths, tumors, etc.). Do surgeons enjoy such social elevation because of the arrogant daring inherent in the act of cutting, the expertise and precision involved in doing it well, the life-protecting potential of such acts, the successful self-presentation of themselves as high priests of the body — or for all these reasons? Is medical specialty status proportional to the level of intrusion into the body?

I thought about how medical students first learn to fragment bodies when they dissect dead people at the outset of their professional training. Their first patients are dead bodies. Perhaps the association is always there, difficult to shake, I imagine: anybody, any body, all bodies, will become dead bodies. I would think this empirical knowledge could be very upsetting, potentially very humbling. But studies of the culture of medical education show that humility rarely plays a part. Medical educators teach students to distance themselves from the dead. "Introspection and reflection are terminal diseases in medical school," Frederic Hafferty writes in his ethnography of medical school (1991: 191). As they practice identifying, labeling, and evaluating the condition of internal bodily elements, the students learn to speak medical language. Peter Finkelstein contends that this language reinforces the view that "one dissects anatomical material; one does not look backward to the person once invested in this body" (1986: 29). Typically, then, doctors craft a disinterested "professional" and "scientific" demeanor; they eschew humility to avoid the pain of association with people, with fear, with the pain of pain, with the pain of loss, and with the pain of death (see Murphy-Lawless 1998). Medical school culture can also promote a more profane set of distancing practices, involving sexual jokes and crude, irreverent treatment of cadavers. So medical professional distance may be edged with habitual contempt.

On a positive note, medical culture can change, as Mary Roach documents in a chapter on gross anatomy lab reforms in the past decade in the United States, in which students are encouraged to behave respectfully toward their cadavers, attend memorial services for them, and confront rather than avoid feeling and thinking about death (2003: 37–57).

Bureaucratic medicalization does not affect only our birth experiences (as I hope my ganglion cyst story and discussion of medical education demonstrates). At its worst, it strips all bodily events claimed to be within its purview of their potential to enhance our lives or make us feel active or powerful. Unfortunately, doctors' professional lack of empathy affects patients; it can itself create a ritualistic process of feeling discounted, invisible, objectified, and, ultimately, humiliated. Doctors often appear unaware that they're participating in and shaping other people's experiences of their bodies or their selves. This lack of awareness and its concomitant appearance of indifference together, at the very least, make medicalized experiences disempowering events for people. The identity-laden aspect of bodily transitions rarely matters to doctors because it seldom registers for them. Doctors simply do not tend to think about affirmation or transformation. They remove the cysts, the babies, whatever. The rest is touchy-feely stuff, not — at least not yet — medicine.

And Now ... Birth

Birth for women can be fraught with a vast array of emotions. Birth can bring up past traumas. It can affect one's relationships with others, one's own bodily competence, one's very sense of self. Pamela E. Klassen writes, "Birth sticks with a woman, remaining in her bones and her flesh as an embodied memory long after the baby has left her womb" (2001: 3). Klassen may overdramatize and essentialize the consequences of birth, but her view that birth experiences have far-reaching magnitude and depth for women and children is common among midwives.

The birth of a baby is also the birth of a mother, so if the experience turns out to be not what a woman expected or hoped for, how will it affect her sense of herself *as* a mother? Women are called upon to produce stories of our own births, and in so doing, we must narrate our successes or explain our failures at achieving positive births (see, e.g., Michie and Cahn 1997). In retrospect, I think, many women deny the complexity of medicalized birth experiences and our ambivalence about them — suppress feelings of vulnerability, powerlessness, incompetence, failure — because we do not want these to be part of the memories we take with us of an experience that is supposed to be beautiful and momentous. It is rarely acknowledged that the accomplishment of beauty and magnitude varies situationally. Many women remain oblivious to the power dynamics involved and feel content to do what doctors want done because they trust in medicine and view birth as their doctors do: as a matter-of-fact getting-out of the baby. This is the least troubling way to view birth, given the omnipresence of medicalization in our culture.

Exposing the philosophy behind the medical model and offering an alternative — as we hope to do by presenting the viewpoints of midwives in this book — may prompt a reevaluation of events that readers previously saw as unproblematic. Birth experiences may seem diminished or flawed when analyzed in this unconventional light. This sort of critical thinking can spark defensiveness, which can give way to disillusionment. Disillusionment can serve as a motivation to work for social change. So we hope.

There is more to this issue than individual birth experiences, a broader medicalization that I believe we need to confront, reform, resist, not only for our own individual good but also for the good of society, however glibly idealistic that sounds. Birth is not the only event that offers the potential for a transformative growth experience (or the opposite), by any means. Our lives are perhaps most medicalized at beginning and end, but all sorts of transitions in life are marked by bodily and health changes. The ways in which we integrate (or don't integrate) these changes, the ways in which we are "treated" (or mistreated) by others during these changes, affects how we become who we become. As Arthur W. Frank writes:

> The bodily vulnerability that medicine resists with honorable dedication is part of what humans *are*; not a contingent and undesired side effect of being human — a wart to be removed — but part of what it is to be human, warts and all. Thus medicine, in its dedication to the human goal of reducing suffering, always risks rejecting a fundamental aspect of our humanity. (2004: 9)

Frank writes of a technician he met during treatment for testicular cancer who told him, "Remember ... everyone who touches you affects your healing" (2004: 27). While not all health-related experiences necessitate healing — in birth, for example, typically there is no injury, no wound, no pathology from which to recover — we would all be better off if approached by health care workers who recognized the importance of "personal acts of generosity" evinced through "people touching each other" (Frank 2004: 29), both physically and otherwise. This is the core of midwifery.

Philosophical Ideals

"Midwifery means *with woman*." We heard this statement countless times while doing interviews with students and midwives. In editorials in midwifery journals and introductions to midwifery textbooks, this definitional claim is virtually universal. Midwives and midwifery students define themselves and their work by implicitly and explicitly contrasting their ideals with the conventional methods of medicine, even when they practice in medical environments. The general message the women I interviewed conveyed was noninterventionist and respectful: the goals of midwifery are to help women to achieve positive birth experiences through supportive and communicative interactions with women. *Births belong to women, not to birth attendants.* Midwives are not in charge. Midwives know that the body and the self change through experience; they see bodily, mental, and emotional existence as inextricably intertwined. Midwives recognize that their work will shape women's perceptions of pregnancy and birth experiences, as well as potentially affecting their identities. Midwives know that help does not consist of telling someone else what to do.

The rest of this chapter is devoted to illustrating midwives' ethics of practice and what they seek to achieve through their work. Rhetorics of *choice* and *love* elucidate their views about power and empowerment, nature and culture, obstacles and aids to achieving ideal practice, and the constraints or freedoms inherent in the situational aspects of birth experiences. Midwives talk about choice in a number of ways: choice as enacting one's desires in one's procreative experiences; choice of birth attendant and birth place; choice as giving in to — or making decisions to resist — conventional medical practice; choice as gaining control or realizing a sense of empowerment during birth. Midwives and mid-wifery students espouse a loving professional stance and evoke stereo-typically "feminine" characteristics such as patience, nurturance, and understanding as central to midwifery care. Together, in the view of participants in our research, choice and love enable "empowerment."

Sometimes participants would say that their ideal is to facilitate whatever women choose, or to protect women's right to make uncon-ventional choices. All the midwives and midwifery students we inter-viewed recognized that medicine constrained their abilities to realize this goal and thus constrained birthing women's choices, even when midwives practiced in states where they were legally recognized as independent practitioners.

Nurse-midwives said they were not always consistently taught in school to honor women's choices, and they did not see it as always possible to accomplish this goal in hospitals. Typically, medical insti-tutions are indifferent or hostile to midwifery because doctors and medical administrators often erect barriers to women's — indeed, all patients' — agency by isolating, anesthetizing, ignoring, routinizing, objectifying, and sometimes even humiliating the people they "serve." Our participants' discussions of choice of practitioner, of place, and of what sort of birth to have all took place against the backdrop of cultural coercion created and sustained by the power of obstetrics and the medical model.

Practice Ideals

I asked midwives and midwifery students to articulate what they saw as the ideals of midwifery, and to describe the way in which they put these ideals into practice. Alona Golden, a home birth midwife, Carrie Ward, a nurse-midwife who had practiced always in hospitals, and Lisette Maddox, a nurse-midwife with experience in home and hospital birth, replied in ways characteristic of the groups we interviewed:

> *Alona Golden:* My first goal is to do as much as I can to guard the safety of the mom and the baby, so ... for me, home birth is never the goal. You know, I say to clients all the time, you don't get pregnant to have a home birth. You get pregnant to have a healthy baby. ... The other principle would be to really have the mother be the center of the care. It's not *my* thing, it's *her* thing primarily. ... People say they empower other people. I don't think you can empower somebody else. I think all you can do is not *take* power and *guide* them to their *own* power. To say you're empowering somebody still implies that you are giving them something that they don't have. ... So, as much as I can, I'm really guiding them to find their own inner comfort, and their own inner strength. So that would be my second principle — having it be really woman-centered. And the third principle would be ... [that it be] family-centered. ... Like a concentric circle.

> *Carrie Ward:* For me ... [the core ideal of midwifery is] loving and giving to women, being of service. Helping them to — this is a little bit off the center of what I'm [actually] doing, but — to know their bodies and to take care of ... themselves. Empower them to be who they want to be. ... I see myself as being a servant to women for their health and their bodies and their childbearing.

> *Lisette Maddox:* Learn to trust birth. We are not taught in midwifery school to trust birth. ... When someone comes to me, my overriding philosophy is: this is your birth, and you invited me to your party — I call it a party — and you write the script. ... I vary my approach depending on who I am servicing. But it's always your birth, and I try my best to honor that.

Ultimately, as they describe it, midwifery promotes the idea of birth as a personal growth experience for women (and their family members) in which choice ideally would actualize into "empowerment." Midwifery facilitates these goals via education, nurturance, love, and support.

Midwives generally see themselves as engaging in a process of informed choice (they inform and women choose) that enhances women's experiences by encouraging self-awareness and comfort in their bodies and in their bodily transitions. This sense of helping women to find their own agency echoes the goals of the feminist health care movement and resonates with what feminist abortion workers want to achieve as well (see, e.g., Ruzek 1978, Simonds 1996). But knowledge and power are not necessarily always directly proportional nor purely objective. Some midwives puzzled over what, how, and how much to tell women. As Mel Sallinger, a nurse-midwife with hospital experience exclusively, said:

> The midwife is a more knowledgeable person in many situations, about the other things — the non-normal. ... It's a very delicate dance between remaining aware of possible problems and supporting normal. And I struggle with this with my students a lot — of them wanting to educate the woman. She doesn't need to know about a lot of the things you know. It's not going to help, in my view, for her to know *all* the possible horrible things that could possibly happen. But the midwife has to know them. And yet, at the same time, she [the woman] needs enough information to make decisions for herself. So you're doing this kind of ballet on one toe! [She laughs.] Sometimes you tip over in one direction or the other. ... How much each person needs to know is also very individual depending on that person and their own approach to health care or to pregnancy. And some people *do* come and want you to make the decisions. Then you have to figure out how to dance *that* dance, because one of my goals is always to move people toward their own decision-making, you know, and power. I don't think we empower people, but I think we can support them to become empowered for themselves.

To take control of the experience away from birthing women — even those who would willingly give it up — is antithetical to what midwives see as most important. Midwives feel most gratified by helping others to feel powerful. Ideally, midwifery enables rather than dictates. All of this might sound hokey, especially given the absence of such talk in conventional medicine. But they mean it.

Medical Problems

When they talked about the overarching goals of midwifery, participants often framed them in direct opposition to medicine:

Rebecca Bernstein (direct-entry student in the program at Downstate): [The goal is] to treat them like a person, not like a thing. Many times I'll see the doctors or medical students treating patients just like a piece of meat, you know — instead of dealing with them as a person and including them in the care — and not talking to them. They talk around them.

Nova Beal (direct-entry student at SMS): I really think there should be a big stamp on hospitals that says: *Emergency use only.* ... I am not saying that women shouldn't give birth in hospitals. ... I fully want to support every woman's choice to labor and deliver where they want to. But I think it is that basic philosophical difference that [sees] birth as disease or birth as natural life process, you know: pregnant woman as different biological species, or pregnant woman as pregnant woman.

As these midwifery students depict it, medicine treats pregnant women like objects, as if they're inconsequential, diseased, or deviant. If one sees birth "as disease," one cannot see birth as a "natural life process." Many participants portrayed the disparate approaches of medicine and midwifery as mutually exclusive polar opposites.

Almost all the women who participated in our interviews offered at least one caveat to soften their critiques (like Nova Beal's claim not to be disparaging all hospital births). Obstetrics has a long history of depicting midwives — especially home birth midwives — as irrational, incompetent extremists. These caveats show that midwives are making reasoned institutional critiques, not giving voice to extremist hatred of obstetrics or obstetricians. The caveats may focus on doctors: there are some good doctors, some great doctors, some wonderful doctors; some of their best friends are doctors; some doctors really are midwives at heart; some doctors act like midwives; some doctors advocate for midwives; some doctors help midwives; some doctors leave midwives alone. The caveats may focus on surgical skills: there are times when someone simply needs surgery; doctors know how to do surgery; and so there are times when you simply need a doctor. The caveats may concern hospitals: there are some good hospitals; some hospitals value midwives; some hospitals allow midwives to function without much interference; some hospitals allow midwives to function without any interference; some hospitals allow midwives to be involved in policy making; and so some good birth experiences might happen in some hospitals. The caveats may deal with technology: sometimes machines can be worthwhile; some machines or surgical techniques can save lives. And last, the caveats might focus on women being culturally influenced or coerced (as in Mel Sallinger's remarks): some women don't question medical authority (whether in the form of hospitals or doctors or medicalization); some women can't get past their fear of pain; some women have been brainwashed not to trust their bodies; thus, some women will feel safest and most comfortable with the status quo.

When asked whether they had experienced conflict with medical practices or hospital protocols, most midwives (or labor and delivery nurses in midwifery school) laughed and said something along the lines of Mel Sallinger's reply: *"Every day of my life!"* The nurse-midwives' ability to achieve their ideals was hampered by bureaucratic demands like hyper-documentation, time constraints because of the number of clients they had to attend to simultaneously, being on call for too long or too often — all conditions and rules antithetical to what they saw as the ideal practice of midwifery. They spoke of how you learn to "choose your battles," and they told about learning how to deal with such conflict, as in these remarks from nurse midwives working in hospital practices:

> *Nell Jameson:* The first strategy I used was *anger* ... which was less than successful, as you may imagine. ... The way I've done things in the past that has been the most successful when there is a conflict is ... I can't respond to the situation right then. ... I need to get all my facts

together, and it helps if you can document that what you're doing has a clinical basis and "here's the literature that applies". ... Do they always agree with me ... [when] I present all the facts, and then everything is hunky-dory and wonderful? Nah!

Renie Daley: Well, you know, I'm in *their* playground. ... I fight doctors a lot less [than I used to]. I mean, some midwives still feel like they have to protect their patients from doctors. If I need a doctor, if it's gone past my scope ... I don't fight 'em. ... I don't expect them to practice midwifery. ... I mean, I'm glad when physicians come around if I need 'em. I don't want to mess with 'em when I don't. I think I have a fairly mature role. I know that there's some things that I have to ask permission to do, just because that's the way the law is; that's the way our practice is. And I don't set myself up to get told to do something that I don't want to do. I can consult in a way that tells 'em what I want to do in a way that doesn't challenge them. ... If I ask them to tell me to practice midwifery or to enhance midwifery, I'm gonna lose, because they're doctors. ... I'd *like* it if they totally honored and respected what midwifery is, but it *scares* them. I mean, trusting normal and trusting women — it's not anything they've ever learned.

Like many other midwives and midwifery students we interviewed, Jameson describes learning to repress anger at doctors or at medical ways of doing things. Daley alludes to this too, when she tells of her conviction not to fight on what she has come to accept as doctors' turf; perhaps she uses the term "playground" to soften the fact that she has come to accept a state of affairs in which she will never share equal power with doctors, and in which what she does may well be disrespected and even countermanded by them. She works around doctors, avoiding them except when she can't. As Jameson describes, her method for dealing with disputes with doctors by producing medical research to substantiate her position may be trumped, ultimately, by their greater authority. They do not have to listen to midwives.

Only a few of the nurse-midwives we interviewed portrayed relationships with doctors as untroubled. Betsy Ettinger replied when asked about whether she'd encountered conflict with doctors or hospital protocols:

No … I'm one of the fortunate ones. … I've always felt accepted as a midwife. Now, I know a lot of people have had trouble, but I haven't. … I think attitude has a lot to do with it. I've always known I needed physicians. I would never be arrogant enough to think I didn't and maybe because I have that belief myself, I've always … been very lucky, you know.

Ettinger inadvertently suggests that midwives who do experience conflicts with doctors bring them on themselves. Yet she also portrays her own lack of problems as serendipitous.

Rarely would a midwife describe working in a situation where doctors did not have greater power than midwives. Athena Cuthbert, who had been trained in Great Britain and owned a birth center in Trinidad, did not experience obstetricians as a recurrent obstacle to achieving midwifery practice ideals:

The midwives do the deliveries, and the doctor's for any complications. … And if there are complications, we are the ones who really send the patient to the MD. The conflict will be now, in the nineties, when we have a higher percentage of young OB-GYN boys coming out of America who are trained, and want to do their own deliveries. And then you will have a little conflict of economy, you know. They want it because of the money involved, and so you have a little conflict of interest there now.

Because of economic differences in the structuring of health care, Cuthbert could enjoy a freedom unimaginable in the United States. But she could also see the "OB-GYN boys" coming, looking for financial opportunities, seeking markets to imperialize.

Throughout the comments midwives made about their relationships with doctors ran a common thread: doctors must be treated carefully by midwives. Their talk reminds me of a subtext of many liberal feminist creeds from the 1970s: great care was taken to palliate, not alienate men. Midwives, like pioneering feminists, take satisfaction in knowing their philosophy is morally superior; they know they provide better care and, in so doing, that they achieve some successes at altering a relatively intransigent system from the inside (nurse-midwives) and from without (home birth midwives).

Evidence-Based Practice

Though midwives offer a critique of medical culture and its objectification of women, medical research and epistemology often escape
criticism. Midwives, in fact, invoke them in their own defense, as
tools they may be able to use in negotiating with doctors, as Nell
Jameson describes documenting the "clinical basis" for her actions
in conflicts with doctors. "Evidence-based practice," a much-touted
approach in midwifery schools and midwifery publications, at its best
offers the hope of hoisting the system with its own petard:

> *Rose Casper (nurse-midwife):* Literature always works because they love
> literature. They love research studies... . When we had physicians that
> were saying, "Well, you know, we're going to induce her because the
> baby is big," ... we were able to, you know, pull out literature ... and
> say, "You know, really, there's five research studies that show that, you
> know, there's no validity to doing that. If you *do* do that, you're going
> to increase the c-section rate and, um, so could we try it this way?" ...
> Evidence-based research works really well.

> *Ruth Russell (SMS direct-entry student):* I want to be able to talk to doc-
> tors, talk to nurses, with a basis for why midwifery is a solid profes-
> sion and is ... evidence-based. And this school stresses evidence-based
> learning and practice. And so the fact that we're reading studies all the
> time is good. It helps — it will help me in that professional aspect.

Some midwives, like Casper or Ettinger, portray (or *hopefully* portray,
as in Russell's comment) medicine as ultimately rational, and doctors
as prone to conversion to the right way of doing things if midwives
handle them logically (by showing them research), solicitously, and
without arrogance. Others, like Jameson and Daley, are less sanguine.
They come to accept, typically over the course of time, that medicine
will change only so much (not much, generally). So they do their best
to avoid it, or to be subtle, and even occasionally use subterfuge to
keep it at bay.

Functioning separately in environments where doctors do not typically oversee midwives but are called when they are needed is the
best arrangement nurse-midwives described. But unfortunately, they

know that some doctors will always see midwives as representing a challenge to their authority and behave accordingly. In stories about controlling, obnoxious doctors, residents featured as the most nasty and domineering, presumably because they were more likely to be insecure *as* doctors, and thus more likely to be competitive with midwives. As Penny Martin, a nurse-midwife, said:

> Residents ... are much more difficult to deal with because they're under pressure themselves and when they get burned, that is the first time the patient goes bad. Then they never forget that. And from then on, everyone becomes a potential for really going bad. And it is very difficult to work with that, to show them that this can be a very normal kind of deal.

The opposing ideological frameworks of midwives and doctors made their empirical realities different. Thus, doctors who mistrust midwifery in the first place for what they see as its philosophical denial of a central place for pathology might well resist "evidence" presented by midwives, as Jameson described.

The recent decline in episiotomies is one example of the success of midwives at presenting evidence that a medical practice causes needless harm. Studies show definitively that episiotomies produce perineal tears rather than reduce them, as obstetricians long claimed (see Goer 1995, 1999, Hartmann et al. 2005). Midwives' opposition to episiotomies may have worked directly or indirectly — through the reporting on the dangers of episiotomies in pregnancy and birth advice books, for instance — to create a demand on the part of pregnant women that doctors avoid doing episiotomies. But the drop in the episiotomy rate is a rare example of a decline in medical interventionism over the past 30 years. The use of forceps has gradually been replaced by roughly equivalent use of vacuum extraction; both technologies cause birth injuries which are vastly underreported, according to midwives we interviewed who practice in hospitals (because of fears of malpractice charges). As noted previously, the c-section rate has rocketed from slightly more than 5% in 1970 to 29.1% in 2003 (the most recent year for which statistics are available; see Curtin and Kozak 1998, Hamilton 2004). These statistics indicate that most OBs are imperious about their habitual practices to adopt invasive techniques and technologies and impervious to medical research that calls these practices into question (and medical research *does* call these practices into question, repeatedly [see DeClercq et al. 2006, Goer 1995, 1999, which show that women's medical risk factors do not cause increases in c-section rates and that c-sections cause a lot more medical problems than they solve]). That is, doctors learn to practice in a certain way, and they tend to continue to practice that way.

Medical textbooks devoted to explicating the process of evidence-based practice are ideologically fascinating. In his introduction to the edited volume *Obstetrical Decision Making* (1982), Emanual A. Friedman (of Friedman's curve fame) writes:

> In the practice of medicine, decision making is commonplace. Almost every patient encounter involves one or more decisions. … They range from simple matters of routine care to complex sequences of diagnostic and therapeutic steps. Inherent in some of the decisions we make is the logic of the basic tenets of medical science. Too many, however, derive from empiricism, dogma, rote, and intuition. Yet every decision should weigh benefits against risks or, more often, the risks of one option against the greater or lesser risks of another. To this end, a burgeoning scientific discipline of decision analysis is developing to quantitate the relative costs (principally monetary) of alternative options. (1982: 1)

Doctors make decisions here rationally and scientifically, with the help of decision trees provided by every author Friedman includes, advising on approximately 200 pathological possibilities that can occur during pregnancy or birth.

Nearly two decades later, the same sort of conceptualization prevails in the text *Evidence-Based Medicine*, edited by Daniel L. Friedland (1998). (This book focuses on medicine in general, rather than on obstetrics alone.) Despite the inroads claimed by proponents of using narratives and active listening in doctor-patient relations, Friedland advises:

> Evidence-based medicine is the practice of making medical decisions through the judicious identification, evaluation, and application of the most relevant information. … First we frame a given medical problem to identify the specific information we need. When this information is identified, we retrieve it and then evaluate it to ensure that it is valid.

Finally, if we believe the information, we need to know how to apply it to the care of our patient. (1998: 3)

Doctors still make the decisions rationally and scientifically. However, two entries in the index of this more recent textbook indicate that patient involvement *can* be a factor: "Patient input, decision tree use and," and "Patient perspective, cost analysis from." In the first example, the authors construe "patient input" as "critical" on the one hand, because "the best decision may depend heavily on how an individual patient values life with a particular disability," yet also potentially irrational: "Many patients value the present much more than they value the future" (38). This "time preference" can be mitigated by making a detailed decision tree: "A decision tree does not merely represent an overview of the problem: rather, it tells us what we should do" (38). As for the second instance of patient input, it concerns class variables: "patients bear different economic burdens for their illness" (86), and it doesn't have anything to do with their participation in treatment decisions. Doctors use the notion of "evidence-based" practice to validate their interventions in texts like these. In the process, doctors silence pregnant women and other patients; whether this is conscious or not is unclear and perhaps irrelevant. Additionally, according to Davis-Floyd and St. John (1998) as well as midwives and midwifery students who participated in our research, doctors may not credit evidence if their presuppositions predispose them against it. "A plethora of studies showing the benefits of various alternative therapies have been successfully completed under appropriate research conditions; the results are ignored if they do not support current prejudice" (Davis-Floyd and St. John 1998: 251). Midwives, on paper and in interviews, claim to value women's voices, needs, and desires. Midwives also advocate "evidence-based" practice, yet they do so primarily in the service of noninterventionism.

Decisions don't really grow on trees. A few of our participants portrayed knowledge and evidence as themselves questionable subjects, as Mel Sallinger did when she offered her dance metaphor to characterize the dynamics between midwives and clients. Dina Wolf, a student in her final term at SMS, presented the strong reliance of midwives and midwifery-educators on evidence-based practice as flawed:

One of the things that I think is problematic about the education that I've gotten ... is ... this kind of hypervaluing of evidence — as in evidence that's in the medical journals ... [and] the nursing journals. You know, really seeing ... the randomized clinical trials as the be-all and end-all. ... And I think that's really problematic. I think there's a lot that midwives do and that midwives have done for centuries that is safe and effective and just, you know, doesn't lend itself well to randomized clinical trials.

Wolf tells how midwifery students are taught to treat evidence — and education based on evidence — as the basis for their clients' choices. But, in her words, "It's just bullshit to even think that you can somehow present this stuff neutrally. Why not own up to your biases?" Midwives, in Wolf's view, ought not emulate the so-called scientific disinterested stance of obstetricians. Informed choice based on the evidence a midwife has to offer in an exchange characterized as a neutral education process was endorsed by almost everyone in our sample who brought it up, except for Wolf and Sallinger, who interrogated it.

Spiritual Midwifery

Nearly universal among the midwives and midwifery students we interviewed was a valuing of the spiritual aspect of birth. This was most pronounced in the narratives of home birth midwives, as in this discussion among advanced students at the FSTM:

Jeri Stockton: That kind of unexplainable spiritual fear, like the fear you're supposed to have of God — not fear like *fear* fear, but that *reverence* of birth. ... We're just *assisting* a miracle. It's not like we're delivering a baby, you know. ... And I think that's it also: that it's a *whole* experience. ... You don't know exactly how it all works. You think you've figured it out. But it just happens. It just *is*. Like the universe. You have to accept that there are planets out there that we can't see with our naked eye, and that there are stars, and you just — there are certain things in life that you have to accept, and birth is one of them. And sometimes things just go wrong, or — I don't even know if it's "go wrong" — sometimes things happen for whatever reasons. They just happen. But birth is just ... a process of life. ...

Hannah Conrad: ... I think of it as sex magic. That there's just — that there's this altered consciousness of birth, sex, and death. And you're talking about a big cosmic energy that is fierce and painful and pleasurable. And it's serious. ... That stuff is *scary*. And — but it's essential. ... And because of this great fear we have of it, it seems really natural, you know, to try to control it. The fact that you label it, and you label it with all of these names — people's names — you know, Mr. Kegel! Or whoever. [They laugh.] ... But we just lose *so* much if we try to tame it. That to be able to take birth into the home and let it be all of those things — let it be whatever it's going to be — is just enriching to all of the parts of your life — to birth, sex, and death, if you can just ride that uncertainty and let it bring all the gifts that it's going to bring.

Next, this conversation moved into how other cultures recognize the awesome spiritual potential of birth, and how U.S. medicalized culture seems particularly thorough in its denial of the potential for depth or wonder in the experience. Birth in hospitals, as Conrad thinks of them, is stripped of its beautiful potential, desexualized, hermetically sealed in a prepackaged format, and made into pathology-waiting-to-happen or pain in need of anesthesia.

Many midwives (especially, but not only, home birth midwives and midwifery students) see their work as honoring the spiritual aspects of birth and facilitating situations in which women can feel empowered through their experiences. Midwives feel that being attuned to modes of personal style and dynamics of interpersonal relations enabled them to work toward these goals. As with doctors, they described themselves as adaptable in their relationships with clients; but with clients they strive for a reciprocal relationship rather than deal with unbalanced power relations. They watch over, tend to, and learn from their work with women.

On Technology

Renie Daley described a program she was running at the public hospital where she worked that was designed to "empower" young pregnant women through a "feminist model of care," which she believed was something only midwives were able to do:

> I don't think very many doctors can do this. We take off our lab coats. We sit, equal, in a circle with women. We share our lives and our experiences with them. We demystify, through information, what is happening to them, and what the risk-assessment part of pregnancy is, so that they take their own blood pressures; they take their own weights. They graph their own weights; they monitor their own weight gains and they have their goals for their weight gains and what they're supposed to be doing about that, and where they're supposed to be going. They calculate their own weeks of pregnancy. They are like *powerful* women. And they act different when they come to the hospital.

In this program, young women are given responsibility for collecting medical evidence on themselves. This strategy, having women learn to use and then take responsibility for procedures that typically are done *to* them, harkens back to the women's health movement. It does matter who does what to whom and how; when you do something yourself, it demystifies — and to a certain extent demedicalizes — that procedure. Daley describes how an implicit critique of medical interactions results in a better way, yet medical processes for monitoring pregnancy remain unquestioned. Ironically, this demystification process also includes reification of the obstetric norm that prenatal care is an ongoing process of risk assessment (where weight gain and blood pressure represent the risk of toxemia). The midwives working in this prenatal program for young women don't teach them to question the evidence itself as the primary valid representation of health in pregnancy or to value equally how they themselves feel, as some more radical midwives might. For instance, Aviva Romm questions the focus on weight in prenatal care:

> Weighing pregnant women has become a ritual in this culture, and one that I think we could easily do without. Lack of weight gain in a pregnant woman is readily apparent to anyone with a bit of experience in the

area, and a "good" weight gain does not ensure proper nutrition. Therefore, much more emphasis ought to be placed on dietary assessment and
improving nutrition. In my practice a woman can tell me her weight if
she wants to, but I do not have women routinely weigh at prenatals, and
I encourage women not to watch the scale at home either. (1998: 50)

Monitoring pregnant women's weight is the tip of the iceberg when
it comes to technologies now conventionally used to size women up
during pregnancy and birth.

When Barbara did her research on midwives doing home birth in
New York City in the 1970s, prenatal testing was primarily comprised
of weighing, blood pressure checking, and urine testing. Since then,
tests during pregnancy have proliferated: sonograms have become
nearly a universal feature of midpregnancy; maternal serum screening tests are routinely offered to pregnant women; amniocentesis is
offered to women 35 and older; continuous electronic fetal monitoring (EFM) has become nearly universal in U.S. hospitals despite
conclusive evidence showing it to be an ineffective indicator of fetal
distress (and one cause of the increase in the c-section rate). Several
scholars have applied Foucault's (1977) theorizing on surveillance
and power to these technological changes (e.g., Armstrong 1995,
Arney 1982, Cheek and Rudge 1994, Sandelowski 2000). Foucault's
panopticon analogy seems particularly apt here. Prisoners in pan-
opticon-prisons can always be seen by (but cannot necessarily see)
guards; they learn to internalize institutionally required behavioral
norms as a result of knowing they can always be watched. The rise in
central monitoring of laboring women means they are observed from
nurses' stations, reduced to tracings of uterine contractions and fetal
heart rates. IV medications and fluids drip themselves into veins,
blood pressure cuffs self-activate, and above all, the clock ticks, and
calculations of whether or not labor meets institutional protocols are
continually produced. Although what motivated feminist scholar-
ship about obstetric practices in the 1970s has changed — women
are no longer knocked out with scopolamine and strapped to their
beds to "be delivered of" their babies in a state of amnesiac unconsciousness — the mechanisms of control have shifted but have not
been eliminated. As a result of this shift in surveillance surgical

interventions have increased dramatically; yet because of its near-invisibility and ubiquity, there has been no great consumer outcry against it as an agent of social control.

How do midwives, whose whole philosophy rests on the notion that birth is "natural," "normal," and in need of intervention in only rare cases, deal with this plethora of "choices" routinized into obstetrics as standard practice, and represented in the culture as safe ways to control outcomes (ranging from identifying fetal "defects" to eliminating pain in labor)? I was especially interested in how midwives would discuss technological issues, because along with their noninterventionist and naturalistic stances, they also promote the idea that midwives should support women in their decision making rather than impose their views on clients. They object to paternalism and authority-wielding expertise. So what do they think about — and what do they do about — women making choices of which they disapprove?

The majority of the midwives we interviewed feel that intervention without cause is unjustified and regrettable, yet for the most part, they tried to avoid making negative judgments about clients' decision-making in favor of interventions. Midwives who practice outside of hospitals are able to avoid interventions in labor for the most part and to refer women out for interventions in pregnancy. Nurse-midwives often describe their work as a balancing act, with medicine and technology on one side and pure principles of midwifery on the other. As in their dealings with doctors and hospital rules, they tell about learning which battles to fight and which to let go. They describe compromise and they describe resistance.

Here is where the caveats about clients come into play. Many midwives believe that women who make what they consider to be bad choices are not aware of the issues (not given full information), do not understand the issues (don't even know they should ask for it), and are, in short, misguided. Renie Daley describes the reasons why women "choose" interventions in pregnancy and labor:

> The technology's there. A certain number of women, probably a pretty high proportion of women think they need it. They don't trust themselves. They think they need all that stuff. They want it. They want the AFP test to tell 'em their baby doesn't have an open spinal cord. They

want that test. Okay? And they're willing to take the risk of being over-diagnosed. They're willing to take the risk of being told, "Well, your baby may have an open spinal cord, now we want to stick a needle in you and take some amniotic fluid out." I don't *think* so! Not for me, person-ally! So women want it. There's definitely a drive. They want epidurals. They want ultrasounds — desperately. They want to know the sex of their babies. They want these things. So it's partially driven by — well, the technology's there. And then the women want the technology. ... They also don't know the risks. And it's just the social thing to do. I mean, you know, if you don't know the sex of your baby, like you can't even have a baby shower!

Daley portrays desire for technological assessments as evidence of false consciousness, reassuring only because women "don't trust themselves" in the first place. The prevalent acceptance of the technology works as an enticement; it takes on a life of its own. Because of this cultural technophilia, women view their bodies as untrustworthy and in need of medical monitoring, and significant others in their lives may reinforce this view by pressuring them to accept interventions. (See Franklin 1995 for an analysis of this phenomenon of bodily mistrust as it relates to assisted reproductive technologies.) While she clearly sees the ruse of prenatal testing as problematic and even silly, Daley didn't feel she could fight it. Mel Sallinger concurred, describing her helplessness in the face of blind acceptance of technological interventionism:

One of the things that I despise most about what's happened to this whole field in the last ten years is the advent of testing for things that we can do nothing about, and the acceptance of this by the medical community, some parts of the midwifery community, and the public. You know, AFP testing to me is absolutely ridiculous. It's not defini-tive. It doesn't tell you, for sure, anything. It's wrong frequently [has a very high false positive rate], and it creates this tremendous level of anxiety in women that I don't think they ever get rid of after ... a nega-tive result. ... I don't know how you get away from doing it or at least offering it in today's environment in the United States. I don't think that nurse-midwives have a *choice* about that. ... So, I really wish that stuff wasn't there. I wish it didn't *exist* because I don't think it's helpful. And I wish it hadn't been promoted the way it's been promoted because people think they're going to know that they have a baby that's fine. And you *never* know. … There are no guarantees in this world that our children are going to be fine. … It's an attitude in our culture about being able to fix everything, and about being able to predict what's going to happen, that's out of control. I think it's totally out of control!

Sallinger next shifted into a technology caveat, telling me how medical technology probably saved her life and her son's life when she had a c-section, and how it also could improve lives (she gave her husband's vision as an example of a medical triumph). Then she lambasted the calculation of gestational age by sonogram, and the routine use of EFM and the cascade effect produced by it. Even midwives who offer scathing critiques of medicine's technophilia maintain that what's bothersome is not the technology itself but the presumption of its universal beneficence.

Midwives and midwifery students said they were "for" technology and medical interventions "when necessary." They offered this caveat to show that they don't oppose technology and innovation because they know they are stereotyped as rejecting it unreasonably. They dislike being portrayed as irrationally censorious. They focus on critiquing the overuse of technology, and the impersonal alienating consequences or false sense of security that technology may generate. They are not Luddites, but most do view the substitution of machinery for hands-on treatment as bad for clients, and they want to convey an unwillingness simply to accept it as good because it produces data.

Margaret MacDonald and Ivy Bourgeault write retrospectively about their study of midwifery in Ontario that "I did not frame the changing relationship of midwifery to medical technology … as a cautionary tale. Rather, I suggest that midwifery is making room for technology, the meaning of natural birth is being redefined by the pragmatic — but not necessary apolitical — choices of midwives and birthing women to include some medical technology" (2000: 161). Midwives have no choice but to make room for medical technology. But they still resist the power dynamics implicit in accepting technology as the answer to any question that arises in pregnancy and birth. In contrast to MacDonald's assessment of midwives as willingly accommodating technology, those who participated in our study expressed a begrudging and helpless acceptance. Technology "has a place," they felt, but it won't ever be in its rightful place in our medicalized, technocratic culture.

On Pain

Quite a lot of intervention could be avoided were it not for the focus on birth as pain and only pain. Arguing for the value of pain in a quick-fix-seeking culture is a challenge. Midwives utilize athletic metaphors for the contractions and pushing involved in labor: this is a physical feat that can teach you that you can surpass what may feel like limits, or what certainly will feel "challenging" in a new way. They liken giving birth to climbing a mountain or running a marathon, and they tout the psychological benefits of getting through this experience as resulting in a sense of empowerment that can change the way you see yourself and confront challenges throughout life. Does pain relief in labor always mean a loss of empowerment? Or is pain relief simply less ideal to midwives because it can produce a cascade effect of interventions and because it introduces new risks?

How do midwives deal with the ironic contradiction presented by women who feel empowered to make choices that midwives see as disempowering, such as choosing an epidural? Midwives do not frame the issue explicitly in this manner, yet they do make occasional disparaging or frustrated remarks about women who get epidurals and then do their nails or watch television while they're in labor. As Elaine Jacobs, a nurse-midwife who runs a birth center, said about women giving birth in hospitals: "Yes, they're out of pain, and they're all just lying there and they're watching television." Such remarks give voice to the notion that women are somehow violating the sanctity of the birth experience, doing passive or trivial activities that demonstrate they don't fully appreciate the momentous occurrence birth represents (to midwives, at least). This is not a choice midwives want women to make, but one with which they must come to terms if they work in hospitals.

Julie Blum described the disillusionment she has experienced on the job:

I really wanted to make it an empowering experience for a woman and her family. And all my idealism sort of has gotten *smacked* in practice. … Number one, a lot of women don't want that kind of birth. They want all the drugs that they can have to numb the experience as fast as they can and they're not motivated *at all* to try *anything* like the bathtub or backrubs or anything. So I have to honor their needs. That's still okay.

Women's desire for pain relief means Blum cannot put her idealism into practice. Her half-hearted endorsement of this situation rings false. On top of women's desire "to numb the experience," Blum tells about doctors pressuring her to speed up births, with their eyes on the clock, urging her to intervene.

Most midwives would like women to embrace the joy, power, and spirituality they believe the birth experience makes possible, and they have difficulty endorsing clients' deliberate avoidance of what they see as wonderfully and essentially awesome, there for the experiencing. But nurse-midwives do resign themselves to taking part in births where what they see as rightful goals may never play a part for the women they serve.

Carrie Ward, another nurse-midwife, described a greater sense of reconciliation with women's desire for pain relief in labor:

My mission is to try and get 'em what they want. If they want to have pain control in labor, have at it! For me to try and dissuade them from what *they* want when it's available for others at [this hospital], I feel like is a disservice to them. And I think that the vast majority of my clients have no conception of the benefits of not having any pain medication. But I don't think they'd *get* it. You know, it's not — it's not part of their understanding of life or birth. So there are a few who *want* that … but usually they want it because they're afraid of an epidural or you know, some other reason, not because "it's better for the baby and I want to be in control and I want to experience this and I want to feel the *power*, the *glory* of giving birth. And watching my body do its thing." … I'm at [this hospital] to help these women have the best experience they can have. And it doesn't usually include being really empowered by the birth experience. That's not part of what they want. You can't force empowerment in that way on people! [She laughs.] And I don't want to.

Ward claims first that to try to persuade women to have unmedicated labors would be a "disservice to them," even though she clearly thinks "control," "empowerment," and enhancing the babies' health are more likely without medication. She has apparently given up on her clients' capability to understand any of this in the face of the general mindset that pain relief is vital, and she judges even the introduction of the subject on her part to be an unwanted and manipulative strategy.

Midwives' ambivalence about what they see as misinformed choices clients make reminds me of the evaluations abortion workers offer of their clients' decision making in choosing abortion (Simonds 1996). Abortion, they believe — as midwives believe about birth — should not be undertaken lightly. While I would argue that a woman who doesn't get upset about her abortion is emotionally healthy, I'm not so sure I would make the same argument about a woman who does her nails or watches television in labor — a woman for whom, as for the hypothetical aborting woman, the outcome is all that matters and who just wants to get it over with.

Alicia Fernandez described widespread ignorance about nonmedicalized options in birth but sounded more hopeful about midwives working to change this view than did Julie Blum or Carrie Ward:

It's really amazing how society as a whole has been kind of brainwashed and it's like, it's a large picture here that we're struggling with. ... It goes *beyond* the medical model. It's the social, economical model of our society these days. Women, they consider that the norm. Because their generation, and the previous generation, that's what they have *known*, I mean the generation that really delivers back at home has been pretty much gone. And we have pretty much the hospital generation, you know, their offspring, and they expect that. I have a lot of patients who think that a c-section is *normal*, you know, or that *request* it, you know, don't want to try labor, you know, don't understand the risk involved because they haven't been *educated* just basically of the risk involved of cesarean sections, how dangerous it can be. They haven't been given *choice* a lot in the past in the medical model. And I believe that's what midwives, certified nurse-midwives, bring to the medical arena. We bring *choice*. We bring

information. We bring consent, informed consent, to the women, so
that they can have the power to choose, and to carry birth differently.

Fernandez describes her work as successful windmill tilting against
the prevalent values of society, not only the medical model. As she
sees it, capitalism and bureaucracy together cement an institutional
health care system in which profit motive, impersonality, quality control, and a lack of autonomy prevail — especially for those with little
status, like the poor minority women whom she served. She was very
optimistic about her ability to fight, and to feel that she would win
at least by exposing women having hospital births to the alternative
values of midwifery.

All the participants in our research judged pain and noninterven-
tive birth to be worthwhile goals — learning experiences, challenges
women would benefit from facing — but none insisted that clients
accept her view. They hoped that the education and information they
provide will make a difference in people's perceptions of what birth
could mean, but often settled on less profound goals than the achievement of power and glory.

In a focus group interview at FSTM, participants including nurse-
midwives, direct-entry midwives, and midwifery activists framed
women's choices of (or lack of protest about) interventions in labor as
historically specific and culturally produced:

Jessie Harris (activist and school director): C-section rates *are not better*
[than in the 1970s]. Episiotomy rates and now epidural rates
— they're sky high.

Celeste Waters (direct-entry midwife and RN): But you know what?
They don't care. The women don't care. It's a different group
of women.

Mona Pickett (nurse-midwife): But they don't know that they're *not*
getting the chance for empowerment.

Waters: I don't think — I don't think it's an issue. I really don't. ...

Pickett: But they don't know that they're giving something up. They
don't know that it's a rite of passage kind of thing. ... You
know, it's not a *real* informed choice.

Liz Jeffords (direct-entry midwife and activist): ... Sometimes I think that maybe they're not as disempowered as my generation was. When I found out how disempowered I was, I was *pissed*! [They laugh.] You know, and now I look at my daughters, and I don't think that they're as disempowered. [They laugh.] ...

Shelley Greenman (activist): I think it's a matter of degree, too. I know when we were first having babies twenty-something years ago, you had to be *put out*. You know, and then it was like, well, are you gonna be awake to see your baby or are you gonna be asleep and wonder what you had? Now, I think, it's all so subtle.

Deanna Gallagher (activist and clinical administrator of the school): Right.

Greenman: You know, that, well, you can have an epidural, you can be awake, you won't feel anything.

Gallagher: They have *walking* epidurals now.

Greenman: Yeah. And so the choices are subtle and it's hard, like to really give good excuses to people who don't want to feel pain, who aren't into really exploring themselves in that way. So, you know, it's a much more subtle issue.

Choosing home birth when many of these women did, in the 1970s, was, as they saw it, a political choice because the mainstream option was so horrendous and degrading to women. They understood hospital birth as part and parcel of patriarchal domination. But at that time, most women did not challenge medical norms. Now, as Shelley Greenman commented, "the choices are subtle": hospitals are no longer overtly barbaric, nor are obstetrical norms overtly misogynistic. Medicine has "lightened up" over the years, making changes in response to consumer demands, and also co-opting the rhetoric of choice popularized by the women's health movement. Thus, childbearing women choosing birth attendants can feel they are exercising consumer choice, without ever conceptualizing birth issues as political power plays, even as the c-section rate climbs steadily toward an unprecedented high of 30%.

Birth Places

Home birth midwives confront technophilia and blind trust in medicine much less directly and less often than nurse-midwives do, but these still constrain their work. These are the midwives who have the greatest chance of realizing their ideals in practice. But with transport rates (ending up moving to the hospital during a woman's labor) ranging from 5% to 20% of women who plan home births, and with some clients wanting prenatal testing, they sometimes end up sharing women's medical encounters in some way.

Regardless of whether they first attend births at home or in hospitals, direct-entry midwives and midwifery students at SMS and FSTM find that their experiences of home birth make them reconceptualize hospital birth negatively. Many do rotations in hospitals as part of their training or have experience as labor and delivery nurses or as doulas. In one of the SMS student focus group interviews, students compared their experiences of home and hospital birth as they sought to articulate the differences:

Allie Cornell: I've found that the difference between the home and hospital birth is much more profound in the States than in other places. And I've seen hospital births, like I was at [a public hospital in Atlanta] actually. It was my first birth. And it was pretty — I mean, the midwives were wonderful, and I cried. It was a wonderful experience. ... And then in Holland, I saw my first home birth, and was, of course, completely blown away with the difference that it was just a completely different world in terms of it being the woman's environment. The woman's in charge. The woman's the most comfortable she can possibly be. The midwife is the guest. But if you have a woman give birth in the hospital there [Holland], it's almost the same. It's not like you become a prisoner of the hospital who's completely given over all power. You're just — you're now in a slightly different setting. Your midwife is still your primary attendant. And you're still calling the shots. And you go home an hour or two after the birth. I mean, it wasn't this wholly different thing. ... I still felt a difference, but I wondered how much of it was our way of doing hospital birth, rather than *just* the location.

Paula Daniels: Hmm. I've only seen two different births in two different hospitals. And I guess major things I noticed that disturbed me ... [were] just watching how the focus was on the [EFM] machine ... the nurses come in, look at the strip, and since I was a student nurse for one of them, she's like, "Get the blood pressure!" So I'd get her vital signs and then I'd write 'em down, and the nurse left the room. I was like, this is really disturbing. First of all, she never even really looked at the woman. She looked at the machine. ... I feel like at least in this country, the hospital tends to take your power away. And your — any sense of self-confidence and any sense of — I mean, you're just completely vulnerable. You're in a robe that isn't yours, that's been worn by hundreds of other people before you. You're just in this totally sterile situation, and ... if it's a teaching hospital — there's people in and out you've never seen before, never will see again. Medical students catching your baby. It's just total craziness. And at home, in a home birth setting ... it's your house and you've invited these people in to help you with your process, and it's *your* process.

Ruth Russell: I want to say one other thing, which is about the actual birth of the baby and after that. That there is a *tremendous* difference in my experience. That at home, the baby's born, there's a respect for this sacred moment and time afterwards. And the family is seen as the — *the* unit — that's the whole focus, is the baby and those parents having their time. And that the midwife is monitoring quietly, but you know, doing what she needs to do to make sure that everything's okay, but that isn't the focus. Whereas in the hospital that I worked in, the baby was taken *right away* to the warmer, and the mother could only look from across the room at her baby. And that's the difference of night and day! That moment is taken away from her that she has worked so hard for.

Echoing the focus on the spiritual quality of birth (discussed earlier), these students contrasted hospital staff's professional indifference with the reverence and unobtrusiveness of midwifery. They depicted hospital routines as routinizing, dehumanizing, and mundane — and as ultimately depriving women of real, true, wonderful birth experiences. The group agreed that hospital births don't have to be this way (as in Cornell's example of the hospital births she observed in the Netherlands), but that U.S. hospitals were unlikely ever to offer women the control over their births they could have at home.

Shana Hess, a faculty member who also trained at SMS, described the difference between home birth and hospital birth in similar terms:

> I think the … differences between the hospital experience here and the out-of-hospital experience here are, you know, very distinct. You know, the technology is always right there. It's pretty much used. Continuous electronic fetal monitoring. Women on their backs. Epidurals … In my training there were two hospital births that were unmedicated, and they went really fast, so there was really no time [laughing]. And actually, these two women didn't want an epidural if they could at all avoid it. … And they did. But all the rest, you know, epidural at what? — three centimeters. Lot of forceps, vacuum extraction, c-section deliveries. No continuity of care whatsoever. You know, we could go through *four* nurses, four shift changes if we were there long enough. I could go on and on. [She laughs.]
>
> And of course the home births … the midwife starts, the midwife finishes. People are comfortable in their own homes. If we need to transport, the midwife goes with them as an advocate, you know, even in situations where it's *clear* that we need to do a c-section, the midwife is still there for the client. When she [the client] goes home, she gets a visit from the midwife at home. She continues postpartum care with the midwife. The midwife does her three-week as well as her, you know, last postpartum check-up. And relationships develop. I think that's a really big key is that, you know, a lot of time these women become *friends*. … It's about relationships. It's not that I want to be best friends with any of my clients, I don't think that's the goal. But it's the kind of care that sort of *develops*, you know, fosters that kind of relationship not intentionally, but just by design. And I think the women are better for it. You

know, they feel like they're supported. They have their needs listened to, addressed.

Most obstetric and nurse-midwifery group practices (and most practices today are group practices) at best offer women the opportunity to meet all the providers who work together in the group. Meeting people once or twice is not the same as knowing them. Knowing someone, midwives repeatedly say, means one is more likely to trust that person and to feel safe with her. Home birth best exemplifies this ethic of "continuity of care." Home birth midwives describe presence through unobtrustiveness: there is something so forceful about *not* taking charge, and simply representing the values that can make someone else who believes in them too feel safe and protected. This is very different from medical paternalism. It is truly, as Shana Hess said, about relationships, about feeling connected with others while you feel most vulnerable, during what could be a potentially very isolating event.

Many home birth midwives and other advocates of home birth feel that moving birth into an alien environment staffed primarily or exclusively by strangers exacerbates the very slow-downs and pathologies in labor that medicine seeks to "correct." As Evelyn Carter, a midwife on The Farm with a nursing degree, said, "I saw more cases of meconium in a year and a half in the hospital than I did in twenty years on The Farm." Meconium, the baby's first bowel movement, when produced before birth signals environmental stress on the part of the birthing woman, Carter felt.

In her book, *Giving Birth: A Journey into the World of Mothers and Midwives* (2002), Catherine Taylor cites one home birth midwife who says: "So many times when I go to a hospital birth I feel like a passive witness to violence, and it's a very hard thing to see. I can't imagine why women would want that" (228). No one we interviewed was quite so forthright about hospitals as malevolent birth places, but we heard repeatedly how, especially for home birth midwives, taking part in hospital births means adapting to an institutionalized setting organized in ways they find philosophically alien. As Serena Davis said:

> Whether these protocols are always necessary or not — you have to fit into them. And sometimes when we see that some of the protocols are

just absolutely ridiculous — I'm not going to — you know, I'm not going
to say you have to *fight*. But, you know, because a lot of the people that
are in the hospital are very territorial and they — sometimes they build
up an attitude or a shield around themselves. ... You don't have to do
[that] at home, you know! One of the nice things about ... having your
baby at home is that you can labor how you want to, you can give birth
how you want to. And what I mean by "how you want to" is basically
what's the most effective for the mother. ... Sometimes, when you're in
the hospital, they don't want you to walk around, they don't want you
to walk outside the bedroom. It's just a lot more rules, more regimens
there. ... In the hospital, they don't want you to deliver in any position:
they want to be able to see, so they can manage. And that's what happens in hospitals: births are managed by machines, by people, by drugs;
whereas at home, it's not being managed by anybody, you know, just the
... the natural flow of the body.

Davis starts out by talking about how it's difficult for *her* in the hospital,
but when she moves into discussing home birth, she shifts from talking about how she feels different at a home birth to talking about how
the birthing woman ("you") experiences the birth. Home birth midwives are especially identified with the women they work with, both
in a personal, idiosyncratic way via the friendships that are formed and
in a kind of womanly solidarity based upon a shared view of birth. In
hospitals, women may feel a connection with staff, and staff may seek
to connect with them, but everyone is subject to obeying institutional
protocols. Even though most births follow the same general course of
events, from contractions to pushing a baby out, home births are deroutinized. They are deroutinized mainly because they take place one at a
time, but also because the overriding philosophy, the general sensibility
of everyone involved, is that they should *not* be routinized.

Alona Golden told the story of a recent transport experience she
had had with a woman who was "not making good progress at all" at
home, was anxious, and then started to develop a fever. She offered
this story as an example of how different the hospital experience is
from home birth:

We got to the hospital. We sat in the waiting room for an hour. She
then was admitted by a nurse — I went in with her — who then took

a full case history. She then got interviewed by an obstetrician, who never looked at the chart, and asked all the same question that this *laboring* woman had just answered on this table in the triage room. She then got taken to ... the birthing room, where *another* attending nurse comes in and asks all the same questions again. ... They are just not paying attention. They're not checking what's already been done. So this woman is now answering the same round of questions *three* times.

We were in the birthing room for two hours. They put her on pitocin, and she had her baby within three hours of when we got to the hospital. ... Seven people in a two-hour period walked into that room and the first thing out of their mouths, before introducing themselves, before saying "hello," before saying "how are you?" they said "Do you want pain medication?" *Seven people!* ... Finally ... this one nurse [the seventh person] ... came up and said, "You're sure you don't want some pain medication, honey? I mean, you really don't have to deal with this." And I turned to the nurse and said, "Look, we are here to support her. You know, she doesn't need pain medication. I'm Epi," and I pointed to my apprentice, "and she's Dural, so you can just leave us be." And she said, real sassy, "What if Epi and Dural get tired?" and I pointed to her husband and said, "Well, his name is Demerol, so we are just fine." And she just looked at me.

For home birth midwives like Davis and Golden and their clients, birth in hospitals involves resistance against institutional norms, and the distinct possibility of being seen as bizarre for their oppositional view. But home birth midwives also emphasize that home birth is not "for everyone." They are careful not to speak in universals. They want every woman at least to have access to midwifery, but they realize that deinstitutionalizing birth would be impossible, given the entrenchment of obstetrics and the prevalence of medicalization.

For nurse-midwives, home birth is something they first (and often only) imagine against a backdrop of hospital birth. Except for the group of nurse-midwives doing home birth whom we interviewed in New York, most of the nurse-midwives and nurse-midwifery students we interviewed intended, expected, or did practice in hospital settings. Carolyn Alexander, a nurse-midwife who trained in the 1960s and established the first hospital-based nurse midwifery practice in her city, was perhaps the most medically inclined among the nurse-midwives we interviewed. Nevertheless, she saw reasons why home birth would be appealing to women:

> No matter how hard we try to make a room look like a homey room, whether it's a birth center, a hospital, or whatever, there are some women I suppose, I've heard, who still want to be in *their* house, in *their* bedrooms, with *their* things around. ... And we'll never be able to offset that. ... And so, that is a legitimate reason, I think, that some women really want a home birth. ... The other [reason] is that if you don't have a birth at home, then the woman does have to ... travel someplace. And that — depending upon what a hospital means or a birthing center means to her or to her family — that can be something that isn't the same as if you stay at home. So I think there are people that really want a home birth and are clear about it, and see differences, as much as we try really hard to make the setting very comfortable.

Alexander suggested that if hospitals could replicate a homelike environment that was in a convenient location, the desire for home birth could be answered by hospitals. And, indeed, this is what many hospitals have striven to provide. Perhaps if environments are homelike enough, people feel more at home. Yet it seems unlikely that hospitals will replicate woman-centered, noninterventionist "birth centers" — a happy compromise many nurse-midwives identified. You can make an institution more aesthetically gentle or luxurious than a conventional hospital room. You can put a tea cozy cover around the monitors. You can put oven mitts on the stirrups. You can domesticate the surroundings by hanging floral wallpaper and providing padded rocking chairs. But redecorating will not alter conventional power dynamics, as long as the precepts of obstetrical monitoring remain in place and the operating room is right down the hall from the labor and delivery room (LDR) "suites." Consider hotel rooms, which are certainly the model hospital redecorators emulate. I think people definitely sleep better and *feel* better in hotel rooms that are clean and comfortable rather than dingy or cramped, that have good beds, good ventilation, and so on. But imagine that they are strapped to a machine and confined to the bed while they're there; imagine strangers coming in and out of their rooms, calculating statistics about the adequacy of their behavior in the room; well, this would significantly affect their hotel stays. "Comfort" is part of what midwifery can offer, but not all. "Comfort" is part of what typical obstetrics doesn't do so well, but not the corrective, say, to a 29% c-section rate, or to the lack of personal connection and denial of patients' autonomy and dignity that often characterize hospital experiences.

Several home birth midwives we interviewed raised the humorous analogy of ordering a man to get an erection in a public setting to point out the absurdities of how birthing women are often bossed around and typically exposed in hospitals. Similarly, Ina May Gaskin (2003) describes an example used by midwife Lisa Goldstein in childbirth education classes to illustrate how difficult it can be to get one's body to perform under impersonal surveillance:

> First she shows them a fifty-dollar bill. Then she places a medium-sized stainless-steel bowl on the floor. ... She then offers that bill to the first man who comes forward and pees in the bowl in front of everyone. In all the years she has repeated this routine, she has never handed over that fifty dollars to anyone (Gaskin 2003: 174).

Most midwives agree that hospitals can produce inhibitions in a way that one's own environment will not.

Yet many of the nurse-midwives we interviewed felt they couldn't imagine doing home births themselves as midwives because the level of responsibility they would have for the well-being of women and babies would be too daunting. They couldn't imagine birth as a situation for which they would not be responsible as *managers* for producing good outcomes. And they showed their fear of birth, which home birth midwives accept and view as integral but not central to their work. Betsy Ettinger, for instance, recognized her uneasiness about home birth as a product of her training:

> I think I have too much medicine and medical background in me to be comfortable in a home birth. Now, I was comfortable in a birthing center, but I had the safety net of a medical center across the street. And I had some wonderful experiences in birthing centers — so beautiful — but I've had beautiful experiences in the hospital. And I guess — and

maybe this is my rationale — but I think the birth experience can be a good experience anyplace.

Many nurse-midwives portray birth centers as an ideal compromise between the unknown perils that could occur at home and the level of constraint of the medical model. Birth centers are more convenient for midwives, too, because they tend to employ larger groups of midwives who can be on call less often than they would be in a home birth practice. However, as we will discuss in more depth in our conclusion, because of malpractice insurance costs in the United States, birth centers are risky business ventures. Home birth midwives or nurse-midwives inclined toward home birth tend to see birth centers as a compromise that can be less than ideal.

In this excerpt from a focus group interview, Megan Wagner, Bella Clark, and Jeannie Nye are labor and delivery nurses in the midwifery program at CNEP. Kate Morrell, a direct-entry midwife, is the only member of her cohort who has attended home births. She worked for years as a direct-entry midwife before seeking a nursing degree. Traci Roeg never used her nursing degree but went straight into midwifery, and has observed a home birth. She hated nursing school and saw it only as a stepping stone to midwifery.

Megan Wagner: I think the whole concept of the litigious atmosphere of birth is a *huge* umbrella over the birth setting. I do. Right now, I think many people would love to practice in a home birth setting, but the litigation now and the legal concerns. … I just think it changes what some of us would like to do. We all — I think some of us will just be resigned to doing things that wouldn't be our first choice.

Bella Clark: As [for] starting out, I think I would be in a hospital setting because for me that would feel *safer* as a beginning practitioner. And — or even a birth center. But I would think the more I'd seen, the more experience I had, that would quite possibly change.

Jeannie Nye [to Kate Morrell]: What do you think, coming from the other side?

Kate Morrell: I don't know. ... It changes as I go along. ... I started out in the home birth setting, and pretty naively, actually. I didn't — we just didn't think much about litigation and we didn't really need to because our clients loved us, and they were taking full responsibility for their actions, and ... we had good outcomes. And then I went directly into city hospitals, and that was, you know, from one end to the other of the pendulum. And now I'm kind of coming back the other direction and I suspect that if my practice, if my home site works out, then I may be delivering in a small, a little tiny hospital in my ... town. And as far as doing births at home again, I say I probably *won't*, but I don't know that I won't, because I really *love* it. I really love it on a deep level like your first love. ... It may not have been right for you, but, boy, you loved it! You know, so I can't say how I'll be. I can't say that I won't do home births. ...

I think it's a matter of comfort for the woman. She is on her *own* territory. She is on her *own* bed. The bed where she snuggles with her husband and her baby and her dogs and her cats — I mean, it's just her own *home* place. It's *her* nest. And everything sort of emanates from that. And so she just starts out in a totally supportive and nurturing environment. You don't have to start creating this nurturing environment [like] when she gets to the hospital, you know, trying to relax her. She starts out that way. ...

Traci Roeg: Even, you know, birth center feels like a hedge, a little bit to me at times. ... The first birth I ever saw was a home birth, and ... I *so* get what you're saying [to Morrell] about it's like the deep love. It's like the shining light for me... .

Morrell: It's on the current, and the current flows differently.

Roeg: Yeah. Yeah. And it's the *birth that made sense.* And it made sense because ... the woman was not inhibited. I mean, she was doing what she needed to do to birth that baby, and that could be anything.

Morrell: She could walk around naked if she wanted to.

Roeg: Exactly.

Morrell: She could go out in the back yard if she wanted to.

Roeg: Exactly.

Morrell: She could squat and pee in the bushes, or whatever she wanted to do.

Roeg: Exactly. And there — the lights can be low. The candles can be going. It just — it just *made sense* to me. It was really — I mean, I don't know how to describe it. Very deep, and very, very different.

Nye: I remember, who was it that said … they were at this birth and they felt like they were *invading* on the couple's intimacy, like they just needed to get the heck out of there — as if they really didn't belong there at all! [She laughs.] … And just, that's so true, 'cause that's what the home birth setting is. And we want to medicalize everything in our society and take that away.

Wagner: In the hospital, you walk into the room and the family members become part of the wall to try and get out of your way, which is such a shame that they feel like that.

The women start this discussion about home birth with the regrettable cautionary tale of malpractice risk as a deterrent to home birth practice, but they express an openness to considering home birth as they (Wagner and Clark) gain experience as midwives. But the conversation shifts when Morrell talks about the way it feels to do home birth and becomes a tribute to freedom that isn't possible or permissible in other environments. Then they come full circle, finally, and end up criticizing the societal constraints that keep midwifery from being more culturally and situationally diffuse and that rob births in institutions of their spiritually illuminating beauty. The situation, as they portray it, is hardly one of boundless choice for women or midwives.

The Rhetoric of Choice

"Choice" language is a variant of "rights" language, culminating in the "right to choose." Justice, as Dorothy Roberts has pointed out in *Killing the Black Body: Race, Reproduction, and the Meaning of Liberty* (1997), carries little weight in the United States, but liberty — a freedom *to* rather than a freedom *from* — is highly valued. Supposedly, it's a free country: people have the right to live where, how, and with whom they choose. Everything a person does is understood as an individual decision; in America, a life is believed to reflect a unique collection of choices.

The value of "choice" was not invented by abortion rights activists, but at this point in time, almost anybody's discussion of almost anybody's right to choose anything will echo the abortion discussion. Framing abortion in terms of "choice" was probably one of the most brilliant rhetorical strategies yet devised in a public debate, at least as brilliant as the rhetorical language of "life." Any discussion of necessity, of need, would have fallen on deaf ears: lots of Americans are in desperate need, do not have many of life's necessities, and that's the way it goes. We see no groundswell of support for people's rights to have their needs met for social justice, in large part because of how deeply embedded the discourse of choice is in our culture. But in capitalist America, how can you argue with choice? It is only life itself that could be used as a justification for an anti-choice position: nothing else would hold up to the power of "choice" as an argument. For most Americans, "choice" and "life" sit in an uneasy balance in the abortion debate. "I wouldn't have an abortion," people say from the relative safety of not having a period that's two weeks late, "but I suppose it's a woman's right to make that choice."

Midwives use the language of "choice" as a rhetorical strategy to justify selecting midwives as caregivers or deciding on the "option" of home birth. Basically, their position is that whatever your procreative experiences, they should be what you choose. It's no one else's business. Yet there's also an irony in the midwifery community's use of "choice," because abortion is a potentially divisive issue within that community. There are midwives who are profoundly pro-choice, who have come to midwifery and their pro-choice positions out of the same commitment to women, out of a vision of feminism. For instance, Kate Morrell said, "I am pro-choice. There's just no other way of thinking for me." Traci Roeg and several other nurse-midwives or nurse-midwifery students imagined midwifery as ideally including an abortion provision: "I also really think of ideal midwifery practice as not just births, [but also as] well-woman GYN, as abortion, as contraceptive stuff — as women's health care."

In contrast, many midwives express profoundly anti-choice senti-
ments and have come to midwifery and their anti-choice position not
only out of a deeply held (usually orthodox religious) worldview, but
also out of a different sort of commitment to women *as* mothers (cf.
Luker 1984). Donna Parker, a home birth midwife, said:

> In my religion, first of all, abortion is murder. ... That's a real strong
> thing for me. ... You know, I've had somebody call me on the phone and
> say "I'm pregnant, can you give me some herbs so that I can abort the
> baby?" I say, "No." I won't even discuss it. You know, my role here is to
> bring a life, you know, a human baby into the world, not to destroy it.

Parker has been a long-term activist for midwifery, both at the local and
national level. She told how midwives strove not to let abortion divide
them as they worked together for legislative and political changes that
would legitimate home birth and support direct-entry midwifery:

> We laugh because there's so many different midwives and so many dif-
> ferent philosophies on stuff and you know. ... My bumper sticker'll say,
> "The Bible says Mary was with child and not tissue." And somebody
> else's will say, "Abortion: Your Choice," you know [she laughs]. And
> our vehicles are all driving along, and then we all get out and just have
> a good ol' time together and everybody looks at us like, "Oh, my gosh!"
> You know, midwifery makes strange bedfellows!

For midwives who oppose abortion, dedication to "choice" does not
extend to all procreative issues. Once pregnancy occurs, they support
procreative decision making about who, when, where, and how prenatal care and birth will occur — but not whether or not to continue
the pregnancy.

Most of the midwives and midwifery students we interviewed were
pro-choice, though many expressed ambivalence about abortion but
remained committed to women's being able to decide for themselves,
as these two comments indicate:

> *Serena Davis (home birth midwife):* I think that if women are taught at
> an early age to have a healthier attitude about their sexuality, that they
> would not find themselves up in abortion clinics, because abortions are
> not healthy. Not only are they not healthy physically, but it's not healthy

mentally, and it's not healthy emotionally, and it's not healthy spiritually. ... If a woman ... needs to have an abortion, I think that option should be given to her.

Keri Wright (CNEP student): It's a very personal decision, I probably, for myself, would not make that choice. However, I don't think it's my right to dictate to other women what they should do with their bodies and their lives. I don't know what's going on in their life at that moment. You know, every pregnancy, every experience, is different.

Midwives and midwifery students who were ambivalent about abortion nevertheless tended to agree that midwives would be better providers of abortion than gynecologists. Many also saw abortion as a contentious issue that could have a negative impact on the public image of midwifery should midwives decide to champion it as part of their scope of practice, and many appeared to be surprised when we asked them about their thoughts on abortion. SMS faculty members Molly Nelson and Lauren Adler, in contrast, saw their involvement in midwifery as emerging out of a dedication to abortion rights and from their experiences counseling women about abortion. They support the idea of midwives performing abortion:

Molly Nelson: I respect the fact that midwives are providers of abortion services in lots of communities around the world. ... Women come to them as resources because they understand a lot of herbal medicine and that they are healers and there with other women. ... Depending on the circumstances I think it would be a good skill to have, within certain guidelines.

Lauren Adler: Yeah, I agree. I mean I think that it's — it has to be in the context of the needs of the community. ... It's not a difficult skill and I think that we probably are going to find ourselves with a shortage of abortion providers if things keep going the way they have been going. ... In the United States, in many communities, access to abortion providers is nil. Women have to travel two hundred miles to find an abortion provider, so that's very concerning — *very*, very concerning. ... When *Roe v. Wade* was announced, I remember exactly where I was. I was thinking, "This is a moment

I will never forget, an important moment in my life and in the life of my daughters to be and my granddaughters." ... I, you know, will so passionately defend abortion rights and feel very, very, very strongly about that. And it is absolutely part of my midwifery worldview as a defender of women, protector of women.

As these midwives (and other midwives and midwifery students who supported abortion rights) see it, procreative choice includes every aspect of procreative behavior, and the availability of abortion and of home birth both are crucial matters of social justice in women's lives.

The Language of Love

The theme of "love" is not, strictly speaking, rhetoric at all: it is not intended to persuade. Love is a way of talking that is directed inward — a way that midwives can understand for themselves and explain to others what it is they do and why they do it. The significance of love as a theme in the talk of midwives emerged for us when I commented to Barbara that midwives kept talking about how they "love women," and that in all my years of hanging out with abortion workers and pro-choice activists, I could not recall hearing that kind of love-talk. Care-talk, justice-talk, yes; love-talk, no. Midwives' talk of love resonates with some of the language of radical feminism — especially what is now denounced as "cultural feminism" — where women's differences from men are essentialized as given and glorified as morally superior. Feminist rhetoric typically avoids the language of love exactly because this sort of discourse risks essentializing women and glorifying motherhood. Midwives do some of both, essentializing women and glorifying motherhood together.

Choice represents a rhetorical strategy that midwives have used, with some success, to legitimize their philosophy. Midwives are offering one more of the many choices today's women should have available to them. And yet choice hardly begins to capture what midwives think midwifery is about. Choice is a language of rationality; midwifery is about birth, which represents an other-than-rational side of life. As midwives see it, birth, like death, is an experience of the body and of the soul, far more than an intellectual exercise or a menu of choices. Working with women through this experience calls forth strong emotion in midwives, emotions they express via the language of love. Loving women, birth, or babies may explain why any given woman would want to become a midwife, but it serves no purpose in public debate. Compared to the rhetoric of choice, the language of love is a far less strategically successful way to promote midwifery or bring about any other social change. In a contested terrain, the language of love is pretty well useless.

And yet midwives do say it; they do feel it. What tends to draw most midwives into midwifery — and to keep them there despite the difficulties and challenges described here — is a love of women, of birth, of birthing women. (They may also love babies, but that is not necessarily the case.) And this love keeps their work meaningful:

Jeri Stockton (direct-entry student): You have to give yourself one hundred percent to them [clients]. You have to be completely open to that person. You have to leave your stuff at the door because it has no place in the birth. And as soon as you walk in that birth, you are there for that experience. … You have to be there to support the woman, and to empower — to help empower her, and to love her.

Alicia Fernandez (nurse-midwife): We're going to give better care in that setting [than doctors do]. … We're going to give TLC and love, and just be there with the woman.

Athena Cuthbert (nurse-midwife and birth center owner): The midwife is there just to support, love, nurture her. It's like a *mamatoto*. You're like a mommy, you know. And that's the ideal.

What does it mean when midwives say they "love" women? What is it that midwives see as essential, the core of "woman"? It is most assuredly not what is understood conventionally as "womanliness" or "femininity" in American culture. Nor do they love some fantasized, idealized woman or mother. Midwives do not claim that all women should be mothers, nor that motherhood is somehow the epitome of womanhood.

Midwives talk about the connection between mind and body, the importance of understanding the social and emotional life and connections of a woman in order to understand her body in birth. The relationship is ever a deeply embodied one; they do not deal with women on either a purely intellectual or purely emotional plane. Yet they do not reduce women to bodies only, as they see obstetrics doing.

While the language of choice positions the individual as "chooser" — an intellectual and emotional being making choices — the language of love goes in a different direction. What is at the core of birth, of life, is what it really means to be alive, to be human and animal: midwives do not see these as contradictory, but as central to who we are. A casual conversation with midwives can incorporate a discussion of piss, vomit, and shit: the body is present. Midwives are dealing with the non-plastic, non-consumerist, non-capitalist essence of what it really means to be alive, from the mundane to the exalted. What midwives love is quite different from "choice" in meaning: choice is about individualism, consumerism, capitalism. "Love" is about whatever is left when consumerism and the lot is taken away. "Love" is about what really matters, about "real" experience, not a manipulated, purchased, smoothed-over, wallpapered version of it. It is this "real" life experience that they love, the "real" in the woman, and in the "animal" act of birth.

Midwives invoke the discourse of choice to persuade others of the legitimacy of midwifery practice. Love, in contrast, is a way of talking within the midwifery community, of claiming legitimacy for themselves for activities — nurturing, caring, indeed, loving — that they know tend to be taken for granted, ignored, or denigrated in U.S. culture. Choice is a political rhetoric; love is a reason for engaging in that rhetoric.

Although choice is a useful strategy, it has profound limitations for midwives. A midwife has no right to practice without some woman's exercising her right to choose a midwife. "Choice" is the province of the individual birthing woman, not the midwife: it is the woman's choice that needs protection in a rights framework. Where does that leave midwives?

Midwives bemoan the fact that women do not know much about midwifery, that in this culture obstetrics is taken for granted as the standard of care and that it really doesn't offer women *care* at all. Midwives talk of women deserving to be "loved and nurtured" during their birth experiences. If women were "educated" properly and understood their choices, midwives believe, women would choose midwifery and loving birth attendants. When midwives talk of loving women, they also mean that they offer women a caring connection: women would not choose to give birth among strangers or near-strangers, midwives feel, if they knew how much better their birth experiences would be among caring friends. Midwives and midwifery students see their care as superior to that of doctors, yet not societally recognized for its superiority because of the ways in which "feminine" skills are culturally devalued rather than considered professional expertise.

Nurse-midwives were most dissatisfied with the conditions hampering ideal midwifery practice in hospitals and in the culture more generally. Participants often remarked on the unfairness of doctors making so much more money than they, or worse, about doctors employing midwives and profiting off their labor. Midwives resent the fact that their malpractice insurance rates were as high as those of doctors — impossibly expensive for most home birth midwives — because they are statistically much less likely to have suits brought against them. Though they complain about the conditions and ideology that created these financial realities, they accept that they can do little to change them.

Midwives experience providing loving care as rewarding, yet they know it can also be depleting. It wears them down and makes it almost inevitable that home birth midwives will struggle to earn a decent living. Hannah Madden, a faculty member at SMS, said:

> I feel like we have gotten ourselves in this country into a style of practice, particularly direct-entry midwives, where it's very difficult, I think, to do midwifery and have a healthy *life*, and have the kind of life we would hope for our clients. You know, a life that is balanced, that is not *guilt-ridden* or co-dependence-ridden, that is adequately supported, adequately compensated. … [That won't happen] until we can be reimbursed by insurance and *really* be reimbursed for our time. … When we do a birth, that means … being with the mom that whole time,

whatever chunk of time that needs to be. And that that is more valuable than walking in and catching a baby and leaving.

Still, most home birth midwives say it is worth it. They often sound proud not to be motivated by what they see as morally a shallow aim, greed:

Marnie Griffin: If somebody goes into midwifery for the money, they got the wrong idea!

Evelyn Carter: ...There's very few direct-entry midwives who looked around and said, "How could I make the most money!" You know! [They laugh.]

Griffin: I walked away from a birth one time with a bag of peanuts. That's what I was paid. And I was happy...

Carter: But yeah, we do births all the time that we know we'll probably never get paid for. But you also get you know, a whole lot in here [hand on heart, laughing].

Griffin: What you get in here [hand on heart also] is amazing.

These midwives, who are long-time residents on The Farm, began attending births in a nearby Amish community after the population of childbearing members of The Farm dwindled in the 1980s. Griffin went on to say:

What we've learned from the Amish ... I couldn't have gotten it anywhere else. I couldn't have learned it in a hospital. I couldn't have learned it in a birthing center. It's something that I could have only learned from that community. And it's valuable beyond explanation. And I wouldn't have given it up for anything. And my kids go to college. My kids go to college on scholarships. That's how they go to college. ... So, you know, when I hear people say they can't send their kids to college if they don't do this and this and this job, you know, there's other ways to figure it out.

Home-birth midwives and midwifery students who participated in our research unanimously voiced the sentiment that midwifery offers invaluable rewards to women and midwives themselves. The labor of midwifery is, quite simply, a labor of passionate love. Athena Cuthbert said:

Let's put it this way. I think it is a very difficult profession for one to choose, to get up 2:00 in the morning to go out there. ... You could never pay a woman to leave her husband in bed, cuddling or doing whatever she's doing, and "twing, twing!" or "beep! beep!" Delivery! Ahh! ... It's something that you love: to go and help someone, to see that she does it, and to help her do it as how she wants to do it.

Midwives believe that their stance of nurturance and outright love should be revered and emulated; that it is how health care should be given. But love is not the standard of care in obstetrics, and love is not what many women think about when choosing a birth attendant.

The connection between "love" and "choice" is the language of empowerment. Midwives want to see women empowered. What midwives love in women is that power, that elemental strength they believe is there in the woman-as-woman, profoundly present in her birthing capacity. Women, midwives feel, may have lost the power, lost the strength, don't know they have that capacity anymore. The cultural portrayal of birth, abetted by obstetrics, depicts it as risky and fearful, and interventions as protecting women against the overwhelming pain and providing control over the uncertainty. What medicine has taken away, midwives believe, is the fundamental knowledge that women can birth without interference, can show such roaring, screaming, overwhelming, engulfing power. Midwives see themselves as the restorative vehicles of women's elemental power: that's what they love.

Birth, to midwives, is not about informed choice with a shopping list of advantages and disadvantages for each possible procedure, drug, position for pushing, and so on. It is about reaching into the power within the woman to birth, to take her body and mind and soul to the limit of where it needs to go. And having done that, having birthed under her own power, with the force of her own strength, the woman knows — forever after — that she has that strength within her. That is what midwives mean by empowerment: not the right to exercise choice, but the power to touch the elemental.

As medical practices have changed over the years, in large part in response to the inroads of midwifery and out-of-hospital birth practice, the balance between love and choice has shifted for midwifery rhetoric. When the choice a birthing woman faced was between being abandoned in a dehumanized hospital or laboring at home among supportive friends and families, midwives felt the choice was clear. They had only to inform women of what they had to offer, and to prove its safety.

The choices a birthing woman is now offered may well include a hospital where she will be promised total pain relief *and* the companionship of friends and family. For middle-class women, at any rate, the ones with the greatest power to make choices, hospitals have become more respectful, potentially pleasant places in which to give birth. Simply offering a woman a "choice" may no longer be self-evidently sufficient. What midwives bring to women — the power, the joy, the spirituality of birth — have come to seem like abstractions. Love, midwives are learning, may not be what a woman chooses.

PART THREE
DISORGANIZED LABOR

5

WOMEN IN WHITE

Obstetricians and Labor-and-Delivery Nurses

WENDY SIMONDS

When I talk about the social construction of birth and the differences between midwifery and the medical model, inevitably someone — a student, a friend, a colleague — will offer up some version of this line of thinking: Why not just hire a *woman* obstetrician? Isn't this the best of both worlds? She would be "better" or "more" trained and thus "safer" than a midwife. Because doctors "know more" about safe birth, the argument continues, surely they have staged the safest conditions for birthing. These imagined women doctors will "understand" better than men doctors could what it means to be a woman in labor, especially if they have given birth themselves. This feminine empathy will soften the harshness of medicalized impersonality: they will be more attentive, more nurturant, and more personable than men doctors, because that's how women generally are. Besides, in hospitals with doctors, there will be the added bonus of *nurses*, women trained to take care of women in that caring, womanly way.

I have attempted to counter this culturally endorsed perspective with several arguments: women physicians are not necessarily less indoctrinated into or less accepting of the conventional power imbalances inherent in the medical model, where doctors are autocratic experts and patients submit; having a woman's body does not guarantee that a person will demonstrate interpersonal relational skills or special caring abilities; even a woman OB who has given birth herself may not necessarily understand the event as anything *other* than a medical event; OBs are not trained *better* or *more* but *differently* from midwives; medical practices in medical environments are correlated with increased, not decreased, morbidity for women and babies; nurses work under doctors and cannot demedicalize medicine even if they want to; and nurses spend much less time providing hands-on in-the-room care than they have in the past, and far more time applying and interpreting monitors and other equipment.

It doesn't matter much what I say or how I back it up. Most people are resistant to persuasion, undaunted even by copious statistics showing the superiority of midwife-attended and home births, not to mention by "soft" evidence of women's powerful and spiritual experiences of unconventional births. I suspect that a major reason people dismiss these arguments is that they know only women who have birthed in hospitals with obstetricians attending, so they think, "How bad could it *really* be?" And what a lot of trouble it must be to try a radically different way, when the weight of the culture is behind medicalization.

I hope that the words of midwives in preceding chapters and of doctors and nurses in this one will effectively illustrate the typical differences between — as well as occasional similarities among — the philosophies of the various birth attendants. In this chapter I draw upon interviews with ten women obstetricians and five women labor-and-delivery nurses. All of these participants were approached as potential participants because they were recommended by midwives or other doctor or nurse participants (who were themselves recommended by midwives). All espoused a positive view of nurse-midwifery, and all had worked with midwives in one way or another.

Obstetrical Decision Making and Outcomes

Eight of the ten doctors who participated in our research said they chose obstetrics and gynecology (OB-GYN) because they liked it best of their rotations in medical school, or because they already had a specific interest in women's health or wanted to work with women. Those who described their preference for OB-GYN recalled a kind of trial-and-error approach to specialty selection. For instance, Harriet Murphy said:

Well, I was attending medical school and I tried to make myself like dermatology and radiology because I thought the hours sounded good, and did an extra rotation in each one of those and didn't like it. Then we just had our regular rotations as junior medical students and I just liked it [OB-GYN] because it was ... a little oncology, a little medicine, and a little endocrinology, a little surgery, mostly healthy people — little of everything. Nice mix.

Murphy was originally concerned with identifying a specialty that would allow her to have a life outside of work ("good hours"), but OB-GYN provided a more interesting combination of activities than the less time-demanding specialties she considered. She recounts her choice as a rational decision-making process, which sounds devoid of the kind of passionate attraction or sense of calling so many of the midwives felt.

Some physicians recalled emotional as well as intellectual motivations for selecting obstetrics as a specialty. Corrine Wood-Daniels, for example, always thought she would become a pediatrician: "That's what I said all of my life. ... I thought that taking care of children would be a wonderful, noble, and gratifying thing to do." In medical school, though, she "was fascinated with learning about the functions of the female. And I thought that the whole reproductive process was just a miracle every time. It sort of held my interest." Nevertheless, she stuck with pediatrics and went to work in a clinic in a small town, and then in an intensive-care neonatal ward in a large city hospital. "It was like an emotional drain a lot of the time. I would just feel so — I don't know — sorry for the kids, the innocent children who were burdened with illnesses. Then I decided that I couldn't go throughout my career being sad and sort of mourning ... each person that I cared for." The emotional demands of pediatrics outweighed the emotional rewards. So Wood-Daniels switched to OB-GYN and found it less distressing, and thus far more personally satisfying. Labor and delivery "was the miracle that I expected it to be every single time. I think the high of delivery — the participating in the birth process with a couple who are really at their worst and their best all at the same time — it was just amazing to me, and it still is." Doctors *can* sound like midwives.

In contrast, Julie Elkmont entered medical school feeling predisposed toward choosing OB-GYN, but then, at first encounter, was turned off by it: "I always thought I wanted to do women — I thought I wanted to be an OB-GYN. And I was in medical school, and I didn't really like OB-GYN, so I was really bummed out." But no other specialty really struck her fancy either, so she gave OB-GYN another go, and this time she found that it did interest her: "I ended up going back and doing a fourth year elective in OB, and [then] I really, really liked it, so that sort of convinced me that that was where I needed to go." The second time around, she came to see the specialty as much more compelling than she had at first encounter: "I like taking care of women. I like the idea that you don't have to deal with chronic medical problems for fifty years — like hypertension, diabetes, and things like that. You get the really nice end-outcome usually, and you can see everyone yearly for their annual exams and stuff like that, but you don't normally have to deal with chronic medical problems." Like Murphy, Elkmont liked dealing with healthy patients. Lois Silverman said, similarly, "It's a field of medicine that's *happy* a lot of the time."

Mindy Fried saw OB-GYN as a way to express her feminist sensibility through her work: "I made my decision to become an MD, I think, in college. And a lot of that was feminist influence, you know, just unhappiness with the kind of care that we were getting from GYNs. So I went into med school thinking I would become an OB-GYN." Fried was the only doctor we interviewed who specifically attributed her professional decision-making to a political orientation that included a critique of the gender politics of conventional medical practices.

Laurie Leland said, "I really think that my decision was very emotionally based." She and Wood-Daniels were the only doctors to characterize their decision-making as other than intellectual; perhaps the others recounted their decisions as "rational" because medicine is generally a profession in which practitioners tend to pride themselves on being "objective" and "scientific." Leland's professional origin story resonates with those of several midwives who traced their professional leanings to adolescent experiences. As a teenager, Leland volunteered at a hospital:

Every time they called for a volunteer on labor and delivery I was the first one there. I just loved being around the babies, the new moms, and ... from about the time I was thirteen, I decided that that's what I wanted to do and never really changed my mind. ... I thought it was just an amazing process — the whole birth process — and I still feel that way, actually.

Leland didn't get to see any births during her volunteer work; she came in contact with patients, their families, and their new babies afterward. Like Wood-Daniels and many of the midwives, she found herself drawn to the intensity of birth experiences: "It just seemed like such an important event in somebody's life, that it would be fun to be a part of that."

Except for Fried and Leland, the obstetricians we interviewed described their choice of OB-GYN comparatively with other specialties by talking about it either in terms of a set of skills they enjoyed, and/or avoiding specialties that were certain to be more emotionally difficult, and/or the rewards it offered. Their talk demonstrates that they do not conceive of an ideal professional identity as involving emotional disengagement from patients; yet they did not sound quite as passionate as the midwives did when they described their paths to midwifery.

Andi Glass described OB-GYN as particularly gratifying to her because it enabled contact with patients across the life course, "so you develop relationships with people." In addition to the happy outcome of a baby, OB-GYNs enjoyed the generally positive results of gynecological surgery as compared with other surgical specialties. Glass said: "It's immensely gratifying to have someone present with a problem and be able to take care of it and a few months later, they're fine, and they no longer have that problem." Silverman liked the sense of closure that the birth of a baby brought about for her, describing how she felt "a sort of immediate completion" that satisfied her. She added, "You know, like you have a problem and you work on it and then you have a baby. And then you're done." None of the midwives or midwifery students attributed the accomplishment of a baby to themselves, nor did midwives speak about their work in this pragmatic manner, as a series of problems to be rectified. Of course, problem-solving is part of any birth attendant's work, yet conceptualizing the birth of a baby as a problem to be addressed, as Silverman did (and many OB-GYNs do), means in all likelihood that she does not see the process of birth as central, as midwives do. In fact, the doctors rarely spoke about birth *as* a process, as the midwives did. Their focus tended to be on the end result. For instance, when I asked Julie Elkmont whether she felt that different birth attendants had "distinct roles to play during childbirth," she said: "No, I think the goal is always the same — to have a good outcome. Healthy mom, healthy baby."

Midwives, of course, concerned themselves with "good outcomes," too, but they tended to celebrate the emotional and spiritual enrichment women could gain from pregnancy and birth experiences, rather than focusing on these processes as fraught with danger. This may well be because they were more likely to talk about what birth could or should be like *for women*, whereas doctors were more likely to talk of their work in terms of the outcomes they produced as deliverers of babies. Each of the doctors we interviewed, even the most midwifery-oriented among them (Fried and Leland), ultimately spoke about birth as inherently dangerous and thus potentially in need of medical management.

Doctors on Conflict

When asked about conflicts they experienced on the job, all but one of the obstetricians we interviewed (Leland) either had difficulty applying the question to the organizational structures in which they worked, or replied by talking about how they dealt with patients' demands. Two OBs were puzzled by my question about conflict:

Wendy Simonds: Have you ever come in conflict with medical practices or hospital rules in the places where you've worked?

Mindy Fried: As an OB? What do you mean? Come in *conflict*?

Simonds: In conflict.

Fried: Medical practice and what? Hospital rules?

Simonds: Hospital rules or protocols?

Fried: In an obstetric sense?

Simonds: Mm hmm.

Fried: Like felt — [long pause] rules or practices? I mean, I'm thinking about I worked in Guam for a while and a big limitation there was we didn't have epidurals for women in labor. That was a hospital limitation. But that's not really a regulation or rule. You're thinking more like routine IVs for everybody and you don't believe in that? Something like that? No, because I don't think anywhere I've been was too rigid in that way. I don't think there were really such fixed protocols ... that we couldn't override.

Simonds: Have you ever come in conflict with medical practices or hospital rules?

Lois Silverman: No. I think the hospital should have *more* rules about not as many people in the delivery room. There are way too many people in delivery rooms now. And that puts a burden on the nurses. I mean, it's very difficult for the nurses because, I mean, you have to wade through ten people to get to the patient when they ask for something. I mean, they often ... will answer for the patient, and it can sometimes be hard to find out what the *patient* actually wants 'cause there are so many people talking for them. So not in sort of the way that you're — like that the hospital says I have to do something and I don't think it should be done that way? [Simonds nods.] I mean ... the rules are generally made up by a committee which consists of physicians, midwives, and nurses. So they're generally amenable to everybody. You know, when a new pathway comes out, you know, there might be, you know, some medicine that wasn't your favorite that was listed first. But there's always a choice and you can always cross things out.

Fried is at first stymied by the question about conflict. She and Silverman both explain that, essentially, doctors *are* the rule-makers and they also can be rule-breakers if they so desire (this view is only qualified in discussions of malpractice and managed care, which will be discussed shortly). Working in hospitals rarely feels to them like negotiating constraining institutions, as it often does to midwives (see the previous two chapters) and nurses. Indeed, to Silverman, who feels there should be "more rules," the authority of health care workers (she gives nurses, rather than doctors, as an example, interestingly) is undermined by what she clearly judges to be too lenient a system. Her example reverses midwives' common complaint that too many health care professionals intrude on women's birth experiences. As she tells it, nurses experience the presence of too many family members and friends as physical impediments who may also attempt to meddle with the care provided. Silverman's call for "more rules" about "too many people in delivery rooms" essentially is a complaint about patient demands; though she does not phrase it this way, she depicts this open policy as leading to the subversion of birthing women's agency by their (presumably) medically untrained guests. She doesn't credit outsiders' views about the birth experiences she manages; she has expertise and they don't, as she sees it.

When asked about their experiences of conflict, several other obstetricians launched into a description of dealing with patients' demands:

Phyllis Fraser: Yeah, I mean you know sometimes patients who want to have more of a natural pregnancy may not want to be monitored, may not want an IV, that kind of thing. And pretty much with things like the vaccinations and things that the baby will get, they have the right to refuse it. The main thing is trying to keep up with the baby's heartbeat, and you know, if everything's looking fine, intermittent observation is okay. … But yeah, I've had a few run-ins. And I don't want to make it so that it's the patient versus the doctor, you know. When people come to me saying, "I don't want this, I don't want that. I don't want this," so I say, "Well, you know, you sound like you really want a home birth. Why don't you do that?" I think what I would prefer patients to do if they really don't want intervention is to take responsibility and have a home birth. Don't try to come to the hospital where we're going to take care of you the way that we know how … and then say, "I don't want any of that." I mean, what's the point of being here [in the hospital]? So I think that if you're going to agree to be under the care of a physician and go into the hospital to deliver, you have to sort of be willing to be flexible. That's the main thing that people need to do. When you're real rigid and you don't want this or that, and

under no circumstances *this* or *that*, those are the people
that tend to wind up with c-sections and fetal distress and
all those kinds of things. If you can learn to be flexible and
try to go with the flow a little bit — you don't have to accept
all of the technology and all that — but if you really want
a home birth, then be woman enough to go and have the
home birth and get you a midwife. Don't come to the hospital and set up a lot of — draw lots of lines in the sand. It's
not necessary, you know.

In Fraser's view, women having hospital births should be "flexible,"
and to her, flexibility means they must accept that anything they want
is contingent upon medical approval. Women who seek to control
the terms of their care in hospitals ought to "be woman enough" to
have their babies at home. Even as she claims to support women's
entitlement to make decisions about their own care, Fraser casts some
patients as dogmatically inflexible, and as likely to fail to achieve their
goals because of it. She portrays birthing women's desire for control as
intransigence. Such rigidity backfires, as she tells it, and these women
end up making their own births into the opposite of what they truly
want; they bring about fetal distress and cause their own c-sections.
(There is absolutely no evidence that women can cause fetal distress in
their babies by being "rigid" about what they want their birth experiences to be; but as far as I know, no one has investigated this hypoth-
esis either.)

Corrine Wood-Daniels expressed a similar annoyance about
dealing with patients who had strong preconceptions about their
birth experiences:

> Now I have a group of six physicians with me, and I therefore take care
> of patients that I don't have that same understanding with. It makes
> it much more difficult. So I try to explain, in layman's terms always,
> the consequences of the decisions and empower the patient to make
> the choice. Almost always they'll end up choosing my recommendation
> when they realize that the choice is theirs. It's very rare for someone,
> when they understand that my training says that [if] we go down this
> road, we do have the risk of compromising the baby, most folks choose

and trust my training. Occasionally, when they don't, it's very difficult, but we can't assault someone, you know!

Wood-Daniels's conflicts have occurred with other partners' patients with whom she has not established an "understanding" in advance of their labors. Wood-Daniels saw her expertise as ultimately trumping patients' contradictory viewpoints. She portrays women's acquiescence as informed and sensible decision making rather than as an act of submission. As she sees it, patients must trust her to be the judge of whether what happens poses a risk to the baby. Like Fraser, Wood-Daniels presents noncompliant patients as irritating and irrational.

Obstetricians continually described their primary role as sentries on the lookout for peril; they encountered conflicts as they heroically attempted to persuade misinformed or poorly informed patients to understand that doctors were the best judges of what is safe:

Lois Silverman: I think keeping safe — I mean safety — keeping everything safe [is the most important goal]. And that becomes
increasingly difficult as patients have access to more information than they really know how to deal with. And they
want to make their own decisions about things that they
really don't know anything about. And you need to spend a
lot of time discussing things with them and with whoever is
there with them. And it's — it's often — you — I mean, you
want to do what your patient *wants* to do, and it's important
to sort of find a balance between what your patient wants
and what really needs to happen. And you know, if your
patient wants to push another hour when you know she
needs a c-section, that's fine, as long as everything looks
good. ... You know, most deliveries are *fine*, but you know,
there's just — there's always that balance between safety and
sort of keeping everybody happy.

Julie Elkmont: I think there are some patients who get very focused on
the process, and all they care about is the process, and there
are probably a lot of midwives that focus in on the process,
you know. But for me, it is the end result. Do we have a
good mom and a good baby? That's what you try to do. You

can't always do that. There are bad things that happen in medicine. Bad things that happen to patients. But we try to limit that.

Silverman and Elkmont contrast their primary focus on "safety" with what they see as secondary concerns of patients (in Silverman's remarks) and midwives (in Elkmont's). Though Silverman, like Wood-Daniels, expresses a dedication to letting patients have decision-making power, she portrays their desires as frivolous and as potentially conflicting with what she decides "needs to happen," because patients don't know enough to make decisions about their own care. Patients may have "information," but they "don't know how to deal with" it, whereas *she* does. Similarly, Elkmont acknowledges that midwives and some clients care about the birth process; but she clearly views the most important element of obstetrical care to be "limiting" "bad things" to achieve a good outcome. Elkmont casts a process-related orientation as clearly less important than her medicalized orientation. She depicts the two orientations as ultimately mutually exclusive; thus, a process-orientation can jeopardize results, and concentrating on results *justifies* not attending to process. Doctors did not represent birth as *only* pathological or risky, by any means, but they depicted it as *always potentially* pathological or risky. If you never know when disaster can strike, you must always be a sentinel. They consistently portrayed their work as guarding against the worst-case scenarios. (This insistence became even more intense when they talked about home birth, with the exception of Fraser.) Within this framework, the most important accomplishment is getting the baby out of the woman.

Harriet Murphy discussed how she balanced achieving her goals and attending to patients' desires. She took an authoritative stance similar to that of Elkmont and Silverman:

I try to discern the type of person she is and then try to, in some way, gear my approach to the person. In other words, there are some people, as far as obstetrics, that consider pregnancy and childbirth just a natural thing. They don't really want to worry about things, and they *don't* worry about things. They just assume everything is going to go along naturally and fine, and "This is a normal thing that happens to people, so why should I worry?" And then there are other people who consider pregnancy an illness. They call you with every little thing. You know: "Are you sure this isn't a sign of a blood clot? I have a pain in my leg, a pain in my toe, my back hurts." ... They have a lot more worries and concerns. So I sort of try to see what their perception is and try to meet their needs. The people that just consider it normal look like you're bugging them if you try to ask them all the little questions. So I try to gear it to the patient. My general feeling, of course, is it's somewhere in-between there.

Murphy, like Silverman and Fraser, presented herself as good-naturedly putting up with patients' questions and worries, working to adapt herself to each women, tailoring her care "to try to meet their needs." Even as she claimed to humor the various attitudes of her clients, she (perhaps unconsciously) depicted her own outlook as a reasonable middle ground between two misguided extremes: dogmatically insisting that childbirth is unproblematic — "just a natural thing," — and griping about every aspect of it as pathological or unpleasant.

Laurie Leland's thoughts about relationships with patients and her own ethic of care sounded much more midwifery-oriented than the stances of these other doctors:

Mainly because I'm a woman — maybe not — a lot of what I do, I do in relation to how I personally would like to have something done if I were in a similar situation. And I do feel very strongly that, in general, obstetrics is a — they're still over-interventional. I think we still medicalize it too much, and I try as much as possible not to do that and to let — to appreciate it as a natural process and try to teach that to the residents and medical students. And sometimes that comes into conflict for me personally because it is such a — in an academic institution where the people want to get experience, there are times when I leave feeling frustrated ... because either a delivery occurs and eighty-five thousand people run into the room — med students and residents — and I really feel like that detracts from the experience for the woman. Or, on the other side, with regards to residents, they want to get the experience doing forceps or vacuum deliveries where I feel like — I appreciate their need to do that and to get the experience in case it's really necessary, but

they want to do it often and at times when it's really not so necessary. ...
I struggle with that personally. ... I'd rather just let it be as much of a
natural process as I can possibly let it be.

In Leland's medical school rotations, students were assigned to
particular women and would stay with them throughout their labors,
as midwives traditionally have done. She objected to the common
practice of doctors arriving at the last minute to catch babies. She saw
this as disruptive and inconsiderate treatment for women and poor
training for medical students, who would not have the opportunity
to connect with patients or to learn about labor. She said she would
talk to medical students about "the importance of being there" with
a woman in labor, and she described her attempts to educate them
as "debriefing" them before they became totally indoctrinated into
the medical model: "The medical students are still closer to being lay
people than the residents are and so I feel like they ... can still see
things from the patients' perspective a little bit more and they haven't
lost it yet." She encouraged students to maintain their ability to identify with patients; to imagine what the treatment they observed would
be like for themselves or for someone they loved; and to act against
impersonality and regimentation.

Doctors on Technology and Interventions

Most of the doctors we interviewed tended to take medical monitoring
and intervention for granted as tools that necessarily produce better
results. They sometimes qualified this belief with an acknowledgment
that technological measurement tools, such as continuous electronic
fetal monitoring (EFM), could lead to unnecessary interventions. For
instance, Lois Silverman said:

> You'll probably get a lot of comments on fetal heart rate monitoring and
> that we ... don't really know what we're doing with it. And we don't.
> But we don't, at this point, have anything else. ... I think it's important
> to monitor babies when you're in labor, because they, you know, babies
> used to die all the time in birth, and be born with problems that may
> or may not have been preventable. ... I think it's important to try and
> assess as best you can and make sure that the baby is doing well. And

unfortunately now all we have are fetal heart rate monitors, and fetal scalp electrodes. And so we can make sure, you know, that their heart rate is doing okay. It's reassuring. And then if it's not, the baby needs to come out. ... There's some evidence that listening to the fetal heart rate every fifteen minutes works just as well as continuous monitoring. You know, I'm not sure that it's less distressing for the patient to have you go in every fifteen minutes and not necessarily find it right away. And I'm not sure if you're in trouble it's better to be *waiting* and think, "Oh, well maybe I just can't find it. Let's go get the ultrasound machine."

Silverman knew that evidence shows EFM to be *imperfect*, but she didn't seem to recognize that it produces ill effects. She depicted it as better than nothing because, to her, doing nothing means unpredictable dangers are more likely to arise than if one does *something*. The equipment, she reasons, enables health care workers to detect and solve problems earlier than they would without the technology and to avert negative outcomes. But studies show no evidence that any of this happens as a result of EFM. Rather, research indicates that women's risk of having unnecessary operative and instrumental procedures done to them and their babies increases with EFM use (see, e.g., Goer 1995, Goer 1999, Sandelowski 2000). Within the discourse Silverman and many OBs use, instrumental and operative deliveries are not conceptualized as *risks to* women, because risk is conceptualized as emanating *from* women's bodies gone wrong or awry, rather than from acts done *to* women's bodies by medical professionals. Doctors tended to characterize performing surgery and instrument manipulations as positive acts of skill undertaken to negate or diminish risk. The specter of impending sudden "trouble" informs the stance of most of the doctors on managing labor, just as their comfort with their role as managers of women's labors informs their view of how best to deal with and prepare for "trouble." It's a vicious circle.

Most of the doctors asserted that even imperfect measurement technologies offer "reassurance." They might grant that detrimental results can occur, but their defenses of the interventions tended to nullify their objections, as when Silverman stated that "babies used to die all the time" or "be born with problems." This remark functions as a comparison with how things are now. She implies that EFM and other interventions have improved outcomes, but this simply isn't true.

Lydia Salvo defends her use of continuous EFM similarly:

> I still would rather have somebody on the monitor than not, and that's just more for my peace of mind. And I know that fetal monitoring hasn't really changed the outcome of deliveries, but I just think, just from being trained that way, I kind of like the technology. I like being able to put an ultrasound on and see what's going on if I have to. ... But I also know that for millions of years, people had babies without any of that.

Salvo's claim that using continuous EFM doesn't change outcomes is only true if one defines outcomes as meaning that healthy babies get born but pays no attention to *how* they get born or the consequences of their mode of birth. EFM *produces* interventions, including major surgery, that are more likely than vaginal birth to have deleterious effects on women and babies. Unlike Silverman, Salvo acknowledges that practitioners' comfort with a technological method results from habitual use, whether or not the practice is effective or justified by evidence.

Most of the doctors espoused a view of technology as inherently progressive, as Silverman did when she counterposed the olden days of lots of dead babies with the present. Salvo sounded less sanguine, yet said she thought that in the future monitoring methods would "get even better," which implies they are already good. She hoped for "some better system to monitor babies and still let people have a little more freedom during labor." In the future, she speculated, technology would become less disruptive of "natural experience" as ways of monitoring become less obtrusive. Thus, Salvo presents a common obstetrical (and cultural) set of views: that technology can improve upon nature; that nature is imperfect and needs monitoring; and that pure nature (associated with pure freedom), *by nature*, can be dangerous.

Most of the obstetricians we interviewed felt that taking measurements of women and fetuses during labor and birth was inherently positive, even if one could generate only imperfect measurements. This opinion makes sense if one weighs interventions only against the ultimate worst outcome: the death of a baby or woman as a result of an unexpected situation arising during labor and birth (which, statistically speaking, is a risk a fraction of a percentage point of the time in the United States). Weighed this way, an unnecessary intervention becomes a minor inconvenience, a justified act of caution that could save lives.

Only one doctor, Laurie Leland, condemned EFM as counterproductive:

> We rely on it too much. … Having the monitor seems … to give people a sense of reassurance. … Studies have shown that it's increased the risk of cesarean section but hasn't decreased the risk of cerebral palsy. So I'm not sure it's done really what I think people had hoped it was going to do. And yet, here it is, so entrenched in our practice now that it makes it impossible to try and get away from it. So that's one of the more disappointing aspects of modern obstetrics in hospitals today.

Unlike Silverman and Salvo, Leland saw medical research as indicating that standard continuous EFM does not make sense, and she thought that the intransigency of medical culture was the problem.

Self-protection from the risk of charges of malpractice charges was one of the most important elements that surfaced in doctors' discussions of the use of technology and interventions during pregnancy and birth. Risks, thus, are not simply present in their talk of threats posed by labor and birth, but in their perceptions of the possibility that patients might turn against them. Ironically, in talking about their resentment of the "litigiousness" that plagues the practice of medicine today, they bemoaned too much interventionism as an unreasonable focus on outcomes. And they portrayed themselves as helpless to resist this trend:

Phyllis Fraser: Well, unfortunately we're in a litigious environment and people want perfect outcomes. And if that doesn't happen, then doctors are at risk for being sued. So we tend to do overkill to protect ourselves. And therefore you have a little too much — probably too much — intervention trying to be on the safe side. I don't feel that probably half of it's necessary, but to practice in this environment you have to do that or else you'll put yourself at risk for financial ruin and possibly lose your license to practice.

Sarah Smithers-Dunn: The fear of being sued and the fear of being
   liable for not doing something, or [for] doing something —
   you just can't really win. So people have tended to be more:
   well, at least if it's looking suspicious, then go ahead and do
   a c-section, because at least you can't be blamed if you did
   the most aggressive thing. And obviously [that] means that
   more people are going to have c-sections and things like
   that. ...

   You're always in the back of your mind thinking not only
   for what is in the patient's best interests, but also what is
   going to be the most protective for me if I do something or
   don't do something. And even though your gut feeling may
   be: I've seen this scenario five thousand times and it always
   turns out fine. But if you *don't* do this, and it's that *one* time,
   when that person has a problem, then you're screwed. So
   people tend to be more defensive. And I think that people
   have been practicing more defensively and just the whole
   morale and the excitement and the fun of it has been a bit
   tarnished because of that.

Doctors' resentment of litigiousness, insurance companies, and
managed care sounds similar to midwives' critique of medicalization:
they portray it as impeding ideal working conditions for themselves
and ideal care for women. In discussions of these institutional limitations, doctors cast interventionism as a mode of self-defense that
results in unnecessary procedures, a stance that sounds contradictory
to some of their comments (earlier in the chapter) defending interventionism as safeguarding babies' lives. Here, malpractice lawsuits
and managed care pose risks: obstetricians may come to see patients
as potential liabilities who could bring about the loss of their professional status and livelihood. They did not acknowledge that some
malpractice claims might be justified, or that the system might offer
needed protection to patients. Nor did they discuss the financial
difficulties of paying for malpractice insurance, just the specter of
financial ruin. Without this coercive and controlling force impelling
them to practice defensively (interventionally) and to devote unreasonable energy to record-keeping (about which midwives and nurses

also complained), they imagined that health care would be better for everyone — doctors and patients — both as they presume it was in an Arcadian past and in terms of achieving goals for a healthier future. Consider these remarks:

Julie Elkmont: I hate managed care. ... I hate the insurance companies. I think the insurance companies are horrible. The CEO gets an eight million dollar home, and yet so-and-so, your patient can't be taken care of. I have patients, they're making me kick them out of the hospital, I think, inappropriately. ... I hope it gets better, but the reality of the situation ... is that ... it *is* a business. And that's what's sad about it for me — when I see it in medicine. ... My father is an internist in solo practice. He is one of those old guys that you don't see anymore. There are no more solo practitioners unless you are in the middle of nowhere. But people really respected him, and looked up to him, and now I don't think people respect me for what I do. I don't think that there is any respect for physicians. ... I think managed care has a lot to do with it. We've done it to ourselves to a degree, too.

Mindy Fried: I think we waste a lot of time — part of the medicaliza-tion and the documentation is wasting a lot of time to protect ourselves medico-legally, which might be spent better in other ways: improving care. You know, more women should get access to prenatal care. All of that should be — there should be more universal access. We've got to decrease the infant mortality rate in this country, which is, you know, so poor compared to other countries. ... I just think HMO care in all ways — for all care in *all* ways — for everything — is a negative. There's some backlash there, though. I think that's going to change. I don't think people are going to put up with managed care forever. ... I've worked in an HMO. When I finished residency ... we [my husband and I] went to Guam and worked in an HMO there for a few months, and I swore I'd never work in an HMO again. It's just this corporate — you know, they tell you everything, what to do. Although my work at [a local university hospital] is very similar, very similar. But at least there you have this academic environment where at least there's this feeling of top-notch, this feeling of you're allowed to go out on a limb to deliver the best care you want to do. Whereas my experience in the HMO was,

"No, we are the boss." You know. Either — both experiences are really limiting, because, for instance, where I am now, I get fifteen minutes to see a [return] patient, and that includes the history, the physical, the counseling. ... Then the women in the waiting room get really angry if you're late. ... So that's very frustrating. And that's, you know, I don't know — is that an HMO per se? No. But that's practicing in a managed care environment.

All the doctors who spoke about this subject portrayed insurance companies and managed care companies as greedy and monopolistic, but they tended not to offer an overarching critique of capitalism nor to suggest a restructuring of medicine. They don't want to be managed or told what to do. They framed their critique as altruistic rather than self-centered, even though they may long for respect, as Elkmont did. As they see it, their loss of autonomy works as a barrier to sound medical practice, imposing requirements and limitations that are not in the best interest of patients.

Nurses on Doctors and Midwives

Four of the five nurses we interviewed worked in hospital labor and delivery (L&D) departments. Monica Harper, the one exception, started as an L&D nurse and worked her way up to directing "maternity services" at a large private hospital that averaged 16,000 births a year at the time of her interview in 2003 and is known locally as a "baby factory." She talked about the differences among doctors and nurses from the unique position of an administrator responsible for coordinating working relationships among health care personnel from the time when midwives first began practicing at her hospital. Difficulties between doctors and midwives did not pose a problem, she said, because midwives began practicing and still practiced there as employees of doctors or supervisees of doctors (in the case of HMOs). She did describe nurses' resistance to midwifery at the outset:

It was hard at first because at that time there were a lot of nurses who had been in labor and delivery for a long time — I mean, I'm talking fifteen, twenty, twenty-five years. They knew these doctors, the doctors knew them, and then all of a sudden [they] got this intervening faction they don't really trust. They don't know what they [the midwives] know. … They immediately assumed that the care that the midwife is going to give is substandard to what the obstetrician would do. It made 'em nervous because they felt like the midwives wouldn't be able to do a section immediately.

Over time, Harper felt, the nurses adapted to the point where they "have gotten very comfortable" working with midwives. (Several midwives described their part in situations like these, where often, L&D nurses initially would perceive them as uppity nurses and would resent their greater power in the chain of command. But eventually they would come around and enjoy working with midwives.)

At the time of her interview, Harper estimated that half of the physician practices that staffed her hospital employed midwives, and that the midwives attended about 40% of the nonoperative births. Harper, like the other four nurses we interviewed, saw midwives and doctors as having different working styles that emerged from their different philosophies and training:

I would say that, in general, the midwives tend to be present in the hospital more often than the physicians are. … I think, in general, they're probably less likely to use some of the interventions, so they're probably a little bit less likely to do Cervadil, a little bit less likely to start pitocin, probably less likely to use internal monitoring versus the external monitoring. So, you know, pretty much all the things that you would expect. Now, I would say if you compared our midwifery group to midwives who practice in a smaller setting, they would be much more in the medical model.

Harper said that she was more medicalized than midwifery-oriented because "a lot of what I learned, I learned from doctors." She had considered pursuing a degree in nurse-midwifery for a while, nonetheless. Midwifery was attractive to her because it would allow her to "function like a doctor without being a doctor." Her attitude differs from that of the midwives and midwifery students we interviewed who started out as L&D nurses: they saw midwifery as ideally distinct from obstetrics and were attracted to it for that reason. Similarly, Amy Widmark planned eventually to go on to become a nurse-midwife because of her ideological commitment to non-interventionist, woman-controlled care. The other three nurses also preferred the ethos of midwifery, but they did not have plans to become midwives. Widmark pointed out that midwives often had to work under the same time constraints as doctors, and because of this "were not so different," but she still felt that philosophically, midwives had "more belief in the woman's capability of giving birth vaginally."

The other three nurses, Kelly Hyde, Ivy Hayden, and Jody Lowell, contrasted the approaches of midwives and obstetricians and spoke about how different it was for them to work with each group:

Kelly Hyde: I much prefer working with midwives ... because they're more willing to work with the patient and to listen to them and try to give them the birth experience that they want, whereas a lot of OBs really push the epidurals. They're not there to attend them throughout their labor; they're just there to attend the delivery. So working with midwives I find much more enriching.

Ivy Hayden: I think it's a better working relationship because midwives come in — most of the ones I work with, anyway — seem more of an equal, and they let you try different things with the patients, and, you know, different ways to have them labor, different things for pain relief, not just necessarily medicines, but just alternative things. Whereas a lot of physicians are very rigid, and you know, you stay in the bed, you stay on the monitor, you can't do this, you can't do that. You know, you can't eat or drink anything. Some of the physicians I work with still want to give them enemas. So I think that the midwives seem to be just a little more relaxed in their care. ... I think they work with nurses a little more closely. It's not just "I'm the midwife, you're a nurse," whereas there is a lot more of "I'm the physician, you're the nurse."

Jody Lowell: Doctors, I think, view labor and delivery as a medical event, as this — as a disease process almost — and I don't see it that way at all. I mean I see it as a very natural thing. ... Midwives: I feel more camaraderie with them because they see it as a natural process and a powerful process and it's, you know, this incredible process. ... It's important to make it a wonderful process for a woman. That even these young girls on Medicaid — that this can be a life-changing event for them. ... You know, maybe give them back some power in their lives. And too often, it just turns into a medical circus.

These nurses depict obstetricians as rigidly hierarchical, dogmatic in their medicalized management of laboring women, and minimally involved in participating in the process of women's births. They see midwives, in contrast, as taking a naturalistic view of labor and birth, as committed to the empowerment of women through birth experiences, and as flexible rather than rule-bound. These comments show that midwives' respect for women's agency apparently plays out in their working relationships with those who are subordinate to them in the chain of command.

Nurses on Conflict

Despite Lois Silverman's claim that all birth attendants work together to come up with rules "amenable to everyone," L&D nurses (like midwives) offered a different take on the situation. Nurses clearly saw their jobs as involving the negotiation of a system in which they wielded little power. Four of the five nurses we interviewed told of their difficulties navigating the standard medical protocols and doctors' demands in ways that were similar to those of the midwives, but they had — as nurse-midwifery students with L&D backgrounds attested in previous chapters — less clout and less autonomy than midwives. Most resented their disadvantaged status in the hospital hierarchy, though Ivy Hayden did remark, "Well, of course the physician is ultimately in charge of what goes on," even as she complained about the dogmatic and dictatorial approach of some physicians with whom she worked.

The other three detailed their frustrations. Amy Widmark, for instance, told me about the frustration she felt with having to get doctors' permission for things she believed she was capable of judging for herself, like whether a laboring woman could have juice or walk around. She explained how she coped with working within the confines of a system that treated birth as a pathological event:

> I come into conflict with rules all the time and it drives me crazy and I pretty much have to — I'm learning and I really have to put my thoughts

on birth really in the back of my head. I've got so much to learn. My goal is to learn this. It doesn't matter how I feel about it or how I think about it because this is the opportunity for me to learn it. ... These women are here giving birth every day all the time and I can — I feel — I really feel like I can help even though I'm constrained in the ways I can help. I'm a sensitive person, and even though I have to do things that I believe are wrong literally, I know that I can help somebody just by really being present with them and just — they know I care about them and I'm taking care of them in the best possible way. In that way I feel good about what I'm doing and I feel like, yeah, I can do this. ... It's not too much of a conflict for me because I have this stuff like this is what I believe and I know that. So I can separate it, I guess.

Widmark struggled to maintain her ideals even as she felt forced, in aspects of her work, to act against them, and she comforted herself with the knowledge that she was doing the best she could within a flawed system. I asked her whether she thought she would "get indoctrinated" into the system as a result of having to act within its confines. At first, she said, "I don't think so," but then conceded, "I know it's changing some things about the way I think, like. ... Okay, so most women get epidurals. Okay, so that's not so bad. ... I'm sure there are ways that I can't see that I've gotten a little bit indoctrinated into that medical view. But basically — really the gut — the whole — the inside — how I feel about it, I don't think that will change."

Amy Widmark and Kelly Hyde worked at the same hospital, and both talked about feeling stretched thin because they were assigned to too many patients at once. Because of the increasing volume (more than 500 births a month, according to Hyde), the prevailing approach seemed to be to speed up women's labor however possible. Hyde said, "It's gotten to the point where we can't let these moms linger a few hours more, because basically, we need the room." She said OBs commonly induced labor and performed amniotomies to make women's labor move faster. Additionally, Hyde said that doctors often would "insist that their patients have epidurals" because it would give them "more control" over when births would occur:

If a doctor's practice is five miles away from the hospital and ... he's got patients to see in his office and he's got a woman laboring, and let's say it's her fourth baby. That baby can come just in a matter of minutes — you know that — and there's no way he's going to make the delivery. ... But if the woman has the epidural, she's not going to have that tremendous urge to push. There's more control. And I'm seeing it more and more where the doctors tell the patients, "This is what I want you to have. It's the best thing." And they'll tell them honestly, "If you don't have it, I will miss your delivery." So they get an epidural.

She told me how she worked to resist what she saw as unnecessary medicalization pushed on patients by doctors, offering epidurals and doctors' increasing off-label use of the drug Cytotec to induce labor as examples:

> If I find the patient using an epidural, for example, does not want the epidural, and she's told me she does not want the epidural, I'll tell her doctor she doesn't want it. And I will encourage her to stick to her guns, you know, "Stick to your rights! You have certain rights: if you do not want it you do not have to have it. He can't *force* you to have an epidural. He misses the delivery, he misses the delivery. There are other doctors here. There's nurses here." ... I'm not going to force her; I'm going to encourage her to do what she wants.
>
> [Regarding Cytotec]: I haven't wanted to give it, I'm just uncomfortable with it at this point. ... Once you give Cytotec, you've got no control — I mean, you've got no control at all. So yeah, I would refuse, and tell them, "If you want Cytotec, you come up and put it in her mouth, I'm not giving it."

Hyde's willingness to stick to her convictions regarding patients' autonomy had developed over a long career (13 years of nursing at the time of her interview). Hyde resisted medical authority by coaching patients to assert themselves; she also felt she could speak up to doctors. Newer L&D nurses such as Hayden and Widmark didn't feel they could be so forthright in their opposition to practices they perceived as less than ideal treatment. Years of experience do not necessarily produce an overt resistance style, however; as midwives' narratives indicate, subterfuge often seems the simplest route. If they do it successfully, they avoid conflict. In fact, Jody Lowell, who had been an L&D nurse for six years, described "disregarding" rules she thought were groundless without seeking permission:

> I frequently go around the rules as much as possible. ... For example, at [the hospital where she works] if a woman's [membranes are] ruptured, they don't let her get out of bed. I think that's ridiculous. ... I mean, I understand the rationale behind it, but if the head's engaged, the danger that they're worried about is not going to happen. So I tend to disregard it. ... I always try to do the right thing, and you know, sometimes I reinterpret the rules. ... And, you know, that's probably not a good thing all the time.

Whether they engaged in outright refusal, clandestine acts of resistance, encouraging patients to resist, or reluctant compliance (or a combination of these styles), the practicing L&D nurses we interviewed all voiced dissatisfaction with the rigidity, depersonalization, and objectification of women's bodies that they saw as inherent in the medical model.

Doctors on Midwives

The doctors we interviewed all endorsed midwifery, mainly nurse-midwifery in hospitals, which tended to be what they knew about. However, when their comments are examined carefully, their support for midwifery appears to be rather lukewarm (see also Langton 1994). Doctors tended to see midwives as functioning in a similar capacity to obstetricians, yet many portrayed midwives as junior to or less expert than obstetricians, as this comment from Sarah Smithers-Dunn shows:

> Midwives, in uncomplicated, low-risk type pregnancies, I think, are wonderful. They do a great job, and they tend to be a little more hands-on in terms of some of the non-definite medication type things, you know, using alternative techniques, encouraging patients to be out of bed and moving around, and kind of being there with them, and that kind of thing, which I think is a very valuable experience for patients that are low-risk patients, and are not complicated patients.

Though Smithers-Dunn complimented midwives, she said twice that their purview was dealing with "uncomplicated" and "low-risk" situations. She rhetorically constructed a continuum on which she situated the work of OBs at the high-skill, difficult end, and midwives at the low-skill, easy, affective end. The continuum is predicated on a gendered division of labor: midwives do womanly, nurturant work, and obstetricians do the edgy, complex, masculine, active work. She talked further about how the hierarchical system should and should not operate:

> When I was in my residency program, that was the first time I was really introduced to midwives. And during that time, it was more of a conflict, in that they were training, and the residents — the physicians — were training as well, so they [midwives] would try to do as much as they could. ... It was a little tough in some of those situations, because you felt that you were only called in once it's gotten really bad. And that was kind of a bad introduction to midwives! But then, on down the line, after having worked with them, and I think as long as they understand their limitations, then it's really not a problem. It's when people think they can do more, or they feel comfortable with the situation when it really should be handed over to medical management, when there's a problem. But I think most experienced midwives know when they are in over their heads, and they need backup or help.

When midwives knew their place and remained cognizant of their "limitations" everything would run smoothly, Smithers-Dunn opined. When they exceeded their station, problems ensued, and doctors would have to rectify the situation.

Also along these lines, Corrine Wood-Daniels remarked: "For midwives that are trained well, I think they add a valuable extension to obstetrical practice." Wood-Daniels implied that midwives are not as well trained as doctors or that some midwifery schools offer inadequate training, and that midwifery is a subsidiary of and a subordinate practice to obstetrics. Nurse-midwives generally viewed the notion that they were "physician-extenders" as insulting. Direct-entry midwives often portrayed nurse-midwives this way when they talked about how overpowering medical indoctrination and medical hegemony could be for those who work in hospitals (see chapter 3). Most of the doctors, though, seemed unaware that midwives' self-conceptualization is determinedly oppositional to obstetrics. For instance, Phyllis Fraser also saw nurse-midwives as quite similar to obstetricians, saying: "The certified nurse midwives, from what I observe, seem to be very much like doctors. They may use herbs more and they may hang out in the labor and delivery suite more a little bit, but in overhearing their conversations, they don't seem much different than us."

The boundaries between situations midwives could handle and those only doctors could handle feel different to doctors and midwives: midwives feel that what they do is deal with "normal" birth, and when situations become "high-risk" or involve surgery, they feel that a wholly different, not more skilled, specialist becomes appropriate. In other words, they see midwives and obstetricians as engaged in two distinct realms of practice. Doctors tend to depict these realms as superordinate and subordinate: they see themselves as having greater expertise and skill, on top of having the ability to handle anything midwives can handle. Most of the doctors saw midwifery as similar to nursing in its ability to relieve doctors by handling what they saw as the tedious aspects of caring for laboring women. Along these lines, Julie Elkmont talked about how glad she was *not* to do what midwives do:

> Maybe it is because I am getting older, and I guess maybe it is [that] the way I do things is differently than the way they do, but I don't get a kick sitting there and breathing with every little contraction the patient has for hours and hours. And I know some midwives do, which is great for them. And I mean, I do believe a lot of patients get a benefit out of the midwives. And they [midwives] can give something that I just don't want to give or that I don't have to give, or have the time to give.... So there's a definite role for midwives, and definite — they add something, or maybe give back to obstetrics that we didn't have before — used to have and took away — whatever. But I just don't get the big thrill out of it. I mean, I ugh — I used to sit there and push with patients for a long time, and I have just learned not to do that anymore. It's so tiring! And I don't know how labor and delivery nurses do it, time after time. ... I can't do it anymore. I can be there for a while, and I try to coach the patients. And if you have someone pushing for three or four hours, it's just draining and it takes a lot out of you. And if you have to do this

every fourth night — I mean, I am on call every fourth night, for years — and it just gets — I can't do it anymore. ... When I was a resident, I couldn't understand why these doctors just show up at the last minute. And I just didn't think that was fair. And now I see why some of them probably do [that]. ... I am probably there a lot more than a lot of doctors are, or a lot of male doctors are.

Elkmont is pleased that midwives want to do what she has come to see as the dull and draining work involved in birth attending. Clearly she believes this sort of care-work is good for laboring women, but she doesn't understand why anyone would be able to sustain an interest in it over time. Still, she asserts that, compared to most doctors (especially men), she probably provides more midwife-like care.

Lydia Salvo expressed her appreciation of midwives' differences from doctors without *initially* undercutting her praise with any sort of remarks that placed midwives below obstetricians:

When I trained, we had a couple of midwives that were on their own and ... we used to be able to go do deliveries with them, and I think in terms of how much time they're able to spend with patients ... [what they do is] different. But I think that's less so here [in the HMO]. Like now that I work more with them, it seems like it's more even. And I don't know if it's just from working with midwives in the past, I've just kind of adopted some of the things they do 'cause I think a lot of things they do are better than what we do. They move the patients around a lot more. A lot of the midwives I know are better at determining like, the true position of the baby, just from doing an exam, than a lot of physicians are. ... I don't know if part of it is being in there with the patient more, but they tend to be better at getting people through without an epidural, you know, just better for pain control. But I think mostly, just, they're much more willing to have people push in different positions or even just have different positions during labor, that a lot of times physicians, you know — they're [patients] not lying flat on their backs.

Salvo said she thought that about half of the OBs in her practice were "tolerant" of the incorporation of midwifery into their practices. Despite her admiration and even appropriation of midwives' techniques, she described the hierarchical arrangements in her practice, saying:

> If they have any questions, they'll come to us. ... Most people [OBs] I think are pretty good. As long as they think everything looks okay, they'll let them [midwives] kind of do what they want to do until they [OBs] decide something else has to be done. And then they'll usually just take over.

Salvo did not appear to consider this power dynamic troubling.

When these doctors discussed their philosophical approaches to birth, they at least paid lip service to birthing women's desires and expectations; but when they discussed the division of labor among birth attendants, birthing women rarely figured as agents. They saw disagreements or conflicts as best resolved by physicians.

Among the obstetricians we interviewed, only Mindy Fried and Laurie Leland discussed their view of midwifery without ever taking a superior stance. In fact, Fried seemed envious of what she perceived as midwives' less hectic and more personally interactive jobs: "I think midwives really offer more comfort and support for the mother. And I think physicians are trained much more with the goal of a healthy outcome. I mean, midwives obviously want that too. It's sort of like them stopping and smelling the roses versus the doctors, you know, are not trained and are not as comfortable and don't have the time, you know, to give that kind of support." Leland identified more with midwives than with OBs; she said: "I feel very much, very akin to midwives. ... The residents ... call me the granola attending [supervisory physician]. I feel, in spirit, often more on that side of the fence than I do on the medical, obstetricians' side of the fence."

Unlike the other OBs, Fried and Leland saw midwifery care as distinct from and superior to obstetrical care because of its greater scope in attending to women's emotional and physical needs. They both became OBs without knowing much about midwifery; if they had known more, they both felt they might have taken that route instead. Fried said: "I would have been much happier as a midwife. ... I like those other parts of OB better. I like the connection. I'd like to have the time to offer more comfort, and I would like getting out of the situation when it's too dire!"

Doctors and Nurses on Home Birth

Many of the obstetricians we interviewed expressed an antipathy to home birth because they viewed birth as a potentially pathological series of obstacles, at best a "natural" process that could go wrong at any time and require correction via medical interventions that were not available outside of hospitals. Consider these responses to the questions: "Have you ever seen a home birth?" and "What do you think about home birth?":

> *Harriet Murphy:* I would have a heart attack if I had to observe a home birth. I would absolutely probably just wet my pants. I *never* would do a home birth. I would think that [only] an idiot would have a home delivery. ... I just can't understand why any reasonable person who loved their child would take a chance with having their child be born dead, which is what they're doing — even if it's a small chance. I have seen too many people go down the tubes in five minutes, and if you weren't in a hospital either the mother could be dead or the baby could be dead.

> *Sarah Smithers-Dunn:* I think that being able to assess the fetal status constantly is much more readily available in a hospital. And you know, obstetrics is generally very nice, very serene, pleasant — it's great. But when something's *not* great, and you need to immediately get back there and do surgery or whatever, you have about six to eight minutes before you can have brain death or things like that from the fetus not getting oxygen supply, you know, or if you have an abruption of the placenta, or something like that, you need to be able to access immediate operative capacity and that's the big problem with home delivery, I think. If you have an emergency, you're just stuck. There's nothing you can do.

> *Lois Silverman:* I think a birth center near a hospital, like *in* a hospital is fine. I mean, I think that nobody today should be laboring far from a room where they can have a c-section. The American College of OB-

GYN recommendation is that you need — in an emergency, you need to have a c-section *done* in thirty minutes. And I think that anyone in labor … *deserves* that level of care. And that means you've got to be there. I mean, you cannot — because you don't know, I mean, you can be having a perfectly nat — normal labor at home, and you think you're just in hard labor, and your placenta abrupts from the strength of your contractions; it separates and you start hemorrhaging. Where are you? You're, like, not in the hospital! You don't have an IV. … Your baby is most likely going to die, and you may not do so well afterwards yourself. I mean, I just don't think it's worth the risk.

Julie Elkmont: I don't believe in home births. … It's risky. I know midwives do that. I don't particularly like that. I mean, what do you do when you are in trouble, and you're home, and things happen? There are patients that get in trouble at the very end, and now you're stuck at home and you're not in a hospital situation. I mean there's a lot of — there's a reason why moms aren't dying anymore. There's a reason why babies aren't dying anymore… . We just don't have that anymore, because we have made a lot of changes. … I don't understand why people feel that they have to suffer. Why do you have to suffer when you are in labor? I guess if you get some kick out of it, or if you feel that you are a stronger woman. I think there are some patients, they feel that they are a better woman for it. It's like, okay, fine, if that's what makes you happy. But not everyone has to believe that. …

What do you do when somebody's bleeding, and you have no drugs to give that patient to help her stop bleeding and she is having a postpartum hemorrhage? What do you do? You're at home. You call an ambulance. You're wasting time. … Birth is a beautiful experience. It's wonderful and everything like that, but it is not benign in every single case. And I have seen too many things happen. That's why I don't think it is necessarily good. But these stars, Hollywood stars, have their births at home, and have all these midwives, nothing bad — it's good that nothing bad has happened to them. Then everyone reads about it in the paper, and is like "Oh, I want to be like so and so!"

Corrinne Wood-Daniels: Well, I do not support home deliveries. I think if a woman should choose not to have the benefit of medical intervention even when it clearly could save her life and the life of her baby, and if she makes that decision, then that is her choice. But she has to understand many of the life-threatening complications of obstetrics come with no warning.

My first inclination was just to include a couple of these remarks on home birth, but the repetitive elements indicate a pattern of thinking, and, I hope, together they make a clear point: these doctors equate home birth with the direst of consequences — life-threatening situations for babies and mothers, and they equate hospital birth with safety for babies and mothers. They see midwives and women who attempt home birth as misguided (even "idiots," as Murphy said or Elkmont implied when she talked about women imitating movie stars), irrationally choosing pain (Elkmont) or irresponsibly risking trouble that could spiral into irreparable emergency (all of them). Even when doctors say that women have the "right" to make this decision, closer attention reveals their frustration with what they see as insensibility (Elkmont and Wood-Daniels). Doctors may even frame the ideology of home birth as masochistic (Elkmont), or as a touchy-feely ruse, cheating women of care they *deserve* (Silverman).

Among the midwives and midwifery students we interviewed who worked outside of hospitals, few spoke about deaths or near-deaths they'd encountered as part of their work. None told of a death that would have been avoided had the mother been in a hospital. This could mean that midwives are reluctant to speak of such matters, but such situations are exceedingly rare, or presumably word would get out. The smear campaigns against home birth midwifery that U.S. doctors have orchestrated at various times do not rely on data that show hospital birth to be safer than home birth, because such data are lacking. One study out of dozens recently showed a higher infant death rate in home births than in other settings (Pang et al. 2002), but critiques of the study refute the claim because the authors did not clearly distinguish between intentional (planned) and unintentional home births (see, e.g., MANA press release 2003 and Vedam 2003). All other studies show superior outcomes in terms of maternal and infant morbidity for home births, and equivalent outcomes in terms of mortality. Most of the doctors we interviewed did not acknowledge that there was any other point of view on home birth but theirs — the story medicine tells about itself that it made birth safer for women and babies, and that home birth is a throwback to a dangerous past practice. This story simply is not true.

Midwives are well aware of the attitude of the medical profession toward home birth and know that if something does go wrong, doctors and family members may well hold midwives and/or the women who choose them responsible. As Elaine Jacobs, a direct-entry midwife who became a nurse-midwife, described how she counseled people who were considering giving birth in her birth center in Brooklyn:

> I can't guarantee anything, and you have to understand that, and you have to understand the guilt element. … If something, God forbid, goes wrong in a hospital, your whole family, everybody, says to you, "You did everything you could. They did everything they could." Whereas if you're in a birth center with midwives, you're going to have to deal with family members — who might not even openly say it: "You should've — how come you didn't go to a hospital?"

Doctors' notion of risk inflates as a result of their interventive training and interventive experience as practitioners. They come to see their interventions as producing (good) results; they never imagine what situations might be like without viewing their (medical, interventive) actions as central. Midwives doing — and women having — home births know that risks exist; the difference is that they view these risks as acceptable, and ultimately preferable to the risks incurred by birthing in hospitals, which doctors do not acknowledge in the first place. What they may do, instead, is talk about how nice hospitals have become nowadays, as Corrinne Wood-Daniels did:

> I celebrate the birthing suites and the sort of residential homey feel of the labor and delivery suite that we have created so that a woman has the best of both worlds. She has cherry wood floors and a mahogany armoire and the television and rocking chair there, as well as the music that she chooses to hear as she delivers. As she labors, the bottom of the bed comes away, she delivers, and everything is fine. And if she becomes unstable, that mahogany headboard goes away. The oxygen is there, the IV fluid is there, the resuscitation equipment is there, and we

have decreased the maternal mortality and infant mortality significantly in the proper setting. So, I do not agree with home delivery. I don't think it's an appropriate choice for women in this age when we have the ability to have a home atmosphere at a high-tech environment.

Home, in Wood-Daniels's view, can be approximated through cosmetic changes: nice furniture, fancy wood floors. She never acknowledges the power dynamics involved. I don't mean to suggest that aesthetic improvements cannot improve people's experiences — they can — but they do not necessarily affect power differentials. They may, in fact, mask them.

Despite their unequivocal endorsement of midwifery, both Laurie Leland and Mindy Fried expressed ambivalence about home birthing:

Laurie Leland: I do feel strongly that we need to … have access to things like an operating room if something went wrong. … You probably wouldn't find me completely on the side of some lay midwives, or whatever. I don't want to jeopardize at all the health of the baby, and I realize that the health of the baby is more important than any — so the issue of trying to make it as natural a process as we can, but still having the benefits of — you know my experience in dealing — when the shit hits the fan on labor and delivery, it really hits the fan and you can't always predict who … it's going to happen to. … As much I want no intervention, I want the ability to do really what we need to do when it comes down to it. So I think an ideal situation would really be … near a hospital or near an operating room or whatever.

Simonds: Do you feel like home births are not safe?

Leland: I don't know — that's — I feel sort of conflicted about that. I've actually chatted with my husband about it. He is more con. I think he would have more resistance to us having a home birth than I would, because I just feel like, you know, I'm a pretty low-risk person for having it. But again, sometimes you can't predict what could happen, and I certainly — I have to tell you I would feel absolutely horrible if something terrible happened to my baby … because I wanted this experience. And I do find that sometimes I see some women that almost seem to be fanatical to the point where ... the experience seems to be more important than the baby, you know. And I definitely don't feel that way, and I think you've got to keep it in perspective ... I think that maybe some sort of compromise [like birthing centers near hospitals] might be ideal. I don't know. I mean I'm so conflicted.

Fried: I'm a little uncomfortable with home birthing. You know, if someone's very low risk and has easy access to a hospital, I think it can be okay. ... I think it must be really *nice* to *not* be in a hospitalized medicalized setting. I think that that could be a real plus. *But,* having practiced high-risk obstetrics for so many years and seen such horrible disasters. ... It creates fear in me to think about it.

The differences between what Leland and Fried said about home birth and what the other doctors said was that the former recognized that home birth could be very appealing and different from hospital birth; they acknowledged ambivalence rather than taking a firm position on the issue; and they recognized that their ambivalence was empirically grounded and institutionally produced. That Leland applied the home birth question to her own future showed that she considered it to be a viable option at least sometimes, even though she had difficulty transcending the paradigm of risk.

Phyllis Fraser was the only doctor we interviewed who had observed a home birth. She said, "It was quite beautiful. . ... It's not for everyone. But for those who want it, I think they should have the right to do it." Only Laurie Leland said she would be interested in providing back-up for midwives doing home births. Fraser seemed unable to imagine anything other than the current situation when she replied to this question: "Because of being sued I really can't. I mean I don't think my malpractice insurance company would allow that."

Nurses expressed more varied views on home birth than the obstetricians did. Two of the five (Hyde and Widmark) clearly supported it, and the other three (Harper, Lowell, and Hayden) expressed ambivalence. Kelly Hyde said, "With medical backup I'm all for it," and talked about positive encounters she had had with home birth midwives in Washington state. Amy Widmark told me about how she had been spending time with Diane Eastman, one of the home birth midwives we interviewed, because her best friend was planning a home birth, which Widmark would attend. She was "really looking forward to it," she said, and told me about how her friend, her friend's partner, and she had discussed with Eastman what would happen if something went wrong:

> We asked her the question about how does that go with the transport. And she said, "You know, most of the time when midwives transport it's not an emergency. It's like, you go in a car. You know what's happening. You know, or you see it coming, and you're like, 'Okay, now we need to go.'" But she said like two percent of the transports are that kind of 911 ambulance thing.

Widmark believed what Eastman said and was open to reframing labor and birth as primarily *not* about risk and impending danger. After the birth of her friend's baby, she told me how wonderful the experience was.

Hayden and Lowell were less positive in their assessments of home birth:

> *Hayden:* I think women do a lot better without the hustle and bustle of the hospital. I think if that's what they want, if they would rather have their babies in a different setting. ... I think a birthing center is a wonderful option. Home births make me a little nervous. ... You may not be close enough to a hospital if there is an emergency. I've seen babies go bad real quick, and there's just not a whole lot you can do if you're fifteen, twenty minutes out. I think if people choose to do that, that's okay. I think it's certainly their right. ... I don't think it should be outlawed. I don't agree with it, but also don't think it should be a law.

> *Lowell:* I've never even seen one out of the hospital. ... I would probably be more comfortable in a birth center setting than at home, and I guess that's because I've probably been too medicalized myself — that fear of what could happen, that fear of the worst-case scenario. That, and then you wouldn't have access to what you needed quickly. And

mostly the baby is what I worry about. I mean, mom I think could get together and get her someplace if she needed it. But the baby is what I'm worried about. I probably need to experience that. I don't know. I really even have a hard time visualizing anything outside of the hospital setting.

Like Leland, Hayden resolved her ambivalence about home birth by endorsing birth centers as a compromise solution. She still conceptualized home birth as a right (like Fraser), though her support for it seemed halfhearted. Like most of the doctors, these two nurses raised the issue of a "worst-case scenario," that, in and of itself, made home birth seem ill-advised. Lowell, unlike Hayden, tempered her anti-home birth stance with the statement that she needed to experience a home birth. She seemed aware that exposure could change her view of home birth; like the more reflective doctors, she recognized that her experience as an L&D nurse in a hospital had shaped her view that hospital birth was the safest option.

Monica Harper responded similarly to Hayden and Lowell, objecting to home birth but not denouncing it altogether:

I really don't think home birth is a good idea. I have a good friend who's a midwife in Florida, and she's in a birthing center practice that's in a house. But they have the ability to monitor, they have a transport situation set up with the hospital, so they've controlled for that. You know, the number of patients who are going to deliver or develop a need for a c-section during the course of their labor — that sometimes can't be anticipated. So I think that's the problem with home birth. ... I just think there's a certain amount of risk, and personally, I don't think it's worth the risk, even if it's a small one. I mean, I see things go wrong here that aren't anticipated and we don't end up with the outcome that we'd hoped for.

These three nurses think that unexpected events can be dealt with in hospitals much better than outside of them. They trust in hospitals, and — like the cautious doctors — fail to mention that medical care can itself cause problems that would not occur in a non-interventionist setting. Harper continued by focusing on the emergency c-section dilemma she mentioned as the presumed solution to sudden

fetal distress. At the time of her interview, the American College of
Obstetricians and Gynecologists (ACOG) had recently come out
against VBACs (vaginal births after cesareans), and Harper segued
into this issue, saying: "Even when you have everybody there that
needs to be there, if you had a catastrophic VBAC rupture, even if
you pick up on it quickly ... you can still end up with a crappy baby
because it's so catastrophic that no matter how fast you are, you can't
get it out in time to not end up with some neuro-damage. That's
why I guess people aren't doing VBACs anymore." She drew upon
her experiences seeing "catastrophic VBAC ruptures" in the hospital, offering them as evidence of why home births make less sense
than hospital births, as well as evidence that VBACs should not be
attempted anywhere. The way she talked about this problem is also
telling: the scar exists because of a previous cesarean, and ruptures
are associated with induction of labor, not with VBAC itself. So the
ruptures are the results of past and present medical intervention,
but her language ("VBAC rupture," not "c-section scar rupture")
masks this. When I objected and said I thought the ACOG statement against VBACs was a mistake because of the correlation of
ruptures with induction, not VBAC, Harper hesitated and seemed
to agree, but then reversed herself:

> Well it probably is [a mistake]. ... I do think that obviously we had far
> more successful good outcomes [with] VBAC than we did not good
> outcomes. But I think that what people found is that, is it worth them
> at all? ... At our volumes, we were having two or three ruptures ... a
> quarter, which is ... very low. ... But when you have one or two a year
> where you have a terrible outcome, it's just not — remember I already
> said I was kind of medical-model!

Inside the ideology of the medical model, undamaged babies are
the end product of the birth process; to ensure a good product, ideally, one must be able to take total control over it should anything go
awry. Medicalized thinkers like Harper and many of the doctors see
access to and use of interventive techniques as providing them with
the greatest amount of control they could possibly have, and they
can only imagine the lack of such access and usage as inappropriate and dangerous. To reject the hospital, to question the medical-

ized formulation of the control issue, to them means inviting what they see as *unwarranted* risk. They simply cannot see outside the hospital box.

Conclusion

When I listened to many of the doctors talk about practicing obstetrics, I was reminded of other institutions that enjoy taken-for-granted supremacy and that can systematically produce negative, even violent effects that occur in such a way that they appear uninitiated by actors, because the institutions have ideological lives of its own. Routines and protocols become taken for granted and appear to need no justification or analysis. Militarism, for instance, comes to seem unauthored and inevitable (see, e.g., Enloe 1990, 2000), as do various forms of inequality (class-based, race-based, gender-based, sexual-identity-based, etc.) under capitalism. Milgram's (1974) experiments in which men and women thought they were administering electric shocks to others, Zimbardo's (1992) simulated prison, and actual "total institutions" like real prisons and mental hospitals (see Goffman 1961) show how easily, seemingly automatically, covert sadomasochistic dynamics are produced when hierarchical power structures become commonplace and taken for granted (see also Chancer 1992, and of course, Foucault 1973, 1977). Within such structures, people rarely question what's happening, and those who do tend to have the least power to effect change. Obstetrics is very much an example of this sort of sadomasochistic institution, even when the actual doctors are nice people with positive intentions. It has taken on a life of its own, as all institutions do. Its ideology and practices evidently do damage to people, but it cloaks itself in a scientific white coat and holds fast to its conceptions and methods. But obstetrics has changed in ways that mask its deleterious effects. Just as subtle or covert racism (or any "ism") may be more difficult to see and to combat, so it is with the sadomasochistic hegemony underlying medicalization.

A few doctors and all the nurses we interviewed could see outside the parameters in which they functioned, but they could only occasionally or murkily imagine a better way. And, for the most part, they felt that the changes that had occurred — wallpaper, hardwood floors, conscious women, the presence of significant others — showed that humanitarianism held sway and progress occurred progressively. So they inadvertently (rather than intentionally) tended to promote the reign of medical authority over women's bodies and pregnancy and birth experiences.

As Judith Lorber (1984, 1993) documents, adding women and stirring doesn't necessarily produce changes in power dynamics within the institution of medicine; women are less likely than men to be in positions of administrative or policy-making power and increasingly more likely to become "rank-and-file professional employees" within highly bureaucratized systems (1993: 68–69).

Some evidence to the contrary does exist. In a study of 60 physician-patient interactions of five women and six men internists, Rita Charon, Michele G. Greene, and Ronald Adelman found:

> (1) Women physicians were more attentive, informative, and supportive to their patients when patients initiated discussion about life events, emotions, and relationships. (2) Women physicians were no different from men physicians, however, in the amount of control exerted in the visit, measured by the percentage of discussions that the doctor initiated. (3) Women physicians offered more comprehensive information to patients in the psychosocial content area. (4) Women physicians were more supportive of patients who raised issues of emotional or relational content. In addition they were significantly more engaged, respectful, egalitarian, and patient than men physicians. (5) Finally, women physicians were more likely to engage in joint decision-making and shared laughter with their patients, and they spent more time with their patients than did the men physicians [slightly less than four minutes longer per visit]. (1994: 215–216)

If these results were generalizable (and they may well be), improvements in doctor-patient relationships among women represent another way in which power imbalances may have softened. Even if medical education and medical practice continue to show more cognizance of the humanity of patients, though, the system remains focused on the premise of pathology waiting to happen and combated via scientifically justified intervention, and doctors still hold the ultimate judgmental and active power. The macro-level power-relations that characterize obstetrical interactions ultimately remain, for the most part, uncontested.

6

THE NEW ARRIVAL

Labor Doulas and the Fragmentation of Midwifery and Caregiving

BARI MELTZER NORMAN AND
BARBARA KATZ ROTHMAN

Of all the conflicted positions women occupy in the birthplace, probably none is more conflicted than that of the doula. In short, the doula provides social and emotional support to laboring women; she provides no medical or clinical care. Essentially, doulas are women hired to be women, to demonstrate every conventional gendered tactic, strategy, stance, and emotion you can imagine. They are there to be supportive of women in labor. They are there not to provide care, but to display care; they are decidedly not "caregivers," or "providers," a role left strictly to the obstetrician or midwife. They are hired for expertise in birth, but not permitted to act on that expertise in anything but their caring support. There is an inherent conflict in this role, expressed by Tanya Graves: "A doula should support a woman regardless — one hundred percent. A perfect birth is a home birth. Any other birth, you're an idiot, you know. That's my personal philosophy. Yet when I go into a birth, it's whatever you want."

It was the failure of husband-coached childbirth that opened the door for today's doula. The Lamaze method supported the hospital and the medical model more than it supported the women, as "the physical trappings and procedures surrounding the American birth were written into the [Lamaze] course" (Rothman 1991: 91); the Dick-Read method originated in Europe and did not account adequately for the lonely reality of American hospital birth; and Bradley placed the husband in a dominant, traditionalist role as "coach," overseeing the woman as she labored (Rothman 1991). Women need to be supported during labor, yet in U.S. hospitals, where midwives comprise a small proportion of care providers, doctors and nurses have not provided support, and fathers or other partners are not prepared adequately to serve effectively in that role. Increasingly, women are looking to hired help to fill the gap.

The word "doula" (pronounced "doo-luh") comes from Greek and translates as "slave" or "female helper." Dana Raphael (1973), a medical anthropologist, first applied the word *doula* to the birth arena when she wrote about the necessity of "mothering the mother" postpartum for better breastfeeding results:

> We use the term "doula" as a title for those individuals who surround, interact with, and aid the mother at any time within the perinatal period, which includes pregnancy, birth, and lactation.
>
> The function of the doula varies in different cultures from a little help here and there to complete succoring, including bathing, cooking, carrying, and feeding. Whatever the doula does, however, is less important than the fact that she is there. Her very presence gives the mother a better chance of remaining calm and nursing her baby. In areas such as the United States, where new mothers are often isolated from their kin, the doula's help is crucial if the mother wants to breastfeed. Her care and handling could save the day. Her presence could save the mother's milk. (Raphael 1973: 141)
>
> We might add that the doula, though most frequently female, experienced and often older, can also be a man. Though inexperienced and young, he may possess the critical ingredients that make a difference — a willingness and ability to be supportive. (Raphael 1973: 24)

Medical researchers later took the term "doula" and moved it out of this familial, communal realm. They used it for "an experienced labor companion who provides the woman and her husband or partner with emotional and physical support throughout the entire labor and delivery, and to some extent, afterward," thereby extending the role beyond familial, personal, and reciprocal relationships to almost exclusively hired helpers (Klaus et al. 2002 [1993]). The word has since been applied to both intrapartum and postpartum (female) helpers but is now most often understood as a hired labor support person, rather than a family member or friend who helps the mother after birth.

This chapter explores the rise of labor support doulas at a defining historical moment in their professional trajectory, focusing on doulas as workers, as caregivers, and as potential agents of social and ideological change. We address the following research questions:

- Who is drawn to this work and for what intellectual and ideological purposes? How are interest and importance organized by the individual actors and by groups/organizations in this field?
- How do doulas reconcile their personal beliefs and ideologies with professional and practical realities? How does this reconciliation affect the doula's sense of self and occupational future?
- What are the implications of "professionalization" and certain occupational practice strategies for doulas, for mothers, for families, and for birth more generally? To what extent are doulas willing to become enmeshed in the existing system? In what ways — if any — do they feel they can effect change?
- How do doulas' perceptions of feminism relate to their work and identification as doulas and as women?

The Doulas

This chapter is based on Bari's in-depth interviews with 30 labor doulas; research was conducted during two distinct phases of data collection. Phase I of data collection consisted of 20 in-person interviews with doulas from New York City and its surrounding suburbs. Phase II of data collection included follow-up telephone interviews with 15 of the 20 initial participants and in-person interviews with another ten labor doulas in Miami. Data were collected between January 2001 and July 2003.

The average age of the 30 doulas Bari interviewed was 39 years (at the time of the first interview). Participants had anywhere from zero to seven children, with an average of two children. Only four of the 30 doulas we interviewed were not mothers. All but three doulas held at least one other paid job to supplement their doula income, and the three women who did not work at another job all said that their doula income was not enough to live on.

Doulas earned an average yearly income of $10,460 from their labor doula work. The median yearly income was $7,000. The median is a better representation of income, as there were substantial differences in fees for services between the two regions. Overall, the average charge for a labor doula was $893. However, in the New York sample, the average charge was $1,084, compared to $457 in Miami. There was also a smaller range in charges in the Miami sample. The spread in the Miami sample was $350, whereas the spread in the New York group was $1,300.

Doulas in this sample attended an average of 15 births per year and had worked as doulas for an average of three years at the time of the first interview. Phase II data revealed that almost an equal number of doulas had left doula practice as had stuck it out. Bari was able to contact 15 of the 20 doulas from the original sample. Eight of these women had either scaled back their doula businesses or stopped practicing completely, while seven were still practicing regularly. Of those still practicing, several had expanded their birth businesses to include services such as childbirth education by the time of the second interview.

Bari drew names of potential participants at random from the membership lists of local and national doula organizations. The criteria for study participation were having attended at least one birth as either an apprentice or a paid doula, and having attended at least one birth as a doula in the 12 months prior to the interview. The response rate for Phase I interviews was 100% — all of the doulas Bari contacted agreed to participate. Interviews usually lasted approximately 60 to 90 minutes and were open-ended.

Certifying Doulas' Relevance

By almost all accounts, having a doula present in labor improves outcomes for the mother and the baby. For example, Klaus, Kennell and Klaus (2002) conducted an analysis of "ten randomized trials of continuous doula support" and found:

The presence of a doula reduces the overall cesarean rate by roughly 45 percent, length of labor by 25 percent, oxytocin use by 50 percent, pain medication by 31 percent, the need for forceps by 34 percent, and requests for epidurals by 10–60 percent.

Clearly, women benefit from the presence of a supportive and knowledgeable labor companion. These studies show that emotional support is crucial for laboring women, a claim that doctors challenging standard obstetric care have argued since at least the 1940s (Dick-Read 1944). But these studies also raise questions about whether there are any significant differences between having a trained doula and having a supportive lay companion. Modern-day birth doulas have been able to penetrate the intimate experiences of strangers' births because, we are told, most people in our lives have little experience with birth and therefore are inadequate mentors for labor support. Hired doulas have therefore taken on a "pseudo-familial" role, as they conduct their work inside medical institutions (Montgomery and Kosloski 1994). Or, it can be argued equally, this social, familial role has taken on an institutional, medical aura in keeping with the deep medicalization of birth in American culture.

The doula community grew organically from a grassroots movement of loosely connected women who were providing labor support regularly to friends, family, and/or clients. Women asked friends to attend their births and childbirth educators accompanied clients who wanted natural births but did not have adequate social support to achieve them. Doulas who entered the field in these ways talk about being doulas long before there was even a name for it. They were going to births because they enjoyed being at them. They weren't compensated financially for their time. The name "doula" was soon attached to those who served in this support role, and doulas eventually organized as an occupational group.

As an occupation emerges and strives to gain legitimacy, it is almost always the case, whether we are talking about key-cutting or bone-setting, that some type of educational credentialing system is created and increasingly imposed. This is of course what happened to midwifery as it reemerged in the contemporary era, and this is what is happening to doula work now.

Though there is currently no mandatory certification or licensing exam for labor support doulas, there is a growing trend toward certification. It was not until the early 1990s that professional[1] doula organizations were up and running to serve members and the public, but certification has already become the typical means of entry into professional labor support. While not required by law in order to practice, certification affords several benefits, including a structured means of entry into doula practice, access to a trainer and/or mentor, a guided curriculum, opportunities for networking and discussion, and "consumer confidence."

The founding of Doulas of North America (DONA) in 1992 is an important milestone in the "professionalization" of the labor support doula. Co-founded by Marshall Klaus, MD, Phyllis Klaus, John Kennell, MD, Penny Simkin, and Annie Kennedy, DONA began as a partnership of sorts between doulas and medical professionals (http://www.dona.org). Some might call it an omen. Kennell and Klaus were the pediatricians whose research gave doulas some early credibility (Klaus et al. 1972). Their study of the effects of a labor attendant on maternal-infant bonding was used, some would argue inappropriately, as "scientific evidence" of the benefits of the labor doula. For instance, Klaus et al. did not study trained labor assistants, per se. Rather, they studied the presence of supportive companions.

On the surface, certification lends credibility and a sense of professionalism to doula practice. Certification also suggests that doulas do indeed possess concrete skills that are certifiable. A closer look, however, suggests that certification has the potential to yield more setbacks than advances for the doula occupation because it is likely to spur divisions from within and regulation from without. Ultimately, certification represents a number of ironies. Though doulas pride themselves on the fact that they developed and maintain control over their certification programs, doula certification is almost indistinguishable from any other traditional certification program. And as in other professions, doulas accuse their professional organizations of bureaucratic aloofness and assert that certification represents little more than a piece of paper — all fairly standard occupational woes.

One byproduct of certification is the creation of a dividing line between those doulas who are certified and those doulas who are not. Although certification is in theory elective, many doulas feel that there is no real choice not to certify. So even though doulas are rarely strong proponents of certification, they tend to do it anyway. Doulas who resist certification are often labeled "radicals." This distinction creates a sense of competing interests between the certified and noncertified. Because there has been no organized resistance to certification, tacit acceptance of it has grown, fueling an increasingly profitable industry.

From its inception, DONA — which changed its name to DONA International in 2005 — has served as a training and certification organization for labor doulas. (Today, DONA certifies labor and postpartum doulas.) DONA's birth story, that of an organization founded not only by childbirth activists and educators, but by physicians as well, mimics the histories of other professional and community birth organizations such as ASPO (the Lamaze organization, American Society for Psychoprophylaxis in Obstetrics) and AAHCC (the Bradley organization, American Academy for Husband-Coached Childbirth). Its beginning foreshadows the strategies the occupation itself adopts as it continues to negotiate its place in American birth. As will become clear in this chapter, rather than distancing themselves from medicalized birth, doulas have elected to operate within the system.

Becoming a Doula

There are two basic ways one becomes a doula. The first is through apprenticeship. Like some direct-entry midwives, these doulas train through experience. For some doulas, as for some midwives, training by apprenticeship and experience is a calculated political decision, a statement against certification. Others just sort of fall into the work, stay busy with clients, and see no need for additional (and repetitive) training. The more popular choice by far is to train via a national organization such as DONA, as part of a formal certification program.

All of the doulas in our sample who got certified did so through at least one of four certification programs: the Association of Labor

Assistants and Childbirth Educators (ALACE), Birth Works, Childbirth and Postpartum Professional Association (CAPPA), and DONA. All four programs require completion of a training workshop, a reading list, attendance at a minimum of two births, and at least two evaluations either from a client, a care provider, or a nurse. The number of births required for certification ranges from two to six, the number of required books ranges from four to eight, and only two of the four organizations require an exam for certification.[2]

Currently, the workshop is the centerpiece of formal certification. The length of a workshop varies over time and between regions and individual trainers. For example, DONA requires that workshops last a minimum of 16 hours, while ALACE and Birth Works list their workshops as three-day commitments. Though the certification workshops are run via the certifying organizations, the details and structure of the training are often left to individual trainers. For instance, DONA trainers set the price for their workshops, rather than DONA setting a flat workshop fee.

In addition to attending a training workshop, doulas-in-training must attend between two and six births, depending on the organization with which they certify. In addition to attending births, the doula-in-training must produce evaluations from either clients, clinical care providers, nurses, or themselves.

Individuals who choose to certify through Birth Works or DONA must also submit essays as part of the certification process. A book report is required for each of the four books required for certification. DONA's written requirements focus on the trainee's experience of providing labor support. They require a 500- to 700-word essay on each certification birth, in addition to a 500- to 1000-word essay on the value and purpose of labor support. DONA's written requirements have increased in the past three years. Of the four profiled organizations, only ALACE and CAPPA require a written exam for certification. CAPPA's exam is open-book and requires an 85% pass rate, while ALACE requires the completion of a written exam.

In short, these programs involve a weekend workshop and additional readings, exams, evaluations, or attendance at a certain number of births. It is as brief an educational program as one can imagine in any field of work, supporting the thesis that doulas are hired simply to *be women* and to put a supportive woman's body in the room with a laboring woman. Doulas are not unlike some other paid caregivers, such as home health care aides, who also fill the caretaker role in the absence of family members. Like doulas, home health care aides undergo minimal training prior to working in the field. However, unlike doulas, who are often supported financially by a spouse or partner to place them firmly in the middle class, home health care aides are primarily working-class people who may or may not have the resources of a spouse.

In spite of the minimal training involved, doulas generally feel passionate about birth and are consumed by their work in the birth world. For some it is, as for some midwives, a calling. When Carole Prado, who had been trained as a massage therapist, first heard of the existence of labor support doulas, "I was like off my feet. I said, 'Oh my God, why didn't you tell me this sooner?' It was apparent in a split second that this is what I was here to do. I took the next available training." And as also happens for some midwives, becoming a doula can be a kind of healing from a traumatic or disappointing birth experience. Bridget Welsh's first birth opened the path to becoming a doula. She had a cesarean section, "which was absolutely 100 percent avoidable. I'm convinced 100 percent that if I had a doula it wouldn't have happened. And that's when I started delving into the whole world of birth and statistics and research and advocacy and activism and the whole nine yards." After a second, vaginal birth with a helpful doula, Welsh became a doula.

Some doulas, like some midwives, come out of feminist politics, sometimes via a formal women's studies background. During Pamela Lenzer's late teens, she was involved in a women's studies self-help group. It was the late 1980s, at a time when "I was real concerned about if women were going to continue to have the right to choose. And I was involved in just trying to figure out, to educate women more about their health care, their own bodies." During this time, Lenzer went to two births in a two-week period. She was asked to go to a friend's birth because she was the only woman her friend knew who had actually seen a birth before. The two experiences could not have been more different; Lenzer found the hospital birth particularly "horrendous." These experiences drew her into the world of birth. Even before she became a postpartum doula, Lenzer attended childbirth and midwifery conferences regularly. By the time she got certified, she had long been part of the alternative birth community. "For a lot of women, doing the training is their introduction to the birth world. ... But for me, it felt like I was already there on a certain level. Not completely, but I ... was busy, already involved in that."

Lenzer, like some other doulas, actually would have preferred midwifery school, but for whatever reasons — often their own pregnancies, births, and demands of motherhood — many women who think they would like to become midwives cannot go to midwifery school and settle for becoming doulas. Two of the doulas we interviewed even discussed a professional interest in obstetrics. Maria Rinaldi came to doula work directly on her path to midwifery:

> I plan to be a midwife eventually. I had years and years of trying to decide between obstetrics and midwifery and I finally decided that midwifery is what I wanted to do. Because c-sections are just not my interest. And so I applied to midwifery school. ... I didn't get in the first year. Both places [I applied] said I haven't shown enough commitment to women's health because I hadn't done volunteer work.

Eventually, Rinaldi stopped volunteering for the midwife she'd started working with and started her own practice as a labor support doula.

Becoming a midwife via a nurse-midwifery program, a direct entry program, or an apprenticeship involves years of commitment and work. Not so for becoming a doula. There are some women who enter doula practice almost by chance during transitional periods in their lives. After spending 20 years in the retail business, for instance, Nicole Bloom found herself at a crossroads and in a midlife crisis. She wanted to start afresh, trying a new career field and even moving to a new city. While on the phone with a friend who lived in another state, she asked, "Tracy, what should I do when I grow up?" Tracy said she thought Bloom would make a great doula. Bloom had no idea what that was. "Without Tracy around, I probably never would have known this existed. Childbirth was not an area that I had a particular interest in — I wasn't disinterested — it just clicked when she said it." Bloom traveled to do the training with Tracy without "do[ing] any research into it." She then decided to certify to become a doula because "it's embarrassingly simple. [It's] really the only reason I was able to make the switch."

The ease with which one can formally certify as a doula is often the primary reason a doula gives for entering the practice, regardless of how she heard of the work in the first place. Whether as a segue to midwifery, because of a strong interest in birth, or just looking for a new job to try out, becoming a doula in the formal sense is not difficult. There is little risk of money or time. No formal schooling is necessary, and the certification workshops usually take place over one weekend. Minimal additional requirements, such as reading books and writing papers, can be completed on one's own timeline. It is indeed "embarrassingly simple."

Doula Work

Doulas come to this work from a variety of occupational and professional backgrounds and with different motivations in mind. Upon their arrival, they find an occupation that is regulated by neither state nor federal legislation. Doulas are not required to be certified (though there are certification programs), to complete either a formal training program or an apprenticeship (though many do), or to be licensed (there is no licensing exam). Given this practice climate, doulas work primarily as independent contractors. In almost all cases, hiring a doula is an out-of-pocket expense for the parent(s), since few insurance companies currently cover doula services. Fees for doula care range from under $500 to about $2,000, depending on the level of experience of the doula and the city in which services are rendered. Level of experience is usually gauged by the number of births attended or years in practice. Some doulas work on a sliding scale, determining their fee based on the client's ability to pay.

In rarer cases, doula services are provided by a hospital. Often the hospital-based doulas who provide these services are volunteers; therefore, the doula services are offered either free of charge or at a significantly reduced rate to laboring women. Of course, these volunteer doulas spend significantly less time with their "clients" than paid ones do, and they rarely meet clients in advance of the birth. Several practicing doulas we interviewed questioned whether these hospital-based doulas were really doulas at all.

Private-duty doulas usually commit to at least one in-person meeting, unlimited phone consultations (need is determined by the client), labor support from the start of labor to a couple of hours following the birth, and a postpartum home visit. Individual doulas may provide more (or fewer) services as part of their basic fee. The crux of the job is understood to be continuous labor support to the birthing mother.

Doulas share as a common goal, virtually universally expressed, the desire to provide women with positive birth experiences that do not undermine their confidence or ability. Given the medical management under which they must provide their services, the unanswered, fundamental question is whether they are making birth better for women, or just making women feel better about their births. Or is there a difference? If a woman has a cesarean section that was unnecessary, but she believes it was a good thing, is there an objective measure by which we can say it is anything but good? Is there such a thing as a "good birth," measured by anything other than the way the woman feels about it? Most midwives and most doulas would say yes: for one thing, a birth that leaves a woman feeling stronger in herself is better, by their standards, than one that leaves her feeling "rescued" by medical intervention.

So what is it doulas actually do? In many ways, doulas are chameleons. Depending on a variety of factors — the doula's relationship with the mother, her familiarity with the care provider, and her opinions about the progress of the labor — the doula tries to help the woman without ruffling the feathers of her institutional care providers. Back rubs and foot massages, warm encouraging words to the woman, the generic "wiping the fevered brow" kind of support is always acceptable. But depending on where they are (at a prenatal appointment, in the labor and delivery room, at home with the mother postpartum) and who is there with them (an obstetrician, a midwife, a spouse/partner, a labor and delivery nurse), what more they can do varies considerably. For instance, in the presence of a medical care provider, a labor support doula will likely be more passive or cryptic (utilizing verbal or nonverbal codes she hopes medical workers will not pick up on) than she would be when alone with her client.

The job of the doulas is not either to challenge or to support the medical model, but to *help the woman*. This is what some call a "humanistic model," which

> speaks of reform rather than revolution. Without overthrowing the dominance of allopathy or undermining popular belief in its efficacy, the proponents of this approach seek to soften the hard edges of techno-medicine. Humanists try to treat patients with compassion and respect, to add the interpersonal dimensions of healing to the allopath's technical expertise. (Davis-Floyd and Sargent 1997: 81–82).

Doulas are in no position to make a revolution: part care broker, part hospital ancillary, and part independent contractor and advocate, with no power to provide alternative care services, doulas are in a curious and difficult place. Doulas find different ways of negotiating these strange demands made on them.

Probably the most widely used stance is passivity: supporting the woman unconditionally, not questioning medical providers, and not themselves advocating for the woman, but doing what they see as "helping women to advocate for themselves." If a doula in a labor room or hospital delivery suite disagrees with the care provider or calls into open question what a midwife, physician, or nurse is doing, she can be asked to leave. And even if she can argue her way, negotiate, plead, somehow manage to stay for that birth, her working relationship with that hospital, doctor, or midwife may well be over. She may not be welcomed back. Because of the imposed silence they feel they are under in the actual labor setting, Brenda Gade sees prenatal meetings and phone conversations as vital to success in the hospital:

> We advocate on her behalf without speaking for her. ... I think that ... prenatal contact comes in so importantly because we can empower her during that. We have that edge over her doctor, who sees her for five or six minutes on average. We have that over the nurse, who's never met her. ... So while I'm an advocate, I'm really clear, both in our written contract and our prenatal meetings, that I'm not there to be her voice. Part of that has got to be that she choose a health care

provider that she trusts. And that she has a responsibility, as well, to be her own advocate.

While this sounds like an ethic of client responsibility and non-paternalism, clearly one of the strongest reasons doulas adopt this approach is that verbal questioning in the birthing room can get them kicked out. In many ways, it is a survival tactic. Maria Rinaldi had one experience early on in her doula career, and it set the tone for her future work:

> I was with the woman and the woman made a comment. She was examined and she was six centimeters dilated. But all throughout labor she's been saying how she's gonna want an epidural, an epidural, an epidural. So when she was I think six and a half centimeters dilated the doctor was in the room. And she says, "Oh, Maria. That's great news. I might not need that epidural." And I said, "Yeah — you might not." The doctor did not like my comment. [They] pulled me out [of the labor room] and the nurse told me what the doctor said, that I should keep my mouth shut, that it's not my opinion to say whether she needs an epidural or not. It was not my first statement, it was her [the woman's] statement. But even so, now you walk around the doctors as if you're walking on eggshells.

Other doulas had stories of either being asked to leave or being taken out in the hallway for a talking-to. Sarah Davis summed up the advocacy conundrum best: "My biggest obstacle is if I'm in the labor room, if I'm really an advocate [laughs], I'll get thrown out." And Peg Marshall put it quite bluntly when she said, "You can just get tossed out on your ear. You know, it's their turf and we're there at their sufferance."

A small minority of doulas take a different approach and do intervene. That was, we found, particularly true of doulas who had had a background in medical work of some sort. Simone Powell, who was a labor and delivery nurse for several years before switching to doula work, said she felt comfortable speaking out. But she lets it be known that she has a nursing background, a strategy that gives her more legitimacy with the medical staff, compared to most doulas:

> A lot of times you pick your battles. I know you can't fight them all and you need to know when you go to the hospital with your client what

really means the most to them. And [I] tell them that I will advocate for them as best I can and that I do feel that part of my role is to run interference for them and, you know, I'm quite happy to just sort of be the bad guy, if necessary, when it comes to dealing with OBs or anesthesia or nursing stuff.

Lee Pate felt that her earlier work experiences in the medical field made her more comfortable questioning medical workers, more generally.

I think of myself as an advocate and I'll go up against a doctor or a nurse if the mother wants something. Very professional. See, I'm not afraid of a white coat. Of course it's my age. I'm older. Kids are younger, going into this. I've been a medical assistant and I've worked in doctors' offices.

Other doulas pick and choose who they will advocate for, depending on the client. Mary Norgren, for instance, is careful, and says she only speaks up "if I know my clients are the kind of people who would allow me to. If she's given me that authority, I will do it. ... Each client's different." But as a rule, most doulas do not advocate on behalf of their clients in the presence of other medical professionals. The risks of being perceived as confrontational, difficult, meddlesome, or even uninformed are too great (see Hwang 2004, and DONA's response at www.dona.org).

What, then, is the job? Doulas are not medical professionals, whether by the doctors' accounting, by the hospital's organizational chart, or by their own self-understanding. It keeps coming back to the language of being present and being supportive: the warm woman's body in the room. Can one turn this deeply gendered role play into a "job," a business? Apparently so. There are doulas who do make a living wage as doulas, becoming entrepreneurial in their doula practice. They incorporate, set up practices with multiple doulas, and offer additional services at an additional charge, such as private childbirth education and preparation classes, hypnobirthing classes, postpartum doula services, lactation consulting, and child care. Even though doulas who function that way are the only ones who tend to make an annual living wage from their birth work, they are sometimes viewed with contempt by other doulas who believe that being a doula should not be about money or financial gain. In keeping with this idealized, essentialist view of women's work and its implicit critique of capitalist business practices, the overt treatment of doula work as a profit-making venture is poor form, according to most of the doulas Bari interviewed. This traditional and essentialist view, wherein money and love are oppositional and incongruous with womanhood and/or femininity, is a common thread in doulas' beliefs about their work, about themselves, and about feminism in general. It is also one of many ironies that characterize this group.

These more entrepreneurial doulas are often accused by other doulas of not giving "from the heart" and focusing too much on the business aspect of things, of being greedy and competitive. In response, the entrepreneurial doulas argue that there are plenty of pregnant women out there who could and would use doula services if only they knew about them. Still, their more proactive approach (some doulas label it aggressive) to getting those clients — via advertising, hiring other doulas to work in their practice,[3] and/or contracting with particular hospitals or OB practices as a preferred but not exclusive service — is perceived as violating the "doula spirit."

It is not that the birth philosophies and practices of the more business-oriented doulas differ from the doulas who criticize their approach. One of the goals of the entrepreneurial doula, aside from building her own business, is to build and market the doula concept more generally, and to get the word and the service "out there" to women on a larger scale. For instance, Bella Cole runs a business in which doulas work through her service, which is the preferred service of a particular hospital. The hospital gives out information on the doula service. Cole organizes meetings where parents can meet all the doulas and then hire the doula they like best. The practice takes a cut of the collected fee, which varies depending on the doula's level of experience. In Cole's opinion, under this set-up, "everybody wins."

Her reasoning is that the hospital wins because it gets to offer an extra, personalized service at no cost to the organization: the clients pay the doulas directly, and the doulas pay to train/certify themselves. The mothers and the doula community-at-large win because more women find out about, have access to, and trust doula services when hospitals promote and support doulas. Individual doulas win because they are not responsible for the advertising or soliciting of clients; the clients come to them, which is particularly attractive for doulas just starting out. And the entrepreneurial doula wins because she is compensated for coordinating the services, the people, and the organization.

Most of the doulas Bari interviewed were troubled by this business model. It is an approach that runs counter to what Carla Reese sees as the essence of being a doula — offering warm, supportive care:

> I like making the money I make. But it's not a business. … For me it loses it where you charge for going to meet the person. … I know people who charge 50 dollars just for them to meet you to see if they like you, or they charge per mile, mileage, driving. It's losing it there for me, you know?… It's a touchy-feely kind of supportive, loving, mothering thing.

They are in a bind: a bind that is familiar to nurses, midwives, foster care mothers, child care workers, social service workers, and so forth. These occupations, whether they require a weekend-long training or postgraduate work, are based on very essentialist notions of womanliness, of *naturally nurturant* womanly behavior. To charge for being womanly, to charge for being motherly, flies in the face of the conventional ideology of gender. And for most doulas, there is much value in conventional gender ideology. These are women for whom being womanly, loving, supporting, and nurturing is a job description.

Values in Practice

The overwhelming majority of doulas Bari interviewed said that their ideal birth is an unmedicated, out-of-hospital birth attended by a midwife. However, since 99% of American births take place in the hospital, and 92% of births are attended by a medical doctor,[4] and more than half of U.S. women receive epidural anesthesia for pain relief during labor,[5] birth is not even close to the way doulas believe it should be (Martin et al. 2002).

Although doulas feel freer to advocate in private prenatal meetings with pregnant women, their clients are still under the primary care of physicians or midwives, and doulas remain second-class birth workers. ("Second-class" is generous, as doulas fall below physicians, midwives, and nurses. Perhaps "fourth-class birth workers" is more accurate.) For instance, one doula said she offered information to clients prenatally but coached them not tell their doctors that the information came from a doula:

> They might ask me, "Well yeah … isn't that [no eating or drinking during labor] necessary to prevent [me] from vomiting and aspirating my vomit?" And I can say, "Well actually no. That's kind of an antiquated dumb notion, you know. But if you talk to your doctor make sure that you tell him that you got that information from a friend of yours, not from your doula."

To avoid appearing confrontational or threatening to hospital staff, doulas may engage in deception as part of their survival strategy, and "make nice with the doctors" and the nursing staff. As Nicole Bloom explained, part of "mak[ing] nice" is "get[ting] what I want from them." It is a calculated, passive-aggressive maneuver with an intended end result. As part of this tactic, doulas attempt to forge relationships with nurses to get them to accept doulas as part of the team and not to see them as adversaries. For instance, Amy Rozen considers it part of her job to befriend the nurses right from the start: "I make it my business to, you know, to make that happen. I mean, to kind of sweet-talk them, if you like … I just really try right from the beginning, [to] like share a snack with them or like ask them, 'Did you have a hard night?' or 'What's going on?'" This "make nice" approach is a form of mediated advocacy that is part of the doula's overall strategy to get a better birth for the woman. Bridget Welsh calculates her movements carefully:

> Then there's also the part of me that is a little passive-aggressive. It's very strategic. … I know how to schmooze and [bull]shit a [bull]shitter, as the expression goes. I know how to play the game. And not all doulas think of it that way. A lot of doulas are like earth mothers, "This shouldn't be a game." But it is.

And so doulas play the "game." But in the process of playing the game — even if they get what they want — they downplay themselves as professionals. Playing dumb is an almost painfully gendered strategy employed by several of the doulas interviewed; for instance, Darlene Wynn asks, "What is that for?" (in a "duh" voice) when an

OB pulls out a hook to break the amniotic sack. But is this necessarily a good strategy to enhance and promote doula services in the long run?

Lenzer calls her approach "a surreptitious kind of advocacy." Kate Tyler, a certified doula with her own practice, relayed a fairly common approach: "I will not say, 'You can't do this to my client,' because that's not my place. ... We generally have little signs ... like I'll clear my throat or do something to let them know that they're about to do something that we talked about and now it's time for you to say, 'No, I don't want this.'" That is, doulas are like mimes, developing nonverbal communicative scripts or nonverbal cues to facilitate communication without a verbal exchange. Similarly, Bella Cole described herself as "the bird that whispers into their ear." Doulas also mentioned stomping on the partner's foot and clearing the throat as "code language" for "Say something now!"

Most doulas, as a general rule, prefer to empower women and families to advocate for themselves. This is the type of advocacy, as described by Phyllis Miller, that is supported by most doula certifying organizations: "I think that the advocacy comes in before the birth when you meet with the mother. ... That's where I feel the advocacy is. ... But in the process [labor], I'm not there for that. I'm there to help them get through it."

Doulas provide (sometimes alternative) information to their clients, but claim not to definitively counsel or advise them in any particular way. When asked if she acts as an advocate for her clients, Tanya Graves said "Yes," but qualified her answer in terms of "rights":

> When I think of advocacy, I think of letting them [clients] know their rights. It's as simple as that. I don't think you have to be ... jumping in front of the epidural or cursing the anesthesiologist or barring the door to be an advocate. Just informing clients of their rights and their choices and [that] they can say, "No." I mean, when I've told people that, their eyes damn near bug out of their head. ... You have to know your rights and that's basically my view of advocacy.

Graves has two views on how advocacy can work: a hands-off, educational model that is based on informing people of their rights, and an interventionist model that involves things like jumping in front of doors. Most doulas prefer to act as educators outside the birthing room, and hope the education takes by the time they get inside of it. This strategy is twofold, as it aims to "empower" women and families and to protect doulas from eviction.

There are other doulas who claim not to play "the game" at all. These are usually doulas who are not certified, who do not see their work as long-term, or who have some other credential, such as a nursing degree, to back them up. Mary Norgren said:

> I hear a lot of doulas say, "Well you have to approach it in a certain way. You have to plant seeds for the next time. You have to watch how you speak." I am [laughs] the only one … vocal enough [about this]. Let's not get tripped up on semantics. I don't want to play word games. I want to just say what it is and where it's at and that's it.

Simone Powell, who used to work as an RN in labor and delivery, left nursing and is now a doula. Based on her experiences in nursing, she feels strongly that her job is to advocate for her clients:

> My experience [in] nursing has taught me that, you know, sometimes I think women in labor can be manipulated a bit into doing things they don't want to do or not getting what it is that they want. And they are not in a good position to advocate for themselves because, you know, they are working really hard — they're in labor and they're in pain. And sometimes a partner isn't always the best person to advocate either because he's concerned about his loved one, who's sitting there and struggling in pain. So I think it's really important if I know what's important to them that I be the one who's willing to talk up. You know, when it's needed.

What some see as an occupational strategy, others see as an occupational trap. Norgren said that several doulas approached her and confided that doulas need to speak up in a more open and honest way to effect change; however, they are unwilling to speak out, either because they lack confidence in their ability to speak effectively or because they are concerned about being perceived as troublemakers or radicals in doula circles. There is trepidation about publicly critiquing the doula community, even at doula group meetings; no one wants to come across as an "anti-doula" doula. And while several other doulas expressed feelings similar to Mary's in their interviews, the public line can be strikingly different.

Nicole Bloom, not committed to being a doula over the long haul, has less to lose if she sticks her neck out. She shared a story of a difficult situation that ultimately worked in her favor:

> So this doctor at the first birth I did with him, did several outrageous things, but the most outrageous was telling my client that that if she didn't have an episiotomy, within the next five years or so, her insides were going to fall out. All her organs would fall out and she would just ... have major problems. And he scared her. He scared her to death. So I waited until he left the room and then proceeded to tell her that he was wrong. That I know I'm not a doctor and he is, but he's apparently not practicing evidence-based medicine and he's wrong. And I worked to calm her down some, and then when the nurse came in I mentioned to the nurse what the doctor had just said so that I could get her another opinion and the nurse said, "That's just plain bullshit!"

In the end, no episiotomy was cut, even though the doctor wanted to do it. It is likely that by speaking up, Nicole really made a difference in the woman's care and effected change in this instance, but she waited until the doctor left to dispute his patently ridiculous claim, and she used a nurse, a member of the medical team, to help convince her client to advocate for herself against the procedure. It was an effective strategy for avoiding an episiotomy; it's markedly less effective at creating a professional place for doulas in birth.

Bloom worked with the same doctor at a subsequent birth. Perhaps believing that she would not contradict him (after all, she did not protest his previous comment regarding falling organs), the doctor took to asking Bloom her opinions in front of her clients. This time, she spoke up:

> At the first birth I never said anything challenging to him at all. I just waited for him to leave the room. At the second birth, I did respond. ... He looked at me and said, "Don't you agree?" And I said, "Well, actually, no, I don't [she laughs]. I realize I'm not a doctor. You are. But you asked me. So I'm going to tell you. I'm going to tell you." And that was the last time he asked me what I thought [she laughs]. But he was cool.

He didn't get mad, he didn't try to make me leave or anything like that. He just stopped asking.

When radical doulas seek support from their colleagues, they often receive the cold shoulder. Susie Shreve told her colleagues about a birth where she got into a heated discussion with the birthing woman and her partner about an invasive procedure that was about to be performed. While Shreve and the client agreed in principle that the procedure was unnecessary, the client still signed the consent form for the procedure. Shreve became frustrated with her client and with her own inability to do anything to alter the situation. As she put it, "I advocated because I *couldn't help it*." Her colleagues told her that she acted "unprofessionally." To that she responded:

> What is unprofessional about being mad as hell? What is unprofessional about advocating for your client? What's wrong with saying, "This is messed up and it's not okay"? You're wheeling a woman in who's crying, saying, "I don't want to do this." And her husband's going, "We don't want to do this." But yet they're still signing the paperwork. ... I was angry and I had every right to be. I loved these people. They loved me.

Shreve used the language of love, of meaningful personal relationships. She had real physical and emotional reactions to this birth, which she saw as a "bad birth." She had parallel positive reactions to good births. For her, as for many, this is personal:

> At a home birth or hospital birth where things are, where a woman's being respected, I'm full when I leave. I'm high. I don't get sick. I go home and write poetry. I'm nice to my kids. When I go home after a bad birth, I'm horrible. I'm angry. I'm torn. ... I get cold sores. ... And I know there are some people who have risen above it and maybe it's a higher state of spirituality where you're not *affected*, but you can be *effective*. But I don't know. I haven't gotten there yet. But it doesn't take me two weeks to recover anymore. It takes me like two days.

Other doulas also report similar "aftershocks" following births gone bad. Pamela Lenzer had this to say:

I just felt heartbroken with the first few births I attended as a doula, a professional doula. One was a forceps delivery. … I mean there was no conflict between me and the doctor. But the father and the doctor got into a screaming match while the mother was pushing. It was just very hard to help facilitate that [birth] and help give the mother the support that she needed in that. I felt like she walked away feeling okay about it, but I needed to cry for several days and go to my [peer support] group and process it.

Advocacy, and doulas' inability to be full advocates during a birth, poses a real problem for some doulas, personally and politically, and the repercussions can manifest in emotional and physical ways. The inability to advocate effectively in the hospital birthing room can breed feelings of powerlessness, which are intricately connected to the ways in which doulas think about their work and their "moral identities" (cf. Kleinman 1996).

Doulas want to see themselves as having the power to effect change in the maternity care system, but they experience their repeated failure at protecting even one woman at a time. Sarah Davis related these feelings of powerlessness:

> The doctors see the doulas are not threatening, they're not coming and, you know, standing between them. Doulas don't have that role, for the most part. Doulas don't have that type of agenda. *We can't*. We don't have that power, even if we wanted. … You can't fight City Hall. Just seeing things happen, knowing how the sprint is going to go and just being there as a doula and just being *powerless* to do anything about it.

Reconciling Work and Values

Every doula we interviewed criticized the routine medicalization of birth, this "natural body process," but few were willing to translate that criticism outright into their doula practices. No doula restricted her practice to "natural" births or out-of-hospital births; few even verbally advocated for their clients in the hospital. They separated their personal ideologies from their professional practices and defined their responsibility to be supporting the choices of their clients, regardless of whether they agreed with those decisions. Oddly — and to us, disturbingly — they draw on a language of "feminism" to support this hands-off, passive stance.

As was true of midwives, there was a contingent of doulas who embraced the term "feminist," although often with some qualification. Identifying with feminism was almost always couched within an acknowledgment that their personal lives were in some sort of conflict with what they thought of as feminist ideology. For instance, Darlene Wynn identified as a feminist, but she raised the issue of her choice to stay at home with her children:

> When I had my kids, I stayed home for two years with the last one and I'm probably going to do that with this one and … it was difficult coming to the conclusion that that was feminism. So the whole doula label where they're like, because doulas are supposed to be very empowered and help empower women, but then they kind of slap you with, "Well what are you going to do when you have your baby?" kind of thing. It's just a very funny place to be.

Despite Lisa Lynch's disenchantment with the politics of her local birth community, she also identified strongly as a feminist. Though her personal life also was fairly traditional (in the middle-class sense), she saw her professional life as exemplifying her feminist ideals:

> I am a feminist. Golly, it means that women can do anything. I mean, just, see, I've been married 26 years and my husband is very male chauvinistic. And I went to a girls' college. … So anyway, that was back when the feminist action first started. But you know, yeah, we can do anything the men can do.

These are not very complex definitions of feminism, but they are at least recognizable as some kind of feminism. Crystal Walker was a traditionally minded doula who embraced the language of feminism, even though she thought that feminists would "cringe" at her kind of feminism. She did indeed push it about as far as it can go:

> It means a woman who promotes and advocates on other women's behalf, and those women's best interests. And so in that sense I would say yes. I am a feminist. I think that as a Christian woman, I've got — I've

come full circle on some issues. There was a time when I believed in a woman's right over her own body and right to have an abortion. I don't feel that way anymore. … My Christian principles have kicked in now. I think that as a married woman in a Christian household, my husband is the head of this household now. … When the final decision needs to be made, I need to leave that role up to him and respect that decision, that he's making it in our best interests — not just his best interests. So in that sense, I think that some feminists may cringe to hear me say that [she laughs], but yeah, I do [consider myself a feminist].

Simone Powell felt there was an inherent feminist statement in being a doula. She was a doula who appropriated the rhetoric of feminism in a way that made sense for herself and for her occupation. She was more willing to identify as a feminist than other doulas; however, she was careful to identify the specific type of feminist she saw herself and her peers as being:

I think anyone who's working as a doula is a feminist. They might not just want to own up to it. And, again, it's with a small "f," not necessarily a capital "f." You know, you don't have to be radical. … But they are [feminists]. I think they just don't realize that, but I think just by saying that I'm going to work as a doula you're making a feminist statement. … I definitely see what I do as a way of enabling women to take back some of their power, you know, when they're laboring and having their babies.

Still, some of the doulas just reject the language of feminism, refuse to apply that word to themselves. Anne Bartlett conceptualized birth and birth issues as human issues, not as women's issues. While she would not reject feminism flatly, she was not comfortable with the label, either. She found it limiting:

I used to define myself as a feminist. I think of myself as a *humanist*. … I mean I think of feminism as a movement that has fought for equal rights for both genders. Both, yeah. So in that way I am a feminist. But I would say that the better word for it is humanist now. I think that at a point it had to be a feminist because women had so few rights. And that we needed to fight for the rights for women. But now I think we really need to fight for the rights of all people. I think fighting for women and husbands to have a choice and information, education about the process of birth, for a human being to be brought into this world in a loving manner, rather than, some of the births — the way these children are welcomed into the world is horrifying. Absolutely horrifying. So I think that being a doula is being an educator and being a supporter of a more humane way of birthing and being born.

Some doulas referred to themselves as "humanists" rather than feminists because they saw themselves as seeking to better humanity, not just the status of (pregnant) women. To them, feminism felt somewhat exclusionary. Also, "humanist" does not have the negative social connotations they saw in "feminist," and so some women were more comfortable embracing that term.

By far, Mary Norgren was the most politically oriented doula Bari interviewed. She expressed great hope and disappointment in doulas' role in American birth. She spoke of doulas' ability to provide accurate information to clients, gather local and national statistics, keep complaint and compliment files on caregivers, write letters, meet with care providers, and get articles written. Doulas have first-hand access to rich data, she argued. However, she said doulas have not taken advantage of these opportunities:

> I've always felt and I *know* … that we were always in a position to make change — *and we haven't*. We haven't at all. And I cannot tell you how disappointed I've been in that. I was always excited about my work because I knew that we could make change. … we were in a position to do so. But I never felt we could do it alone, that any of us could do it alone.

The strategy that doulas have employed, unconditional support of women's choices, is where the doula issue became clearly feminist for Norgren, who said that, along with "unconditional support," another overarching feminist principal of doula care is "unconditional respect." She added:

> But that comes with a lot of tentacles. Respect is not just doing whatever, support the woman in whatever she's being told. Respect is also spending some time alone with that woman, saying, "You really don't want this. Don't do it." Support her, not what's around her, even if it

looks as if she wants that. Find out for sure what she wants. Unconditional support, see that's become a feminist issue now.

Based on her experiences providing care and her experiences behind the scenes, Norgren framed birth and the politics of it as larger social issues — not just feminist issues — and chose to identify on that basis:

> So in terms of the feminist issue, yeah, it's a social issue, it's a cultural issue. It's not just women, men, babies. It's everybody (laughs). I see the world through the eyes of a doula. I've learned a lot about the rest of the world applying these principles to birth that I see out in the rest of the world and it's shit, everywhere. Everywhere power's being taken away from people.

Some doulas evade extrapolating from the power dynamics of the birth scenes they witness to larger societal inequities — for example, deliberately leaving patriarchal marriage uninterrogated (as Crystal Walker did) or glossing heteronormativity and equal rights together into "humanism" (as Anne Bartlett did). Yet many doulas seek to intervene (whether passive-aggressively or, occasionally, directly) to enable women to feel less disempowered (if not actually powerful) than they otherwise would be in medicalized birth experiences. The variation can be explained in doulas' general uncertainty regarding the future of their occupation. It is our sense that doulas as a group see themselves as hanging by a thread, with privileges and access to the birthing room ready to be taken away from them at any given moment, at one misstep. They'll knowingly be pushed (sometimes tacitly, sometimes overtly) into staying quiet, acting surreptitiously or behaving well — ironically, the very thing that they're trying to get their clients *not* to do — all in the hope of effecting some sort of change, some sort of philosophical shift.

Conclusion

On the whole, doulas have reconciled divisions they have experienced between their personal beliefs about what makes for a good birth, and the professional practices their clients actually encounter, by enabling more mainstream approaches. They work in hospitals, sit and chat with women who have had epidurals, or nod supportively as women are sent into unnecessary cesarean sections. Those who have not adapted to the medical marketplace have had a difficult time. Many of the women who had identified themselves as more radical or change-oriented doulas had either scaled back their doula practices significantly or left the field entirely. Some went on to midwifery school. The professional leadership has chosen to work within the system rather than trying to change it; they have chosen to play by the rules. On its website, DONA specifies that labor "doulas should be facilitators in the birthing environment. We do not speak on behalf of the mother nor do we make decisions for her." Doulas who speak up in the birth environment are violating DONA's standards of practice. Those who chose to challenge the rules have been fingered as jeopardizing the future of the profession, "ruining it" for everyone else.

Without organizational support from within the medical institution or from outside it, doulas who are unwilling to facilitate status-quo decision making find themselves outnumbered and alienated from many of their colleagues. Without a critical mass of support from other doulas or from the professional doula organizations, effectively challenging the biomedical status quo is nearly impossible. Doulas are appropriated by the system. As Bella Cole said: "If, for some reason, she [a woman] needs to give birth in, you know, Cesarean Hospital with Dr. Knife, if that's what she needs to do, then that's what she needs to do and I'm just there for what's going on with her." How can this approach improve birth for women?

Like nurse-midwives, doulas must generally play by the hospital rules. Most notably, they aim to stay in the good graces of the hospital staff: they do not want to get kicked out of the labor room, the doula equivalent of losing hospital privileges. And although several doulas specifically acknowledged the problematic situation of nurse-midwifery, they saw their situation as doulas to be different, since doulas do not directly compete with obstetricians for business. However, these doulas encourage mothers to be less obeisant, and that may prove to be a similarly daunting threat to physicians. Despite their best efforts, doulas may become enmeshed in the system, indistinguishable in their practice from the conventional, medical birth attendant.

Certification reinforces the authority of medicine. In the absence of state laws and regulation of doula services, hospital administrators have taken matters into their own hands, creating hospital-based doula programs. Not surprisingly, hospitals with doula programs require that doulas be certified. This keeps non-certified doulas out of some hospitals and gives hospitals even greater say in how doulas should operate their businesses. The distinction between lay and expert, which certification symbolizes, underscores an irony in the doula certification debate. That is, one intended effect of certification is to differentiate between lay servants and professional servants, with doulas being professional servants. Yet doulas support women's choices, regardless of their possibly contrary expert and personal opinions. Like genetic counselors or others in counseling positions, they are there to help people reach their own goals, not to set the goals for them. So what exactly is their expertise? In what is a weekend-trained doula "expert"? And does she ever assert her expert knowledge and opinions?

There is a difference between an expert in birth and an expert in companion skills. Midwives are birth experts, with finely honed and trained companion skills. If doulas are experts in companionship and support, their goals toward a reformed maternity care system are less obvious and robust. They are just there as companions, and they could just as easily — as some of the doulas we interviewed suggested — be doulas for root canal, knee surgery, or any other instance in which someone needs companionship, especially in a medical setting.

On the other hand, if doulas want to position themselves as experts in birth, they need to take a clear stand on how they think birth should be, not only in theory but in practice as well. Part of the problem is that doulas try to deflect attention from the activist nature of their work. They sell themselves to their clients as being there, being present at a birth, only to support the woman in her choices. However, their work is inherently political, activist work simply *because* they are working in the birth field. They believe that birth matters, and they do believe that there are "good births" and "bad births." For doulas to think that they can enter the birth scene without making some sort of political statement, as many of them believe, makes for an unclear mission. Why are they there, if not to help promote good births and decrease bad births?

With certification and third-party reimbursement being the primary goals of doula organizations such as DONA, their mission for birth is increasingly vague and business-oriented. This lack of clarity results in the absence of a calculable measure of success or quality, a significant gap in the certification of labor assistants. What signifies good practice or preparation? Fewer interventions? Client satisfaction, regardless of interventions? Institutional support and approval? Increased use of doulas? A greater trend toward unmedicated childbirth? How can we judge success?

Ultimately, certification underscores an important strain in doula work: doulas have an activist, social movement-oriented philosophy that leans toward "natural" and even out-of-hospital birth. At the same time, they have chosen to organize themselves as an occupation within the medical institution, attending women primarily in hospitals; they have not limited their work to out-of-hospital births, to midwifery clients, or to natural births. Occupationally, they accept their position inferior to clinical caretakers, as evidenced in their hands-off type of advocacy in the birth room. Yet doulas still seek general legitimation and authority of their own within the medical context.

In short, doulas want to change birth, but they do not want to be labeled as change makers. They want authority in the medical marketplace, but they shun the traditional medical approach to birth. They want insurance to cover doula services, but they don't want insurance companies to restrict their practice. While they have tried to elicit change quietly from within — the strategy they have chosen to employ — the overall result has been an enabling effect. That is, in trying to make quiet waves, doulas ultimately help along the current medicalized system of birth.

Working within the system has also meant overwhelming support for the formal certification of doulas. This is the case, despite several doulas' expressed interest in traditional midwifery training. Time and money, however, were typically obstacles to midwifery for this group. Indeed, many doulas considered the certification procedure for doulas to be inadequate preparation and praised empirical training in the field as the best preparation and training for their work. But consumers respond to (and some hospitals require) the certification credential, leaving many doulas to opt for a more mainstream path in an effort for quicker, greater acceptance. One implication of this strategy is that certification has become all but compulsory. Doulas who reject certification on principle have received little support from colleagues or professional doula organizations, which depend on fees for training courses.

One area in which doulas have been somewhat more resistant is in the proliferation of hospital-based doula programs. These programs are hospital-approved and create a more formal work structure for affiliated doulas. The typical hospital program, however, structures its doula program so that women do not have a prior relationship with their doula; some programs cannot even guarantee continuous support from the same doula. Although hospital programs charge lower rates than most private-duty doulas, and so make the service available to more people, doulas are not subsidized by the hospital. The doulas thus become more clearly low-level, underpaid workers in the hospital system. Thus far, hospitals have only been willing to sponsor labor support in name and to pledge minor structural resources. They stop short of offering monetary resources to provide labor support for women who labor and birth in their facilities. The doulas we interviewed generally rejected the hospital program model as inappropriate for laboring women.

Continuous support is the one thing doulas offer that distinguishes them from anyone else providing birth services. And it is in prenatal meetings that doulas have the most freedom of speech and the greatest chance of affecting decisions made by the mother. Take those two things away, and what do you have besides a woman's body in the room? Is putting one more person in the birth room, one weekend-trained, warm woman's body to stand by while medicine proceeds as usual, going to make a difference?

Doulas are trying to be more than just that. Most of them are passionately committed to the idea of a good birth, a non-interventionist, woman-centered birth. Given the medical management under which they must provide their services, our original question remains unanswered: Are doulas making birth better for women, or just making women feel better about their births?

7

CONCLUSION

An Unending Labor of Love

WENDY SIMONDS AND
BARBARA KATZ ROTHMAN

The Past, Present, and Future of Birth

A British midwife recently said to Barbara, "I'm about to retire, and I'm trying to come to terms with the fact that every single thing I care about, every single thing I worked for over the course of my career, has gotten worse."

Fortunately, we're American. Things were so unthinkably bad in the world of birth in the United States until quite recently — a world in which Barbara has been involved as scholar, activist, and mother for over 30 years — that we can never say that. Anything — yes, even a 70% or higher epidural rate and a 29% cesarean section rate — is better than leather straps, twilight sleep, and locked-down nurseries.

That said, the current situation is rather depressing. When Barbara started, it looked as if home birth and out-of-hospital birth centers were the lunatic fringe, nearly unheard of. Then, by the early 1980s, they seemed to be the coming thing, on the rise, a new horizon of possibility. When Wendy entered the world of procreative health as a scholar, activist, and mother in the 1990s, it was back to the lunatic fringe! In a way, in most of the United States, now it's even harder to contemplate a home birth than it was in the 1970s. People have heard of home birth, they know that's an option — but for fanatics, for lunatic fringers. It's unimaginable not in principle, not as too far out to be done, but as unnecessary for sensible people. The propaganda tells American women that they can get the coziness, all the home-like advantages, all that a home birth or a birth center can offer — all at their charming local hospital, with good feminist obstetricians or nurse-midwives to boot.

The kinds of compromises that were made, the ways institutional-ization played out, and the ways revolutions settled into business as usual were, in hindsight, probably quite predictable. The larger power structures adapted, adjusted, took in what was useful, and lost the rest. Birth choices and birth plans became part of a consumer movement, each option one more purchasable commodity. Water birth? Epidu-ral? Videotaping? Siblings present? Hospital, doctors, and nurse-mid-wifery practices advertised the availability of consumer choices. All choices, though, were contingent on "safety" — as the doctors defined it. And so medical authority remained intact, and medical interven-tion in birth actually increased, as demonstrated, for example, by the alarming increase in the cesarean section rate between 1970 and now — from slightly more than 5% to 29.1% in 2004 (Curtin and Kozak 1998, Hamilton et al. 2004, Martin et al. 2005). Doctors have become more aggressive about doing c-sections for first births, and the vaginal birth after cesarean (VBAC) rate has dropped precipitously (a 67% decline since 1996) to 9% (Martin et al. 2005).

As midwives moved into hospitals, midwifery achieved legitimacy. As the work became professionalized and increasingly institutional-ized, it inevitably became more medicalized. As midwives found them-selves facing the demands of hospital-based practice, some aspects of traditional midwifery care inevitably fell by the wayside. Where is the time for a midwife to be "with the woman," to travel with her from home to hospital and back again, to sit with her through a long labor, to come to know her and her family, when she works in a group prac-tice that sees hundreds of clients each month, and when she typically has three or more laboring women to attend to at once in the hospital (plus reams of paperwork to complete)?

It's a fairly classic example of co-optation: medical care has brought in enough of the showier aspects of midwifery care to maintain its hegemony. The days of women birthing alone or in impersonal "mater-nity wards" are over. The presence of significant others, especially fathers, has become taken for granted in hospital birth. In *Birthing Fathers: The Transformation of Men in American Rites of Birth* (2005), Richard K. Reed looks at what happens to men in American hospital births, and it is (no surprise) not altogether lovely. The cover photo perhaps says it best: a newborn hand touching an adult man's hand — against the background of a fetal monitor strip. Nary a mother in sight. A whole generation of birthing women has watched men bond with the fetal monitor, and Reed shows us just how and why it happens: "In the end, men often find themselves co-opted by physicians, reinforcing the power of the medical process to enact its own rituals of transformation over the mother, and accomplishing this same purpose with the father in the process" (2005: 33).

When we tell the story of birth in terms of mothers laboring and fathers attending them, gender seems to be the issue. But what if we were also to interview the women family members who attend women in birth, as sisters and mothers, or, even more to the point, as the lesbian partners of laboring women? Their experience, we firmly believe, will be much the same as that of these men. It's not just birth: consider women who are trying to take care of their mothers or their husbands or their children in hospitals; they face the same situation that fathers do in births, and they have many of the same responses: begging, arguing, and colluding with power. What else is there to do?

The power dynamics haven't changed much, but they manifest differently. The days of the bossy maternity warden are over, at least for middle-class women. Pleasant nurses, kind doulas, and respectful-sounding physicians work with the woman and her partner in the room to explain what they are doing. Like a contemporary well-educated parent talking to a child, the doctor explains his practice and tells the woman and her partner what he's going to do. But what he — or just as likely she — is going to do is just the kind of medical intervention that doctor thinks best. Given the pleasant, warm, benevolent atmosphere, it has come to seem foolish, even greedy, to ask for more, to move outside the hospital. With lovely floral wallpaper and attractive rockers in the corner, with polished wood floors and custom-ordered post-partum dinners, hospitals look so cozy and comfortable. Yet it's this cozy, comfortable institution that produces that 70% epidural rate and that 29% cesarean section rate.

The governing notion of risk and the power dynamics — the two dominant forces in birth — have not changed. In fact, they have become in some ways more intransigent, as malpractice "risks" have become intertwined with intervention protocols. That's a polite way of saying that doctors blame high intervention rates on patients' imagined potential litigiousness. A spirit of mistrust lurks at the core of the health care system, apparently. Medicalization is so complete that it sets the terms of the discussion, determining what's reasonable and what's risky, what's necessary and what's self-indulgent. No matter how solid the data, even the medically mediated data, that a particular medical practice is wrong, still it stands.

Episiotomies might be the best example. Every ten years or so for the 30 years that Barbara's been watching this, a new, big, carefully constructed medical study comes out showing that episiotomies are not a good idea: more likely to create than to prevent tearing, and causing worse tears than would have happened without them. And the practice rolls on: the rates are perhaps lower than in the heyday of forceps birth and almost universal episiotomies, but even now, some doctors routinely do episiotomies to avoid tears. Rather than stop the episiotomies, they believe even more fervently that they are necessary and think tearing would be worse without them. So more episiotomies are done. And another study comes forth. And the cycle repeats itself, with very gradual, incremental reductions in episiotomy rates.

Or take fetal monitoring. Research clearly indicates that it leads to unnecessary interventions. Nevertheless, it shifted medical discourse in the name of saving babies. The old days of doctors telling women to do what they say, to follow orders, to lie back and be still — those are gone. Now it's not the voice of the doctor — or the midwife; it's the printout of the authoritative machine that dictates practice. Lie back, dear, and let me do a cesarean; the fetal monitor says your baby needs it. Monitoring, ranging from various quality-control tests in pregnancy to EFM in labor, has become increasingly insidious. Foucault would have a field day.

The ideology of the risk society, or the culture of fear, can nowhere be seen as clearly as in childbirth practices. Obstetrical management shifted from controlling the woman, particularly with drugs to sedate her, to controlling risk itself. The woman, in this arrangement, becomes the locus of risk. By making risk the issue, doctors obscured power dynamics in a new way. Rather than wielding power over women as patients, doctors now present evidence of risk as justification for interventions, and the women become willing, perhaps eager consumers of medical technology. The doctors' objectification of women's unconscious or sedated bodies has transformed into a shared objectification — performed by women along with doctors — of bodies as sites of risk, ever teetering on the brink of pathology. This is, of course, how hegemony works, as many feminist scholars studying procreative practices in the United States over time have shown (see, e.g., most of our bibliography).

The question arises: Are we worse off now than we were in the 1970s? What counts as progress? Birthing women — and again, treatment varies with race and class — are not as infantilized, not as overtly disrespected by medicine as they were in the not-so-distant past.

Some women are active participants — but in *what*, exactly? In a better system for getting babies out of women's bodies, or in the colonization of their bodies by medicine? It does, we are sure, feel better to be a woman who chooses a cesarean when faced with the data produced by an electronic fetal monitor than to be a woman who is literally knocked out and tied down with leather straps. It must feel better to have a baby born with an epidural while one watches in a mirror than to emerge groggy from twilight sleep unsure of what happened. So no, things have not gotten consistently worse here in the good old U.S. of A.

Conflict and Rivalry

Try to think of analogous situations in which different occupational groups compete to perform a service around the same event and in the same setting, yet base their praxis in such radically opposed foundational ideologies. Here are some instances: the juvenile court system, for example, or drug courts, began with radically different ideologies, housed within the larger legal system. In side-by-side courtrooms, you can find judges working with a strictly punitive legal system, judges working with a developmental psychology model, and judges working with a medical model. Over time, some have argued, these too become subsumed under the larger, more punitive legal system, and juvenile detention comes to look remarkably prisonlike; drug court is progress, but certainly compromised.[1]

Is this what happens to nurse-midwives? They're slotted into the system. Whatever underlying ideology, values, and beliefs they bring, they are functioning — like the juvenile court judge in relation to the regular judges — in a position parallel to that of the obstetricians, in a larger system. But they are not, of course, really parallel: obstetricians retain the ultimate power, and the midwives, however professional, certified, trained, and approved, practice under the authority of the medical professionals and typically observe many of the same norms. As the home birth midwife Alona Golden said:

> I think that a lot of times you get an improvement over the OB [with a nurse-midwife], because you're getting much more woman-centered care. But a lot of times you are still getting a fifteen–twenty minute visit; you're still getting the same protocol, it's just a nicer version of it. It's still the allegiance to the hospital protocol. I've seen situations where somebody said, "Well, my nurse-midwife said they weren't going to do this, and they weren't going to do that, but when it came down to it, the hospital policy is what ruled." And you still don't know who you are going to get for your birth. You know, you might be in a practice of three or six nurse-midwives. ... So I don't see it as an ideal model.

One of the strongest criticisms that the direct-entry midwives offer of the CNMs' practice is that they are not, never will be, cannot ever be, truly independent practitioners. They are not autonomous but must defer to the obstetricians. OBs set the conditions of practice, from simple design of the setting to specific protocols. Nurses and CNMs may well participate in protocol committees, but no one ever has cause to question where ultimate authority rests.

The CNMs are cognizant of this; they are not blind to the controls under which they must work. They know they are caught up in a hierarchical system in which they are assuredly not at the top. As the nurse-midwife Renie Daley said about the differences between the two groups, home birth midwives "know midwifery. And they practice midwifery. We know midwifery, and we also have to function in medicine. And some of us function more in medicine than we do in midwifery. Because we've been caught, you know, bought out by the — we're in a system that's stronger than we are." But nurse-midwives working in hospitals at least are there, as they often point out: they are "where the women are."

Even very home-birth-oriented nurse-midwives saw their practical goals of reaching more women by working within the system as noble praxis. Sheila Marks, who was training through CNEP to become a nurse-midwife after first learning and practicing home birth, asserted:

> I believe that if a woman does feel more comfortable having her baby in the hospital, she should have it in the hospital. I will do everything to educate her about epidurals and the problems with drugs, and breastfeeding, and you know, I'll give her all the statistics, you know, and I'll hope and pray that she'll make the decision that she doesn't want that, but if she wants that, that's her decision. And I cannot place judgment on that.

She wondered if she would be able to handle practicing in ways that might compromise her midwifery-oriented ideals, and added, "Ultimately, when I practice, I don't know if I'll be — if I'll survive in the hospital very long!"

The overwhelming majority of American women give birth in hospitals. Most CNMs (without a personal connection to home birth midwifery) see direct-entry, home birth midwives as offering a kind of luxury service, reiterating the accusation of self-indulgence. But it's more complex: it's the midwives, more than the home birthers whom they see as self-indulgent, enjoying their work, free to love birth and women — but not down in the trenches where the hard work needs to be done.

Direct-entry midwives may well think of themselves as the very paragon of what true, pure midwifery should be. They can be woman-centered, they can love women, they can offer all the nurturance in the world. But to whom? To a few select women who are concerned enough, educated enough, and determined enough to seek them out. If they are not there doing that, midwifery is really gone in America;

but is doing it for just a few women enough? Round and round we go: Is it better to provide ideal midwifery, to do birth as birth ought to be done for a small minority, or is it better to make as many compromises as need to be made to spread bits of midwifery care to as many women as possible? We cannot, in America, as things are now, supply real midwifery care to all women.

Whatever the midwives do, whichever side of the argument one falls on, it's not a satisfying situation. Bad choices all around, bad situations. And bad situations create bad politics. It's an impressive statement of the dedication that all of these types of midwives feel, that they can rise above internecine bickering and get past the inevitable sniping to express a strong sense of commonality. All of them do want midwifery care for all women.

Despite the common goal, of course each group has to worry about how the work of the others might interfere with achieving that end. Some CNMs see the direct-entry midwives as unregulated wildcats and fear that their behavior — their occasional flaunting of the accepted rules of practice — will reflect poorly on all midwives. It's a kind of accusation we've all heard, common among oppressed groups: those with more status fear that the outliers, the least privileged, will "bring us all down." It's also reminiscent of what happens in families when there are rifts, class-based or otherwise. As one nurse-midwife commented about the exclusive practices of the ACNM, "I feel like my mother didn't invite my sister to Thanksgiving dinner." A direct-entry midwife interviewed by Catherine Taylor invoked a more politicized analogy, describing the rift between and differences among home birth midwives and nurse-midwives as "kind of the classic, virgin-whore dichotomy of one woman who is having sex for money and a place to live is a wife and in another situation she's a prostitute. It just depends on whether or not you play by the rules" (Taylor 2002: 227).

The direct-entry midwives, for their part, also have reason to fear that the CNMs will be destructive of the larger goal: co-optation is scary. It's scary because it works. Move a few CNMs into the local hospital, or let the local OB hire a couple of CNMs in her practice, and of course the direct-entry midwives lose clients and community support, and become seen as the lunatic fringe. It is hardly surprising that the accusation the direct-entry midwives level against the

CNMs, when they are at their angriest and most damning, is that the CNMs are selling out for money, prestige, and job security. While a direct-entry midwife can take a perverse pride in her struggle and her comparative poverty, CNMs in hospital-based practices take home a regular salary, and that has to be noted. There are undoubtedly some CNMs who started as nurses and went the midwifery route the same way other nurses become nurse-anesthetists or go into surgical nursing. It's a career path upward. In contrast, nobody goes into direct-entry midwifery for careerist reasons, and nobody would go into it for the money. They're paid peanuts — sometimes literally. One Farm midwife told us: "I walked away from a birth one time with a bag of peanuts. That's what I was paid, and I was happy." She added, smiling, that it was a *big* bag of peanuts, "It was like a bushel!"

There's a nobility to working for love and not money, an anticapitalist sensibility you'd expect on The Farm — the Birkenstock, tie-dyed aspect of it all. These are not just different occupational groups competing. These are different worldviews, different value systems, despite their common source. And the difference is not necessarily between the types of midwives but between the systems in which they operate. So while their attention may be drawn to each other and their fears may be for the damage each can do the other, it is the medical system that creates the conditions under which these conflicts arise. As Charles Rosenberg writes in *The Care of Strangers: The Rise of America's Hospital System*:

> We cannot seem to live without high-technology medicine; we cannot seem to live amicably with it. Yet, for the great majority of Americans, divorce is unthinkable. Medical perceptions and careers still proscribe or reward behaviors that may or may not be consistent with the most humane and cost-effective provisions of care. And despite much recent hand-wringing, it still remains to be seen whether physicians will be edged aside from their positions of institutional authority. (1987: 351–352)

Systems take on lives of their own. And it really is about systems, not individual people. The obstetricians Wendy interviewed were the ones midwives recommended to her, the good ones. They were women themselves, had many positive views about birth, tried not to pathologize pregnancy or labor, saw themselves as helping women have good experiences, and liked being part of that. Yet even they rarely questioned their place at the top of a hierarchy of birth workers. They thought that the hierarchy had become increasingly inclusive of midwifery. And perhaps it has. But as in any social hierarchy, people at the bottom have a much clearer view of the limitations to fluidity than do those at the top. Yes, midwives do practice in their hospitals, and yes, they do have a greater voice than they did 20 years ago in hospital practice: they have all the voice the obstetricians allow them.

These obstetricians — as good as you're going to find, midwife-endorsed, as open-minded as obstetricians are going to get — however inadvertently, did tend to describe their practice experiences in deeply medicalized terms. Birth is about outcome; technologies are useful tools for the ultimate goal of getting the baby out of a situation that can go wrong at any moment; and the threat of litigation is justification for any intervention. Scratch a doctor, Barbara always says, and you find a doctor. Most of them were nervous about home birth, troubled by any questions that fundamentally challenged the medical model. They countered such questioning from Wendy with a return to the rhetoric of risk.

Nurse-midwives' discussions of turf battles show that doctors may experience their presence as a threat: they walk a fine line and have to be careful not to appear threatening. The main way that obstetrics has handled this threat has been to co-opt and fragment what midwives offered. Feminist obstetricians, or at least women obstetricians, appeal to the values of independent women. Doulas provide a new, cheap, deskilled version of midwives, entirely without power in the birth setting. Because having doulas present results in less costly births, and because deskilling is a fundamental technique for cost control, doulas are probably going to be more and more widely used in the future. Warm and pleasant, spa-like services appeal to middle-class consumers, and doulas, providing back rubs and pep talks, fit right in. They represent an acceptable self-indulgence. To ask for more — to ask for power, power for mothers or power for midwives — would be asking too much.

These are the people — these are the best versions of the people — who set the stage on which all these other players must act. The others either find a way of negotiating accommodations they can live with, as most of the nurse-midwives and doulas have, or avoid the arena as much as they can, as most of the home birth midwives do.

But these are not the only players. The almost invisible, taken-for-granted presence in the hospital is the nursing staff: they were there long before the midwives arrived; they've watched each new set of players come on. They make space for whomever they have to: fathers come to watch; children are permitted in; grandmothers stay close; and in that odd space between familial and institutional, the doulas do too. In the ever-increasing fragmentation of care, it is the nursing staff who struggle to hold it all together, even as their own labors are fragmented. Dana Beth Weinberg (2003) provides a passionate indictment of a new medical management strategy entitled, ironically, "team nursing." Essentially, team nursing entails instituting a hierarchy of workers who fit into a chart that divides nursing into "pieces that could be performed by workers with varying levels of skill. In so doing, it defined nursing practice not as a holistic practice of providing care but as a series of tasks to be carried out" (Weinberg 2003: 49). Moved away from doing the hands-on care themselves (mundane, not skill-based work), nurses supervise its provision by lower-status workers, monitor the monitors, and serve as administrative support staff for people offering the actual "care."

And oh, yes, one more set of players have to function under obstetrical control: the mothers.

What Do Women Deserve?

Midwifery care, truly woman-centered, family-centered care, sounds self-indulgent. Putting the emotional and social as well as physical needs of women and their babies first sounds like the call of a generation of spoiled brats. Our culture encourages us to think of mothering as a sacrificial project: we give up whatever we have to in the interests of our children and babies. The idea of an adversarial relationship between mothers and fetuses has taken over.

Medicine has developed technologies that treat mother and fetus as separate beings trapped together, taking measurements on one body or the other (fetal heart tones; maternal contractions), letting us listen to the heartbeat of the baby over a speaker removed from the woman, and making us turn away from the woman to see the baby on a screen. We read recurring newspaper stories of drug-exposed babies, of abandoned babies, and uncaring mothers. And of course, and maybe most divisively, the cultural positioning of abortion as uncaring mothers killing their innocent babies has gained credence in a conservative political climate. All these images of mothers as the natural enemies of their children or potential children cement the idea that measures must be taken to protect fetuses and babies from irresponsible mothers. This plays out in childbirth management in increasing medicalization and in burgeoning technological control in obstetrics.

And yet, we know: we who read the scientific research, we who read the social research, we who look at the census data on infant mortality and morbidity, we who think, we who know that what our babies most need is healthy — and happy — mothers. Care for the mother, meet her needs, and you've done the single best thing you can do to make healthy children.

Interestingly, and ironically, one of the best hopes we've had is that midwifery care is cost-effective. Far from indulging or spoiling mothers, caring for them is actually cheaper. For years now, we've had studies on that too. Clearly midwifery care results in fewer cesarean sections and other interventions. Clearly fewer interventions result in lower costs.

Without question, this is true on the straight and clear-cut physical issues, such as medical costs in the perinatal period, but it may well also be true on the "softer" outcome measures. Women who've had positive, ego-building as well as health-building pregnancy and birth care may well become more competent mothers and raise healthier children than they would have otherwise. Research indicates — to us, convincingly — that woman-centered care makes for stronger mothers and children, in lots of ways. You'd think, given the data, that as a society we'd have turned away from high-tech, high-intervention, high-cost maternity care and toward midwifery care.

And yet, why hasn't that happened? Why, in a country that constantly talks about the need to save costs in health care, does the cost of this health care service, like the others, continue to rise (Perkins 2003)? With all the good economic reasons arguing for it, why hasn't an empowered, enabled midwifery emerged in America?

It's happened elsewhere. We don't have to look only at the ever-cited Netherlands, where midwives somehow, despite all of European and Western "progress," maintained their independence. Nor do we have to look just at England, Japan, Germany, the countries of Latin America, and most of the rest of the world, in which some kind of midwifery has maintained its presence and the ongoing struggle has been to avoid excessive Americanization of birth practices.

But we are not the only country that lost its midwifery, allowed medicine to take over. It has happened elsewhere, and midwifery has been recreated, reborn. With the strength of the women's movement, both Canada and New Zealand found ways to reestablish midwifery. In both places, there are troubling race politics, a situation that should be familiar to any American. But in both countries, middle-class white women became the empowered midwives — for empowered, middle-class, white birthing women. And some women of color and some poor women did benefit by getting some of the spillover, as has happened even in the United States with its far more limited midwifery movement. But in no way can our puny number of midwives — nurse-midwives, direct-entry midwives, all kinds of midwives together — be understood as true competitors for the vast number of births in this country.

What distinguishes the United States are at least two things. One is the utter absence of a national health care system. Each state has its own regulations. No single payer oversees the standard of care. But there is something else that is unusual in the United States: we lost our midwifery not just to medicine, but specifically to obstetrics. Whereas in most of the world it has been family practitioners who attended uncomplicated births, and obstetricians just stepped in to manage problems, in the United States the "ob/gynies" completely took over the health care of women, declaring themselves primary practitioners. Our midwives thus stand not as a viable threat to a small segment of the medical profession, as they did in New Zealand or Canada, but as a weak threat to a single mighty profession.

Medicalization remains a threat to midwifery everywhere. In the United Kingdom, for example, Fiona MacVane Phipps writes in an essay entitled "Educating Midwives: Where Do We Go from Here?": "We are fortunate in having a long tradition of midwifery where midwives are the acknowledged experts in the 'normal' and where that function is protected in law" (2003: 12). Nevertheless, she adds, "It is clear that the midwifery profession has allowed medicalisation to encroach upon our knowledge, skills, and practice" (2003: 12). Others evaluating the British scene are far less sanguine:

> Many midwives are no longer even semi-professionals, but merely service workers driven by prevailing whims of government schemes which privilege both medical control and business management objectives over the development of independent midwifery practices. (Mason 2003: 17)

> Good midwifery is good for women. But what is being widely practiced in UK hospitals is not good midwifery — it is obstetric nursing, a professional compromise constructed largely out of fear instead of concern for women's needs. ... Indeed, many proponents of traditional midwifery have now left the profession, frustrated by their inability to work as fully independent practitioners. (Thomas 2003: 18)

Obstetricians in some Latin American countries have begun to emulate those in the United States in perverse ways: cesarean section rates among wealthy urban women giving birth in private hospitals far surpass that of the United States (Villar et al. [2006:] report private hospital c-section rates over 50% in Nicaragua and Paraguay, over 60% in Ecuador, and over 70% in Mexico). Perhaps industrialization will inevitably mean increased medicalization, no matter where. The particular configuration of pre-industrial birth practices, the economic situation of the locality, and the societal status of women will all affect the shape and magnitude of the outcome, but medicalization will continue to transform birth practices globally.

Ideals and Predictions

We want to ask for it all. We want the damned revolution.

We know it is dissatisfying to get to the end of a book and have the authors say that the only way out is total change and ask their readers to accept a completely different path, a way diametrically opposed to the dominant discourse. Books on poverty and policy shout: *Look at Sweden!* In the realm of birth, feminist scholars shout: *Look at the Netherlands!* The irony here, of course, is that we have perfect midwifery going on in little underground and even aboveground pockets around the United States. We can say: *Look at the state of Washington! Look at Florida!* But the kind of work facing it, the amount of change — cultural, political, economic, social, and educational — that would have to happen to have midwifery flourish in the United States is, sadly, almost unimaginable.

Not that we can't imagine it. Thirty years ago, Barbara ended *In Labor* by calling for the elimination of obstetrics. She called for midwives as health workers, connecting to medical services when needed — surgeons to do the necessary cesarean section, certainly — but also to the social services we thought, back then, we could someday have. (Back to "Look at Sweden!") But she didn't really expect that revolution. It was small changes that she hoped for and did expect: women refusing episiotomies and doctors seeing that they weren't necessary, women sitting up in labor and doctors rethinking delivery tables. Some of those have happened. *In Labor* concluded:

> That is the most optimistic conclusion I can draw from my research; that maybe, by accident, things will get better. Careful planning is bringing us regionalization of maternity care; the sorting and matching of women and hospitals in risk categories; more and fancier technology; and a well-thought out attempt to co-opt midwives and the home birth movement. Maybe they will just put flowered sheets on the beds, hang a plant on the IV pole, and go on about business as usual. But maybe it will backfire. Maybe the attempt to co-opt those seeking alternatives will end by creating change in the medical institutions, as doctors and nurses work in the new settings. Maybe obstetrics will go through some changes too. (Rothman 1982: 287)

Neither of us is that optimistic now.

Is that just because we're older and wiser (or older and more cynical)? Or is it that things really have gotten worse in the larger political and social world of the United States, and we can feel the repercussions in the world of birth? A little of both, surely. We're thinking

about birth, midwifery, the childbirth movement over the long haul
— not just Barbara's 30 years, Wendy's 15, Bari's entry. We're thinking about the course of American history, and the place birth takes
in that. Midwifery history is very much part of gender history, race
history, and class history. Its ups and downs reflect the ups and downs
in each of these stories.

We're a long way from the days when surgeons smuggled forceps in
under cloaks so women couldn't see the wonderful new tools. We're
a long way from the days of twilight sleep and drugged babies. We're
farther away from the days of the frontier nurses, riding out, women
to women, birthing by kerosene lantern. And we've left behind the
black grand midwives, the many and varied old-country midwives
who brought their techniques and tools and skill with them to this
country, where they were traded in — like their own recipes for Betty
Crocker's — for the wonders of modern technology.

Our hopes lie now with what Robbie Davis-Floyd likes to call the
postmodern midwife, the midwife with her cell phone in one hand,
her Internet networks, international conferences, online educational
programs and licenses, her teas and herbs, and her research studies
on hands-and-knees positions for breech births. She pulls together,
across nations and times, across cultures and polities, whatever it is
she needs to be with women.

We do want the revolution, yes. We want a revolution in which
she, that postmodern midwife, is in charge of birth. We want obstetricians, doulas, and nurses, all listening to her as she listens to women.
We want her wisdom and experience and values there in the service of
the women she serves.

Yes, we do get sloppy and sentimental about those midwives, a bit
over the top. But hell, you have to believe in something. And midwifery, laboring on over the centuries, is about the best that we can
hope for.

Notes

Chapter 3

1. Nursing historians tend to replicate Breckinridge's view of rural midwives; for example, Philip A. Kalisch and Beatrice J. Kalisch write: "As a group these untrained midwives were grossly superstitious and knew nothing of prenatal or postnatal care" (1995: 277), and drawing on Breckinridge, they detail some of the midwives' backwater practices: "Soot was used extensively as a medication. ... Generally recommended preventive procedures included placing an ax under the delivery bed with the blade straight up" (1995: 278). Similarly, Dammann dismisses local midwives as appropriate caregivers.

2. "Sex on The Farm meant marriage and that meant forever, so single life there was far from the image of a free-sex hippie commune" (Gary Rhine in Fike 1998: 50). There were several group marriages, referred to as "Four Marriages," which formed "when two couples united as one after going through a shared psychedelic experience," but they all eventually "dissolved" (Doug Stevenson in Fike 1998: 54).

3. I interviewed Sheila at The Farm conference, not at the CNEP training I attended. She was part of a different cohort than the women I met in Kentucky.

4. Names of participants were difficult to keep track of throughout the interview because the group was so large.

Chapter 6

1. In this chapter we use the words "profession" and "professional" because this is the language doulas use to describe their occupation and their work.

2. CAPPA and DONA require three births and evaluations from the client, clinical care provider, and nurse at each of the births. Birth Works requires evaluations from two clients, and ALACE requires a total of three evaluations, which can be from either clients, clinical care providers, or nurses. ALACE also requires that trainees submit written self-evaluations pertaining to each of the six required births attended for certification.

3. The typical arrangement in such practices is that the doula attends the birth and passes on a portion of her fee to the service. One service, for instance, took 40% and the doula kept 60% of the fee.

4. This is compared to 7.8% of all births attended by midwives (including certified nurse-midwives and direct-entry midwives) for the same year. Further, 9.5% of all vaginal births in 2000 were attended by CNMs.

5. National statistics on the usage rate of epidural anesthesia for pain relief during labor are more difficult to pin down. One estimate is "more than 50%" nationally (NIH). Many hospitals report epidural rates in the 80% range and higher. Combined with the rate of narcotics use, the usage rate of pain medication (epidural anesthesia [including spinal] and narcotics) often reaches the 90% mark.

Chapter 7

1. Barbara thanks Rebecca Tiger and Mike Jolley, CUNY graduate students, for pointing this out to her in their dissertation work.

References

Apgar, Virginia, and Joan Beck (1973). *Is My Baby All Right?* New York: Trident.

Applebaum, Richard M. (1975). "The Obstetrician's Approach to the Breasts and Breastfeeding." *Journal of Reproductive Medicine* 14: 98–116.

Arms, Suzanne (1975). *Immaculate Deception: A New Look at Women and Childbirth.* Boston: Houghton Mifflin.

Armstrong, David (1995). "The Rise of Surveillance Medicine." *Sociology of Health and Illness* 17: 393–404.

Armstrong, Elisabeth A. (2000). "Lessons in Control: Prenatal Education in the Hospital." *Social Problems* 47: 583–605.

Arney, William Ray (1982). *Power of the Profession of Obstetrics.* Chicago: University of Chicago Press.

Ashford, Janet I. (1990). "The History of Midwifery in the United States." *Mothering* 54 (Winter): 64–71.

Baker, James T. (1987), "Revisiting 'The Farm': From Commune to Suburb." *Christian Century,* 21 October, 918–920.

Banks, Amanda Carson (1999). *Birth Chairs, Midwives, and Medicine.* Jackson: University Press of Mississippi.

Bastien, Alison (2002). "Apprenticeship in Medicine and Midwifery." In Jan Tritten and Jennifer Rosenberg (eds.), *Paths to Becoming a Midwife: Getting an Education.* 3rd ed., 124–126. Eugene, OR: Midwifery Today.

Bing, Elizabeth, and Marjorie Karmel (1961). *A Practical Training Course for the Psychoprophylactic Method of Painless Childbirth.* New York: ASPO.

Blum, Linda (1999). *At the Breast: Ideologies of Breastfeeding and Motherhood in the Contemporary United States.* Boston: Beacon.

Bohjalian, Chris (1998). *Midwives.* New York: Vintage.

Borst, C.G. (1995). *Catching Babies: The Professionalization of Childbirth.* Cambridge, MA: Harvard University Press.

Boston Women's Health Collective (1971). *Our Bodies, Ourselves: A Book by and for Women.* New York: Simon & Schuster.

Brack, Datha Clapper (1976). "Displaced: The Midwife by the Male Physician." *Women and Health* 1: 18–24.

Breckinridge, Mary (1981 [1952]). *Wide Neighborhoods: A Story of the Frontier Nursing Service.* Lexington: University of Kentucky Press.

Brendsel, Carol, Gail Peterson, and Lewis Mehl (1979). "Episiotomy: Facts, Fiction, Figures and Alternatives." In Lee Stewart and David Stewart (eds.), *Compulsory Hospitalization or Freedom of Choice in Childbirth?* Marble Hill, MO: NAPSAC.

Brown, Denise, and Pamela A. Toussaint (1997). *Mama's Little Baby: The Black Woman's Guide to Pregnancy, Childbirth, and Baby's First Year.* New York: Plume.

Bullough, Vern (1966). *The Development of Medicine as a Profession: The Contribution of the Medieval University to Modern Medicine*. New York: Karger.

Burst, Helen Varney (1990). "'Real' Midwifery." *Journal of Nurse-Midwifery* 35 (July/August): 189–190.

Burtch, Brian (1994). *Trials of Labor: The Re-emergence of Midwifery*. Montreal and Kingston: McGill-Queen's University Press.

Casper, Monica J. (1996). *The Making of the Unborn Patient: A Social Anatomy of Fetal Surgery*. New Brunswick, NJ: Rutgers University Press.

Center for Nursing Advocacy (2003). "Mary Breckinridge (1881–1965)." www.nursingadvocacy.org/press/breckinridge.html.

Chabon, Irwin (1966). *Awake and Aware: Participation in Childbirth through Psychoprophyaxis*. New York: Delacorte.

Chambliss, Daniel F. (1996). *Beyond Caring: Hospitals, Nurses, and the Social Organization of Ethics*. Chicago: University of Chicago Press.

Chancer, Lynn (1992). *Sadomasochism in Everyday Life: The Dynamics of Power and Powerlessness*. New Brunswick, NJ: Rutgers University Press.

Charon, Rita, Michele G. Greene, and Ronald Adelman (1994). "Women Readers, Women Doctors: A Feminist Reader-Response Theory for Medicine." In Ellen Singer More and Maureen A. Milligan (eds.), *The Empathic Practitioner: Empathy, Gender, and Medicine*, 205–221. New Brunswick, NJ: Rutgers University Press.

Cheek, Julianne, and Trudy Rudge (1994). "The Panopticon Revisited? An Exploration of the Social and Political Dimensions of Contemporary Health Care and Nursing Practice." *International Journal of Nursing Studies* 31: 583–591.

Clarke, Adele E., and Virginia L. Oleson (1999). *Revisioning Women, Health, and Healing: Feminist, Cultural, and Technoscience Perspectives*. New York and London: Routledge.

Coltrane, Scott (1996). *Family Man: Fatherhood, Housework, and Gender Equity*. New York: Oxford University Press.

Cunningham, F. Gary, P. C. MacDonald, and N. F. Gant (1989). *Williams Obstetrics*. 18th ed. Norwalk, CT and San Mateo, CA: Appleton and Lange.

Cunningham, F. Gary, et al. (1993). *Williams Obstetrics*. 19th ed. Stamford, CT: Appleton and Lange, 1993.

———— (1997). *Williams Obstetrics*. 20th ed. Stamford, CT: Appleton and Lange.

———— (2001). *Williams Obstetrics*. 21st ed. New York: McGraw-Hill.

Curtin, Sally C., and Lola Jean Kozak (1998). "Decline in U.S. Cesarean Delivery Rate Appears to Stall." *Birth* 25 (December): 259-262.

Daly, K. J. (1996). *Families and Time: Keeping Pace in a Hurried Culture*. Thousand Oaks, CA: Sage.

Dammann, Nancy (1982). *A Social History of the Frontier Nursing Service*. Sun City, AZ: Social Change.

Davis-Floyd, Robbie E. (1992). *Birth as an American Rite of Passage*. Berkeley, CA: University of California Press.

_____ (2002). "The Ups, Downs, and Interlinkages of Nurse- and Direct-Entry Midwifery: Status, Practice, and Education." In Jan Tritten and Jennifer Rosenberg (eds.), *Paths to Becoming a Midwife: Getting an Education*. 3rd ed. Eugene, OR: Midwifery Today.

Davis-Floyd, Robbie E., and Carolyn Sargent (eds.) (1997). *Childbirth and Authoritative Knowledge: Cross-Cultural Perspectives*. Berkeley: University of California Press.

Davis-Floyd, Robbie E., and Gloria St. John (1998). *From Doctor to Healer: The Transformative Journey*. New Brunswick, NJ: Rutgers University Press.

Dawley, Katy (2003). "Origins of Nurse-Midwifery in the United States and its Expansion in the 1940s." *Journal of Midwifery and Women's Health* 48(2): 86–95.

DeClercq, Eugene R., et al. (2002). *Listening to Mothers: Report of the First National U.S. Survey of Women's Childbearing Experiences*. Conducted for the Maternity Center Association by Harris Interactive.

DeClercq, Eugene, Ray Menacker, and Marian MacDorman (2006). "Maternal Risk Profiles and the Primary Cesarean Rate in the United States, 1991-2002." *American Journal of Public Health* 96 (May): 867-872.

DeLee, Joseph B. (1920). "The Prophylactic Forceps Operation." *Journal of Obstetrics and Gynecology* 1: 34–44.

DeVries, Raymond G. (1996). *Making Midwives Legal: Childbirth, Medicine, and the Law*. 2nd ed. Columbus: Ohio State University Press.

DeVries, Raymond G., Cecilia Benoit, Edwin R. van Teijlingen, and Sirpa Wrede (eds.) (2001). *Birth By Design: Pregnancy, Maternity Care, and Midwifery in North America and Europe*. New York and London: Routledge.

Dick-Read, Grantley (1944). *Childbirth without Fear: The Principles and Practices of Natural Childbirth*. New York: Harper and Row.

Donegan, Jane B. (1978). *Women and Men Midwives: Medicine, Morality and Misogyny in Early America*. Westport, CT: Greenwood.

Donnison, Jean (1977). *Midwives and Medical Men: A History of Inter-Professional Rivalries and Women's Rights*. New York: Schocken.

Dubos, René (1968). *Man, Medicine and Environment*. New York: New American Library.

Dye, Nancy Schrom (1984). "Mary Breckinridge, The Frontier Nursing Service, and the Introduction of Nurse-Midwifery in the United States." In Judith Walzer Leavitt (ed.), *Women and Health in America*, 327–344. Madison: University of Wisconsin Press.

Ehrenreich, Barbara, and Deirdre English (1973). *Witches, Midwives and Nurses: A History of Women Healers*. Old Westbury, NY: Feminist Press.

Eisenberg, Arlene, Heidi E. Murkoff, and Sandee E. Hathaway (1991). *What To Expect When You're Expecting*. 2nd ed. New York: Workman.

Enloe, Cynthia (1990). *Bananas, Beaches and Bases: Making Feminist Sense of International Politics*. Berkeley: University of California Press.

_____ (2000). *Maneuvers: The International Politics of Militarizing Women's Lives*. Berkeley: University of California Press.

Erickson-Owens, Debra A., and Holly Powell Kennedy (2001). "Fostering Evidence-Based Care in Clinical Teaching." *Journal of Midwifery and Women's Health* 46 (May/June): 137–145.

Fee, Elizabeth (ed.) (1982). *Women and Health: The Politics of Sex in Medicine.* Farmingdale, NY: Baywood.

Ferree, Myra Marx, William Anthony Gamson, Jurgen Gerhards, and Dieter Rucht (2002). *Shaping Abortion Discourse: Democracy and the Public Sphere in Germany and the United States.* Cambridge: Cambridge University Press.

Fike, Rupert (ed.) (1998). *Voices from The Farm: Adventures in Community Living.* Summertown, TN: Book Publishing Company.

Finkelstein, Peter (1986). "Studies in the Anatomy Laboratory: A Portrait of Individual and Collective Defense." In Robert H. Coombs, D. Scott May, and Gary White Small (eds.), *Inside Doctoring.* New York: Praeger.

Fiscella, K. (1995) "Does Prenatal Care Improve Birth Outcomes? A Critical Review." *Obstetrics & Gynecology* 85: 468.

Firestone, Shulamith (1970). *The Dialectic of Sex: The Case for Feminist Revolution.* New York: Morrow.

Foley, Lara, and Christopher A. Faircloth (2003). "Medicine as a Discursive Resource: Legitimation in the Work Narratives of Midwives." *Sociology of Health and Illness* 25: 165-184.

Foucault, Michel (1973). *The Birth of the Clinic: An Archaeology of Medical Perception.* A.M. Sheridan Smith (tr.). New York: Vintage.

_____ (1977). *Discipline and Punish: The Birth of the Prison.* Alan Sheridan (tr.). New York: Pantheon.

Fox, Bonnie, and Diana Worts (1999). "Revisiting the Critique of Medicalized Childbirth: A Contribution to the Sociology of Birth." *Gender & Society* 13 (June): 326–347.

Frank, Arthur W. (2004). *The Renewal of Generosity: Illness, Medicine, and How To Live.* Chicago: University of Chicago Press.

Frankin, Sarah (1995). "Postmodern Procreation: A Cultural Account of Assisted Reproduction." In Faye Ginsburg and Rayna Rapp (eds.), *Conceiving the New World Order: The Global Politics of Reproduction.* Berkeley: University of California Press.

Fraser, Gertrude Jacinta (1998). *African American Midwifery in the South: Dialogues of Birth, Race and Memory.* Cambridge, MA: Harvard University Press.

Freedman, Emmanuel (1959). "Graphic Analysis of Labor." *Bulletin of the American College of Nurse-Midwifery* : 94–105.

Friedan, Betty (1963). *The Feminine Mystique.* New York: W.W. Norton.

Friedland, Daniel J. (ed.) (1998). *Evidence-Based Medicine: A Framework for Clinical Practice.* Stamford, CT: Appleton and Lange.

Friedman, Emanual A. (ed.) (1982). *Obstetrical Decision Making.* Trenton, NJ: B.C. Decker.

Gaskin, Ina May (1990). *Spiritual Midwifery.* 3rd ed. Summertown, TN: Book Publishing Company.

_____ (2003). *Ina May's Guide to Childbirth*. New York: Bantam.

Gaskin, Stephen (1972). *The Caravan*. New York: Random House.

Gesell, Arnold, Frances Ilg, and Louise Ames (1943). *Infant and Child in the Culture of Today: The Guidance of Development in Home and Nursery School*. New York: Harper and Row.

Glaser, B.G., and A.L. Strauss (1968). *Time for Dying*. Chicago: Aldine.

Goer, Henci (1995). *Obstetric Myths versus Research Realities: A Guide to the Medical Literature*. Westport, CT: Bergin and Garvey.

_____ (1999). *The Thinking Woman's Guide to a Better Birth*. New York: Berkley.

Goffman, Erving (1961). *Asylums: Essays on the Social Situation of Mental Patients and Other Inmates*. Garden City, NY: Doubleday.

Greer, Germaine (1970). *The Female Eunuch*. New York: Bantam.

Guttmacher, Alan (1962). *Pregnancy and Birth: A Book for Expectant Parents*. New York: New American Library.

Hafferty, Frederic W. (1991). *Into the Valley: Death and the Socialization of Medical Students*. New Haven, CT: Yale University Press.

Hahn, Robert A. (1987). "Divisions of Labor: Obstetrician, Woman, and Society in *Williams Obstetrics*, 1903–1985." *Medical Anthropology Quarterly* 1: 256–282.

Haire, Doris (1972). *The Cultural Warping of Childbirth*. Seattle, WA: International Childbirth Education Association.

Hamilton, Brady E., Joyce A. Martin, and Paul D. Sutton (2004). "Births: Preliminary Data for 2003." *National Vital Statistics Reports* 53. Hyattsville, MD: National Center for Health Statistics.

Harlow, Harry F. (1973). "Love in Infant Monkeys." In William T. Greenough (ed.), *The Nature and Nurture of Behavior: Readings from Scientific American*. San Francisco: Freeman.

Hartmann, K., M. Viswanathan, R. Palmieri, G. Gertlehner, J. Thorp, and K.N. Lohr (2005). "Outcomes of Routine Episiotomy: A Systematic Review." *Journal of the American Medical Association* 293: 2141–2148.

Hausman, Bernice L. (2003). *Mother's Milk: Breastfeeding Controversies in American Culture*. New York and London: Routledge.

Hellman, Louis M., and Jack A. Pritchard (eds.) (1971). *Williams Obstetrics*. 14th ed. New York: Appleton-Century-Crofts.

_____ (1976). *Williams Obstetrics*. 15th ed. New York: Appleton-Century-Crofts.

Hochschild, Arlie (1997). *The Time Bind: When Work Becomes Home and Home Becomes Work*. New York: Metropolitan.

Hughes, Edward C. (ed.) (1972). *Obstetric-Gynecologic Terminology*. Philadelphia: Davis.

Hwang, Seiun (2004). "Mother's Helper: As 'Doulas' Enter Delivery Rooms, Conflicts Arise." *Wall Street Journal*, 19 January, p. A1.

Hytten, Frank E., and Tom Lind (1973). *Diagnostic Indices in Pregnancy*. Summit, NJ: CIBA Geigy.

Inhorn, Marcia C., and Fran Van Balen (eds.) (2002). *Infertility around the Globe: New Thinking on Childlessness, Gender, and Reproductive Technologies*. Berkeley: University of California Press.

Jeffries, Elizabeth (1998). "Hearing the Call to Nursing." *Nursing* 28: 34–35.

Jordan, Brigitte (1993). *Birth in Four Cultures: A Crosscultural Investigation of Childbirth in Yucatan, Holland, Sweden, and the United States*. Rev. ed. Prospect Heights, IL: Waveland.

Kahn, Robbie Pfeufer (1995). *Bearing Meaning: The Language of Birth*. Urbana: University of Illinois Press.

Kalisch, Philip A., and Beatrice J. Kalisch (1995). *The Advance of American Nursing*. 3rd ed. Philadelphia: J.B. Lippincott.

Karmel, Marjorie (1959). *Thank You, Dr. Lamaze: A Mother's Experience in Painless Childbirth*. New York: Doubleday.

Kelleher, Christa (2003). *Postpartum Matters: Women's Experiences of Medical Surveillance, Time and Support after Birth*. Waltham, MA: Brandeis University.

Kirkham, Mavis (1999). "The Culture of Midwifery in the National Health Service in England." *Journal of Advanced Nursing* 30: 732–739.

Kitzinger, Sheila (1980). *Pregnancy and Childbirth*. Harmondsworth, UK: Penguin.

Klassen, Pamela E. (2001). *Blessed Events: Religion and Home Birth in America*. Princeton, NJ: Princeton University Press.

Klaus, Marshall H., P. Jerauld, N. Kreger, W. McAlpine, M. Steffa, and John Kennell (1972). "Maternal Attachment: Importance of the First Postpartum Days." *New England Journal of Medicine* 286: 460–463.

Klaus, Marshall H., John H. Kennell, and Phyllis H. Klaus (2002 [1993]). *The Doula Book*. Cambridge, MA: Perseus.

Kleinman, Sherryl (1996). *Opposing Ambitions: Gender and Identity in an Alternative Organization*. Chicago: University of Chicago Press.

Kobrin, Frances (1966). "The American Midwife Controversy: A Crisis in Professionalization." *Bulletin on the History of Medicine* 40: 350–363.

Kuhn, Thomas S. (1962). *The Structure of Scientific Revolutions*. Chicago: University of Chicago Press.

La Leche League International (1997). *The Womanly Art of Breastfeeding*. 6th rev. ed. New York: Plume.

Langton, P. A. (1994). "Obstetricians' Resistance to Independent, Private Practice by Nurse-Midwives in Washington, D.C. Hospitals." *Women and Health* 22: 27–48.

LaRossa, Ralph (1983). "The Transition to Parenthood and the Social Reality of Time." *Journal of Marriage and the Family* 45: 579–589.

Lay, Mary M. (2000). *The Rhetoric of Midwifery: Gender, Knowledge, and Power*. New Brunswick, NJ: Rutgers University Press.

Leavitt, Judith Walzer (ed.) (1999 [1984]). *Women and Health in America: Historical Readings*, 2nd ed. Madison: University of Wisconsin Press.

———— (1986). *Brought to Bed: Childbearing in America, 1750 to 1950*. New York: Oxford University Press.

Litt, Jacquelyn S. (2000). *Medicalized Motherhood: Perspectives from the Lives of African-American and Jewish Women.* New Brunswick, NJ: Rutgers University Press.

Lorber, Judith (1975). "Good Patients and Problem Patients: Conformity and Deviance in a General Hospital." *Journal of Health and Social Behavior* 16: 213–225.

———— (1984). *Women Physicians: Careers, Status, and Power.* New York: Tavistock.

———— (1993). "Why Women Physicians Will Never Be True Equals in the American Medical Profession." In Elianne Riska and Katarina Wegar (eds.), *Gender, Work and Medicine: Women and the Medical Division of Labor,* 62–76. London: Sage.

Lowman, Kaye (1977). *The LLLove Story.* Franklin Park, IL: La Leche League International.

Luker, Kristin (1984). *Abortion and the Politics of Motherhood.* Berkeley: University of California Press.

MacDonald, Margaret, and Ivy Lynn Bourgeault (2000). "The Politics of Representation: Doing and Writing Interested Research on Midwifery." *Resources for Feminist Research* 28(1/2): 151–168.

MANA press release. "Obstetricians Use Dubious Method in Attempt To Discredit Home Birth." http://www.mana.org/WAHomeBirthStudy.html. February 11, 2003.

Mason, John (2003). "An Analysis of Midwifery Education." *Midwifery Matters* 96 (Spring): 16-17.

Martin, Emily (1987). *The Woman in the Body.* Boston: Beacon.

Martin, Joyce A., Brady E. Hamilton, Fay Menacker, Paul Sutton, and T.J. Mathews (2005). "Preliminary Births for 2004: Infant and Maternal Health." Health E-stats. Hyattsville, MD: National Center for Health Statistics.

Martin, Joyce A., Brady E. Hamilton, Paul D. Sutton, Stephanie J. Ventura, Fay Menacker, and Martha L. Munson (2003). *National Vital Statistics Report, Births: Final Data 2002.* Hyattsville, MD: National Center for Health Statistics.

Martin, Joyce A., Brady E. Hamilton, Stephanie J. Ventura, Fay Menacker, and M. M. Park (2002). "Births: Final Data for 2000." *National Vital Statistics Reports* 50(5).

Matthews, Sandra, and Laura Wexler (2000). *Pregnant Pictures.* New York and London: Routledge.

McGregor, Deborah Kuhn (1998). *From Midwives to Medicine: The Birth of Ameican Gynecology.* New Brunswick, NJ: Rutgers University Press.

McKay, Donald (1974). "Alternative Points of View." In Duncan E. Reid and C. D. Christian (eds.), *Controversies in Obstetrics and Gynecology 2.* Philadelphia: Saunders.

Mead, Margaret (1978). *Blackberry Winter.* New York: Pocket Books.

Mehl, Lewis E., J.R. Ramiel, B. Leininger, B. Hoff, K. Kroenthal, and G. Peterson (1980). "Evaluation of Outcomes of Non-Nurse Midwives: Matched Comparisons with Physicians." *Women & Health* 5: 17–29.

Melosh, Barbara (1982). *The Physician's Hand: Work Culture and Conflict in American Nursing*. Philadelphia: Temple University Press.

Michie, Helena, and Naomi R. Cahn (1997). *Confinements: Fertility and Infertility in Contemporary Culture*. New Brunswick, NJ: Rutgers University Press.

Milgram, Stanley (1974). *Obedience to Authority: An Experimental View*. New York: Harper and Row.

Millman, Marcia (1977). *The Unkindest Cut: Life in the Backrooms of Medicine*. New York: Morrow.

Mills, C. Wright (1959). *The Sociological Imagination*. New York: Oxford University Press.

Mills, Nancy (1976). "The Lay Midwife." In David Stewart and Lee Stewart (eds.), *Safe Alternatives in Childbirth*. Chapel Hill, NC: NAPSAC.

Mitchell, Lisa M. (2001). *Baby's First Picture: Ultrasound and the Politics of Fetal Subjects*. Toronto: University of Toronto Press.

Montgomery, Rhonda, and Karl Kosloski (1994). "Strangers in Intimate Spaces: Home Care Workers as Pseudo-Family." Paper presented at conference of the American Sociological Association.

More, Ellen S. (1999). *Restoring the Balance: Women Physicians amd the Profession of Medicine, 1850–1995*. Cambridge and London: Cambridge University Press.

Morgen, Sandra (2002). *Into Our Own Hands: The Women's Health Movement in the United States, 1969–1990*. New Brunswick, NJ: Rutgers University Press.

Murphy-Lawless, Jo (1998). *Reading Birth and Death: A History of Obstetric Thinking*. Cork, Ireland: Cork University Press.

Myers-Ciecko, Jo Anne (1999). "Evolution and Current Status of Direct-Entry Midwifery Education, Regulation, and Practice in the United States, with Examples from Washington State." *Journal of Nurse-Midwifery* 44: 384–393.

Mykhalovskiy, Eric (1996). "Reconsidering Table Talk: Critical Thoughts on the Relationship between Sociology, Autobiography and Self-Indulgence." *Qualitative Sociology* 19 (March): 131–151.

National Research Council, Committee on Maternal Nutrition (1970). *Maternal Nutrition and the Course of Pregnancy*. Washington, D.C.: National Academy Press.

Oakley, A. (1980). *Woman Confined: Toward a Sociology of Childbirth*. New York: Schocken.

———— (1984). *The Captured Womb: A History of the Medical Care of Pregnant Women*. Oxford: Blackwell.

Page, Lesley (2003). "One-to-One Midwifery: Restoring the 'with Woman' Relationship in Midwifery." *Journal of Midwifery & Women's Health* 48: 119–125.

Palmer, Gabrielle (1993). *The Politics of Breastfeeding.* 2nd ed. London: Harper Collins/Pandora.

Pang, J.W., J.D. Heffelfinger, G.J. Huang, T.J. Benedetti, and N.S. Weiss (2002). "Outcomes of Planned Home Birth in Washington State." *Obstetrics & Gynecology* 200: 253–259.

Perkins, Barbara Bridgman (2003). *The Medical Delivery Business: Health Reform, Childbirth, and the Economic Order.* New Brunswick, NJ: Rutgers University Press.

Petchesky, Rosalind Pollack (1990). *Abortion and Woman's Choice: The State, Sexuality, and Reproductive Freedom.* Rev. ed. Boston: Northeastern University Press.

Phipps, Fiona MacVane (2003). "Educating Midwives: Where Do We Go from Here?" *Midwifery Matters* 96 (Spring): 12–16.

Pope, Rosemary, Lesley Graham, and Swattee Patel (2001). "Woman-Centered Care." *International Journal of Nursing Studies* 38: 227–238.

Pritchard, Jack A., and Paul C. McDonald (eds.) (1976). *Williams Obstetrics.* 15th ed. New York: Appleton-Century-Crofts.

_____ (1980). *Williams Obstetrics.* 16th ed. New York: Appleton-Century-Crofts.

Pritchard, Jack A., Paul C. MacDonald, and Norman F. Gant (eds.) (1985). *Williams Obstetrics.* 17th ed. Norwalk, CT: Appleton-Century-Crofts.

Quilligan, Edward J. (1975). "Prenatal Care." In Seymour L. Rombey et al. (eds.), *Gynecology and Obstetrics: The Health Care of Women.* New York: McGraw-Hill.

Raatikainen, Ritva (1997). "Nursing Care as a Calling." *Journal of Advanced Nursing* 25: 1111–1115.

Raphael, Dana (1973). *The Tender Gift: Breastfeeding.* Englewood Cliffs, NJ: Prentice-Hall.

Reed, A. (1997). "Trends in State Laws and Regulations Affecting Nurse Midwives: 1995–1997." *Journal of Nurse-Midwifery* 42: 421–426.

Reed, Richard K. (2005). *Birthing Fathers: The Transformation of Men in American Rites of Birth.* New Brunswick, NJ: Rutgers University Press.

Rich, Adrienne (1995). *Of Woman Born: Motherhood as Experience and Institution.* New York: W.W. Norton.

Ringler, N.M., et al. (1975). "Mother-to-Child Speech at Two Years: Effects of Early Postnatal Contact." *Journal of Pediatrics* 86: 141–144.

Roach, Mary (2003). *Stiff: The Curious Life of Human Cadavers.* New York: W.W. Norton.

Roberts, Dorothy (1997). *Killing the Black Body: Race, Reproduction, and the Meaning of Liberty.* New York: Pantheon.

Romm, Aviva Jill (1998). *Pocket Guide to Midwifery Care.* Freedom, CA: Crossing.

Rooks, Judith P. (1997). *Midwifery and Childbirth in America.* Philadelphia: Temple University Press.

_____ (1998). "Unity in Midwifery? Realities and Alternatives." *Journal of Nurse-Midwifery* 43: 315–319.

_____ (1999). "The Midwifery Model of Care." *Journal of Nurse-Midwifery* 44: 370–374.

Rosenberg, Charles (1987). *The Care of Strangers: The Rise of America's Hospital System*. New York: Basic Books.

Roth, Julius (1963). *Timetables: Structuring the Passage of Time in Hospital Treatment and Other Careers*. Indianapolis: Bobbs-Merrill.

Rothman, Barbara Katz (1991 [1982]). *In Labor: Women and Power in the Birthplace*. Rev. ed. New York: W.W. Norton.

_____ (2000). *Spoiling The Pregnancy: The Introduction of Prenatal Diagnosis to the Netherlands*. Bilthoven, Netherlands: Catharina Schrader Stichting of the Dutch Organization of Midwives (KNOV).

Ruzek, Sheryl Burt (1978). *The Women's Health Movement: Feminist Alternatives to Medical Control*. New York: Praeger.

Ruzek, Sheryl Burt, Virginia L. Olesen, and Adele E. Clarke (eds.) (1997). *Women's Health: Complexities and Difficulties*. Columbus: Ohio State University Press.

Sandelowski, Margarete (2000). *Devices and Desires: Gender, Technology, and American Nursing*. Chapel Hill: University of North Carolina Press.

Schlinger, Hilary (1992). *Circle of Midwives: Organized Midwifery in North America*. Privately printed.

Shaw, Nancy Stoller (1974). *Forced Labor: Maternity Care in the United States*. New York: Pergamon.

Shostak, Arthur B. (1996). *Private Sociology: Unsparing Reflections, Uncommon Gains*. Dix Hills, NY: General Hall.

Shroff, Farah M. (ed.) (1997). *The New Midwifery: Reflections on Renaissance and Regulation*. Toronto: Women's Press.

Simonds, Wendy (1996). *Abortion At Work: Ideology and Practice in a Feminist Clinic*. New Brunswick, NJ: Rutgers University Press.

_____ (2002). "Watching the Clock: Keeping Time During Pregnancy, Birth, and Postpartum Experiences." *Social Science & Medicine*, 55(4) (Aug): 559-570.

Simonds, Wendy, and Barbara Katz Rothman (1992). *Centuries of Solace: Expressions of Maternal Grief in Popular Literature*. Philadelphia: Temple University Press.

Spock, Benjamin (1946). *The Commonsense Book of Baby and Child Care*. New York: Duell, Sloan and Pearce.

Starr, Paul (1982). *The Social Transformation of American Medicine: The Rise of a Sovereign Profession and the Making of a Vast Industry*. New York: Basic Books.

Sudnow, David (1967). *Passing On: The Social Organization of Dying*. Englewood Cliffs, NJ: Prentice-Hall.

Tanzer, Deborah, and Jean Libman Block (1987). *Why Natural Childbirth? A Psychologist's Report on the Benefits to Mothers, Fathers and Babies*. New York: Schocken.

Taylor, Catherine (2002). *Giving Birth: A Journey into the World of Mothers and Midwives*. New York: Perigree.

Thomas, Pat (2003). "The Midwife You Have Called Knows You Are Waiting ..." *Midwifery Matters* 96 (Spring): 18–19.

Tritten, Jan, and Jennifer Rosenberg (eds.) (2002). *Paths to Becoming a Midwife: Getting an Education.* 3rd ed. Eugene, OR: Midwifery Today.

Vedam, S. (2003). "Homebirth v. Hospital Birth: Questioning the Quality of Evidence for Safety." *Birth* 30: 57–63.

Vellay, Pierre (1966). "The Psycho-Prophylactic Method: Its Evolution, Present Situation and Prospects." In *Report of the Fourth Biennial Convention.* Milwaukee WI: ICEA.

Verrilli, G. E., and A. M. Mueser (1993). *While Waiting.* Rev. ed. New York: St. Martin's Griffin.

Villar, Jose, Eliette Valladares, Daniel Wojdyla, Nelly Zavalete, et al. (2006). "Caesarean Delivery Rates and Pregnancy Outcomes: The 2005 WHO Global Survey on Maternal and Perinatal Health in Latin America." *The Lancet* 367 (June 3-9): 1819-1829.

Wagner, Marsden (1994). *Pursuing the Birth Machine: The Search for Appropriate Birth Technology.* Camperdown, Australia: ACE Graphics.

Walzer, Susan (1998). *Thinking About the Baby: Gender and Transitions into Parenthood.* Philadelphia: Temple University Press.

Webb, D.A. and J. Culhane (2002). "Time of Day Variation in Rates of Obstetric Intervention to Assist in Vaginal Delivery." *Journal of Epidemiology and Community Health* 56 (Aug.): 577–578.

Weber, Max (1992 [1930]). *The Protestant Ethic and the Spirit of Capitalism.* Anthony Giddens (tr.). London and New York: Routledge.

Weinberg, Dana Beth (2003). *Code Greed: Money-Driven Hospitals and the Dismantling of Nursing.* Ithaca, NY: Cornell University Press.

Wells, Sharon (2002). "Direct-Entry Midwifery Education: Caught in the Middle." In Jan Tritten and Jennifer Rosenberg (eds.), *Paths to Becoming a Midwife: Getting an Education*, 3rd ed., 162–166. Eugene, OR: Midwifery Today.

Wertz, Richard W., and Dorothy C. Wertz (1989 [1977]). *Lying-In: A History of Childbirth in America.* Rev. ed. New Haven, CT: Yale University Press.

Wickham, Sara (2002). "An Interview with Ina May Gaskin." *Practicing Midwife* 5 (January): 38–39.

Williams, Kristi, and Debra Umberson (1999). "Medical Technology and Childbirth: Experiences of Expectant Mothers and Fathers." *Sex Roles* 41: 147–168.

Williams, Deanne R. (1999). "Preserving Midwifery Practice in a Managed Care Environment." *Journal of Nurse-Midwifery* 44: 375–383.

Winship, Daniel H. (1975). "Gastrointestinal Diseases." In Gerald N. Burrow and Thomas F. Ferris (eds.), *Medical Complications during Pregnancy.* Philadelphia: Saunders.

Zerubavel, E. (1979). *Patterns of Time in Hospital Life.* Chicago: University of Chicago Press.

Zimbardo, Philip (1992). *Quiet Rage: The Stanford Prison Experiment.* Stanford, CA: Stanford University Press.

Index